The Drama Handbook
A Guide to Reading Plays

The Drama Handbook

A GUIDE TO READING PLAYS

John Lennard and Mary Luckhurst

OXFORD
UNIVERSITY PRESS

OXFORD
UNIVERSITY PRESS

Great Clarendon Street, Oxford OX2 6DP

Oxford University Press is a department of the University of Oxford.
It furthers the University's objective of excellence in research, scholarship,
and education by publishing worldwide in

Oxford New York

Athens Auckland Bangkok Bogotá Buenos Aires Cape Town
Chennai Dar es Salaam Delhi Florence Hong Kong Istanbul Karachi
Kolkata Kuala Lumpur Madrid Melbourne Mexico City Mumbai Nairobi
Paris São Paulo Shanghai Taipei Tokyo Toronto Warsaw
with associated companies in Berlin Ibadan

Oxford is a registered trade mark of Oxford University Press
in the UK and in certain other countries

Published in the United States
by Oxford University Press Inc., New York

British Library Cataloguing in Publication Data
Data available

Library of Congress Cataloging in Publication Data
Data available
ISBN 0-19-870070-9

Typeset in ITC Stone
by RefineCatch Limited, Bungay, Suffolk
Printed in Great Britain by
T.J. International Ltd., Padstow, Cornwall

For

DAVID EDGAR

Playwright
Director and Professor of Playwriting Studies
University of Birmingham, 1989–1999

In friendship

and with gratitude for his pioneering and generous work

in drama education

Contents

Figures and display boxes

Figures

Display boxes

Acknowledgements

In writing a book like this many debts are incurred, not least to the students who have over the years harassed us into clarity and made us sharply conscious of the need for a reliable short guide to reading plays. Particular thanks are due to those brave students who have allowed their timed work to be published, so that readers may judge for themselves, and to Andrew Goreing for more than fulfilling his brief. The photoquotation from the Oxford Shakespeare *Hamlet* in Chapter 3 is reproduced with the kind permission of Oxford University Press, and the exam questions in Chapter 32 with the kind permission of Cambridge University. We would also like formally to thank those without whose cheerful friendship, professional conversation, dramatic libraries, and generous assistance we could not have started, let alone finished—a long list, but heartfelt thanks:

Alan Ayckbourn; Anne Barton; John Barton; Richard Beadle; Philip Bird; Dan Burnstone; Jean Chothia; Roland Clare; Peter Cochran; Christopher Cook; Mike Cordner; John Creaser; April de Angelis; Ljubica Dimitrevich; Helena Dollimore; David Edgar; Donna Fulkerson; Lucy Garcia; Gabriel Gbadamosi; Gabriella Giannachi; Janine Goedert; Chris Goode; Andrew Grant-Taylor; Tess Grant-Taylor; Fiona Green; Tony Harrison; Natsu Hattori; Margaret Hebden; Emma Hebden; Alison Hennegan; Anne Henry; Peter Holland; Julia Hollander; Romana Huk; Francis Ingledew; Kevin Jackson; Marion Kant; Nick Kaye; John Kerrigan; Mark Kilroy; Wendy Lesser; Alex Lindsay; Jonathan Lloyd; Bernard Luckhurst; Marcello Magni; Simon Mills; Charles Moseley; Conrad Nelson; Helen Nicholson; Joan Norris; David O'Shea; Julia Pascal; Peggy Paterson; Adrian Poole; Steve Poole; Leonardo de Arrizabelago y Prado; Helen Raynor; Dan Rebellato; Richard Rowland; Barrie Rutter; Cathy Phillips; Davina Silver; Maggie Silver; Zoë Silver; Tim Pigott Smith; Claire Preston; Hanna Scolnicov; John Singleton; Max Stafford-Clark; Tristram Stuart; Richard Todd; Lloyd Trott; Patrick Tucker; Mark Turnbull; Chloe Veltman; Harriet Walter; Stephen Walton; Graham Whybrow; Steve Waters; Maja Zade.

Abbreviations

< [page number]	see [page number] above
> [page number]	see [page number] below
→	becomes, is the etymological source of
ABC	American Broadcasting Company
a.k.a.	also known as
b.	born
BBC	British Broadcasting Company
BCE	Before Common Era (= BC)
c.	*circa*[1]
CBS	Columbia Broadcasting System
CCTV	closed-circuit television
CD	compact disc
CE	Common Era (= AD)
cf.	*conferro*[2]
ch.	chapter
d.	died
dir.	director, directed by
DVD	digital versatile disc
ed.	edition, editor, edited by
eds	editors
esp.	especially
et al.	*et alia*[3]
etc.	*et cetera*[4]
EU	European Union
F (1, 2, etc.)	(the 1st/2nd etc.) folio-text (of a particular work)
F1	Shakespeare's First Folio (1623)
ft	foot, feet
fol., fols	folio(s)
gen. eds	general editors

---

[1] Latin, 'about' or 'approximately', usually before dates.
[2] Latin, 'compare'.
[3] Latin, 'and other people'.
[4] Latin, 'and (the) other things'.

Ibid.	*Ibidem*[5]
k.a.	known as
l(l).	line(s)
lit.	literally
m	metre(s)
MAT	Moscow Art Theatre
MLA	Modern Language Association of America
n(n).	note(s)
NBC	National Broadcasting Company
n.d.	no date (of publication)
NT	National Theatre, London (see also RNT)
OED2	*Oxford English Dictionary* (2nd ed.)
o.s.d.	opening stage-direction
p(p).	page(s)
perf.	performed
pub	public house
pub.	published
Q (1, 2 etc.)	(the 1st/2nd etc.) quarto-text (of a particular play)
Qq	quartos
r.	recto (the front-side of a page)
RADA	Royal Academy of Dramatic Art, London
rev. (ed.)	revised (by/edition)
RCT	Royal Court Theatre, London
RNT	Royal National Theatre, London
RSC	Royal Shakespeare Company
RST	Royal Shakespeare Theatre, Stratford-upon-Avon
sc.	scene
s.d.(s)	stage-direction(s)
Sh. OED	*Shorter Oxford English Dictionary*
sig., sigs	signature(s)
STC	Pollard & Redgrave, *Short-Title Catalogue 1475–1640*
TEQ	traditional essay-question
TLN	Through Line Numbering
trans.	translator, translated by
TV	television
UK	United Kingdom of Great Britain and Northern Ireland
US(A)	United States (of America)
v.	verso (the reverse-side of a page)
VO	voice-over
vol.	volume
vols	volumes
vs	versus
Wing	Wing, *Short-Title Catalogue 1640–1700*
wr.	written

---

[5] Latin, '(in) the same (place)'; the same reference as in the previous note.

Introduction

This book is born of frustration. For full-time students of drama there are many books on text and elements of performance; but for students of English Literature, who may in their studies at school or university encounter one classical Greek, one mediaeval, several Renaissance, and a variety of later plays, and for the general reader or playgoer, there is no good, short guide to all the basics. Our remit therefore is what all such readers need to know to avoid misunderstanding drama, and to develop their reading in ways that promote better connections with their experiences of spectating and auditing.

Those familiar with John Lennard's *Poetry Handbook* (OUP, 1996) might expect something closely similar, but with drama it is not possible to select a single work for exemplary analysis nor to treat technical elements abstractly. The communal and performative nature of drama means plays are inseparable from theatrical conventions, architectures, and technologies specific to the cultures that produce them, and in teaching a significant part of the problem is a general ignorance of theatre-history. Most graduates in English know a potted history of English poetry ('alliterative—Renaissance—Metaphysical—Augustan—Romantic—Victorian—Modernist'); some know a potted history of English prose ('Malory—Bacon—Browne—Johnson—Austen—Dickens—James—Woolf'); but if most know a little about Shakespeare's theatre, perhaps from visiting *Globe III* in London,[1] few can say much about the history of drama. Yet theatres shaped by specifically modern conditions are not remotely like *Globe I* and it is misleading to read older texts as if they were written for modern performance conventions. Both omnipotent *directors* and dimming

---

[1] Globe I was the original, 1599–1613, when it burnt down; *Globe II* was the replacement, 1613–42, when it was closed down; and Globe III is the replica opened in 1997 near the same site.

house-lights for performance, for example, date only from the late-nineteenth century; and the conditions of most mainstream productions, from lengthy *rehearsals* to professional *reviews* and long *runs*, are now profoundly alien to the performative tenor of Shakespearean texts. Equally, the peculiar, almost parodic endings of some of the plays of Henrik Ibsen (1828–1906), the heroine abruptly shooting herself in *Hedda Gabler* (1890) or Nora Helmer walking out in *A Doll's House* (1879), seem less peculiar read against the wild endings of mid-century plays like *Lady Audley's Secret* (1863)[2] by C. H. Hazlewood (1823–75), against which Ibsen was reacting (41–5 >). Playwrights also often write for particular theatres/companies, as Shakespeare (1564–1616) did for the *Lord Chamberlain's* (later *King's*) *Men*; and to know about them helps. A full theatre-history would be another, much larger project, but one purpose of this book is to introduce perspectives on theatre-history that alert you to new ways of thinking about the plays you read and see. We provide dates for every new person and play we mention to help readers place them in context; personal dates are also given in the index of persons, and where helpful in the glossary.

A second part of the problem, addressed throughout, can be summarised as 'object/process'. Many readers treat plays as static objects, complete in themselves, but from writing and rehearsal to performance and revival drama is an open-ended process, constantly dynamic and never complete. Performing and spectating are intrinsically collaborative, and drama is in many ways more like music than like poetry or prose—all of which can be deployed performatively within a play that demands a more complex approach than any one of its component forms. It is hard for readers without dramatic experience or training always to respect this dynamism and complexity, but to approach any drama, printed or performed, as only an object is often to court disaster and almost always to miss the point.

A third consideration is the need to introduce and define technical words that enable readers to think (and students to write) <u>precisely</u> about what they read and see. Jargon can be abused, but technical vocabulary is essential: how could anyone discuss music without names for the notes, keys, and instruments? A lot of drama jargon is commonplace: 'act', 'scene', 'line', 'stage-direction', 'director',

---

[2] Hazlewood adapted Mary Braddon's 1862 novel, available in Oxford World's Classics; the play is in Rowell, ed., *Nineteenth-Century Plays*.

'auditorium'. Some is falsely familiar and badly used: 'downstage', 'tragicomedy', 'realist'. Some is commonplace but hazily understood: 'stage-business', 'naturalistic', 'tragedy'. And some may be new: 'senex', 'dramaturg', 'thrust-stage', 'corpsing'. Each technical word is *italicized* on its first appearance, and all such words are gathered in the glossary at the end, with page-references to their use. We have therefore not italicized but underlined words we want to emphasize; foreign words and titles, however, are italicized in the usual way, so Hamlet is the rôle and *Hamlet* the play.

One term we don't use is *dramatic irony*, because we have both become weary of finding it used by critics and students as an all-purpose term without specific meaning. Irony itself is hard to define exactly, and the most useful rule-of-thumb definition, that irony is 'the preservation of distance' (with the rider that if you are going to use the word you should be able to say between what and what a distance is being preserved),[3] is tricky in drama because distances between actors and the people they play, and between the stage and the worlds represented there, are common to all theatrical representation. Of itself, therefore, while it may seem to point to a particular quality of a particular bit of text, 'dramatic irony' does not often clearly distinguish one moment of performance from another; and we have not found it hard to avoid. But we do not of course mean to suggest that irony is not present in play-texts, or in performances: Mark Anthony's repeated observation (in his great "Friends, Romans, Countrymen" speech in *Julius Caesar, c.*1599) that "*Brutus* is an Honourable Man" (3.2.82, 87, 94, 99) is plainly in some sense ironic. Or rather, in many senses: Mark Anthony almost certainly thinks Brutus to have been deeply dishonourable in killing Caesar (a gap between the speaker's words and belief), and is using his verse-oration to political ends (a gap between what he professes to be doing, and is perceived to be doing); the Roman citizens on stage to hear him begin by insisting he speak no ill of Brutus, but are persuaded that Brutus did ill by hearing Brutus apparently praised (a gap between the intentions and reactions of the Roman crowd); and the paying spectators at *Julius Caesar* may or may not appreciate Mark Anthony's strategy, and may or may not think Brutus to have been dishonourable (gaps between

---

[3] See Lennard, *Poetry Handbook*, p. xvii.

what they have seen, how they hear it described, and what they themselves think). Moreover, depending on the styles of production and performance, the gaps between the actors playing Mark Anthony and the citizens (living people in the present), the rôles they are playing (dramatic parts written by Shakespeare), and the historical figures or pluralities they represent (dead people in the past), may or may not be made evident to the paying spectators, who may or may not be aware of them anyway. So there are surely ironies! And <u>any</u> of these ironic gaps might properly be attended to in a discussion of *Julius Caesar*, but the blanket term 'dramatic irony' seems to us usually to block, not to promote, closer scrutiny and clearer thought.

Our methods, therefore, are the provision of history and terminology and an emphasis on process. In choosing examples we stick fairly closely to texts students and general readers may encounter or need to know about, using the main Western theatrical canon from the Greeks to Beckett; most of the plays we mention are therefore reasonably available in libraries and bookshops—and (especially as *copyright* fees mean we quote less modern drama than we would like) it is important, when we mention a work you don't know, that you look it up sooner rather than later and test what we say against what you read yourself. You can of course read us as you will: but be aware that while chapters can stand alone, they are designed to accumulate. Readers without previous dramatic knowledge will certainly get most benefit by reading in order, looking plays up as necessary, and going on to the next section only when happy with the last—and students who try to read the book fast, as a crash-course, will probably waste their time. There is also a final section on exams, of use to anyone who has to write on drama but specifically written for students who face examinations or must otherwise provide work for assessment.

Finally, some explanation about texts, the editions we use, and the forms of references:

- For older plays we quote from *early editions,* and for Shakespeare from the *First Folio* (F1), his first collected plays, published in 1623, a decision explained in Chapter 3 (23–35 >).[4]

---

[4] There is a reference system for F1 called *Through Line Numbering* (TLN) which counts all lines from 1, ignoring act- and scene-divisions; but without a *facsimile*, act.scene.line references are needed to find the passage in modern editions: we therefore give references to the equivalent passage in the *Riverside Shakespeare*.

- Full titles of Shakespearean plays are also given in F1 title-page versions, sometimes unexpectedly different, but when we simply mention a play modernized short-titles are used: thus *Much adoe about Nothing* and *A Midsommer Nights Dreame*, but *Much Ado* and *Dream*.

- The editions of modern plays we use are specified under 'Play-texts' in the bibliography (which includes modern editions of older plays). Details in the bibliography are not duplicated in footnotes.

- Any ellipses which we introduce into quotations are crotcheted, thus: [. . .]. Suspension-marks which are not crotcheted are authorial.

- *Act.scene.line references* are in arabic numerals, as 3.2.4–5 (*act 3, scene 2, lines 4–5*), not roman ones (III.ii.4–5), but work in exactly the same way. Some plays have *scene-divisions* without *act-divisions*, and references of the form 2.7 (scene 2, line 7). Anything odder is footnoted.

- In cross-references (9 >) = 'see p. 9 below'; (< 12n.2) = 'see p. 12, note 2 above'.

JCL, ML
June, 2001

I

PERFORMANCE, NOTATION, TEXT

CLOV: What is there to keep me here?
HAMM: The dialogue. [*Pause.*]

Samuel Beckett, *Endgame* (1957)

Thou tellest my flittings; put my tears in the bottle;
    are not these things noted in thy book?

Book of Common Prayer, *Psalm 56:8* (1662)

Notes are often necessary, but they are necessary evils.

Samuel Johnson, *Preface to Shakespeare* (1765)

1

Performance: process and the ephemeral

Drama is not like poetry or prose, though it contains both. If you read a poem or passage of prose silently to yourself your reading is not necessarily incomplete. With drama it will be, for plays and other dramatic texts do not simply exist on paper to be read but are written to be performed, and for most dramatists written text is a by-product, necessary for production and a vital means of disseminating work and generating income but secondary to what happens in rehearsal and on stage.

For poets, novelists, and most authors of non-fictional work, writing is solitary, and the process of publication begins with sending their work to a publisher, by arrangement or in hope. Once it is accepted for publication, the people involved will include an *editor* (the author's main contact who oversees the process), a *copy-editor* (who checks the typescript for inconsistencies and marks it up for the printer), *compositors* (who set type), and a *proof-reader*, usually the author (to ensure there are no errors). The process ends with printed and bound copies, which in theory represent the author's 'final intentions', and have both authorship and authority (author-ity).

All these people will also be involved in printing a dramatic text, but with new work another very complicated process will overlap with the processes of writing and printing. In the case of a stage-play this process begins with the author/s sending a *script* to a particular theatre: it may go to a *literary manager* (who deals with new plays) or straight to a director or *artistic director* (who decides what plays will be put on), and any of these functionaries may read it themselves or refer it to a *play-reader* for a report on its quality and suitability. Once a play is accepted and scheduled for production (and it is far harder to get a play professionally performed than to get a book published), a director will be appointed, with much greater freedom to demand or impose cuts and alterations than most editors. A *designer*, who creates the *set* (the fixed elements of the staging) and probably the general look of the costumes and props, is also likely to be appointed. The author will negotiate with the director, and may have to cut or rewrite bits that s/he doesn't think will work, or that pose other problems. The play must also be *cast* (choosing and hiring *actors*[1] for each *rôle*), and the rest of the production and technical crew hired or assigned, including any or all of assistant directors, dramaturgs, set-makers and -painters, costume-designers and -makers, wig-makers, wardrobe managers, prop-designers and -makers, a make-up team, voice-coaches, movement-coaches, lighting-designers and assistants, sound-engineers and assistants, a musical director and musicians, a stage-manager and stage-hands, a programme-designer and production team, a publicity and sales team, and other front-of-house staff.[2] Once rehearsals begin the script is likely to change further as the director focuses more sharply on individual moments, and actors begin to speak lines and *walk-through* actions. The author may or may not want to attend rehearsals, and may or may not be allowed to do so. Actors may ask director or author for changes, which may or may not be granted, or suggest changes themselves, which may or may not be accepted. The *stage-crew* may simply do what a director or designer orders, or make suggestions and become a significant creative influence. The artistic director may monitor the rehearsal process and intervene if there are things they don't like, or think the theatre's audiences will not like. Eventually there will be a full *technical rehearsal*, using lights and sound, and a *dress-rehearsal*, in costume and make-up, and then the play will open: but in professional theatre today the very first performance will probably not be the *first night*, the official opening, but a *preview*, for which tickets may be cheaper because it is anticipated that some things will go wrong. Only after several previews, and a *press-night*, to which reviewers are invited, will the production officially begin—and even then it will continue to

---

[1] Because the word 'actress' has often been used pejoratively or dismissively, most critics now refer to actors, specifying male or female actors as necessary.
[2] These functionaries are discussed in Chapter 21 (202–6 >).

change, because each performance will inevitably differ from every other performance, and because actors continue to explore text as they perform, finding some bits weak or troublesome, needing further cuts or adaptation, and some bits under-developed, suggesting in performance further possibilities and refinements.

By the first night there may be a printed text for sale in the *foyer* and in bookshops (and if so an editor, a copy-editor, compositors, and a proof-reader will have been involved in its production), but this is principally a marketing ploy, and outside mainstream theatre it may be years before a printed text becomes available. But even if the text is for sale in the foyer it may not be exactly what is being spoken on the stage and heard in the *auditorium*, because a version of the text had to be sent to press weeks before, while the text on stage continued to evolve in rehearsal; the actions of the plot will probably be the same, but the *stage-business* of the production (the little things worked out in rehearsal, such as action with *props* or the timing of fights and comic sequences) will probably not be recorded in print; and for any *revival* (a subsequent production of the play) a printed text will be only a point of departure, as the author's script was for the first production. In any case, the actors, director, designer, set, and all the other elements of the *mise-en-scène* will be different in every production, and even productions that seem similar will differ far more than editions of a classic novel. To come down to cases, Shakespeare's *Hamlet* exists in many different printed texts (Arden, Oxford, Riverside, etc.), none of them exactly what Shakespeare wrote, and however many performances of however many productions of *Hamlet* you see, none will correspond exactly to any of those printed texts. Even the marathon film of *Hamlet* (1996) by Kenneth Branagh (b.1961) is only one possible version and has no exact equivalent in print. So what does it mean to 'read' *Hamlet*? And when you sit down with a copy of the Arden or Oxford edition how should you set about 'reading' what is before your eyes?

This is a serious question. Philosophers draw a distinction between *ontology*, what things are in themselves, and *epistemology*, how we know or perceive them, and in their relation to performance dramatic texts are both ontologically and epistemologically distinct. Costume provides a good example: what is Hamlet wearing when he first meets his father's ghost? and what is the ghost wearing? If Shakespeare had written a novel rather than a play, and omitted to say what folk wore, a reader would be free to imagine Hamlet in whatever seemed appropriate and the ghost in best ectoplasm. As it is, the only Shakespearean clue we have to Hamlet's costume in 1.4–5 is that since his father's death he has habitually worn "suites of solemne Blacke" (1.2.78), and was so dressed earlier in the day when he talked to his mother and stepfather at a formal reception. Everything else is up to the director and designer, and though many people think of Hamlet wearing black leather boots, black hose, and a fancy shirt, that is only a particular costume used by many directors and popularized by the *Royal Shakespeare Company* (RSC) in Stratford and on film. For all that Shakespeare says Hamlet <u>could</u> be wearing <u>anything</u> in 1.4–5: no longer on display to the King and Queen, and going outside at night, he may well have changed; on a castle guard-platform at midnight, waiting in the cold for a ghost, it may be important that he wears a thick coat or cloak and shivers inside it—but that is a decision for the director, and it might make better sense in a particular production for Hamlet <u>not</u> to feel the cold upon which those with whom he is waiting remark. The point is that while a reader does not and <u>cannot</u> know exactly how Hamlet is dressed or whether he shivers, a director, equally ignorant, nevertheless <u>must</u> clothe Hamlet in something, and the actor playing Hamlet <u>must</u> shiver or not shiver—and the audience then knows from observation things about Hamlet that Shakespeare did not tell them. Ontologically Hamlet <u>in the play</u> remains an uncertainly dressed fiction, but Hamlet <u>on stage</u> is an actor who dresses and acts in a particular way; and epistemologically the audience learns only about the Hamlet <u>on stage</u>, not the Hamlet <u>in the play</u>. It is vital not to confuse what you can learn by reading a text with what you may learn from a particular production.

For the ghost the problem is different. The text repeatedly insists that the ghost wears full armour (1.1.47–64, 1.2.199–200, 1.4.52), and that was Shakespeare's choice. There were several conventional ways in which his theatre indicated that an actor was playing a ghost: then as now, the simplest was to be draped in a white sheet, or when the character now returning as a ghost had been seen alive earlier in the play, to be white-faced and obviously bloodied (Banquo's ghost in *Macbeth* is still often done like this). Hamlet's father dies before *Hamlet* begins, and the audience would not know who this ghost was if

Horatio and the watchmen did not tell them—so there was no pre-existing reason for Shakespeare to insist on armour, and one is left asking why he did so. It can make for impressive spectacle, and is probably meant to signal a vengeful ghost on the warpath (he wasn't wearing armour when he died); it also raises an interesting question about the noise of the ghost's footsteps, sometimes solved in practice by felting the soles of silver-painted boots. But for any theatre that is not rich and well equipped the ghost's armour is likely to be plastic and partial, not matching very closely the descriptions of the armour in the text; and in that case members of the audience who know that full armour is specified in the text will probably use their knowledge to amplify the unpersuasive breastplate and helmet they see an actor wearing. Ontologically, the 'ghost' in the play may be the ghost of Hamlet's father (whatever ghosts are), or, as Hamlet fears, a devil pretending to be that ghost (whatever devils are); the ghost on stage is ontologically almost always an actor, but could be a projection or hologram. Epistemologically, readers and audiences know it to be (an actor playing) a ghost from *stage-directions* and because those on stage describe and react to it as if it were one.

This common sense can be surprisingly difficult to keep straight in one's head. The great temptation is in reading to slide past all the uncertainties and instabilities of drama in process, and concentrate on the text as if it were a novel or narrative poem; and in watching performance to treat it as a finished and fixed product that is or is not 'faithful' to the text—as if the text were a mould, and each production a better or worse replica from that mould. For reviewers, and many teachers, simplifying things makes life much easier; but it also kills the drama and much of the interest. Consider, for example, the still common school essay-title, 'Write about the character of Lady Macbeth' (or Gloucester, or Hedda Gabler, or whoever), in which *character* always means "Mental or moral constitution" and "A detailed report of a person's qualities" (*Sh. OED*), as if one had an omniscient novelist's judgement of and insight into their minds. But with dramatic 'characters', or more properly *rôles*, we have only a sequence of lines that they say plus what other 'characters' (rôles) say about them, and perhaps a few clues in stage-directions; <u>and</u>, if we are lucky, a stage or film performance in which an actor helps us to imagine one of the possible ways that rôle could be played. As used by teachers and reviewers the 'character' question tends to impose a *naturalistic* approach, one that treats rôles as real and fixed people about whom a reader/spectator must 'find out' the 'truth', yet wilfully forgets that on the page the rôle of Lady Macbeth is a framework, a skeleton alive only for the few hours that 'she' is fleshed out on stage by an actor who may be male (as in the first productions of *Macbeth*, when all female rôles were played by boys) or female, and will always be part of a collaborative enterprise. This doesn't mean that either in the text or in performance Lady Macbeth has no character: for the duration of reading or performing she lives and dies, saying and doing some things in particular ways, failing to say and do other things in equally particular ways, and through her words and deeds, accents and pauses, movements and stillnesses, conveying a representation of a thinking and feeling woman. It does mean, however, that there is not, never has been, and never can be *a* Lady Macbeth; instead there are as many Lady Macbeths as there are performances and texts.

The way to read *Hamlet* as a play, then, is not to try and fix any definite reading, but to read each line and scene with the constant understanding that you are looking only at a skeleton or plan, and that every moment is rife with possibilities capable of being realized only ephemerally. You can't imagine them all, but you can and must remember that at first you are imagining only one or two, and be prepared as your reading and theatregoing experience increases constantly to be open to further possibilities and more variations.

2

Notation: documentation, layout, and the preserved

Writing was for centuries the only way of recording a spoken text. Most actors need a *cue-script*, a copy of their lines and *cues*, from which to learn a rôle; and all revivals depend on the availability of the play-text (and perhaps also on the survival of costumes, sets, or a star-actor associated with a rôle). Text can now be stored electronically and printed as necessary, but must still be available; and since the Renaissance there has been a steadily growing trade in the sale of play-texts, both in individual and omnibus or collected editions, in whatever medium currently sells best. But sit down with pen, paper, and video of a theatrical performance, trying to transcribe what you see/hear, and it rapidly becomes clear that what goes down on paper and what is recorded on video are not easily interchangeable. Sit with a printed text in your hand and watch the video, and a different kind of gap appears. Video, like photographs, lighting- and sound-charts, and other forms of theatrical *documentation*, is an alternative to but not a substitute for writing; and writing is an alternative to but not a substitute for other means of recording a production. We instantly recognize the documentation of music (notes) or movement (*Laban notation*) as special systems needing interpretation; but because play-texts are in familiar language many people fail to recognize that they are also highly specialized documents.

The basic assumption underlying the formatting of modern printed play-texts is that *dialogue*, words spoken by actors, is primary, and it is almost always given in *lower case* roman letters. It has to be clear who says what, and each speech therefore has a *speech-prefix*, usually but not always a name conventionally printed in UPPER-CASE LETTERS or **bold type**. Each line after the first is usually slightly indented, so that every speech is distinct on the page, and there is often a blank line between speeches. Stage-directions, authorial instructions for action or verbal *delivery*, are also distinguished, usually by italics and within speeches by *lunulae* (round brackets); stage-directions between speeches are also italicized and often centred, but not bracketed, and any rôles named within them are in upper-case or bold.

Enter stage-right JONES, *reading a book. Enter stage-left* SMITH, *watching him.*

JONES: Now, where on earth was it? (*riffles the pages, looking*) No . . . no . . . bother . . . ah! That's it, I think—

SMITH: Found it, have you?

JONES starts, stares at SMITH.

JONES: What the hell are you doing here?

These simple elements create a powerful, flexible system, conveying a great deal of information besides the words themselves and the identities of the speakers. The *suspension-marks* (. . .) imply pauses as Jones turns the pages, and contrast with the final *dash* of that speech ("I think—"), which signals that Smith interrupts (if it were 'I think . . . ', Jones's voice would tail away into silence before Smith spoke). Jones's "where on earth" and "bother" suggest impatience or irritation, which grows when he is interrupted and says "What the hell are you doing here?", rather than just 'What are you doing here?' or 'Hello'. By contrast, Smith's unnoticed entrance and his interruption seem aggressive, or sly; and the entrances from left and right suggest an opposition[1] which grows as they speak and in production would probably be expressed by moving closer together and towards the audience. But already we are beginning to infer things which it might not be possible to realize in production—if, for example, the space used has only one entrance/exit—and there are many aspects of production about which one knows nothing. Lighting could be influential (is Smith in darkness? is Jones trying to read in the dark?), as could costume (Jones in a suit, Smith in football-kit?), sound (a song playing over loudspeakers?), and, if obvious to the audience, what Jones is reading (the Bible, pornography?). It may seem easily possible to include this information:

---

[1] Villains often enter *stage-left*, and heroes *stage-right*.

Enter stage-right JONES, *wearing a dark suit, white shirt, and bowler-hat, reading the Bible; a spotlight follows him. Enter stage-left* SMITH, *wearing football-kit and boots, in relative darkness, but carefully watching* JONES.

Madonna's Like a Virgin *audible over loudspeakers*

JONES: (*distractedly, reading*) Now, where on earth was it? (*riffles the pages, looking*) No . . . no . . . bother . . . ah! (*pauses, moving towards downstage-centre*) That's it, I think—

SMITH: (*interrupting him and walking rapidly towards downstage-centre, his football-boots loud on the boards*) Found it, have you?

As he speaks a second spotlight comes up on SMITH. JONES *starts, stares at* SMITH, *noticing his clothes and scowling. They now face one another downstage-centre, so that the circles of their spotlights just fail to meet.*

JONES: What the hell are you doing here?

As you see, in practice if you include all this information the dialogue is rapidly drowned in stage-directions, and it is not obvious that this is clearer or better to read than the simpler version. It's certainly longer, and applied to *Hamlet* would turn a long play into a young encyclopaedia. For an actor or director it is much worse, because they increasingly become slaves to the text, obeying its instructions rather than being free to try to make it come alive; and most playwrights learn the hard way that if they want the willing co-operation of top-quality actors and directors much must be left for those actors and directors to do. For wholly practical reasons actors also prefer very lightweight books with as much dialogue as possible on each page, and by meeting those criteria Penguin editions of Shakespeare have influenced performance far more than anything in any sense heavier weight.

And where do you stop? Suppose that on the press-night of the play in which Smith and Jones appear, Jones (very anxious to make an impression) manages to drop his Bible when Smith speaks, and as he jumps in surprise kicks it straight into Smith's hands. Spontaneous applause and laughter erupt, and all reviews lead with this wonderful moment; of which there is no mention in the text on sale in the foyer, but which becomes such a success in performance that Smith and Jones make sure it happens every night of a sell-out run, and both dine out on it for years. How soon will that text in the foyer change, and how should the drop-kicked Bible be added? How about '*Pause for laughter and cheering.* SMITH *and* JONES *may, if they wish, take a bow at this point'*. Is that a suitable stage-direction? Where do you stop? And how do you lay out the information on page or screen? The academic answer is to provide *notes*, usually in smaller type beneath the main text. Many editors would reprint the text available in the foyer that first night, and perhaps mention the Bible-kicking incident in a footnote, or print the added stage-direction from a later edition in an appendix. This is sensible, especially with modern graphics skills and technology, but depends on the quality of *annotation* (the provision of notes). There are many modern paperback editions of Shakespearean and other Renaissance plays; all contain helpful basic annotation—definitions and comparable uses of words, *glosses* of tough or grammatically ambiguous lines, historical references, and so on; and more recent ones are beginning to pay proper attention to stage- and performance-history. But these editions unavoidably privilege text above action, usually in a form closer to our first version of Smith and Jones. Theatre-practice offers a different answer, and for professional productions there is a special copy of the text (known as *the Book* or *prompt-copy*), sometimes rebound to include blank leaves, on which cuts, additions, and technical cues are marked up, and many notes on delivery and stage-business more or less neatly added. An experienced reader could reconstruct from the Book one or more performances with reasonable fidelity, and if it were supplemented by full (multi-camera, multi-performance) video and audio, and complete technical charts, high fidelity could be obtained—but to what end? How long do you have to spend reading? *Hypertext* offers a third answer, but there is a technical bottleneck in the megabytes required for full video, and even in the *hyperverse* (the web-world of hypertext) there are major advantages in primarily verbal and iconic information-display.

Considering all of which, the real question is what <u>kind</u> of information annotations supply. Suppose with Smith and Jones that you were told, perhaps with the help of a photograph, that Jones's black suit and bowler hat make him look like a tramp, after Charlie Chaplin (1889–1977) or Buster Keaton (1895–1966); and that (like Chaplin's) his walk was deliberately comical. How might the scene play now? Are you sure the drop-kicked Bible was only a happy accident? Where does helpful information shade into opinion or fact into accident? Theatre is a live business but pages don't move; and what an editor (or author) admits to the printed page is subject to much ideological (and technical, practical) pressure. SMITH and JONES are very bare speech-prefixes: suppose they were REVEREND JONES and SIR WEASEL SMITH? Or VICAR and FOOTBALLER? Or 1 and 2? And as academic editors have felt free to add stage-directions at will, now always in *crotchets* [square brackets] to signal an emendation to the 'authoritative' text, the result of their control has too often been (as in the *Arden 2* Shakespeares)[2] to banish almost all consideration of Shakespeare's plays as plays, to be acted on stage, and create instead a sham-show of the missing action in a plethora of additional stage-directions. To be fair, some editors have experience of directing, often student productions; but to be truthful, many would like to direct much more than they have, and their frustrations can become professionally misplaced.

Nor is it only older plays that are affected. The Chaplin image is a good example, not with Smith and Jones, but in the plays of Samuel Beckett (1906–89). Many people know that the two main rôles in *Waiting for Godot* (French 1952, English 1955), Vladimir and Estragon (a.k.a. Didi and Gogo), are hanging about waiting for someone who never comes; but people who see the play in England often leave with no idea that it is (potentially) hugely funny (as well as wintery), and draws on the same funny-and-simultaneously-sad music-hall figures who inspired Chaplin, and the great French actor Jean-Louis Barrault[3] (1910–94) and *white-face mime* Marcel Marceau (b.1923). On the other hand, given the po-faced, stiff-jointed productions of Beckett we have sometimes seen, everyone stock-still and plodding monotonously through their lines like daleks with flat batteries, there is little to suggest it could be funny.[4] The work of Wole Soyinka (b.1934) is less well

---

[2] There are three sets of Arden Shakespeares: *Arden 1* (1899–1944), now all out-of-print; Arden 2 (1946–82), of which about two-thirds are still current; and *Arden 3* (1995–), of which about fifteen volumes are now available. The standard format of Arden 2 introductions exemplifies a very scholarly but untheatrical approach to Shakespeare (and Renaissance drama in general) by many mid-twentieth-century British academics. (234–5 >).

[3] Best known in the UK and US from the film *Les Enfants du Paradis* (1944).

[3] In many ways Didi and Gogo are *clowns* (175–6 >), but the director of the British première, Peter Hall (b.1930), made them into figures more often described as 'tramps'. He probably had Chaplin in mind, but the label has perhaps served more to mask than to point the comedy.

known, despite his Nobel Prize, but in plays such as *The Road* (1965) and *Madmen and Specialists* (1970) there are, as well as specifically Nigerian rôles, figures clearly related to Chaplin, Keaton, French white-face mimes, and (through *Pierrot* and the *Harlequinades*) to *Commedia dell'Arte*, a Venetian play-form whence *Pantalone* comes, and *Pulcinella*, who in England became Mr Punch in *Punch-and-Judy shows*. Soyinka, too, suffers from po-faced productions that lack dramatic intelligence and cultural respect, so that to see a good (probably Irish, and strongly physical as well as cleverly verbal) Beckett, or a Soyinka by a company (probably Nigerian) that understands the form and style of his plays, is a revelation. Or many revelations.

One major issue raised by Beckett is timing. How long does it take you to read a page of Beckett? And how long would it take to perform? The regularities of printing create identical spaces between speeches, but in life (and certainly in Beckett) speeches overlap, or draw apart, and the regularity of the page must not survive in performance. Typography always has an uncertain relationship to timing in performance: playwrights and play-readers often reckon typescripts (double-spaced A4 paper, not the printed page of a book) at one minute per page, but it is plainly true that the same page of Beckett might take 45 seconds in one production, 2 minutes in another, and 5 in a third, and that all or none might be good, or bad. Shakespearean *blank verse* (the unrhymed five-beat lines of *iambic pentameter*) does give a certain consistency, but can be consistently slow or (more profitably) fast, and in either case needs to be set against the speed of any prose in the play, and of other verse-forms that may be used (couplets, songs, doggerel). Great blocks of speech can send actors manic or clog them up, and both Beckett and Harold Pinter (b.1930) famously insist with three-dot, four-dot, and five-dot pauses that actors respect and cultivate a repeated precision of silence.

And silence is critical, for one thing which the printed page (though itself silent) can never capture, and that even at its greatest height and intensity will be as brief as the glimpse of a wild creature, is the potency of silence, especially an extended silence in a full theatre. Stories of great dramatic silences are often told, not least because Shakespeare was a master of them and his later work demands in performance moments of utter stillness and deep silence in which his art seems at its most profound. But no living human silence has ever lasted, and the printed page can in its nature only gesture towards silence with white space.

One can try for special effects—Caryl Churchill (b.1938), for example, has influentially experimented with various ways of indicating that speeches should *overlap*[5]—but in commercially printed and distributed work there is a strong pull to the conventional and a strong aversion to anything troublesome or requiring capital investment. Most printed drama appears typographically similar, allowing for the differing *house-styles* of individual publishers, but experiences of drama in performance are at least as profoundly different from one another as they may in other ways be similar. As a reader of drama you must bring that knowledge of variety and potential to the limiting convenience and uniformity of a printed text.

[5] See Churchill, *Plays 2*, p. 195, and Crimp, *Plays 1, passim.*

3

Text I: editing and reception

Edit 1. To publish, give to the world.
2. To prepare an edition of. **b.** To prepare, set in order for
publication. Sometimes euphemistically for: To garble, 'cook'.

Sh. OED[1]

Editing is always an intervention between reader and text. If there is
only one previous edition of a play, or a text *seen through the press* by
the author which may be taken to represent the author's intentions, it
will usually be chosen as the *copy-text* for the new edition (the basic
source compositors follow) and reprinted closely. But should obvious
mistakes be reproduced? If the copy-text reads 'That's very wind of
you.', do you change it to 'That's very kind of you'? Probably yes, and
probably rightly; but matters get tricky fast.

Not all mistakes are obvious; and between what might be a mistake
on the page and what is possible on stage is a great gap which editors
may or may not respect. *Entrances* and *exits* are a good example: suppose in the copy-text there is a long scene with three speakers (A, B,
C), and for the first 100 lines all three are speaking, but for the second
100 lines A and B speak directly to one another with no reference
whatever to C. The copy-text provides no mid-scene exit for C, implying s/he is still on stage, silent. In practice directors may tidy C off
stage by adding a mid-scene exit, or keep C on stage (watchful? prowl-
ing? trying to speak but not able to get a word in edgeways?). Should
the editor also add an exit? Many do, but it isn't a neutral decision: in
act 5 of *Measure, for Measure*,[2] for example, the drunkard-murderer

---

[1] This quotation has itself been edited (but not cooked) for convenience. Some
material has been omitted but nothing has been added or made up.

[2] The unexpected comma is not a pause, but probably serves to insist that it is
'Measure *for* Measure', not 'Measure f' Measure'.

Barnardine says nothing for the last fifty lines and is often made to exit, but when he stays can be an electrifying presence, especially if mobile.

With some Renaissance playwrights, particularly Shakespeare, matters are genuinely complicated, for there are multiple early editions none of which has authority in any direct sense. These texts may be *quartos* (the paper is folded twice, to give four pages per sheet) or *octavos* (paper folded three times, eight pages per sheet), which are usually small books, editions of individual plays; or they may be *folios* (paper folded once, two pages per sheet), larger books which are usually collected works. If there is more than one quarto edition they are referred to as Q1, Q2, etc.; and it may be obvious that Q2 was set from Q1, Q3 from Q2, and so on, in which case only Q1 really matters. But there may also be material in a Q2 that is <u>not</u> in Q1, implying that the compositors of Q2 had another source, perhaps the Book of a production or authorial *foul papers*. Similarly, an F-text may obviously derive from a Q-text, or be significantly different, omitting material and adding new lines which appear in no quarto. There may also be multiple F-texts, referred to as F1, F2, etc.: Shakespeare's Second, Third, and Fourth Folios were printed in 1632, 1663, and 1685 (232 >), but his F2–4 all derive from F1 so only F1 really matters.

It is easiest to understand the scale of the problem with a concrete example, so on pages 24–7 are *photo-quotations* of the 'same' passage in *Hamlet* 5.1 from the Q1 (1603), Q2 (1604), and F1 (1623) texts; each offers many distinct readings between which an editor of *Hamlet* must choose. Please read each text carefully, identifying as many differences as you can and pondering what effects those differences have on the page and might have on stage.

Lear. So, I tell thee churlish Priest, a miniftring Angell
fhall my fifter be, when thou lieft howling.
Ham. The faire *Ofelia* dead!
Queene Sweetes to the fweete, farewell:
I had thought to adorne thy bridale bed,faire maide,
And not to follow thee vnto thy graue.
Lear. Forbeare the earth a while: fifter farewelle
Leartes leapes into the graue.
Now powre your earth on *Olympus* hie,
And make a hill to o're-top olde *Pellon*:   *Hamlet leapes*
Whats he that coniures fo?   *in after Leartes*
Ham. Beholde tis I, *Hamlet* the Dane.
Lear. The diuell take thy foule.
Ham. O thou praieft not well,
I prethee take thy hand from off my throate,
For there is fomething in me dangerous,

                       Which

Prince of Denmarke.

Which let thy wifedome feare, holde off thy hand:
I lou'de *Ofelia* as deere as twenty brothers could:
Shew me what thou wilt doe for her:
Wilt fight,wilt faft, wilt pray,
Wilt drinke vp veffels,eate a crocadile? Ile doot:
Com'ft thou here to whine?
And where thou talk'ft of burying thee a liue,
Here let vs ftand : and let them throw on vs,
Whole hills of earth, till with the heighth therof,
Make Oofell as a Wart.

William Shakespeare, *The Tragicall Historie of Hamlet Prince of Denmarke. As it hath beene diverse times acted by his Highnesse servants in the Cittie of London: as also in the two Universities of Cambridge and Oxford, and else-where.* (At London printed for N. L. and John Trundell. 1603)
[Q1, sigs I1v–I2r]

Laer. Lay her i'th earth,
And from her faire and vnpolluted flesh
May Violets spring : I tell thee churlish Priest,
A ministring Angell shall my sister be
When thou lyest howling.
Ham. What, the faire *Ophelia*.
Quee. Sweets to the sweet, farewell,
I hop't thou should'st haue been my *Hamlets* wife,
I thought thy bride-bed to haue deckt sweet maide,
And not haue strew'd thy graue.
Laer. O treble woe

Fall

The Tragedie of Hamlet

Fall tenne times double on that curfed head,
Whose wicked deede thy most ingenious sence
Depriued thee of, hold off the earth a while,
Till I haue caught her once more in mine armes;
Now pile your dust vpon the quicke and dead,
Till of this flat a mountaine you haue made
To'retop old *Pelion*, or the skyesh head
Of blew *Olympus*.
Ham. What is he whose griefe
Beares such an emphesis, whose phrase of sorrow
Coniures the wandring starres, and makes them stand
Like wonder wounded hearers : this is I
Hamlet the Dane.
Laer. The deuill take thy soule.
Ham. Thou pray'st not well, I prethee take thy fingers
For though I am not spleenatiue rash,   (from my throat,
Yet haue I in me something dangerous,
Which let thy wisedome feare ; hold off thy hand,
King. Pluck them a sunder.
Quee. Hamlet, Hamlet.
All. Gentlemen.
Hora. Good my Lord be quiet.
Ham. Why, I will fight with him vpon this theame
Vntill my eye-lids will no longer wagge.
Quee. O my sonne, what theame?
Ham. I loued *Ophelia*, forty thousand brothers
Could not with all theyr quantitie of loue
Make vp my summe. What wilt thou doo for her.
King. O he is mad *Laertes.*
Quee. For loue of God forbeare him.
Ham. S'wounds shew me what th'owt doe :

Woo't weepe, woo't fight, woo't fall, woo't teare thy felfe,
Woo't drinke vp Esill, eate a Crocadile?
Ile doo't, Iooll come heere to whine?
To out-face me with leaping in her graue,
Be buried quicke with her, and fo will I.
And if thou prate of mountaines, let them throw
Millions of Acres on vs, till our ground
Sindging his pate againft the burning Zone

Make

Prince of Denmarke.

Make Offa like a wart, nay and thou'lt mouthe,
Ile rant as well as thou.

William Shakespeare, *The Tragicall Historie of Hamlet, Prince of Denmarke. Newly imprinted and enlarged to almost as much againe as it was, according to the true and perfect Coppie* (At London, Printed by J. R. for N. L. and are to be sold at his shoppe under Saint Dunstons Church in Fleetstreet. 1604) [Q2, sigs. M4r–N1r]

Laer. Lay her i'th' earth,
And from her faire and vnpolluted flefh,
May Violets fpring. I tell thee(churlifh Priefl)
A Miniftring Angell fhall my Sifter be,
When thou lieft howling?
   Ham. What, the faire *Ophelia*?
   Queene. Sweets, to the fweet farewell.
I hop'd thou fhould'ft haue bin my *Hamlets* wife:
I thought thy Bride-bed to haue deckt(fweet Maid)
And not t'haue ftrew'd thy Graue.
   Laer. Oh terrible woer,
Fall ten times trebble, on that curfed head
Whofe wicked deed, thy moft Ingeniousfence
Depriu'd thee of. Hold off the earth a while,
Till I haue caught her once more in mine armes:
         Leaps in the graue.
Now pile your duft, vpon the quicke, and dead,
Till of this flat a Mountaine you haue made,
To o're top old *Pelion*, or the sky:fh head
Of blew *Olympus*.
   Ham. What is he, whofe griefes
Beares fuch an Emphafis? whofe phrafe of Sorrow
Coniure the wandring Starres, and makes them ftand
Like wonder-wounded hearers? I his is I,
Hamlet the Dane.
   Laer. The deuill take thy foule.
   Ham. Thou prai'ft not well,

I prythee take thy fingers from my throat;
Sir though I am not Spleenatiue, and rafh,
Yet haue I fomething in me dangerous,
Which let thy wifeneſſe feare. Away thy hand.
 King. Pluck them : funder.
 Qu. Hamlet, Hamlet.
 Gen. Good my Lord be quiet.
 Ham. Why I will fight with him vppon this Theme.
Vntill my eielids will no longer wag.
 Qu. Oh my Sonne, what Theme?
 Ham. I lou'd *Ophelia*; fortie thoufand Brothers
Could not (with all there quantitie of Loue)
Make vp my furmme. What wilt thou do for her?
 King. Oh he is mad *Laertes,*
 Qu. For loue of God forbeare him.
 Ham. Come fhow me what thou'lt doe.
Woo't weepe? Woo't fight? Woo't teare thy felfe?
Woo't drinke vp Esile, eate a Crocodile?
Ile

The Tragedie

Ile doo't. Doft thou come heere to whine;
To outface me with leaping in her Graue?
Be buried quicke with her, and fo will I.
And if thou prate of Mountaines; let them throw
Millions of Akers on vs; till our ground
Sindging his pate againft the burning Zone,
Make *Offa* like a wart. Nay, and thoul't mouth,
Ile rant as well as thou.

The Tragedie of Hamlet, Prince of Denmarke, in *Mr William Shakespeares Comedies, Histories, & Tragedies. Published according to the True Originall Copies.* (London: Printed by Isaac Jaggard, and Ed. Blount. 1623) [F1, TLN 3429–81, sigs PP5v–6r. 5.1.238–84]

There are some obvious features of all these early editions which no modern edition preserves. The *long-s* resembling an f (but with only half a crossbar) fell out of use during the eighteenth century, and retaining it would only confuse modern readers—but even so one needs to remember that an 's' could look like an 'f', and a line like Donne's "As a worme sucking an invenom'd sore" (Elegy VIII, 1. 44)[3] could look comically rude to an Elizabethan and was probably meant to do so. u/v and i/j have been distinct letters since *c.*1630, but

---

[3] C. A. Patrides, ed., *The Complete English Poems of John Donne* (London: Dent, 1985 [Everyman]), p. 151.

before that were alternative graphs of the same letter: v and i were used initially (vnto, Iohn), u and i medially (loue, maior), and u and j terminally (glou [glove], viij). There are also the *catchwords* at bottom-right of each page/column which warn readers what the first word of the next page/column is—a civilized and helpful habit which also disappeared during the eighteenth century. Speech-prefixes are abbreviated and may vary confusingly from one use to the next. All modern editions except facsimiles are *modernized*, and that modernization begins with the choice of a new *fount* of type (one which looks clear and modern, such as this, 𝔫𝔬𝔱 𝔞 𝔡𝔢𝔩𝔦𝔟𝔢𝔯𝔞𝔱𝔢𝔩𝔲 𝔬𝔩𝔡-𝔩𝔬𝔬𝔨𝔦𝔫𝔤 𝔟𝔩𝔞𝔠𝔨𝔩𝔢𝔱𝔱𝔢𝔯 𝔬𝔯 𝔤𝔬𝔱𝔥𝔦𝔠 𝔣𝔬𝔲𝔫𝔱), the alteration of *orthography* to post-eighteenth century norms (long-s, u/v, i/j, and fewer 'e's—'fair' instead of 'faire', for example), and the provision of conventional modern layout with capitalized speech-prefixes, centred stage-directions, etc. This is helpful and uncontroversial: but even so there may be a cost to making a play look modern on the page.

The Q1 text is the shortest, and is often called a *Bad Quarto* or *memorial reconstruction*.[4] It is believed the text was stolen and dictated to a printer's *scribe* by an actor or actors who had been in the play and remembered some lines accurately, some inaccurately, and others not at all; which would imply that the cuts (relative to the longer Q2 and F versions) were accidental. Q1 *Hamlet* probably <u>is</u> a memorial reconstruction, but has also been recognized as an *adaptation*, a formal reworking and <u>deliberate</u> cutting to produce a shorter, more easily staged text, perhaps for touring outside London on temporary and simple stages. An editor might choose Q1 as a special version, but would probably choose Q2 (a *Good Quarto*) or F as copy-text, and faced with the variants in Laertes's first speech would accept Q2/F1, and regard the short Q1 version as 'corrupt':

> *Lear.* So, I tell thee churlish Priest, a ministring Angell
> shall my sister be, when thou liest howling. (Q1)
>
>   *Laer.* Lay her i'th earth,
> And from her faire and unpolluted flesh

---

[4] For recent views see Kathleen O. Irace, *Reforming the "Bad" Quartos: Performance and Provenance of Six Shakespearean First Editions* (Newark: University of Delaware Press/London and Toronto: Associated University Presses, 1994); and Laurie Maguire, *Shakespearean Suspect Texts: The 'Bad' Quartos and Their Contexts* (Cambridge: Cambridge University Press, 1996).

May Violets spring: I tell thee churlish Priest,
A ministring Angell shall my sister be
When thou lyest howling. (Q2)

    Laer. Lay her i'th'earth,
And from her faire and unpolluted flesh,
May Violets spring. I tell thee (churlish Priest)
A Ministring Angell shall my Sister be,
When thou liest howling? (F1)

Q1's 'corruption' is not only its omission of "Lay her . . . spring", but also its *lineation* (arrangement into lines), for it prints the speech as prose but in Q2/F1 it is verse whose iambic (ti-TUM) beat is easily heard ('I TELL | thee (CHURL- | ish PRIEST) ‖ A MIN'- | string AN- | gell SHALL | my SIS- | ter BE,').[5]

The 'problem' is thus reduced to the much lesser differences between Q2 and F1, both claiming to be set from the "*true and perfect*" or "*True Originall*" copy, which in this speech affect the punctuation but not the words or lineation. Some of these differences are interesting, especially for an actor who must learn and deliver the lines: the lunulae around "churlish Priest" in F1, for example, were conventional for a *vocative*, a call to someone by name or title, and F1 has plenty of "(Sir)"s and "(my Lord)"s; but they also suggest possible variation in delivery. Conversely there may be little aural difference between F1's full-stop after "spring" and Q2's colon—both require pauses—but there is to the eye a difference between two distinct units and one in which two ideas are bound together. Other differences are trivial, such as F1's "i'th'earth" and Q2's "i'th earth" (which may simply be a mistake in Q2). But in most modern editions of Shakespeare the general policy of modernizing means that all punctuation-marks in early editions are removed, the whole text (often composed of *periods*) being repunctuated according to late-twentieth-century ideas (as if composed of *sentences*). In Laertes's speech the new punctuation would often coincide with F1 (a full-stop after "spring", for example) but would also remove F1's *capitalization* (Violets, Priest, Ministring

---

[5] There are also obvious errors such as the meaningless "Make Oosell as a Wart"; Q2 reads "Make Ossa like a wart", and F1 "Make *Ossa* like a wart". F1's italics indicate a proper name, Mount Ossa in Thessaly, mentioned in Homer's *Odyssey* and the proverbial phrase 'to pile Pelion upon Ossa', meaning 'to add difficulty to difficulty'. Laertes mentions Pelion at 5.1.253; Hamlet picks up the reference and means 'make one mountain on another look like a mere wart'.

Angell, Sister), as well as any italics, both of which can helpfully suggest stress (for actors) and the movement of thought and argument (for actors and readers). The editor of *Hamlet* in the series might agree or disagree with these decisions, but would have to accept them.

This speech is relatively easy to sort out, posing no severe problems; but how do you choose between Q2's "O treble woe" and F1's "Oh terrible woer" (i.e. woo-er, one who woos)? or between Q2's "hold off thy hand" and F1's "Away thy hand."? In both cases both alternatives are possible on page and stage alike, and one must pay one's money and take one's choice. Trickier still is to ask who says "Good my Lord be quiet"? Q2 and F1 agree it is said, but Q2 gives the line to Horatio and F1 to an anonymous, otherwise silent "*Gen.*" (Gentleman). As the funeral is attended by a King and Queen there are likely to be extra gentlemen standing about, one of whom could easily speak the line; but there is a good case in performance for preferring Horatio as the speaker (he is otherwise silent throughout), and it is suggestive that in Q2 the previous line is "*All.* Gentlemen.", a general shout which F omits—or half-omits, accidentally transforming "Gentlemen" into the next speech-prefix? The F1 reading may be an error, but is possible; and a worse editorial headache starts with the stage-directions.

The idea that Laertes and Hamlet fight <u>in</u> Ophelia's grave is widespread, and the play is often staged that way: but while Q1 and F1 agree that *Laertes* leaps into the grave, Q2 gives no explicit stage-directions at all,[6] and only Q1, the 'Bad Quarto', makes <u>Hamlet</u> jump in. The most interesting explanation is based on staging: at Globe I the grave was probably a *stage-trap*, a trap-door in the *stage-boards* which could be opened as necessary during performance; but it seems unlikely that the Globe's stage-trap was big enough to allow <u>two</u> people to jump into it and fight, so at the Globe a staging in which Laertes jumps in but gets out again to fight Hamlet next to the open grave was probably used. This would seem to be what is indicated in F1, while Q2, giving no instructions, is ambiguous. But Q1, remember, is probably simplified for touring, and on a touring-stage without a stage-trap the grave could be off the front of the stage, in which case there <u>would</u> be enough room for both Laertes and Hamlet to jump and

---

[6] It still has its embedded stage-directions: Hamlet says to Laertes "I prethee take thy fingers from my throat", so Laertes must put his fingers there first.

fight. A modern director might have a decision made for them by the stage they were using; but what should an editor do?

On pages 32–3 is an opening from the Oxford Shakespeare *Hamlet* (1987), edited by G. R. Hibbard (1915–92), which shows most of this passage. Please now look at and read all of it carefully. Hibbard has a 'Textual Introduction' (pp. 67–130) in which he considers all three early editions, and explains his decisions to adopt F1 as his copy-text and to emend it as he thinks fit with readings from Q1 and Q2, or later editions, or of his own. The single-column block of notes immediately below the play-text on each page is the *textual collation*, recording some rejected readings, including variant stage-directions; and below that in double-column are the annotations. As in all paperback Oxford editions the type, layout, orthography, and punctuation are modernized: but the second word on p. 332, "minist'ring", suggests how odd such modernization can be. In both Q2 ("ministring") and F1 ("Ministring") an iambic rhythm can only be fully sounded if 'ministering' is pronounced as two syllables (mins-tring), rather than three (min-is-tring) or four (mi-ni-ster-ing); but how to speak the line is left up to the actor. Hibbard should modernize the spelling by adding an 'e' (ministering), but recognizes that that spelling enforces four syllables and so opts instead for an *apostrophe* (') indicating the *elision* of the 'e' he was supposed to introduce. The problem for an actor is not just the 'e' but the second 'i', because iambic rhythm demands 'min'-st'ring' not 'mi-ni-st'ring'): in Q2/F1 the whole word is printed and an actor must make it fit as they will, but Hibbard's "minist'ring" seems to say 'omit the e but not the second i', and so may misdirect an actor or reader specifically to sabotage the iambic rhythm.

Equally dubious are the extra stage-directions about Gertrude "(*scattering flowers*)" and Hamlet "(*coming forward*)": certainly it makes sense for Gertrude to carry and leave flowers, but must she scatter them? And surely Hamlet comes forward, but must he do it then? In the matter of leaping Hibbard follows Q1 and has Hamlet follow Laertes into the grave (though he alters the timing slightly); he notes that "A 'grave' that was both shallow and wide would seem to have been essential", but does not worry about how this could have been done at Globe I, where *Hamlet* was often performed. Another stage-direction, "⌈*grappling with him*⌉", is placed in *broken brackets*, which are

5.1   *The Tragedy of Hamlet*

A minist'ring angel shall my sister be
When thou liest howling.
HAMLET   What, the fair Ophelia!
GERTRUDE (*scattering flowers*) Sweets to the sweet. Farewell.
I hoped thou shouldst have been my Hamlet's wife.
I thought thy bride-bed to have decked, sweet maid,
And not t'have strewed thy grave.
LAERTES   O, treble woe
Fall ten times treble on that cursèd head
Whose wicked deed thy most ingenious sense
Deprived thee of.—Hold off the earth awhile,
Till I have caught her once more in mine arms.   240
    He leaps into the grave
Now pile your dust upon the quick and dead,
Till of this flat a mountain you have made
To o'ertop old Pelion or the skyish head
Of blue Olympus.
HAMLET (*coming forward*) What is he whose grief
Bears such an emphasis, whose phrase of sorrow
Conjures the wand'ring stars, and makes them stand
Like wonder-wounded hearers? This is I,
Hamlet the Dane.

233 *scattering flowers*] not in FQ2Q1   Sweets to the sweet. Farewell.] Q2 (Sweets . . . sweet,
farewell,) Q1 (Sweetes . . . sweete, farewell:); Sweets, . . . sweet‸ farewell. F   236 t'have] F;
haue Q2   treble woe] Q2; terrible woer F   237 treble] F (trebble); double Q2   240.1 *He leaps
into the grave*] F (*Leaps in the graue*) Q1 (*Leartes leapes into the graue*); not in Q2   243 To o'ertop]
FQ1; To'retop Q2   244 *coming forward*] not in FQ2Q1   grief] Q2; griefes F   246 Conjures]
Q2; Coniure F

232 **howling** i.e. howling in hell. Compare   cited by *OED*)
   Measure 3.1.128–9, 'those that lawless   244 **blue** Shakespeare is the first English
   and incertain thought | Imagine howl-   writer cited by *OED* to use this adjective
   ing'.   with reference to mountains, flames, and
238 **ingenious** quick of apprehension   the veins of the body.
241–4 **Now pile . . . Olympus** The allusion is 245 **emphasis** violence of utterance
   to the war of the gods and the giants in   246 **Conjures** puts a spell on (*OED* v. 7)
   Greek mythology. In the course of it the   **wand'ring stars** planets
   giants attempted to scale Olympus by   **stand** stand still
   piling Mount Ossa upon Mount Pelion.   247 **wonder-wounded** wonder-struck (Shake-
   Virgil's mention of the story, *imponere*   spearian compound)
   Pelio Ossam (*Georgics* 1, 281), became   248 **Hamlet the Dane** In calling himself *the*
   proverbial (Tilley O81)   *Dane*, i.e. King of Denmark, Hamlet as-
243 **skyish** lofty, sky-high (earliest instance   serts his right to the throne.

                            332

William Shakespeare, *Hamlet* (ed. G. R. Hibbard, Oxford and New York: Oxford
University Press, 1994 [World's Classics]), 5.1.231–66. The edition was first published in
1987.

The Tragedy of Hamlet   5.1

He leaps in after Laertes

LAERTES ⌜*grappling with him*⌝ The devil take thy soul!

HAMLET Thou pray'st not well.

   I prithee take thy fingers from my throat;   250

   For though I am not splenative and rash,

   Yet have I something in me dangerous,

   Which let thy wiseness fear. Away thy hand.

CLAUDIUS Pluck them asunder.

GERTRUDE   Hamlet, Hamlet!

ALL THE LORDS Gentlemen!

HORATIO   Good my lord, be quiet.

HAMLET

   Why, I will fight with him upon this theme

   Until my eyelids will no longer wag.

GERTRUDE O my son, what theme?

HAMLET

   I loved Ophelia. Forty thousand brothers

   Could not, with all their quantity of love,   260

   Make up my sum—What wilt thou do for her?

CLAUDIUS O, he is mad, Laertes.

GERTRUDE For love of God, forbear him.

HAMLET 'Swounds, show me what thou'lt do.

   Woo't weep? Woo't fight? Woo't fast? Woo't tear thyself?

   Woo't drink up eisel, eat a crocodile?

---

248 *He leaps in after Laertes*] Q1 (*Hamlet leaps . . . Laertes*); *not in* FQ2   *grappling with him*] *not in* FQ2   251 For] Q2Q1; Sir F   and] F; *not in* Q2   252 something in me] FQ1; in me something Q2   253 wiseness] F; wisedome Q2Q1   Away] F; hold off Q2Q1   255 ALL THE LORDS Gentlemen!] Q2 (*All*. Gentlemen); *not in* F   HORATIO] Q2; Gen⟨tleman⟩ F   264 'Swounds] Q2; Come F   thou'lt] F; th'owt Q2; thou wilt Q1   265 Woo't fast] Q2; *not in* F; wilt fast Q1

248.1 *He leaps in after Laertes* Q1 is very definite about what happens here; and so, in agreement with it, is the author of the elegy on Burbage quoted at p. 15. A 'grave' that was both shallow and wide would seem to have been essential.

251 **splenative** quick-tempered. The spleen was regarded as the source of anger.

253 **Which let . . . fear** i.e. which your own good sense should warn you to treat with caution

257 **wag** move. Movement of the eyelids is one of the last signs of life in a dying man.

263 **forbear him** leave him alone, i.e. don't take up his challenge

264 **'Swounds** F's *Come* is an evident case of 'purging'.

265 **Woo't** wilt (a colloquial form of the 2nd person singular of *will* (*OED v.*[1] A 3δ)). The form seems to have been associated with challenges and the like in Shakespeare's mind. Compare *2 Henry IV* 2.1.54–5; *Antony* 4.2.7.
   Woo't fast The omission of these words from F is the result of eye-skip.

266 **eisel** vinegar (regarded as the quintessence of bitterness). See *OED* for numerous examples and for the wide variety of spellings.
   crocodile (probably included here on account of the toughness of its skin, which, according to Nashe, 'no iron will pierce' —*Have With You to Saffron-Walden* iii. 96)

not explained in Hibbard's edition but elsewhere in the series are used when alterations to the copy-text's stage-directions and speech-prefixes are "not indisputable" or "likely to be regarded as contentious".[7] Presumably, therefore, Hibbard felt that he was taking a chance in making Laertes grapple, but not in making Hamlet jump—which is odd, because grappling is implicit in all three early editions ("I prethee take thy hand from off my throate", etc.) while Hamlet jumps only in Q1. In the textual collation *"grappling with him"* is listed as *"not in FQ2"*, wrongly implying that it is in Q1, which it isn't. Horatio gets his line back from the mysterious gentleman, but the Q2-only "Gentlemen." is inserted, its speech-prefix (*"All."*) becoming "ALL THE LORDS"—which suggests that any commoners present (Horatio, and sometimes the Grave-Diggers) stand aloof from a general shout. And so on. Overall, as well as making unavoidable choices about the existing stage-directions, Hibbard chose to intervene decisively and direct the scene on the page; but is it an editor's job to do so?

We're not trying to knock Hibbard's particular choices. His edition is helpful and often thoughtful: but he made very extensive decisions on your behalf, and if the textual collation is there, the effects of those decisions are writ very much larger. Problems and alternatives may be considered in the notes: but the stage-directions that appear in the text are imposed on the action, and for most readers the text they happen to have is 'how the play is'. To counter this editorial and typographical foreclosure on meaning it is always worth looking at any quarto-texts and the F1 text of any Shakespeare play you are working on intensively, especially if you are an actor as well as a reader; but the point isn't to abandon modernized editions, only to remember they are not neutral, and the decisions they make, even if logical and sensible, are also commercial and ideological, and always consequential. Modernized editions are helpful, available, and often invaluable; but if you only read one, and assume 'that is how the play is', you are making a big mistake. It is for that reason that we almost always quote Shakespeare in the F1 text (with long-s, u/v, and i/j

---

[7] William Shakespeare, *Julius Caesar* (ed. Arthur Humphreys, 1984; Oxford and New York: Oxford University Press, 1998 [World's Classics]), p. 86; *Anthony and Cleopatra* (ed. Michael Neill, Oxford and New York: Oxford University Press, 1994 [World's Classics]), p. 136.

modernized): it too is only one version among many, but it is the most consistent and careful of the early editions, and often pointedly open and helpful to actors where many modern editions are closed and unhelpful.

Finally, a word about the *reception* of editions, the responses readers and others have to them. A publisher will not invest in a new edition unless they think they can sell it, preferably in large quantities, and that means competing in the academic and general market-place. This is one of the things that makes editors, especially of Shakespeare, vulnerable to ideological pressures, for one of the largest markets is school use—Shakespeare is a compulsory element of the National Curriculum in the UK and taught throughout the Anglophone world—and parents and politicians alike have strong ideas about what it is suitable to teach schoolchildren. This is now unlikely to affect editorial decisions about the text, but will affect decisions about what is or isn't mentioned in the notes. Obscenity is an obvious example, as when Hamlet says to Ophelia "Do you thinke I meant Country matters?" (3.2.116), and quite clearly puns on 'cunt'. Hibbard, as it happens, does note that Hamlet "quibbl[es] indecently on the first syllable of *country*", and the Oxford Shakespeare, aimed more at university students than schoolchildren, is usually quite good about admitting obscenity; other editions of *Hamlet* do not mention the pun, and some teachers seem to think that obscenity is beneath Shakespeare or shouldn't be mentioned in class. Such attitudes affect whole plays, the prime example being *A Midsommer Nights Dreame*, often the first Shakespeare play schoolchildren are introduced to, at about 14. Most people now think of fairies as little fluttery things, like Tinkerbelle in the Walt Disney *Peter Pan*, and some of Shakespeare's images, fairies sleeping in flowers or jousting with bumble-bees, support that conception; but there is also the consideration that Titania, Queen of the Fairies, is made to fall in love with Nick Bottom, an adult male human whose head has been turned into a donkey's. Add the ideas that in the first productions Titania (like all female rôles) would have been played by a boy, and it is not rude or stupid to wonder if the sight of a *cross-dressed* donkey-man and fairy-queen-boy embracing might be sexually charged. Some modern productions explore this option, and it is not unknown for Bottom to be very amorous (or visibly 'hung like a donkey'), and for (the now female actor playing)

Titania to bare her breasts, generating a rather X-rated *Dream*. But such ideas, almost by definition, continue to be excluded from most editions intended for school-sale, and all editions are likely in one or another way to reflect commercial, social, and political constraints, as much as any individual editor's sensible or insensible choices.

4

Text II: the process of reading

Everything we have said so far applies to each moment (speech, action) of a play in itself, and to write accurately about drama one must maintain in reading a constant awareness of the filters and interventions which affect every word of every play. But another aspect of reading works outward from each moment, connecting an individual line or action with what one already knows of the speaker and auditor(s), the plot, themes, verbal motifs, and theatrical ambitions on show. Plays are relatively short works which need economic construction, and in most canonical plays every moment is both itself and resonant with other moments. In performance an audience may be offered cues to connect widely separated moments—a particular colour of light, a repeated gesture, sound, or arrangement of actors—but readers must cue themselves. Though often used interchangeably, a script (from Latin *scribere*, to write) is simply something written, and hence linear, but a text (from Latin *texere*, to weave) is something woven, which has warp and weft and goes sideways and back as well as forward and across: and readers of texts must always be about their weaving.

Consider, for example, an apparently trivial moment late in Shakespeare's *The Second part of King Henry the fourth* (*c*.1598). The speakers are the host, Robert Shallow (once a law student in London, where he knew Falstaff, and now a Country Justice in the Cotswold hills in Gloucestershire); his trusted servant Davie, a local man; and Bardolfe, an unsavoury (but not unlikeable) Corporal with a drinker's red face and nose, one of Falstaff's London-based crew of rogues-turned-soldiers (who are in residence). There is also a *mute*, a page-boy whom Shallow calls "my little tyne [tiny] theefe":

> *Shal.* Honest *Bardolfe*, welcome: If thou want'st any thing, and wilt not call, beshrew thy heart. Welcome my little tyne theefe, and welcome

indeed too: Ile drinke to M. *Bardolfe*, and to all the Cavileroes about
London.
  Dav. I hope to see London, once ere I die.
  Bar. If I might see you there, *Davie*.
  Shal. You'l crack a quart together? Ha, will you not M. *Bardolfe*?
  Bar. Yes Sir, in a pottle pot.
  Shal. I thanke thee: the knave will sticke by thee, I can assure thee that.
He will not out, he is true bred.
  Bar. And Ile sticke by him, sir.
  Shal. Why there spoke a King: lack nothing, be merry.   (5.3.55–70)

Shallow (like Polonius) is as his name suggests a great talker, whose
words often mean little but sometimes mean a lot, and in all the
Gloucestershire scenes (3.2, 5.1, 5.3) there is a bittersweet comedy in
Falstaff's plans to cheat Shallow and Shallow's generosity as a host,
here extended to Bardolfe. There is also a general comedy in seeing
Bardolfe, a haunter of taverns repeatedly twitted about his large red
nose, so enthusiastically encouraged to drink and so unfailingly dignified as "M[aster] *Bardolfe*". But something else begins with Davie's
wistful desire to "see London, once ere I die.", at first also comic (the
première was in London) and familiar (a "pottle pot" is a four-pint
tankard, fitting Bardolfe's thirst for beer) but sharpening when
Shallow affectionately calls Davie a "knave". This harks back to an
exchange between Shallow and Davie in 5.1, where Davie begs
Shallow "To countenance *William Visor* of Woncote, against *Clement
Perkes* of the hill": Davie admits that Visor is a knave but explains he is
also "mine honest Friend", and Shallow promises that Visor "shall
have no wrong" (5.1.38–52). Davie's justification for his request, that
"I have serv'd your Worshippe truely sir, these eight yeares: and if I
cannot once or twice in a Quarter beare out a knave, against an honest
man, I have but a very litle credite with your Worshippe.", and
Shallow's granting of it, are triumphs of loyalty and affection over
consistency and law, deplorable in the abstract but attractive in the
particular instance. This earlier exchange (drawn by the word 'knave')
resonates in Shallow's concern that Davie be looked after in London
and Bardolfe's self-interested and unreliable but not unkind promise
to do so; and both exchanges follow one in the first Gloucestershire
scene when Bardolfe accepts bribes to exempt some men from being
drafted (3.2.220–40), an equally understandable but improper and
venial subversion of law. Perhaps in choosing who must go to war and

who may stay at home Bardolfe was speaking like a king, but one would hardly have thought it then; hearing it now said by Shallow, and knowing all one knows of Bardolfe, one might be moved to approve the sentiment—a king should indeed be understanding and promise protection—even if doubting Bardolfe's capacity to deliver on his words. But a nasty surprise is in store, for when in the play's last scene there enters a real king—the just-crowned Henry V, with whom (as Prince Hal) Falstaff and his crew have long kept company, and whose accession they greet with greedy joy, anticipating riches and revelry—he speaks very differently:

> *Falst.* My King, my Jove; I speake to thee, my heart.
> *King.* I know thee not, old man: Fall to thy Prayers:
>   How ill white haires become a Foole, and Jester?   (5.5.46–48)

As in *Henry V*, when he refuses to save Bardolfe from being hanged for looting, Henry as king will set aside neither law nor the public propriety and justice he knows is demanded of a king. Is he wrong? Is Shallow wrong to respond to Bardolfe's promise of a shared concern for Davie with generous praise? Are readers wrong to find in Henry's principled abandonment of his knavish friends something deeply unlikeable? Or do we ruefully understand that kings must in their office be unlikeable, and in their nature are so unlike others they can have no friends?

Nor can the weaving end there. To begin with there intervenes between the first and second Gloucestershire scenes the whole of Act 4, largely concerned with (1) an encounter of armies in Gaultree Forest, in which the rebels against the ailing Henry IV are betrayed by one of their own, who does not come, then persuaded to sign a treaty and lay down their arms, after which they are promptly arrested and condemned to death—a fine pattern of loyal friendships and kingly dealings engineered by the cold Prince John, who unlike Prince Hal is a well-behaved and 'honourable' son; and (2) the *mock-death* of Henry IV, mistakenly thought to have expired by Prince Hal, who takes the crown—to the bitter distress, on waking, of his father, who thinks it shows his son and heir impatient for his death. Hal is himself mortified by his mistake and his father's rebukes, and his rejection of Falstaff after his father's true death and his own coronation, however unlikeable, venerates his father's advice in a way hard to condemn, and fuses with tremendous dramatic power a shattering personal experience and the public need for impartial justice. This strand of the play, the Gaultree episode, and the Gloucestershire scenes are set in rich contrast and constant resonance with one another; and the whole complex of concerns boils in and under an untrue but heartfelt compliment from a loving-foolish Justice to a streetwise-knavish Corporal: "Why there spoke a King: lack nothing, be merry.".

And this is, after all, 2 Henry IV. For those who started with *1 Henry IV* (*c*.1597) there are other connections to be made: Shallow and Davie appear only in the second part, but Falstaff, Bardolfe, Hal and his trusted servant-companion Poins, and Henry IV all wind with many others through both plays, and the concerns which Shakespeare invented Shallow and Davie to serve wind with them. Henry IV's mock-death, for example, is a reverse-echo of Falstaff's self-serving mock-death (or lying doggo) at the battle of Shrewsbury (*1H4* 5.4)— another 'corpse' mistaken by Hal: but on that occasion, when Falstaff spins a great yarn to claim credit for killing the rebel Hotspur (actually slain by Hal himself), the Prince does not speak as he will when king, but is of Davie's mind: "For my part, if a lye may do thee grace, / Ile gild it with the happiest tearmes I have." (5.4.157–58). In each part 2.4 is set in the Boar's Head in Eastcheap, a low area of London, home territory for Falstaff and Bardolfe but not for Hal, seen in both scenes slumming with men he treats as cronies but from whom as Prince he remains detached; in both he also overtly plays rôles, in the first 'acting' his father-as-king in a jesting rebuke to Falstaff for misleading a Prince, and then having to lie in earnest to cover for Falstaff when a Sheriff appears; and in the second disguising himself as a servant to hear what Falstaff says about him behind his back before confronting Falstaff with rebukes which anticipate the limit of their friendship. Both *Henry IV* plays, moreover, are themselves framed by *Richard II* (*c*.1596) and *Henry V* (1599) in Shakespeare's *second tetralogy*, and scenes from both could be brought to bear on Shallow's line, particularly the paired 4.1s—in *Richard II* the 'mirror scene' in which Richard abdicates, and goes from speaking as a king to speaking otherwise; and in *Henry V* the 'cloak scene', in which Henry, wistfully remembering on the night before the battle of Agincourt what it was to be Hal, disguises himself so that he can talk with his troops without anyone knowing "there spoke a King". And the whole second tetralogy is itself a prequel to Shakespeare's *first tetralogy*—*1, 2, 3 Henry VI* and *Richard III* (*c*.1592–4)—in which he began his investigation of what kings might be and how a dramatist can profitably have them speak, and have others speak like them.

This is a deliberately extended example, and while there are many other paired plays Shakespeare's historical tetralogies are exceptionally dense. On the other hand, the more Shakespeare one knows the more numerous and interesting the connections that appear between all his plays: serious readers of his work as a whole constantly find (un)expected echoes and contrasts which illuminate the workings of his drama, and critically interact with knowledge of the actors for whom he wrote multiple rôles in successive plays. The same is broadly true, allowing for differing circumstances of composition and performance, of most dramatists who produce sustained bodies of work: but the awareness of these larger patterns must be grounded in the full reading of individual texts. The warp and weft are there to be traced in every text, signalled overtly in dialogue or stage-direction or implicit in structure, but we have both become pressingly aware in teaching that many students have difficulty recognizing those signals: and we end this section therefore with two further examples, of plays often read but less often read productively.

The first is Ibsen's *Hedda Gabler* (1890), at the end of which Hedda (whose married name is Tesman, though she is still frequently identified as the daughter of General Gabler) commits suicide aged 29 by shooting herself in the head. Here are the last 12 speeches: the speakers are Hedda herself; her husband of about six months, Jörgen Tesman, a somewhat fatuous and insensitive academic whom she does not love; Mr Brack, a judge, outwardly very proper but intent on quietly supplanting Tesman in Hedda's bed; and Mrs Elvsted, a younger contemporary of Hedda's at school, who recently left her husband for another academic, Ejlert Lövborg (to whom Hedda was close before her marriage). Tesman's maid Berte comes in at the end, but does not speak; both Lövborg (mentioned as 'Ejlert') and Tesman's Aunt Rina have just died; and the "melancholy task" at which Tesman and Mrs Elvsted are busy is the attempted reconstruction of Lövborg's last book, the manuscript of which he lost while drunk but told Mrs

Elvsted he had destroyed, and which was in fact found by Tesman and burned by Hedda.

> [HEDDA *goes into the inner room and pulls the curtains together behind her. A short pause. Suddenly she is heard to play a wild dance tune on the piano.*]
>
> MRS ELVSTED [*starts up from her chair*]. Oh . . . what's that!
>
> TESMAN [*runs to the doorway*]. But Hedda, my dear . . . don't play dance music, not tonight! Do think of Aunt Rina! And of Ejlert, too!
>
> HEDDA [*puts her head out between the curtains*]. And of Auntie Julle. And of all the rest of them . . . . I shall be silent in future.
>
> [*She draws the curtains together again.*]
>
> TESMAN [*at the desk*]. I don't think it's good for her to see us at this melancholy task. I'll tell you what, Mrs. Elvsted . . . you'll have to move in to Aunt Julle's. Then I'll come up in the evenings. And then we can sit and work there. Eh?
>
> MRS. ELVSTED. Yes, perhaps that would be the best . . .
>
> HEDDA [*from the inner room*]. I can hear what you're saying, Tesman. And how am I supposed to survive the evenings out here?
>
> TESMAN [*leafing through the papers*]. Oh, I expect Mr. Brack will be kind enough to look in now and again.
>
> BRACK [*in the armchair, shouts cheerfully*]. I'll gladly come every single evening, Mrs. Tesman! Don't you worry, we'll have a fine time out here together!
>
> HEDDA [*clearly and distinctly*]. Yes, you're looking forward to that, aren't you, Mr Brack? Yourself as the only cock in the yard . . .
>
> [*A shot is heard within.* TESMAN, MRS. ELVSTED, *and* BRACK *all start to their feet.*]
>
> TESMAN. Oh, now she's playing about with those pistols again.
>
> [*He pulls the curtains aside and runs in.* MRS. ELVSTED *follows.* HEDDA *lies stretched out dead on the sofa. Confusion and shouting.* BERTE, *in alarm, comes in from the right.*]
>
> TESMAN [*yelling at* BRACK]. Shot herself! Shot herself in the temple! Think of that!
>
> BRACK [*half prostrate in the armchair*]. But, good God Almighty . . . people don't do such things!

(pp. 263–4)[1]

---

[1] In Ibsen, *Four Major Plays*. This translation by Jens Arup was first published in 1966.

Many critics and more students, finding the ending an incoherent shock, confidently assert that Hedda is 'mad': but this is simply not so. We have already suggested that Ibsen's endings relate quasi-parodically to the genuinely incoherent (but thrillingly spectacular) endings of much mid-nineteeth-century drama, against which he reacted (< 2); and one aspect of that reaction was to write plays in which sensational things do not happen merely for effect, but grow remorselessly from circumstance and character. Every line of this ending echoes earlier lines, and "those pistols" are an adventure in themselves: on the back wall of the inner room, visible throughout the play, is a portrait of General Gabler, from whom Hedda inherited a pair of cased pistols (p. 198); act 1 ends with Hedda remarking that she still has them, and act 2 begins with her loading them and firing at Brack (pp. 198–9); she has previously threatened at least once to shoot Lövborg (pp. 191, 219), and gives him one of the pistols with which to kill himself "beautifully" (pp. 245–6); and just before her own suicide she has learnt from Brack that far from dying beautifully Lövborg was shot in the stomach, perhaps by accident, in a brothel. Nor is the impulse to fire a gun the only sign of Hedda's capacity for violence: at school she once threatened to burn off Mrs Elvsted's hair (p. 186), the previous night again threatened to do so while man-handling Mrs Elvsted out of the room (p. 227), and imagined the manuscript she burnt as not only Mrs Elvsted's hair but also her child by Lövborg (p. 246). Stage-directions, moreover, refer explicitly to Hedda's 'anger', 'frenzy', and 'desperation' whenever she is pressed or teased about her putative pregnancy (pp. 178–9, 209, 251).

The exact status of her sexual relations with Tesman, more interested in paper than flesh, are uncertain, but Brack's view of Tesman as a capon and his predatory intent to satisfy Tesman's wife himself are made clear in act 3, when Hedda first calls him "the only cock in the yard" and says that any relationship with him will be tolerable only "so long as you don't have any sort of hold over me" (p. 239). Speaking to Lövborg she acknowledges that she doesn't love her husband but explicitly rejects any "kind of unfaithfulness" (p. 217); and in the same conversation confesses her acute fear of scandal (p. 219). But scandal now threatens her and gives Brack his hold, for he, shown it as a judge, has recognized the pistol with which Lövborg was shot and threatened Hedda with a scandalous court appearance to explain her gift of it (pp. 261–3)—to all of which Tesman is utterly blind: so the implication of the exchange about Tesman's future evening absences and Brack's future presences, registered in the stage-directions, is that the "fine time" to help Hedda "survive" will comprise sexual demands she will be powerless to refuse.

Consider, then, Hedda's circumstances: trapped in a loveless marriage, betrayed by and bereaved of the man she did perhaps love, faced with a choice between potentially ruinous scandal and forced sex, and possessed of an efficient and ritual means, should her hand and nerve be steady enough, of making the honourable officer's exit. Consider also what exactly she does: withdrawing from company and her husband to the room dominated by her father's image; playing a last tremendous blast of music that is wholly about living and celebrating; staging her own exit-line and last withdrawal through the curtains; doing what she can "[*clearly and distinctly*]" to dump the scheming Brack right in it; and acting with steady hand and nerve, the heavy pistol exactly to her temple, her body aesthetically reclined on a sofa to present, when the curtains are pulled back, those among whom she cannot live (and the paying audience) with a perfect *tableau* (a standard nineteenth-century ending). And where is the madness in that? One might add that Brack's famously nonplussed final line ironically echoes a line (and lie) of Hedda's in act 1, when she tells Mrs Elvsted in a "*cold and collected*" voice that "People don't have such things [as pistols] here." (p. 191); and that the "*wild dance tune*" reaches still further back, to the tarantella famously danced by Nora Helmer in *A Doll's House* (1879).[2]

It is of course true that the performative tenor of Ibsen's ending is unstable, combining the suicide of a young and perhaps pregnant woman with a grotesque social comedy of mutual blindnesses and misunderstandings, in a manner that invites comparison with *Grand-Guignol*, the fused sensationalism and farce popularized in Paris from 1895 by the theatre of that name. But that is only to say that readers (and theatre-practitioners) should be aware of Ibsen as a playwright of his time, and should respect the multiple and contradictory emotions which permeate the play and find what resolution they can in this resolute self-staging of a death. To track those emotions all one need

[2] Ibsen, *Four Major Plays*, pp. 58–9.

do is read Ibsen's stage-directions as carefully as his dialogue, and allow them authority to undermine, offset, ironize, or flatly deny what is (and is not) said. In our second example, however, Beckett's *Waiting for Godot* (French 1952, English 1955), the stage-directions are barer, and the weight of reading falls rather on verbal and structural repetitions.

Waiting for Godot[3] has two acts, in each of which Vladimir and Estragon wait fruitlessly, pass the time playing verbal games reminiscent of *music-hall* routines, are interrupted by Pozzo and his slave Lucky, and are eventually told by a boy that Godot will not come today but will come tomorrow. Act 1 is set on *"A country road. A tree. Evening."* (p. 11), act 2 is *"Next Day. Same Time. Same Place."* (p. 53), and almost everything comes, or seems to come, around twice in a terrible vision of futility. Stage-directions, though plentiful, are usually brief: many concern stage-business or impose pauses, some are negative (as *"Without turning"* and *"Without anger"*, pp. 18, 52), and all have a functional feel which makes it difficult to run the play emotionally in one's head. But against this brisk monotony Beckett orchestrates so many variants, minor and not so minor, that the two acts can seem like a pair of 'Spot the Difference' pictures.

To begin with, the tree in act 2 has *"four or five leaves"* (p. 53) that it lacked in act 1, suggesting a passage from winter to spring, not the passing of one day. The difference affects Vladimir and Estragon: in act 1 they consider hanging themselves from the tree and Estragon becomes *"Highly excited"* at the idea that doing so will give him an erection (pp. 18–19); in act 2 only Vladimir, who notices the leaves, remembers the conversation (p. 56). (Which of them is more hopeful?) On his first appearance Pozzo makes Lucky, whom he holds on a rope, perform in various ways, culminating in the delivery of a long tirade (pp. 42–3); but on his second he is blind, going in the opposite direction, and dependent on Lucky, who is now dumb—which Pozzo seems not to notice. (What kind of luck has Lucky had? And has Pozzo been punished?) Only one boy is specified in the list of characters, and only one is usually cast, but the boy who arrives in act 2 says he did not come yesterday (p. 85). (Do you believe him?) And, most famously, each act ends all but identically:

[3] Beckett, *Complete Dramatic Works*, pp. 7–88.

[*Silence.*]
ESTRAGON: Well, shall we go?
VLADIMIR: Yes, let's go.
[*They do not move.*]

CURTAIN (p. 52)

[*He pulls up his trousers.*]
VLADIMIR: Well? Shall we go?
ESTRAGON: Yes, let's go.
[*They do not move.*]

CURTAIN (p. 88)

As well as swapped lines and invariant immobility, there is the greater difference of the precedent moments and stage-directions, expressed also in Estragon's act–1 comma ("Well,"), a ruminative ending of the silence, and Vladimir's act–2 question-mark ("Well?"), a friendly enquiry about Estragon's successful raising of his trousers—other than which nothing whatever seems to have been accomplished.

Waiting for Godot is notorious as a play in which nothing happens twice, and in many ways that is quite true. By comparison with Shakespeare or Ibsen the paucity is astonishing: no plot, barely any character and certainly no moral or emotional character development, no revelations, and no climax: but the facts remain that on stage and page alike it can be wholly compelling, and that its structural, cyclical, rhythmical, and philosophical means of being so are available to the attentive reader of its densely woven text.

II

READING STRUCTURES

Why is this thus? What is the reason of this thusness?

Artemus Ward (1834–67)

5

What is genre?

Genre means "a type of literary work characterized by a particular form, style, or purpose" (*OED2*). It derives, via Latin *genus* ('birth, race, racial stock') and Old French *gendre* ('gender'), from Greek γένος (*genos*, 'race')—one of many words from that root, including 'generation', 'genetic', 'genocide', and 'genus'. Word families of this kind are prone to ambiguities and overlaps of meaning, and the problems with 'genre' are severe, because the modern sense dates only from the late-nineteenth century but is applied to all texts, and often used very sloppily.

In one way that makes it easy to use: 'What genres do you like?' 'I like *comedies* and *thrillers*.' 'And what genres does she like?' 'Oh, she prefers novels.' The meaning seems clear, but 'novel' is not the same kind of category as 'comedy' or 'thriller', and the confusion is plain if you compare artistic genre with scientific genus. In the Linnaean classification of living things 'genus' occupies a specific place in a descending order—kingdom (animals), sub-kingdom (metazoa), phylum (chordates), sub-phylum (vertebrates), class (mammals), order (primates), sub-order (anthropoids), family (hominids), genus (humans), and species (*homo sapiens*). In the case of *homo sapiens* genus and species are effectively the same, for human beings are the only living hominids; but there are extinct members of the family and genus (such as Neanderthal Man) and every possible level of classification may be needed to distinguish one species from another. To say that two animals are of the same genus is to make a precise statement about relatedness which could be scientifically proven and expressed, for example, as a percentage comparison of the animals' DNA. But in the arts there is no such chain of classification, and although genre is distinct on one hand from *form* (one-act play, sonnet, concerto), and on the other from *medium* (performance, print, music), to place two artworks in the same genre is at best a very imprecise statement about their relatedness. *Oedipus the King, Macbeth, Hedda Gabler, The Crucible, The Godfather,* and *Twin Peaks* are all in some sense *tragedies,* and *Lysistrata, As You Like It, The Importance of Being Earnest, Blithe Spirit, Manhattan,* and *Friends* are all in some sense comedies. But in what sense, <u>exactly</u>? and why is it helpful to say so?

The crucial thing is not <u>what</u> any particular genre is or might be, but <u>how</u> to think about genre in general. Even if definitions of particular genres were universally agreed, existing writing about types of artwork from Aristotle to the present would remain to be interpreted, for dead authors could not be made retrospectively to think as we had decided to think. The word genre is relatively new, but a tendency to compare art-works and argue about their dis/similarities is very old; and in classical or mediaeval discussions it is clear that although their words and way of arguing are other than ours, the problems both they and we soon run into are identical.

The most famous illustration of those problems is probably by Polonius in act 2 of *Hamlet*:

> The best Actors in the world, either for Tragedie, Comedie, Historie, Pastorall : Pastoricall-Comicall : Historicall-Pastorall : Tragicall-Historicall : Tragicall-Comicall-Historicall-Pastorall : Scene individable, or Poem unlimited. *Seneca* cannot be too heavy, nor *Plautus* too light, for the law of Writ, and the Liberty. These are the onely men.
>
> (2.2.396–402)[1]

In performance this catalogue of genres is usually a laugh at Polonius's expense: he starts confidently, often ticking the genres off on his fingers ("Tragedie, Comedie, Historie, Pastorall"), but as he reaches the two-genre combinations he gets more frantic ("Pastoricall-Comicall : Historicall-Pastorall : Tragicall-Historicall") and finally lumps everything together in a great waving of hands ("Tragicall-Comicall-Historicall-Pastorall"). The image is of Polonius getting into a mess, but his whole point is that the actors who have arrived at Elsinore are "The best Actors in the world" precisely because they can do <u>all</u> these genres, and any others you might care to imagine. Titus Maccius Plautus (*c.*250–184 BCE) and Lucius Annaeus Seneca (*c.*4

---

[1] Pastoricall-Comicall : Historicall-Pastorall] pastoral comical, historical pastoral Q2; Pastoricall-Comicall-Historicall-Pastorall F.
individable] Q2; indivible F.

BCE–65CE) were both famous Roman playwrights, but Plautus wrote only comic plays and Seneca only tragic ones; yet these actors can do *Plautine and Senecan* work to the highest standard as well as everything in between, so much so that the quality of their performances reveals the inadequacy of the system of classifying plays. In other words Polonius goes wrong deliberately, and it would be wiser to laugh <u>with</u> him than <u>at</u> him, for the classificatory problems he illustrates are ones with which we are still struggling.

The system runs into trouble with the combination-genres because it assumes genres are mutually exclusive, so that the same play cannot be both tragedy and *history*, and if it seems to be so must 'actually' be a new genre, tragi-history (or histo-tragedy). *Exclusivity* thus leads to *proliferation*, the constant creation of new genres; and proliferation creates a third problem, *hierarchy*, or how all these genres relate to one another. The underlying model is of genre as a system like the pigeon-holes used for letters at universities and hotels, etc.: there have to be as many pigeon-holes as there are categories represented; you can't put one letter into two pigeon-holes at once; and different sorts of label can be applied to identical pigeon-holes. These problems cannot be solved by rearranging the pigeon-holes, building them of plastic rather than wood, or re-thinking the labels on each compartment; they can only be solved by something much more radical which avoids the idea of physically separate boxes altogether.

Imagine instead a large electronic scoreboard, like those at major sportsgrounds. On it you could easily show, simultaneously and superimposed, a triangle, a square, and a circle, and everyone could see and distinguish all three shapes. Every lightbulb, lit or unlit, would contribute to all three patterns; and if all three were set in motion, filling with colours, rotating, separating, recombining, mutating, and freezing again, only very dull people would argue the overall pattern was 'really' triangular or 'really' square.

Literary genre is much more like this than like pigeon-holes, and it is vital to remember that genres are <u>not</u> mutually exclusive: that any two (or ten) genres can combine within the same work in parallel, in series, or in fusion, because genres are <u>not</u> pseudo-boxes into which art-works can be put, but processes of understanding.[2] If we ask

---

[2] Genres-as-boxes is an *essentialist* theory, while genres-as-scoreboard is *anti-essentialist*.

students to define a particular genre, say *westerns*, they often list various common elements (the American West, cowboys and Indians, horses, gun-fights, a sheriff, a saloon-bar brawl, etc.) as if these were necessary ingredients; but a given western can lack any element ('Spaghetti westerns' were largely filmed in Spain, *The Outlaw Josey Wales* has no cowboys, etc.), and the point is not that 'All westerns are like this', but that the idea of westerns links these various elements so any one of them leads a reader/viewer to expect some of the others— an expectation that may be fulfilled or disappointed. If a film opens with a vista of open plains and a man on a horse, you expect Indians, a wagon-train, or an arrival in a frontier-town with a saloon and a jail, but also that the various characters will behave in a manner appropriate to a western, saying the right things in the right way, fighting with fists and guns, ordering whisky at the bar, and so on. And if a giant cartoon foot suddenly squashes the man and his horse; or a spaceship lands; or when the man gets into a town he changes into a dress and orders a cup of tea at the bar; or the town turns out to be 1960s New York, then your understanding of the film's genre will change, differently in each case, as will your expectations of what is likely to happen next. The giant foot would suggest *Monty Python's Flying Circus*, and the idea of westerns might vanish completely, but in the other examples the idea of westerns might remain, combined with science-fiction (*Wild, Wild West*), undermined by *satire* (*Blazing Saddles*), or contrasted with a modern urban world (*Coogan's Bluff*). Your new expectations might or might not be fulfilled, and if you were lucky there might be a genuine *twist*, by definition that which cannot be (or has not been) expected. That is what happens, for example, in Shakespeare's *dark comedies*, late *Elizabethan* plays like *The Merchant of Venice* (*c*.1598) and *Measure, for Measure* (*c*.1603), which invoke the framework and expectations of comedy but pointedly qualify or flatly fail to deliver satisfactorily comedic endings, and in Ibsen's *A Doll's House* (1879), which invokes the framework and expectations of tragedy but is written in prose (until then rarely used for tragedy) and at the end of which Nora walks out on her husband and children, but does not die. Expectations, fulfilments, and consumers' satisfactions are tied together, and it is in relating our experiences of them to one another that a sense of genre develops.

This way of understanding genre is harder work than pigeonholing, for you cannot say "Ah, this is a ——", and 'know where you are', but instead must wonder how many genres are being invoked, and how closely your various expectations are being fulfilled. On the other hand it's more fun, much more rewarding, and we do it in practice all the time as we argue about films or books, watch advertisements, and appreciate sketches. In reading drama, though, the ontological problem of drama's incompleteness on the page compounds the problem, for dramatic genres (like plays themselves) are substantially created only in performance. It is not enough in any medium for an element of a genre to be present: it must also be <u>appropriately</u> present, so in drama actors must individually and collectively (inter)act with the set, props, and audience in an appropriate style. You wouldn't want horror-film mannerisms in a TV *sitcom* except as a joke, nor comic TV routines in a tough-minded thriller. It's obvious: but the complexities are great.

Classical Greek tragedies, for example, contain elements with no functional modern Western equivalent, such as the normative use of *masks*, a *chorus* (many people playing a compound but unitary rôle) and *dithyrambs* (sacred choric dances); and modern attempts to stage these works are plagued by difficulties in finding a mode of performance to suit the text. The *theatre-space* is usually very different from anything the Greeks used, and we know little of how actors and chorus related in classical antiquity. Some directors try to re-create 'classical' performances; others openly modernize, cutting bits they can't make work and adapting action to modern theatres and performance conventions. But if we don't really know how to perform it, what does it mean to say that a classical play invokes or exemplifies this or that genre? And how do you read its surviving text? Nor is it only very old plays that are affected: *Hamlet* undoubtedly has funny lines and humorous action, including the blackly comic fight at Ophelia's funeral (< 24–7)—but should actors play those bits for laughs and revert to being 'tragic/serious' for the finale? Or should they stay 'tragic/serious' throughout, leaving Shakespeare's jokes to fend for themselves? Some *Restoration tragedy* (from the decades following the restoration of King Charles II in 1660) poses an even greater problem: heroic plays filled with extremes of pathos can now easily seem comic, and no one has found a modern style of performance that could make them accessible as tragedies—so they are rarely performed. Another striking example is the problem with Beckett's *Waiting for Godot* (< 19), where productions may contain every line and stage-direction yet clearly lack a kind of acting, or style of performance, that would release the richness of Beckett's words and action.

All these examples posit a style or styles that are somehow demanded by a particular text, and wherever there has been a strong and particular theatrical culture it will always be helpful in studying its drama to understand as much as possible about its conditions and styles of performance. To know the approximate dimensions and layout of a classical Greek amphitheatre, or of Globe I, is (whatever the remaining problems) a helpful and substantial beginning; and to know what there is to be known about how choruses behaved, or to understand how differently actors respond to a three-sided stage like the Globe's compared to a one-sided stage, is another major step. But the real trick is to remember that a complicated process of expectations and fulfilments or disappointments can no more be fixed than can the play itself: dramatic genre inheres in performance as well as text and every performance is different, so genre can be different in every performance even if the text is supposedly 'the same'.

When in 1590 the printer of Marlowe's two-part *Tamburlaine* registered his right to the text he called it *"two comicall discourses"*, but three months later he printed it as *"two tragicall discourses"*—not because he changed his mind, but because comic stage-business in the performances was cut from the text; on stage it was comical, and on the page tragical. A director can also decide to perform a text in a style for which it was not originally intended—white-face, for example, or as a *promenade* performance (in which audience follows actors from place to place)—and in so doing may deepen the genre(s) achieved in the first performances or change them altogether. It may be a disaster or may rescue a play from (un)deserved oblivion, as a 1995 *RNT* production by Stephen Daldry (b.1960) rescued *An Inspector Calls* (1947), an old moral chestnut by J. B. Priestley (1894–1984).[3] Written for post-war London, it became a hit in the 1990s through a strikingly *Expressionist* set-design, full of fascinatingly distorted perspectives. In continental Europe, where such sets are commoner, the trick might

---

[3] See Lesser, *A Director Calls*.

not have worked, and its success in the UK is a cultural exchange, as Japanese or Zulu performances of Shakespeare are, adapting the stories and images his plays offer with styles of performance he couldn't have imagined, and making them welcome there.

You must therefore ask yourself continuously as you read or spectate what expectations you have, and why, and whether they are fulfilled. Each (set of) expectation(s) will suggest a genre at work, and it is by the author's, director's, actors', and readers' or spectators' skills at manipulating dynamic interactions between genres, on page or stage, in the mind or auditorium, that dramatic success stands or falls. For contemporary work your own knowledge of contemporary genres is as good as or better than ours—few students need much help with the e-mail scene in *Closer* (1997) by Patrick Marber (b.1964)—but authors also invoke and exploit older genres, as older plays must also do, and some knowledge of the genres available to the author, the expectations that the first audiences brought to the theatre with them, is necessary for perceptive reading. The chapters in this section provide a starter-kit for that knowledge, which is inevitably of many kinds for the generation of genre begins with authorial, actorly, and audience knowledge of the venue, cast, and occasion, and extends to critical discussion of plays first performed 2,500 years ago: but all of it contributes, in one way or another, to the patterns of understanding, anticipation, and surprise that authors, actors, and audiences collectively create in performance, and so to a reader's ability to sense in a text the structures, traces, forces, and potentials of performance. Understood as a shorthand for such patterns the names of genres become a useful language and critical tool-kit; but as the nameplates of supposedly exclusive categories of text they are blindingly worse than useless.

6

Classical genres:
tragedy, comedy, satyr-plays, and epic

Tragedy and comedy are 'supergenres', infinitely varied and adapted to the cultures that generate them. Ideas of a unified comedy or tragedy extending from European classical antiquity to the present are often challenged but have never quite been defeated: the pervasive influence of Aristotle (384–322 BCE), who discussed *tragedic*[1] theory in his *Poetics*, partly explains a sense of continuity, but equally important are the analytical opposition of tragedy and comedy (symbolized in the paired masks 😩 and 😃), and their links with politics and society.

Only blunt formulations can have much general truth, and the bluntest of all, that tragedies end in death and comedies in marriage, is true enough if understood to mean that tragedies habitually lead their consumers to expect a death,[2] and comedies to expect a loving union. Sexuality and mortality are human constants, corresponding with other basic oppositions—joy/grief, company/solitude, rise/fall—and many post-Aristotelian definitions of comedy and tragedy combine these terms, for example to label tragedy as concerned with the fall of individuals, and comedy with the joys of company. Sex (lovers united) and death (struggle over) are common and satisfying ways of ending narratives, and very many works in many media end with a flavour of comedy or tragedy; but for the terms to be of serious practical use in reading the comedies and tragedies of different times and cultures an appreciation of how the genres have evolved, and more

---

[1] Tragedic means only 'to do with tragedy as art', and retains a far more specific sense than tragic; similarly, *comedic* is narrower than comic.

[2] Even in tabloid journalism an accident is 'tragic' if someone is killed, and 'a tragedy' usually means multiple deaths.

localized knowledge of dramatic theories and performance-practices, especially in ancient Athens, are necessities.

The earliest known drama developed in Athens in the fifth century BCE, not as a recreational option but as a religious and civic duty in which any male citizen might at one or another time participate as a member of a chorus, and regularly as an auditor; perhaps half the adult male citizens, 15,000–20,000 people, attended any given performance. Tragedy, literally 'goat-song' (from Greek τράγος, *tragos*, 'a billy-goat', + ᾠδή, *ode*, 'ode'), developed from the worship of Dionysus, the god of wine, in dithyrambs, and is thought to take its name from a prize-goat for which the first choruses competed. Its principal subjects were largely from Homer's *Iliad* and *Odyssey* and from 'myth' (which in Greek means 'speech, story; that spoken by mouth'), the doings of gods and heroes with particular emphasis on fate, authority, defiance, and sacrifice. The major competitive annual performances of tragedy at the five-day spring festival known as the *City Dionysia* profoundly combined politics with religion: Day 1 probably comprised opening ceremonies and dithyrambs, Day 2 the performance of five comedies, and on each of Days 3–5 the performance of three linked tragedies and a *satyr-play*; winning was a major honour, and for those involved in performances, especially of tragedies, the process of preparation was a major duty of the preceding year. Performances were probably sanctified by animal sacrifice, performers were masked and robed, and the whole business was intrinsically serious; but the central emblem of the Dionysia was an erect phallus, and classical gravity of purpose did not imply modern prudery.

Satyr-plays and comedy (from Greek κῶμος, *komos*, 'a revel') probably developed in complementary opposition to tragedy. Satyrs, servants of Dionysus with a horse's tail and ears, thickly-haired legs, permanent erections, and prodigious appetites for wine, mixed the divine, human, and bestial; only one complete satyr-play-text survives (Euripides's *Cyclops*), but it seems likely that, following each day's third tragedy, the *pendant* satyr-play (performed by the same actors and completing the *tetralogy*) served as exuberant relief from the strain of tragedy and perhaps as a means of returning actors and audience from a sacramental to an earthly frame. They contrasted with the preceding tragedies much, perhaps, as Ben Jonson used an *anti-masque* to contrast with and elevate his *masques*, or as one colour can be used to heighten another. The modern term *satire*, art that mocks or denounces, used to be thought to derive from satyrs: a later Latin word, *satira*, meaning a medley, work in a mixed style, is now preferred as the source, but satyrs too are mixed forms and there are probably connections. Satyr-plays were not, however, satirical in the modern sense; that was part of comedy and more fundamentally opposed to the tragic. Comedy had its own lesser winter-festival, the *Lenaia*, as well as its day in the Dionysia, was set in contemporary Athens with ordinary citizens and street-life, and celebrated the fantastical and absurd, enjoying wide licence to mock individuals, civic preoccupations or problems, and even gods. Its main emblem was the limp phallus, attached to the costume of every male rôle to render dignity all but impossible. Tragic actors addressed the audience but tragedy maintained a barrier between performers and audience, while in comedy that barrier was far more porous and at moments deliberately breached. This distinction corresponds with one in costume, between the smooth, full-length robes of tragedy, and the bared flesh and rough, phallused outfits of comedy; perhaps also to different aspects or conceptions of the bodies beneath. Similarly, in satyr-plays and comedy the masks all actors wore were distorted, for example with exaggerated *volumes* of nose or chin, but in tragedy were relatively *neutral* (without unnatural volumes), requiring the audience to project on to the masks the emotions they read from posture and gesture and heard in dialogue.

In both comedy and tragedy the principal actors, theatre-professionals who could include the playwright, were few in number but interacted with a chorus, of 12 (later 15) in tragedy and 24 in comedy, citizens generally trained and specifically rehearsed in co-ordinated movement, dance, and speech. Tragic choruses were accompanied by an *aulos*, something like a modern flute, and/or a lyre. Modern Western-trained directors almost always *distribute* choric lines so that only one chorus-member speaks at a time, delivering a full speech between them, and because few modern actors can speak persuasively or pleasingly in unison directors find it hard to believe that classical choruses could have done so; but the utterly co-ordinated chanting and dancing prominent, for example, in traditional Zulu culture or a first-rate musical chorus-line, may be the nearest surviving equivalents to the classical chorus. The balanced and/or pointed self-arrangement of the chorus within the playing-space probably constituted a further universally understood language of drama, accompanying text and music (which used both 'western' and 'eastern' scales, or *Dorian* and *Phrygian* modes).[3] Jacques Lecoq (1921–99), a great practitioner of dramatic movement, used an exercise in which chorus-members had to imagine their stage to be balanced on a central pivot, so that to remain level they must position themselves to keep the stage in balance. One among them was the *coryphaeus*, a kind of conductor and focus; so Lecoq varied his exercise by deeming a coryphaeus to weigh five times more than other chorus-members, requiring all to reposition themselves to maintain the stage-balance. The exercise helps one to imagine possibilities—how a choric circle, say, would be forced when the coryphaeus's 'weight' was increased to move into a triangular formation on the opposite side of the pivot, or to scatter and reform as the coryphaeus approached or crossed the central spot; and how the opposition between coryphaeus and others could be instantly transformed into powerful and accusing unity if, for example, facing his chorus at the end of a passage of movement/dance as the apex of a triangular formation, the coryphaeus abruptly turned, aligning himself with them as all addressed in unison an actor just entered. The combination of symbolic abstraction with potent multiple presence makes the chorus the central mystery of Greek drama, which in reading one must both try to imagine and acknowledge as an experience lost to the post-classical world.

The theatrical and cultural practices we have described are those of fifth-century-BCE Athens in the period of democratic empire between the defeats of the invading Persians at Marathon (490 BCE) and Salamis (480 BCE), and the surrender to Sparta at the end of the Peloponnesian war (404 BCE). There had been earlier dramatic performances at the City Dionysia, and one significant name survives—Thespis (whence *thespian*), credited with inventing in the 530s BCE

---

[3] Western post-Renaissance music, with polyphony and harmony as well as monody and melody, is probably inappropriate for use in classical tragedy, and the most successful modern performances we have seen used Middle-Eastern scales and vocal techniques. Similarly the extravagant public mourning of breast-beating, ulu-lation, etc., conventional in many Islamic cultures, would probably be familiar to classical Greeks, while modern Western funerals would be a mystery.

the solo actor as distinct from the coryphaeus—but no texts and little other information. It seems likely that the threat from and triumph over Persia fuelled the development of tragedy and the suddenly urgent importance of ritual drama; the first great surviving tragedian, Aeschylus (*c.*525–456 BCE), fought at Marathon, and a distinction (first articulated in tragedy) between civilized Athens and the barbarism of non-Greeks is often vital. Surviving fragments and the one surviving tragic trilogy, Aeschylus's *Agamemnon, Choēphoroe* (*Libation-Bearers*), and *Eumenides* (*Kindly Ones*), collectively known as the *Oresteia*[4] (458 BCE), defines with the other three or four plays by Aeschylus that survive[5] a first state of tragedy, usually with only two actors on stage at any one time (the *protagonist* and *deuteragonist*) and the chorus. The two great later tragedians, Sophocles (496–406 BCE) with seven surviving plays[6] plus fragments, and Euripides (484–407 BCE) with 19,[7] increased the actors to three and then four, and Euripides is associated with a shift of emphasis towards the investigation and rhetorical expression of individual character. Other contemporary and later Athenian tragedians survive only as names, and the major influence on later drama was the Roman Seneca, particularly associated with *revenge-tragedy* which (in keeping with Roman notions of entertainment) demands *on-stage* enactments of bloody horror. In Greek tragedy murder and violence were almost always performed *off-stage*, heard but not seen, and Seneca provides the main link between classical and Renaissance tragedy: but the society for which he wrote differed from that of Athens and his plays may well have been *closet-drama*, written primarily to be read or recited rather than performed.

For comedy the record is slightly fuller, and three periods of Greek comedy are distinguished: in *Old Comedy*, of the fifth century, principally the 11 surviving works of Aristophanes (*c.*450–385 BCE),[8]

[4] The pendant satyr-play, *Proteus*, is lost.

[5] *Persians, Prometheus Bound* (authorship disputed), *Suppliants*, and *Seven against Thebes*.

[6] *Electra, Women of Trachis, Philoctetes, Ajax, Oedipus the King, Oedipus at Colonus,* and *Antigone*. The last three are sometimes called 'The Theban Plays', but do not form a trilogy.

[7] *Alcestis, Medea, Hippolytus, Andromache, Hecuba, Trojan Women, Phoenician Women, Orestes, Bacchae, Rhesus, Helen, Electra, Children of Heracles, Heracles, Suppliant Women, Iphigeneia in Aulis, Iphigeneia in Tauris, Ion,* and *Cyclops*.

[8] *Acharnians, Knights, Clouds, Wasps, Peace, Birds, Lysistrata, The Poet and the Woman, Frogs, The Women's Assembly,* and *Plutus*.

street-life is mixed with wild fantasy, pungent satire of contemporary figures, including the powerful, and the full use of the comedic chorus. Aristophanes was an innovator, however, and his last plays, in which the chorus begins to lose its functionality, belong to *Middle Comedy*, between the fall of Athens in 404 BCE and *c.*321 BCE, which had no single outstanding dramatist but saw crucial changes, including a decline of the chorus into something much closer to a modern *prologue*, the introduction of five-act structures, and (probably) the abandonment of the padded, phallus-bearing costumes once central to comedic performance. The fantastical and satirical were also eroded, and in *New Comedy* (*c.*321–*c.*264 BCE), associated with Menander (*c.*342–*c.*291 BCE),[9] largely disappear, supplanted by plots of love and intrigue featuring a collection of rôles that can reasonably be called *stock-characters*, much used in later comedy—the father, the suitor, the married woman, the *clever slave*, and so on. Greek New Comedy was directly adapted in the Roman comedy of Plautus and Publius Terentius Afer (k.a. Terence, *c.*190–?158 BCE): only six complete plays by Terence survive,[10] revealing a potent use of colloquial language and concern for an overall dramatic shape; 21 plays by Plautus survive,[11] in which the character of the clever slave is enormously developed, and from these *Commedia dell'Arte* is partly descended. Two Plautine stock-characters, the *senex* (old man) jealous of his wealth and his daughter's chastity, and the *miles gloriosus* (braggart soldier) endlessly brave in talk but in action a complete coward, have been especially important: they became in *Commedia Pantalone* (Pantaloon) and *Il Capitano* (the Captain), and in Shakespeare are clearly visible in Polonius and Falstaff (among others).

The subsequent histories of tragedy and comedy are infinite subjects. Both are products of high culture, and little work of dramatic significance is preserved from the 'Dark Ages' between the fall of

---

[9] One complete play, *The Curmudgeon*, survives, with substantial fragments of six others, lesser fragments of another eight, and about 900 quotations preserved in other authors.

[10] *The Girl from Andros, The Mother-in-Law, The Self-Tormentor, The Eunuch, Phormio,* and *The Brothers.*

[11] *Stichus, Pseudolus, Cistellaria, The Braggart Soldier, Truculentus, Epidichus, Bacchides, The Rope, The Merchant, The Jar Play, Threepence, The Spook Play, Casina, The Ass Play, The Menaechmuses, The Prisoners, Curculio, The Persian, Amphitruo, The Wretch from Carthage,* and the fragmentary *The Wallet Play.*

Rome and the Renaissance; but since then both have flourished. Zealous study of Aristotle by Renaissance scholars recovered some interesting tragedic words whose meaning is still debated, including *hubris* (presumption against the Gods), *hamartia* (traditionally but wrongly 'tragic flaw'), and *catharsis* (emotional purgation effected by seeing tragedy performed); they also insisted on the *neo-classical* or *Aristotelian unities*, a supposed requirement for 'good' plays to have unity of time (occurring within one day), place (one location), and action (no *sub-plots*). Many classical plays have these unities but some (especially comedies) do not, and as a supposed set of rules they were absurdly restricting to European secular year-round theatres with high, commercially driven demand for new plays. Neo-classicists also tended to polarize tragedy and comedy, emphasizing their sharp separation in classical thought and insisting that generic *decorum* (from Latin *decorus*, 'seemly'), 'appropriate' combinations of plot, character, and dialogue, should always be maintained; but without the religious and civic structures which supported the Athenian separation of genres maintaining any absolute distinction was impossible.

In consequence much *Early Modern*[12] European drama can be helpfully investigated through tensions between neo-classical theory and theatre-practice, including the work of Spaniards Lope de Vega (1562–1635) and Pedro Calderón (1600–81), and Frenchman Pierre Corneille (1606–84). In these writers there is perennial tension between elevated ideas of Aristotelian tragedy and the more contemporary materials from which many of their own plays were fashioned. The slightly later Frenchmen Jean-Baptiste Poquelin (k.a. Molière, 1622–73), a great comedian, and Jean Racine (1639–99), an equally great tragedian, observed generic decorum more closely. The elaborate revenge-tragedies of Englishmen Thomas Kyd (1558–94) and Thomas Middleton (1580–1627) can be performed with tragic decorum but their performative registers are uncertain, often inviting knowing laughter; similar problems may attend apparently decorous tragedies by George Chapman (*c.*1560–1634) perhaps undermined in performance by *children's companies*. Ben Jonson (1572–1637) seems to maintain generic decorum in his Roman tragedies *Sejanus, His Fall* (1603)

---

12 1300–1500 = *Late Medieval*, 1500–1700 = *Early Modern*, and 1700 + = *Modern*.

and *Catiline* (1610), but was freer in style in his *comedy of humours*, as he and others were in the related *citizen comedy*. The 'tragedies' of Christopher Marlowe (1564–93), including *Tamburlaine* and *Doctor Faustus*, consciously mix genres. So too does Shakespeare: all his *history plays* combine comedic and tragedic scenes, and he exploits mock-deaths and failed courtships in comedy (e.g. Hero in *Much Ado*, Berowne and Rosalind in *Love's Labour's*), while using distorted comedic stock-characters in tragedy (e.g. Polonius in *Hamlet*, the Fool in *Lear*). Thomas Heywood (*c.*1574–1641) and John Ford (1586–1639 +) experimented with *domestic tragedy*, rejecting Aristotle's specification of high-ranking protagonists. Some of these practices might properly be thought to constitute a distinct genre, *tragicomedy* (80–5 >), but neo-Aristotelian critics continue to debate whether this or that play is 'really' comic or tragic, for Shakespeare using the labels *problem plays* for *Troilus, Measure*, and *All's Well* as if the 'problem' were obstinate generic indeterminacy,[13] and *Romances* for the late plays (*Pericles, Cymbeline, Winter's Tale, Tempest*) which 'so defy categorisation they require a genre of their own'.

The world of the Shakespearean stage ended with the closing of the theatres in 1642: musical performances began to be allowed in the mid–1650s and travelling players surreptitiously performed *drolls*, short excerpts from plays; but in 1660 a restored monarch and court, familiarized in exile with early Molière, brought female actors (established in *Commedia* and French practice) and new performance conventions to the stage. *Restoration comedies* by George Etherege (1636–92), Aphra Behn (the first female professional playwright, 1640–89), William Wycherley (1641–1715), John Vanbrugh (1664–1726), and William Congreve (1670–1729), are typically set in the status-conscious milieux of fashionable London and often satirical, with much dizzying wit and verbal volleying. Plot-lines expose (and apparently condone) the hypocrisy of a sex-obsessed society where women feign virtue in public while sinning in private and men invest

---

[13] The term 'problem plays' emerged from the debate about Ibsen in the 1870s and 1880s, and referred to plays such as *An Enemy of the People* (1882) which concern a real problem (the discovery that the spring-waters in a spa-town are polluted) not in its nature susceptible to generic resolution (neither death nor marriage will 'solve' it). It was transferred in that sense to Shakespeare by F. S. Boas (1862–1957), but has subsequently been very loosely used.

their egos in their gift for seduction; and if plots usually climax with at least one impending marriage, conjugal life is generally represented as a matter of social advancement rather than love, and social conventions are seen to rule all aspects of public life. Older scholarship tends to characterize it as a 'comedy of manners' (a late-nineteenth-century term associated with novels) and identify 'typical' stock-characters such as the *Rake*, a vigorous, witty libertine, and the *Fop*, dandified, vain, and gullible. Such rôles certainly exist but are not ubiquitous, and particular actors were at different times more important than has been allowed: in the 1660s the partnership of Charles Hart (d.1683) and Nell Gwynn (c.1650–87) produced *screwball comedies* with a *madcap couple*, and in the 1670s–1680s James Nokes (d.1696) and Anthony Leigh (d.1692) were renowned both for smart/smart and smart/stupid pairings.

Restoration comedic acting, associated with the *forestage* (140 >), was not the elaborate caricature often supposed: it was certainly self-conscious, but a principal actor's mediation of the fiction of his/her character to an audience was subtler and more decorous than is often claimed, and an actor's excellence was judged by finesse in this regard; acting in Restoration tragedy was more formal, codified in its use of gesture, and dependent on skills of grand oratory.[14] There was a strong tendency for comedies to be set in Britain, often London, while tragedies were set overseas, so in some respects the distinction of the supergenres sharpened in comparison with Renaissance practice; but it never became as absolute as in Athens.

Eighteenth- and nineteenth-century Anglophone theatre, distorted by the enforced distinction between *legitimate* and *illegitimate* drama (89 >), has until recently been critically marginalized, producing something of a 'black hole' between Restoration theatre and the dramatic flowering associated with Ibsen. In the nineteenth century tragedy became strongly associated with the novel, and much of the stage-work now being recovered is *melodrama* (92–3 >), but English Romanticism produced high tragedy, particularly *Manfred* (pub. 1817, perf. 1834), *Marino Faliero* (1821), and *Cain* (wr. 1821, not perf.) by Lord Byron (1788–1824), and *The Cenci* (pub. 1819, perf. 1886) by Percy Bysshe Shelley (1792–1822). These contain fine poetic speeches

---

[14] See Holland, *Ornament of Action*, pp. 55–99.

but as the commonly delayed performance-dates suggest were (and in some cases still are) difficult to stage, because of their content or their poetic and/or dramatic form; all continue to be read but their influence on drama has been limited. In Germany, however, (proto-) Romantic tragedy inaugurated a specifically German national drama: Gotthold Lessing (1729–81), Friedrich Schiller (1759–1805), Friedrich Hölderlin (1770–1843), and Heinrich von Kleist (1777–1811) all produced notable tragedies, Schiller being particularly celebrated for historical drama with sharp, contemporary political applications. The great name, however, is Johann Goethe (1749–1832), whose two-part *Faust* (1808, 1832), building on and transcending the relatively simple story told in the sixteenth-century *Faustbuch* (Marlowe's source), incorporated many poetic metres, challenged dramatic form, and in redeeming Faust at the last created a theatrical and moral conundrum which continues to provoke audiences.

With Ibsen stage-tragedy was renewed, and the twentieth century saw many, particularly in connection with *social realism* (98, 248–52 >) and in the USA, where writers in all genres were persistently troubled by the place of tragedy in the New World. The outstanding American tragic forms are musical (notably Blues) and cinematic (notably westerns), but three major twentieth-century American playwrights specialized in tragedy: Eugene O'Neill (1888–1953) in *Mourning Becomes Electra* (1929–31) and *Long Day's Journey into Night* (1939–41), Tennessee Williams (1911–83) in *A Streetcar Named Desire* (1947) and *Cat on a Hot Tin Roof* (1955), and Arthur Miller (b.1915) in *Death of a Salesman* (1949) and *The Crucible* (1953). These works are, like Shakespeare's, in tension with Aristotelian ideas: can a self-deluding, authoritarian second-rater like Willy Loman in *Death of a Salesman* satisfactorily star in a tragedy? or does the loving, damaging self-effacement of his wife cut closer to the quick? Are Blanche's rape and institutionalization at the end of *A Streetcar Named Desire* fates less than, equivalent to, or worse than death? How does Williams's modulation of domestic tragedy compare with Ibsen's? Or Miller's?

The persistent bickering with Aristotle has led to complex developments in tragedic theory particularly associated with Romanticism, the philosophical criticism of Friedrich Nietzsche (1844–1900), and the moral crises of the *Sho'ah* and nuclear weaponry. However, the dominant features of tragedic practice since *c.*1700 have been (i) the proliferation of media and forms (notably opera, the novel, prose-drama, radio, film, and television), associated with a greatly increased range of protagonists; (ii) the direct encounter with female bodies, denied in classical Greek and Elizabethan practice by the use of male actors for all rôles but artistically and commercially exploited in operatic and cinematic tragedy; and (iii) encounters between non-European cultures and European tragedic theory and practice exemplified in Wole Soyinka (b.1934) and some of Derek Walcott (b.1930). Comedic theory, lacking any explicit classical source (the second book of Aristotle's *Poetics*, on comedy, is famously lost),[15] has been sporadic and uncertain, but comedic practice has also proliferated in forms and diversified in new media. Sex and death, *pratfalls* and betrayals, remain the stuff of drama, and most dramatists deal, sooner or later and one way or another, with the legacies of Athenian drama.

One other classical genre should be mentioned, *epic*, primarily a term for long poems usually concerned with great personal or tribal conflicts, and since the *Aeneid* of Publius Vergilius Maro (k.a. Virgil, 70–19 BCE) associated particularly with national origin-myths. No Aristotelian would apply epic to drama, but much Athenian tragedy drew material from Homeric epic, and for modern readers, all classical Greek culture being at this distance entwined, the worlds of Homer and the Athenian dramatists are mutually supportive. The issue matters because the German Marxist playwright, poet, and director Bertolt Brecht (1898–1956) used *epic theatre* as a consciously *anti-Aristotelian* label for a co-ordinated, theorized practice of writing and staging (101–3 >), and it is important not to confuse the classical and Brechtian meanings.

Finally a word about translations of Greek (or any) drama, which when scholarly and well annotated are unfortunately likely also to be dramatically un-speakable. When Aeschylus's Agamemnon is stabbed to death off-stage, in Philip Vellacott's 1950s Penguin translation he cries, "Help, help! I am wounded, murdered, here in the inner room!", and "Help, help again! Murder—a second, mortal blow!"[16]. In a 1960s

---

[15] For a fictional account see Umberto Eco, *The Name of the Rose* (1980; London: Picador, 1984).

[16] Aeschylus, *The Oresteian Trilogy* (Harmondsworth: Penguin, 1956 [Penguin Classics]), p. 89.

version by the American poet Robert Lowell (1917–77) he shouts, "I've been stabbed. Help me, I've been killed." and "I've been stabbed twice. Help me, I am dying."[17] Neither translation (so far as we know) has ever been staged; and in one that has, by Tony Harrison (b.1937) in 1981, both Agamemnon's lines become on the page simply "ah!", and in performance whatever an actor and/or director make of those two letters.[18] Which is the better translation, and which the better drama? The criteria depend on the intentions of the translator and the purposes of the reader, but it is vital not to confuse an unactable translation with an unperformable play.

---

[17] Robert Lowell, *The Oresteia of Aeschylus* (London: Faber, 1979), p. 41.

[18] Harrison, *Theatre Works 1973–1985*, pp. 222–3.

7

Religious genres:
the liturgy, Mysteries, and Moralities

All drama may begin in religious ritual, and in many religions artistic performance of text and/or movement is central: Buddhism and Hinduism in particular have active concepts of sacred dance, as do some Jewish sects. In Islam modesty-codes make public female performance other than mourning unusual and some imams think acting an abdication of self-control like drunkenness. Christianity, especially Protestantism, has a history of *anti-theatricality*: theatre is associated doctrinally with the commandment against graven images (Exodus 20:4) and socially with supposed licentiousness, but the *liturgy* (the structure and formulae of a service including Communion) is itself performative, involving dialogue between priests and congregation, choric speech, and audience-participation in a mystery. Throughout the Middle Ages Christianity maintained substantial power over performance, harnessing vast amounts of money, labour, and artistry to create the great abbeys and cathedrals as settings for highly structured performances of worship; there must have been secular entertainments at festivals and fairs, and local traditions of popular performance, but secular theatre-buildings existed only as classical ruins, and scripted secular plays seem for centuries to have been virtually unknown.

Collective Christian worship requires not simply that an audience/congregation attend, but also that they become directly involved. Classical Greek dramatists developed a form of dialogue called *stichomythia*, in which performers exchange single lines in quick alternation, like a sudden clash of swords (see, for example, Cassandra and the Chorus in Aeschylus's *Agamemnon*, ll. 1203–14), and similar *antiphony* (alternating voices) is common in the liturgy, affirmations of belief performed by priest and congregation as call-and-response. Shakespeare also used stichomythia, most famously when Richard of Gloucester woos Queen Anne, whose husband and father he killed:

> *An.* I would I knew thy heart.
> *Rich.* 'Tis figur'd in my tongue.
> *An.* I feare me, both are false.
> *Rich.* Then never Man was true.
> *An.* Well, well, put up your Sword.
> *Rich.* Say then my Peace is made.
> *An.* That shalt thou know heereafter.
> *Rich.* But shall I live in hope.
> *An.* All men I hope live so.
> [*Rich.*] Vouchsafe to weare this Ring.
> [*An.* To take is not to give.]   (*Richard III* 1.2.192–202).[1]

Richard III has many classical features, including a trio of lamenting queens who sometimes resemble a chorus, so it makes sense to read this stichomythia as another such feature; but it also makes sense to hear the influence of antiphonal structures within the liturgy and Anglican marriage-service, with which Shakespeare and his audiences were far more deeply familiar. Just as in the quasi-stichomythic sonnet which Romeo and Juliet famously construct between them (1.5.93–106) the subject is faith (trust, belief), and the outcome is a kind of unity, rare in classical stichomythia but the very purpose of most liturgical antiphony.

The overall form of the liturgy, and the invariant parts of Catholic Masses—the *Kyrie* (plea for divine mercy), *Gloria* (praise of God), *Credo* (statement of belief), *Sanctus* (angelic hymn), *Benedictus* (request for blessing), and *Agnus Dei* (invocation of Christ as redemptive sacrifice)—place Communion within the story from which it takes its logic. This structure is itself highly dramatic, and can be used theatrically, as director Deborah Warner (b.1959) did in framing her production of Shakespeare's *Richard II* (RNT, 1995), which ends with Richard's death, as a *requiem* Mass, one said for the soul of a dead person: the stage was a *traverse*, with the audience in two facing halves, like a church choir; an *Introit* (entry) of the kind with which Masses may begin was played before the lights went down; and parts

---

[1] The crotcheted speech-prefix and line, omitted in F1, are supplied from Q1 (1597).

of the Mass were audible during performance, culminating in the presentation of Richard's coffined body and an *Agnus Dei*. For audience members aware of this structure Shakespeare's acute questions about Richard's doom, his kingly status as a divinely sanctioned leader, and whether his sacrifice would redeem or damn his kingdom were deepened by Warner's parallel invocation of the Christian narrative, so much so that Shakespeare's story began to seem deliberately patterned as much on the gospels as on any historical source.

Yet there is a fundamental difference between sacred ritual drama and secular theatre most clearly visible in their attitudes to time. In secular theatre there is no intrinsic confusion between the time of performance and the time represented in performance, or between the actor and the rôle they play, but ritual drama maps a religious master-narrative on to the calendar, and is concerned less to represent than to re-present that story, affirming continuity or even identity with the present. Modern school *nativity-plays*, representing the birth of Jesus, the Three Wise Men, etc., are only performed at Christmas, just as *passion-plays*, representing Christ's crucifixion and resurrection, are associated with Easter; in the Late Mediaeval church there was an annual round of services and associated drama in which many elements of Christian belief were celebrated on particular days and in their proper order. Evidence predating 1100 is scant, but it appears that services in which parts of the gospels were celebrated began to acquire in some abbeys theatrical trappings, so that, for example, monks singing words by the Wise Men or the Virgin Mary adopted costumes and stood separately from the choir; from these beginnings a rich popular sacred drama developed which lasted in full measure from the twelfth to the sixteenth or seventeenth century (depending on country), and some aspects of which survive today.

This drama was pan-European. Evidence survives from Poland, Hungary, Croatia, Bohemia, Germany, Switzerland, Scandinavia, the Low Countries, Scotland, Ireland, Cornwall, Italy, and Spain; and especially from France and England. Hundreds of texts suggest very varied forms, and though some evidence survives about staging almost nothing is known of delivery, performance-styles, or stage-business. Even basics are moot: were women (outside nunneries) allowed or required to participate? Were actors allowed or encouraged to *ad lib*, embellishing learned rôles with their own topical additions?

But the critical distinction between *Mysteries* (which concern the religious mysteries of creation and incarnation and are often *cycles*) and individual *Moralities* is a necessary starting point.

Cycles deal episodically with two major sacred narratives, Creation to Doomsday and, often inset, Christ's life from Annunciation to Resurrection: the surviving English cycles, York, Chester, Wakefield/Towneley, and Coventry/N-town are each of 10,000–14,000 lines and took one to three days to perform, while some French cycles exceed 50,000 lines and took over a month. The biblical episodes to which component plays were devoted vary but commonly include Adam and Eve, Cain and Abel, Noah, Abraham and Isaac, Jacob, and Christ's annuciation, glorification by the Magi, flight to Egypt, baptism, temptation, miracles (especially Lazarus), betrayal, crucifixion, resurrection, Harrowing of Hell, and ascension. Some cycles may have been performed on fixed stages, but many seem designed for *pageant-wagons*, as in modern Mardi Gras and *carnival* processions; individual plays were sponsored by particular guilds (craft associations) and performed by guild members. Texts consequently take work-a-day perspectives, reflecting the concerns of the sponsors and the interests of a mass audience: the use of shepherds in nativity-plays is a familiar example, but others, such as the concern in some crucifixion-plays with the working lives and attitudes of the men who had to nail flesh to wood and physically raise the cross, are deeply disconcerting. Major rôles running through many plays, like those of Satan and Christ, were perhaps taken by professional actors, but each play in a cycle provided many small rôles for the amateurs of the guild. Texts are largely in *alliterative verse* and the local vernacular, including dialect words and grammar (which helped memorization), but also use Latin and prose, particularly for stage-directions; in the Wakefield Cycle the work of a skilled writer-reviser, the *Wakefield Master*, is acknowledged, and in the York cycle a hand dubbed the 'York realist'; but in general authorship is anonymous, and what survives probably combines the work of minor clerics with accumulative, collaborative composition by generations of performers.

Performances took place on different days in different cities, but there were particular associations with Whitsun (seventh Sunday after Easter), commemorating Pentecost, the Holy Spirit's gift to the Apostles of speaking in tongues, and Corpus Christi, the Feast of the

Body of Christ (eighth Thursday after Easter). Corpus Christi, instituted in 1264, was from the early-fourteenth century widely celebrated in Europe as the major early-summer festival; but it was specifically Catholic, and as Protestantism became entrenched as the state religion in England Corpus Christi performances were denounced and in the 1560s–1570s suppressed. Shakespeare <u>might</u> have seen a performance, and the 'Drunken Porter' scene (2.3) in *Macbeth* (*c*.1605–6) echoes scenes from Harrowing-of-Hell plays in which Christ hammers on Satan's gates; but under determined state-censorship traditions were rapidly lost and Mysteries vanished from English performance. European performance continued, and at Oberammergau in Bavaria there is a continuous history of productions every tenth year since 1634, but in the UK there was no revival until the mid-twentieth century. Initially driven by post-war civic rebuilding, renewed scholarship, and amateur civic and university drama, it later extended to professional performance. *The Mysteries*, an adapted synthesis of all four cycles by Tony Harrison (b.1937), begun in 1976 and first performed complete at the *National Theatre* (NT) in 1985, was a hit, and if you find the original texts difficult to imagine in performance Harrison's version offers a stunning guide to their dramatic force. More recently Northern Broadsides, who perform in northern English accents, have revived Harrison's texts, often at Easter or Christmas, and civic productions of Mysteries continue in various places, including York. The writer-actor-director Dario Fo (b.1926) also had international success with *Mistero Buffo* (*Comic Mysteries*, 1969), a one-man adaptation (with satirical and political commentary) of material from the Italian cycles.

For individual plays the picture is complex and uncertain. *Saints' plays*, the lives and martyrdoms of a particular saint, were performed on the feast-day of that saint, and like *miracle-plays*, dealing with miraculous happenings at shrines, etc., seem an adjunct of the cycles, associated with guild- as well as church-performance and Protestant suppression; only one English miracle-play and two Saints' plays survive (French evidence is stronger), one of which, *Mary Magdalene* (*c*.1475–1525), has elaborate stage-directions for special effects requiring a fixed stage and probably semi-professional production.[2] Moral-

---

[2] The other Saints' play is *The Miracle of Saint Paul*; the miracle play is *The Croxton Play of the Sacrament*.

ities take a much larger step away from ritual drama, abandoning biblical episodes for allegories in which an Everyman-figure (Mankind, Youth) is beset by devils and personified sins (Belial, Lust-liking) and helped by virtues (Wisdom, Piety).[3] The earliest complete surviving Morality, *The Castle of Perseverance* (*c*.1400–25), is anonymous,[4] as are *Mankind* (*c*.1470)[5] and *Everyman* (from the Dutch *Elckerlijc*, pub. *c*.1515); but later authors tend to be recorded. Printed in the early sixteenth century, *Nature* (pub. *c*.1530) by Henry Medwall (b.1461) is a full-blown morality, as is *Magnyfycence* (1515–18) by John Skelton (*c*.1460–1529), but Medwall's *Fulgens and Lucres* (pub. 1512) is far more secular; the surviving plays of John Bale (1495–1563) and John Heywood (*c*.1497–1580), and in Scotland *Ane Satire of the Thrie Estaitis* (perf. 1540, pub. 1602) by David Lindsay (1490–1555), also show marked development of comedy and satire; as do *Lusty Juventus* (1550) by Richard Wever (dates unknown), *Inough is as good as a feast* (?1565) by William Wager (dates unknown), and *Like wil to like quod the Devel to the Colier* (1568) by Ulpian Fulwel (1546–*c*.1585). Vernacular verse continued to be used, but the alliterative line was lost. All are now called *interludes*, a loose fourteenth-century term for anything played between the parts of something else, whether brief diversions offered during what we would call an *interval*, or whole plays performed during an 'interval' in a banquet; the term is now used to refer collectively to sixteenth-century work of uncertain genre because it usefully labels a growing secularity.

Two crucial developments occurred in the Moralities and interludes: the shifting attitude to time from re-present-ation to representation, which implies a changing relation of actors to audience and changing authorial and performance-styles;[6] and entwined with those changes the evolution of the *Vice*, a rôle partly deriving from that of the devil/tempter/mischief-maker in early Moralities but drawing on gaudily dressed *Fools* in popular entertainments.[7] Devil-tempters of Everyman-figures had to involve the audience, making

---

[3] The basic plot of these plays is called the *psychomachia*, a Greek word meaning 'soul-battle'; cf. the *Quem quaeritis* trope.

[4] There is also an anonymous fourteenth-century fragment, *The Pride of Life*.

[5] *Perseverance* and *Mankind*, with *Wisdom* (*c*.1455–70), are sometimes called the *Macro plays*.

[6] See Righter, *Shakespeare and the Idea of the Play*.

[7] 'Vice' was first used as a rôle-designation by John Heywood in 1532.

them recognize their own sinfulness and vulnerability to evil, and Fools (not to be confused with *natural fools*, who are merely foolish) were entertainers who at carnival-time could become masters-of-ceremony, directing ritual fun. Both functions require actors to have considerable discretion in performance, including licence to ad lib at will; both are readily compatible with Plautine clever-slave rôles; and successive Vices, from Mischief in *Mankind* to Neither-lover-nor-loved in Heywood's *Play of Love* (perf. ?1529, pub. 1534) and Ambidexter in *Cambyses* (1570) by Thomas Preston (1537–98) illustrate a new fusion. Mischief dominates when on stage, and through his involvement in creating an *inset-play* is able to navigate and control levels of 'reality', so that, for example, the audience's payment to attend is conflated with robberies that Mischief carries out; Ambidexter provides running commentary on the action and he (or the actor playing him) speaks to a 'cousin' supposedly pick-pocketing in the audience. Because Vices *improvised*, their performances are largely lost and printed scenes can seem bald: this is from Fulwel's *Like wil to like; Luc.* is Lucifer and *N. New.* is the Vice, Nichol Newfangle:

> *The Devil entreth.*
> *Luc.* Ho ho ho mine own boy, make no more delay:
> But leap up on my back straight way.
> *N. New.* Then who shall hold my stirop while I go to horse?
> *Luc.* Tushe for that doo thou not force.
> Leap up I say leap up quickly.
> *N. New.* Who ball who, and I wil come by an by.
> Now for a pair of spurres I would give a good grote:
> To try whether this Jade doo amble or trot.
> Farwel my masters til I come again,
> For now I must make a journey into spain.
> *He rideth away on the Devils back.*[8]

Fortunately a description of the stage-business with which "Who ball who" was fleshed out survives in a *Declaration of Egregious Popish Impostures* (1603) by Samuel Harsnet (1561–1631):

It was a pretty part in the old Church-playes, when the nimble Vice would skip up nimbly like a Jacke an Apes into the devils necke, and ride the devil a

---

[8] Ulpian Fulwel, *An Enterlude Intituled Like Wil to like quod the Deuel to the Colier* (London: John Allde, 1568), F1v; Happé, ed., *Tudor Interludes*, p. 362. The original is in blackletter, and as a verso has speech-prefixes to the right of each first line, which have been silently repositioned.

course, and belabour him with his woodden dagger, til he made him roare, wherat the people would laugh to see the devil so vice-haunted.[9]

Both the service of evil and the link with Fools (who also had wooden daggers and a wooden ladle with which to beat people) are plain, and in Elizabethan drama the Vice-rôle underlies and informs not only Fool-rôles like the Fool in *King Lear* (*c.* 1604), Feste in *Twelfth Night* (1600), and Lavache in *All's well* (*c.*1605–6), but also self-conscious, manipulative villain-rôles like Richard III and Iago in *Othello* (1601).

It used to be thought the Moralities vanished with the Mysteries, and they were often characterized as a crudely didactic mediaeval form wholly superseded by Renaissance drama. It now seems that at least some Moralities continued to be performed in England until the closing of the theatres in 1642, and no clear distinction can be maintained between evolving Moralities and the emergent theatre of Shakespeare's age.

---

[9] Quoted in F. P. Wilson, *The English Drama 1485–1585* (Oxford: Clarendon Press, 1968), p. 64.

8

Renaissance genres:
Commedia dell'arte, tragicomedy, masque, and opera

The Renaissance or rebirth of classical culture was founded on its physical recovery: statues were dug from the ground, texts systematically rescued from obscurity and saved from progressive physical decay. As recovered knowledge flowed north from fourteenth-century Italy to sixteenth-century England, artistic practice and theory, like national/cultural self-perceptions, were profoundly altered. Painters developed perspective, musicians harmony, poets rhyme and stanza-forms, and prose-writers a new punctuation leading to the grammatical sentence; joined-up writing replaced gothic scripts, printing began international standardization and revolutionized the commerce and materiality of written texts, and recognizably modern science began, prompted by classical architecture, engineering, and medicine. In theatre too the recovery of classical drama played a vital part, combined (as in all arts) with survivals and legacies of mediaeval practice; but Renaissance theatre was birth as much as rebirth. In 1576, when James Burbage (*c.*1531–97) built *the Theatre*, the first durable building designed for professional actors to perform to paying audiences,[1] in Shoreditch, just east of the City of London,[2] he began a theatre continuous with the present and distinct from everything past.

Much without classical antecedents was necessary for that devel-

[1] An earlier but probably temporary structure, the Red Lion, was erected in 1567 in Stepney, probably for Burbage; it is sometimes credited as the 'first' theatre in London.

[2] The 'City of London' is the area within the mediaeval city-wall, now the financial district known as 'the City'.

opment. Burbage had to borrow money to build and to recruit players, which required new financial instruments and lenders who saw theatre as a profitable investment. It is not chance that actors form a *company*, and profit depends on a sufficiently large and nearby potential audience willing and able to pay, repeatedly, to hear actors perform: a dense, thriving, and culturally receptive populace. Late-sixteenth-century London, with a population nearing 250,000, was only one-twelfth the size of ancient Rome at its height, but still the largest city in Europe since Rome fell, and growing fast; yet it was mediaeval in layout and appearance (its neoclassical buildings post-date the Great Fire of 1666), and the nation whose politics and economy it increasingly dominated was in many respects a new kind of polity. It was also, as today, the 'Big Smoke' (cf. 'Big Apple'), a place of danger and opportunity attracting hopeful writers and performers to supply the emergent theatre with plays and actors.

The term Renaissance points to classical culture and scholars of Early Modern literature often stress classical inheritance, but mediaeval influence, innovation, and the fusions of all three were central to theatre-practice. Renaissance dramatists may seem distant, 'classic' writers, but Elizabethan and *Jacobean* theatre[3] was exceptionally dynamic, responding to audience tastes, technical advance, and European influence, and a small number of plays written for Londoners around 1600 have been in almost continuous production ever since, not simply as great plays, but because they embody a new set of conditions and conventions which dominated European theatre well into the twentieth century.

The first great theatrical achievement of the Renaissance was *Commedia dell'arte*, pan-Italian but particularly associated with Venice. The term was coined by playwright Carlo Goldoni (1707–93) to distinguish an *improvised* (unscripted, invented in performance) and masked form from scripted and unmasked *Commedia erudita* ('learned comedies'), but the practice dates to at least the 1550s. *Dell'arte* means 'of artists/craftsmen', reflecting the training necessary for masked improvisation, and *Commedia dell'arte* combined stock-characters

---

[3] The terms are often conflated as *Jacobethan* (1558–1625), which with *Caroline* theatre (under Charles I) constitute the *Shakespearean stage*, from the opening of the Theatre in 1576 to the closing of the theatres in 1642.

with specific names, traits, and types of mask[4] and typical starting points (e.g. a love problem) and *dénouements*, final unravellings of plot (e.g. the revelation of a disguise). Actors knew what rôle they were playing (including costume, props, stance, walk, movement, gestures, voice, and motivations) and where the action had to end, but plot-details, dialogue, and most longer speeches were invented in performance, individual actors developing routines and stage-business for the rôle in which they specialized. One source of stock-characters was Venetian *Carnivale* (lit. 'farewell to meat'), the Shrove Tuesday (Mardi Gras, Pancake Day) feast when foodstuffs forbidden during Lent were finished off; others include the *patter* of street-salesmen and fairground *barkers* who assemble and hold a crowd, and early *Commedia erudita*, which drew heavily on the Roman comedy of Plautus and Terence and through them on the Greek New Comedy of Menander.

The mixed origins and improvisation mean that all *Commedia* rôles vary considerably, and as companies toured Italy particular rôles, stage-business, or dialogue associated with a region would be played up in performance, but the core relationship remained the Plautine pairing of master and servant, usually spanning a generation. Companies visited Germany, France, Spain, England, and Russia, absorbing new character-traits and influencing emergent national dramas, and many *Commedia* rôles survive with adaptations to the present, Pedrolino and Pulcinella having developed into central figures in other drama. The practice of *Commedia* fell into disuse in the eighteenth century, but the twentieth saw many revivals of its techniques, including influential projects by Edward Gordon Craig (1872–1966), Vsevolod Meyerhold (1874–1942), Jacques Lecoq (1921–99), and Ariane Mnouchkine (b.1938). It is therefore well worth being familiar with the major Masks (see Display box 1) and wondering with any play you read whether any of its rôles derive from *Commedia*. In Shakespeare, for example, constables like Dogberry in *Much Ado* and Elbow in *Measure*, who habitually *malapropize* (use the wrong word) to ribald effect, are versions of Tartaglia—which can help you imagine how those rôles might be played. Similarly, the Sebastian/Cesario confusion in *Twelfe Night*, which results (5.1) in a surprise beating for

---

[4] In *Commedia* such rôles are also called *Masks*, the capital M distinguishing them from 'masks', the physical objects.

DISPLAY BOX 1

The principal Masks in *Commedia dell'arte*

1. The principal older/master figures are *Pantalone*, the <u>Pantaloon</u>, authoritarian, rich, miserly, and jealous, often father of one of the lovers, against whom servants and the young struggle; and his neighbour/rival, *Il Dottore*, the Doctor (often named Gratiano), corpulent, pompous, pedantic, supposedly learned but actually a quack, if married usually a cuckold, and sometimes father of one of the lovers.

2. The lovers or *Innamorati* are usually two couples with names such as Silvio, Fabrizio, Florindo, Silvia, Isabella, Lavinia; hopelessly infatuated, full of exaggerated language and sighs, their love, the obstacles in their way, and their eventual triumph usually drive the plot.

3. The servants are <u>*zanni*</u> (→ 'zany'), a diminutive of 'Giovanni' (John); a common lower-class name in northern Italy, it is both singular and plural. Zanni is a name in its own right, but at least two zanni are needed, and other named zanni include <u>*Brighella*</u> (from *brigare*, to intrigue), clever, bossy, and dominant; <u>*Arlecchino*</u> (Harlequin),[5] a complex rôle combining a limited mind with an exceptionally agile and clever body, a tendency to unrequited love, a readiness to adopt disguise, and a *slapstick*; and <u>*Scapino*</u> (from *scappare*, to flee or scarper), always ready to get involved and still readier to run away. All zanni function as messengers and create havoc by delaying or misdelivering their messages. Their main female counterpart is <u>*Colombina*</u>, maid to the first female lover, clever, kind, calm, sensible, and often the exasperated target of Arlecchino's romantic devotion or attempted seduction by Pantalone.

4. Other important Masks include <u>*Il Capitano*</u>, the braggart soldier, full of boast and short on courage; <u>*Il Cavaliero*</u>, the cavalier, a genuine soldier who may be mistaken for a *Capitano* and dish out a beating; <u>*Pedrolino*</u>, little Peter, the youngest, least well-treated son, who wears white-face not a mask (the main source of the French Pierrot); <u>*Pulcinella*</u>, sometimes a potent zanni but also a small trader or shopkeeper (the main source of Mr Punch in *Punch and Judy*); <u>*Scaramuccia*</u> (Scaramouche), a stirrer and often a thief; and <u>*Tartaglia*</u> (from *tartare*, to stammer), a *utility figure* who may be a lawyer, minor official, or policeman whose stammering is a constant source of comedy and obscenity.

---

[5] The name probably means 'little devil', and may have originated in a fusion of the zanni-type with a mediaeval French 'wild man' characteristically covered in leaves (hence the coloured Harlequin costume; cf. *motley*).

Sir Andrew and Sir Toby, is a version of the *Capitano/Cavaliero* confusion, which helps to explain the prolonged 'duel' (3.4) that sets it up. Molière was also deeply influenced by *Commedia*: in (*L'Avare, The Miser*, 1668), based on *The Jar Play* (*Aulularia*) by Plautus, Harpagon is a particularly grim Pantalone. At the other end of the spectrum, the character of Michael Corleone in *The Godfather* (1972) owes a surprising amount to Pedrolino, while the opening, Don Vito Corleone unable to refuse any supplicant's request on his daughter's wedding-day, tags the Godfather himself as another version of Pantalone, identifications which offer a very different way of analysing the film.

The usual centrality and triumph of the lovers kept most *Commedia* comedic, but pathos may complicate the generic mix and sixteenth-century *Commedia* was paralleled by a development of *tragicomedy*. There can be no formal definition of tragicomedy, and the label has been used for anything that seems to mix genres as well as more specifically for tragedies which avert or transcend terminal deaths and comedies which abort anticipated marriages, but its Renaissance form is particularly associated with the Italian Giovan Battista Guarini (1538–1612), whose play (*Il Pastor Fido, The Faithful Shepherd, c.*1582–4) enjoyed wide European popularity for more than a century.[6] As its name suggests it is a *pastoral*, originally a classical genre of poetry featuring refined love in a rural setting (*Arcadia*) with a cast of shepherds, country maidens, etc., which usually ended happily but lacked the coarse and physical humour of comedy. In his *Compendio della poesia tragicomica* (Summary of Tragicomic Poetry, 1601), Guarini argued for pastoral as a place where tragedy and comedy could mix, defending his own practice with hundreds of classical examples which challenged neo-classical dicta about generic decorum. Dramatists and actors who were fiercely criticized for anti-Aristotelian practice welcomed Guarini's support, and he is credited with influencing Shakespeare, John Fletcher (1579–1625), Philip Massinger (1583–1640), and James Shirley (1596–1666) in England; Corneille in France; and Lope de Vega and Tirso de Molina (*c.*1579–1648) in Spain. All probably knew Guarini's work, but the Spanish playwrights and Shakespeare exceeded Guarini in practice before his theories were published, and though he is interesting his importance

---

[6] A modernized text of the 1647 translation by Richard Fanshawe (1608–66) is included in Penman, ed., *Five Italian Renaissance Comedies*.

to professionals dependent on commercial success has been over-stated. Companies offering daily performances in permanent theatres had to provide a mixed repertoire and needed actors capable of both tragic and comic rôles; dramatists writing for such companies had to use actors' strengths and provide parts for the talents available; and mass audiences for whom theatre is recreation do not usually have purist views about what they want to see.

Shakespeare's practice was from the first polygeneric and none of his plays maintains decorum. The nine histories written in the 1590s combine the story of a king (appropriate for tragedy) with crowd scenes of army and popular life (appropriate for comedy);[7] and may alternate between tragedic and comedic scenes or fuse them in mem-orable moments like the 'trial' of the Clerk of Chatham in *2 Henry VI* (4.2.84–110) and the scene in *3 Henry VI* which opens with the stage-direction "*Alarum. Enter a Sonne that hath kill'd his Father, at one doore: and a Father that hath kill'd his Sonne at another doore.*" (2.5.o.s.d.). The extraordinary figure of Richard III, simultaneously a Vice who glee-fully addresses the audience, a deformed clown, a king, and a tragic figure who pays for his ambitions and crimes with his life, is what he is precisely because he explodes generic decorum. He owes much to Marlowe's Tamburlaine and Barabas (in *The Jew of Malta*, *c*.1589), but has been hugely influential and remains visible in the stylish, exag-gerated villains we love to hate in action-movies. Equally astonishing is Falstaff in the two-part *Henry IV*, combining the Vice and *Il Capitano* from *Commedia* (or the Plautine *miles gloriosus*) in a figure of such generous deceits that audiences usually love and pity him when the logic of state requires the newly crowned Henry V to abjure him. The lines that reduce Falstaff to "a Foole, and Jester" (< 39) signal the end of his power as a Vice—the proper upbeat ending of a Morality: but with that dismissal a deep melancholy is set against the triumphant coronation that ends *2 Henry IV*, and any comedy profoundly qualified.

Shakespeare's 'comedies' are similarly mixed. Even the sunniest have complications—in *A Midsommer Nights Dreame* (*c*.1595) the love-plot is 'resolved' by leaving one lover spellbound—and some pose profound problems: how can *The Merchant of Venice* (*c*.1598) be a

---

[7] *The Famous History of the Life of King Henry the Eight* is *c.* 1613. *Richard II*, wholly in verse, is close to decorous tragedy, but the Aumerle episode in act 5 is ludicrous.

'comedy' given the villainy and forced conversion of the Jewish Shylock? In *All's Well, that Ends Well* (a provocative title) how can the vicious Bertram be an acceptable husband for the heroine, Helena? If these questions really mean 'how can these plays be made generically decorous?' the answer is they can't, and Shakespeare's complexity has much to do with generic tensions. He has common ground with Guarini in that while all classical comedy is urban, Shakespearean comedy, after acts 1 in courtly or urban settings, the *first world*, often heads to the countryside, greenwood, or sea for any or all of acts 2–5, and this *green world* is clearly related to pastoral. As in Guarini tragedy and comedy meet there, but Shakespearean green worlds are also places of theatre, like the wood in *Dream* where the actors rehearse or the Forest of Arden which provides Rosalind with a performance-space in *As You Like It*—places where you can guise and disguise, be open to encounter, and undergo transformation, losing yourself to find yourself. Such *metatheatre*, especially in the full form of inset-plays where some actors act actors and others act audience, is itself a primary method of manipulating genre.

Shakespeare's dark comedies could also be called light tragedies, and there is no deep structural difference between his 'comedies' and 'tragedies'. In *Measure* there is a prison where the green world would be expected, and in *All's Well* a battlefield, but both turn out to have many green-world properties; in *King Lear* and *Macbeth* the blasted heaths where Lear suffers the storm and Macbeth meets the witches are also green worlds of a kind, though in *Macbeth* the heath is *de facto* the first world and Macbeth's castle the place of actings and disguise. As Shakespearean comedy features Vices so his tragedy features Fools and pantaloons: even Lear, however bitter and bleak the play, is (like Polonius) a type of Pantalone, and the unique agony of *King Lear* is partly a result of knowing that a clown undergoes a prolonged tragic fate. Tragedy had, before Ibsen, a strong affinity with verse as an 'appropriately' elevated form of language, and Shakespeare's characteristic mix of passionate verse, inventive prose, and powerful song records his indecorum. Of all his plays only *The Comedy of Errors* (*c.*1592) and *The Tempest* (*c.*1610) observe the unities: *Errors*, directly modelled on a Plautine play, was an early exercise in form, but *The Tempest*, traditionally regarded as his last major work, seems far more an ironic gesture towards neo-classical rules which all his plays systematically and inventively break.

Tragicomedy has flourished ever since as a satisfying and challenging frame for practitioners and a default position for critics, becoming associated with playwrights as diverse as Ibsen, George Bernard Shaw (1856–1950), Anton Chekhov (1860–1904), Luigi Pirandello (1867–1936), Federico García Lorca (1898–1936), Beckett, Eugène Ionesco (1909–94), and Friedrich Dürrenmatt (1921–90). The label means something different in each case, but consider the opening of act 2 of Chekhov's *The Cherry Orchard* (1903–4):

> *In the open country. A small, tumble-down old chapel long ago abandoned. Near it a well, some large stones which look like old tombstones and an old bench. A road can be seen leading to* GAYEV's *estate. Dark poplar trees loom on one side and beyond them the cherry orchard begins. There is a row of telegraph poles in the distance and far, far away on the horizon are the dim outlines of a big town, visible only in very fine, clear weather. It will soon be sunset.* CHARLOTTE, YASHA *and* DUNYASHA *are sitting on the bench.* YEPIKHODOV *stands near them playing a guitar, while the others sit lost in thought.* CHARLOTTE *wears a man's old peaked cap. She has taken a shot-gun from her shoulder and is adjusting the buckle on the strap.*

CHARLOTTE [*meditatively*]. I haven't any proper identity papers. I don't know how old I am and I always think of myself as a young girl. When I was little, Father and Mother used to go on tour round all the fairs giving performances, and very good ones too. I used to do the dive of death and lots of other tricks. When Father and Mother died a German lady adopted me and began educating me. Well, I grew up and became a governess. But where I come from and who I am I've no idea. Who my parents were I don't know either, very likely they weren't even married. [*Takes a cucumber out of her pocket and starts eating it.*] I don't know anything. [*Pause.*] I'm longing for someone to talk to, but there isn't anyone. I'm alone in the world.

YEPIKHODOV [*playing the guitar and singing*].

> 'I'm tired of the world and its bustle.
> I'm tired of my friends and my foes.'

How nice it is to play a mandolin.

DUNYASHA. That isn't a mandolin, it's a guitar. [*Looks at herself in a hand-mirror, and powders her face.*]

YEPIKHODOV. To a man crazed with love it's a mandolin. [*Sings softly.*]

> 'If only my heart were delighted
> By the warmth of an ardour requited.'

> [YASHA *joins in.*]

CHARLOTTE. The awful way these people sing—ugh! Like a lot of hyenas.

DUNYASHA [*to* YASHA]. You're ever so lucky to have been abroad, though.

YASHA. Yes, of course. My sentiments precisely. [*Yawns, then lights a cigar.*]

YEPIKHODOV. It stands to reason. Abroad everything's pretty comprehensive like. Has been for ages.

YASHA. Oh, definitively.

YEPIKHODOV. I'm a cultured sort of person and read all kinds of remarkable books, but I just can't get a line on what it is I'm really after. Shall I go on living or shall I shoot myself, I mean? But anyway, I always carry a revolver. Here it is. [*Shows them his revolver.*]

CHARLOTTE. Well, that's that. I'm off. [*Slings the gun over her shoulder.*] Yepikhodov, you're a very clever man and a most alarming one. Women must be quite crazy about you. Brrr! [*Moves off.*] These clever men are all so stupid, I've no-one to talk to. I'm lonely, oh so lonely. I'm on my own in the world, and—and who I am and what I'm for is a mystery.[8]

Charlotte's opening speech at first seems tragic, and her shotgun (usually a man's weapon) might be expected to go off, as guns on stage almost always do sooner or later, but the cucumber is incongruous and its sudden appearance comically startling. Yepikhodov's behaviour with his "mandolin" (the instrument of Italian love-serenades) is full of pathos, but the gun he suddenly produces while casually suggesting he might kill himself may also go off. Charlotte's "hyenas" is also unexpected, either comic exaggeration or very unpleasant insult, and the juxtaposition of 'deep' statements with 'shallow' chat, tragic expectation and comedic incongruity mutually denying generic predictability, was for Chekhov a vital method of construction. Charlotte, moreover, identifies herself as a performer and refers specifically to the "dive of death", a fairground attraction where someone undertakes an apparently unsurvivable fall: but do fairgoers really expect a death? Is it the possibility of a real accident that makes excitement? As in Shakespeare self-conscious inset-performance confuses expectations, and Charlotte's memory of death-defying childhood stunts alerts audience and readers to Chekhov's game without granting any relief from uncertainty either to them or to Charlotte herself, who finds her own life and function a "mystery".

The Cherry Orchard premièred at the *Moscow Art Theatre*, a

---

[8] Chekhov, *Five Plays*, pp. 258–9.

high-profile company run by Constantin Stanislavski (1865–1938), Russia's most famous *actor-manager* and a major theorist of acting. The tensions between Stanislavski's style (which Chekhov thought overstated), the way to perform a "dive of death", and the way this scene needs controlled <u>under</u>statement to work are intentional, and Chekhov perhaps learned to manipulate metatheatre from Shakespeare, whose inset-plays are always stylistically distinct from their framing plays. The amateur performance of *Pyramus and Thisbe* in *Dream* is hopelessly incompetent by the professional standards of Shakespeare's company, requiring a different inset-style; the performance of *The Murder of Gonzago* is by a travelling company and unlike *Hamlet* is preceded by a *dumb-show*, a form as antiquated for Shakespeare as silent film is for us and equally requiring a very different performance-style.

In some plays Shakespeare inset a distinct contemporary form, the masque, in part performed (like *Commedia erudita*) by amateurs, usually aristocratic, and particularly associated with the Jacobean and Caroline courts. Originating in ritual court-welcomes and masked entertainments, masques were usually performed only once as lavish spectacles commercial theatre could not match, and so were a place where technical innovation was welcome. The great names of English masque are Ben Jonson, who from 1609 developed the anti-masque as a foil, an enactment of disharmony to heighten by contrast the harmonious masque proper; and the architect-designer Inigo Jones (1573–1652), who introduced to England *perspectival scenery, raked* (angled) stages, the *proscenium arch* (framing the action), and many other stage-devices. Masques were performed in temporarily adapted halls, but increasingly elaborate designs led to Jones's creation of the Banqueting House in Whitehall (1619–22), temporarily the most mechanically advanced theatre-space in the world, and the Cockpit-in-Court (1629–30), a beautiful small theatre also used by professional companies for *command-performances*; the proscenium-arch theatre-designs of 1660–1945 (exemplified in most theatres in London's West End and on Broadway) owe much to Jones.

The techniques and spectacle of masque are suggested in Shakespeare's masques in *The Tempest*, where "*Iuno descends*" (4.1.74.s.d.), and in *Cymbeline* (*c*.1610), where "*Iupiter descends in Thunder and Lightning, sitting vppon an Eagle*" (5.4.92.s.d.); *descends* means lowered by wire from the stage-roof, drawing oohs and aahs from the audience as fireworks do. The fact that in both plays (as in the masques of Hymen in *As You Like It* and of Amazons with Cupid in *Timon of Athens*, c.1607) it is gods or goddesses who descend reflects the classical *deus ex machina* ('god out of the machinery') ending, but also parallels the association of court-masques with a semi-divine monarch and their consequent political function.[9] Recent work has animated the politics,[10] noting, for example, that some of Jones's perspectival scenery could only be properly viewed from one seat, the king's, and that for other spectators the spectacle was not the masque alone but the king watching the masque. That suggests interesting things about Hamlet's plan to watch a king watching a play, and the nearest modern equivalents of masque may be overtly political: TV coverage of military parades or celebrity funerals, for example, is usually divided between footage of the event itself and of those watching, who become part of the spectacle; when a British monarch stands on the balcony of Buckingham Palace is the monarch performing for the crowd or the crowd for the monarch?

Modern productions of plays featuring masques often downplay the form, making inset-masques continuous with their framing-plays, but clear stylistic changes (delivery, posture, gesture) as well as distinctive light and music may offer a better guide to how they functioned.[11] A further clue is provided by *opera*, a late-sixteenth- and seventeenth-century Italian development, not formally related to masque but similarly élite, solemn, highly stylized, restricting to actors, and requiring specialized theatres (to accommodate the orchestra). The musicology of opera is beyond the scope of this book, but as a Renaissance form which requires performers strictly to obey the composer's instructions and survives with far less change than any non-musical drama, opera offers many useful challenges to imaginations of sixteenth- and seventeenth-century performance. With stage-plays, for example, we now tend to assume that actors should be

[9] In classical use the phrase *deus ex machina* is neutral, simply stating what happens, but is now usually critical, implying a forced contrivance by which a dramatist improbably overcomes a plot difficulty.

[10] See Orgel, *Illusion of Power*.

[11] See e.g. Derek Jarman's film of *The Tempest* (1979), a dark, often relatively silent, and moody piece into which a Busby Berkeley style dance routine and a performance of 'Stormy Weather' by Elizabeth Welch are abruptly cut.

about the same age as those they play, and the idea of casting a 50-year-old as an adolescent or vice versa sounds crazy: but this is a function of film and TV, which depend on the *close-up*, and does not apply in opera, where the only issue is the quality of a singer's voice. Singers do not mature fully until their later 20s or 30s, and while a voice remains there is no notion that a singer is too old, too young, or the wrong shape for any particular rôle: a large middle-aged diva can play a dying teenager without anyone objecting to non-naturalistic casting, which makes it easier to understand, for example, how the great Restoration actor Thomas Betterton (*c*.1635–1710) could play Romeo in *Romeo and Juliet* for nearly fifty years, giving his final performances when over 70, and Mrs Patrick Campbell (1865–1940) appear at 49 in the première of Shaw's *Pygmalion* (1914) as the teenage heroine, Eliza Doolittle.

Grand opera, in which all dialogue is sung, largely maintains generic decorum (tragic or comic), and though widely attacked as élitist, particularly with regard to ticket-prices, has since 1945 attracted many distinguished theatre-directors, including Peter Hall (b.1930), Jonathan Miller (b.1934), and Peter Stein (b.1937). *Light opera*, with spoken dialogue, usually tragicomic, and often produced (as grand opera is not) by amateur and university clubs, was in various forms very popular during the nineteenth century, and in England culminated in the *Savoy operas* of William Gilbert (1836–1911) and Arthur Sullivan (1842–1900); but distinctions between light opera, *melodrama*, and *musicals* are arbitrary, more to do with artistic snobbery and conditions of performance than structural difference (92–4 >).

Both masque and opera demand highly stylized acting which has not survived in commercial theatre but influenced many Renaissance and post-Renaissance playwrights: and that influence is worth remembering if you read scenes that cannot be (or you cannot imagine as) naturalistic. Both élite genres also exerted disproportionate influence on theatre-architecture: their concerns with spectacular *illusion* and the primacy of sound were fused in the design of proscenium-arch theatres, and remain a basic influence on most commercial theatre today. Popular Renaissance theatre, conversely, was rooted in a form of theatre building which had a diminishing influence on subsequent architecture; but the exceptional general quality of the drama produced by Shakespeare and his fellows, and the pervasive influence in particular of his handling of stock-characters and generic indecorum, have made that popular theatre as central an influence on later playwrights as the élite genres were on theatre-design.

9

Eighteenth- and nineteenth-century genres:
burlesque, sentimental and gothic drama, pantomime, melodrama, music-hall, farce, and well-made plays

In 1662 William Davenant (1606–68) and Thomas Killigrew (1612–83) were granted exclusive rights to perform drama in London, rights inherited by their successors, extended by the 1737 Licensing Act, and ended only when the 1843 Theatre Regulation Act abolished *theatrical monopoly*. The relevant laws governed only non-musical drama, and other theatres found ways of operating by including songs, dancing, and musical interludes in their performances: thus *legitimate* and *illegitimate theatre* competed throughout the period 1662–1843, and theatrical monopoly profoundly affected generic developments.

The major legitimate genres were *burlesque* and *sentimental* and *gothic drama*. Burlesque resembles parody and satire in seeking ridicule through distortion, but extends to the *pastiche* of a serious genre. It took independent shape in seventeenth-century French rejections of neo-Classical rules; but the Pyramus and Thisbe scene in *Dream, Isle of Gulls* (1606) by John Day (1574–?1640), and *Knight of the Burning Pestle* (1607) by Francis Beaumont (*c.*1584–1616) are English antecedents. *The Rehearsal* (wr. 1665, perf. 1671) by George Villiers, Duke of Buckingham (1628–87), burlesqued plays by Davenant and was modified to mock the heroic drama of John Dryden (1631–1700), especially *The Conquest of Granada* (1671). Its enormous success made it a model whose legacy remains visible in *The Critic* (1779) by Richard Brinsley Sheridan (1751–1816), the Savoy operas of Gilbert and

Sullivan, and even the films of Buster Keaton and the Marx Brothers. There is also a long tradition of burlesquing Shakespeare, particularly vigorous in the nineteenth century and clearly visible today, both used to serious purpose, as in the 15-minute and 90-second *Hamlets* in *Dogg's Hamlet* (1979) by Tom Stoppard (b.1937), and for fun, as in the Reduced Shakespeare Company's performance of all 37 plays in two hours.[1]

In 1698 the clergyman Jeremy Collier (1650–1726) lambasted Restoration comedy in his *Short View of the Immorality and Profaneness of the English Stage*, and many dramatists were stung (or pressurized) into cleaning up their language. Collier's influence is easily overstated, but he struck a chord with both the public and the authorities; as the eighteenth century progressed there was a trend towards softer satire, less ebullience, and overtly moral plotting, while censorship strengthened under the *Lord Chamberlain* (who replaced the *Master of the Revels* in 1737). The new dispensation was reflected in sentimental drama, concerned to show the tribulations and triumphs of (Christian) virtue: rôles were simple and sharply polarized, dyed-in-the-wool villains versus anaemic, hypersensitive heroes, while dialogue expressed distress rather than frailty and virtue always triumphed; examples, many Anglo-Irish, include *The Conscious Lovers* (1722) by Richard Steele (1672–1729), *False Delicacy* (1768, starring Garrick)[2] by Hugh Kelly (1739–77), *The Good-Natured Man* (1768) by Oliver Goldsmith (1728–74), and a dozen plays by Richard Cumberland (1732–1811), mocked in *The Critic* as Sir Fretful Plagiary.

Gothic drama built on the sentimental, but sought to combat anaemia by adding aspects of the sensational and amoral which audiences (especially in the 1790s) again found enthralling as well as disturbing. Horace Walpole, Earl of Orford (1717–97), is credited with inventing the gothic novel[3] in *The Castle of Otranto* (1765), and transferred his invention to drama in the incest tragedy *The Mysterious Mother* (1768), a closet-drama so shocking that even private readings caused offence; later examples include *The Castle Spectre* (1796) by

---

[1] See *The Reduced Shakespeare Co. presents The Compleat Works of Wllm Shkspr (abridged)* (New York: Applause Books, 1994).

[2] David Garrick (1717–79) dominated acting for thirty years.

[3] The label 'gothic' (rather than 'Romantic') novels encodes a critical distaste easily transferred to 'gothic drama'.

'Monk' Lewis (1775–1818), *De Montfort* (1798, perf. Kemble/Mrs Siddons,[4] 1800) by Joanna Baillie (1762–1851), thought too disturbing to have been written by a woman, and another closet-drama, Shelley's incest tragedy *The Cenci* (1819). Typical settings, as in gothic novels, were castles, dungeons, forest-glades, stormy lakes or seas, and remote rustic dwellings where fearful heroines battled evil or supernatural events and characters. Themes, often extreme, included sexual or social taboos and plots were predicated on the disruption of social order by psychological experience.

The first great illegitimate genre, peculiar to Britain but with origins in fairground-performance and *Commedia dell'Arte*, was *pantomime* (often called *panto*). Puppet-shows had long been staple fairground-entertainments (as in Jonson's *Bartholomew Fair*, 1614), but from at least 1662 a distinctly English form developed, the Punch-and-Judy Show, hook-nosed Mr Punch combining the mediaeval Vice with Pulcinella.[5] Early in the eighteenth century John Rich (?1682–1781) began adapting well-known *Commedia* scenes and characters to English settings: he played Harlequin, an anglicised Arlecchino, as a figure of knockabout fun and clownish agility, scoring a major hit with *The Necromancer or Harlequin Dr Faustus* (1723). Panto has been the staple Christmas diet of many English theatres ever since, and most English children's first experience of theatre; it has evolved continuously, the need for topical jokes ensuring regular rewrites. In the nineteenth century the narrative thrust was influenced by fairy-tale, usually a rags-to-riches story like Cinderella, and many current conventions of performance and *audience-participation* began with the Victorians, particularly the active encouragement of spectators to join in by warning hero/ines of danger, hissing at villains, singing songs, and cheering good or jeering lame jokes. In the twentieth century the biggest developments were the importance in casting of radio and TV stars, and the vast international success, following its 1953 Disney adaptation, of *Peter Pan* (1904) by James Barrie (1860–1937); but plots still end with the honest hero and beautiful heroine kissing in a grand

---

[4] The brother/sister team of John Philip Kemble (1757–1823) and Sarah Siddons (1751–1831) were renowned from the 1780s to the 1810s.

[5] By the 1780s the scenarios familiar today had largely developed, including Mr Punch beating Judy and the adventures of his dog Toby with sausages (and later policemen).

finale. Major rôles include the *Pantomime Dame*, a comic, well-meaning, interfering elderly woman always played by a male actor; the *Principal Boy*, played by a female actor, who rescues the innocent heroine; the *Chief Villain*, pleasingly flamboyant; a *Benevolent Agent*, often a usefully magical fairy(-godmother); and the *Pantomime Horse* (or other animal), two actors in one costume.

The importance of music to evade the licensing laws has become subordinate in panto; the other major illegitimate genre was dominated by the need for music. The term *melodrama* (Greek, μέλος, *melos*, 'song' + drama) was first used in France by Jean Jacques Rousseau (1712–78) to describe his play *Pygmalion* (1766), in which music was not a setting for dialogue but used for background effect. French audiences were enthusiastic, demand for similar plays grew, and the term arrived in England with *A Tale of Mystery* (1802) by Thomas Holcroft (1745–1809), adapted from the French *Coelina* (1801) by Réné Charles Pixérécourt (1773–1844). From then to *c.*1900 melodrama was a dominant form, and many of its features continue to inform drama today (B-movies and low-budget soap operas, for example, rely on it heavily): the central aim was to arouse *pathos*, music was vital to create mood and manipulate emotions, and every moment was wrung for maximum sentimental effect. Casts were large, dozens of actors being used for crowd-scenes, but stock-characters became the norm and in the *stock-companies* actors were employed specifically to play such rôles as hero, heroine, villain, patriarch, comic man/woman, good old man/woman. Endings were expected to be *coups de théâtre*, and frequently rendered as a tableau: *Lady Audley's Secret*, for example, ends with the sudden demise of the lady herself who "*Falls—dies—Music—tableau of sympathy—*GEORGE TALBOYS *kneels over her.* CURTAIN".[6]

Reading melodrama presents many challenges since plot and character obeyed contemporary conventions of dramatic sensation and not logic; what we today may find unacceptably contrived or implausible added to atmospheres of unpredictability and suspense. Sudden fits of madness or transformations of personality were not unusual; characters returned from the dead, revealed dark secrets out of the blue, were reprieved from extreme circumstances, or met through far-fetched coincidence. Words were not the most important element,

---

[6] Rowell, ed., *Nineteenth Century Plays*, p. 266.

and scripts not carefully crafted literary works but rough-and-ready blueprints for production; what mattered above all was combining dramatic visuals with music, sentimental manipulation of emotion, and lavish spectacle, an actor's repertoire of melodramatic gestures counting more than rhetorical talents. Yet from the 1830s melodrama increasingly reflected contemporary social concerns—familial, domestic, professional, and class issues—and unlike most sentimental drama treated poor and lower-class rôles with compassion. Oppression, injustice, exploitation, crime, poverty, and abuses of power were common themes, villains were often wealthy or titled, and connections between behaviour and social circumstance were implicit. For all its unreality melodrama anticipated and galvanized *realist* concerns about setting and characterization, and when the theatrical monopoly ended was well placed to take advantage of changing theatre-architecture and the increasing concerns of legitimate theatre with *pictorial* illusion, elaborate set-design, and complex stage-machinery. So-called *sensation drama* became a passion, and playwrights created extreme scenarios, train crashes, avalanches, and shipwrecks illusionistically staged to great effect; playwright Dion Boucicault (1820–90) in particular made a name for himself in the 1850s–60s.

The end of the theatrical monopoly allowed musical genres to develop in their own right. Like its American cousin *vaudeville*, music-hall grew out of tavern entertainment with alcohol usually available throughout, and though initially associated with prostitution and low-life was very popular with all classes, gradually became more respectable, and ended in large halls built specifically for it. It incorporated set-pieces and sketches by different actors, impersonations, mime, acrobats, juggling acts, comic songs, recitations, and dance-numbers; turns lasted about twenty minutes, and famous music-hall artists included *black-face* comedian G. H. Chirgwin ('the white-eyed kaffir', 1854–1922); raconteur Dan Leno (George Galvin, 1860–1904); male-impersonator Vesta Tilley (Matilda Towles, 1864–1952); and the Scottish balladeer Harry Lauder ('Hoots, mon, there's a moose loose aboot the hoose', 1870–1950). Music-hall flourished from the mid-nineteenth century to the First World War and largely died out by 1950; but the comic physical routines in Beckett's *Waiting for Godot* owe much to music-hall, *Krapp's Last Tape* (1958) was famously played by actor Max Wall (Maxwell George Lorimer, 1908–90), trained in music-hall, and *The Entertainer* (1957) by John Osborne (1929–94) expresses nostalgia for its style.

Musical comedy, light-hearted plays intercut with songs and dancing, evolved from light opera, at its height from 1870–1918, and the two cannot always be distinguished. Gilbert's and Sullivan's string of successes made them household names, and Savoy operas such as *HMS Pinafore* (1878), *The Pirates of Penzance* (1879), and *The Mikado* (1885), are still regularly performed by amateur groups; Gilbert is famous for brilliantly witty lyrics which earned him a reputation as a nonsense-poet with subversive and satirical edges. Musical comedies often borrowed plots from (and readily blur into) one another, but like melodrama can make deceptively simple reading: texts appear uncomplicated but the most significant narratives of movement, dance, and song are not notated in detail and the performative complexity of these genres often goes unrecognized. After 1918 musical comedy became faster paced, with more dancing and less romance, but the greatest changes came in America via a generation of outstanding composers including Jerome Kern (1885–1945), Cole Porter (1892–1964), George Gershwin (1898–1937), and Richard Rodgers (1902–79). Rodgers's partnerships with lyricists Lorenz Hart (1895–1943) and Oscar Hammerstein II (1895–1960) produced the *Broadway* greats of the 1930s–50s, including *Oklahoma!* (1943), *South Pacific* (1949), *The King and I* (1951), and *The Sound of Music* (1959), developing musical comedy into the genre now called *musicals*. The interest in integrating singing, dancing, and spoken words reached its apotheosis with *West Side Story* (1957), a musical version of *Romeo and Juliet* by Leonard Bernstein (1918–90) and Stephen Sondheim (b.1930), but since 1945 the growth of the musical has been the major phenomenon in Western theatre. Andrew Lloyd Webber (b.1948) now dominates: internationally famous for *Jesus Christ Superstar* (1970), *Evita* (1976), *Cats* (1981), and *The Phantom of the Opera* (1986), he effectively copyrights productions by insisting his shows are identically formatted wherever they open. Musicals are now a multi-million-pound global industry at the core of London's *West End*; academically slighted, they are arguably the only form of mass entertainment to which Western theatre can still lay claim.

One other genre should be noted. *Farce* began in Greek and Roman theatre, and both Shakespeare's *Comedy of Errors* (*c.*1592) and Jonson's *The Alchemist* (1610) are sometimes so described; but modern farce derives from French dramatists Eugène Labiche (1815–88) and Georges Feydeau (1862–1921), and was popularized in England by Arthur Wing Pinero (1855–1934) and Henry Arthur Jones (1851–1929). Pinero's *The Magistrate* (1885) and *The Schoolmistress* (1886) were particularly successful, and the advent of silent film made farce international through such stars as Stan Laurel (Arthur Jefferson, 1890–1965) and Oliver Hardy (1892–1957), and Buster Keaton. In Latin *farsa* means 'stuffing'; farces are typically stuffed with ever more intricate scenes which become increasingly frantic in pace and relation to plot. Associated with comic buffoonery, farce demands great skills of timing and physical clowning from actors; tending to anarchy, it can abound with scatalogical and sexual references: A twentieth-century English tradition of *bedroom farce*, focused on complicated sexual machinations, was at its height at the Whitehall Theatre in the 1950s and 1960s (hence *Whitehall farces*), and in the *Carry On* films. Ben Travers (1886–1980) became known for his *Aldwych farces* (after the Aldwych Theatre) mixing absurd plots and bizarre characterization with social satire. Other notable farces include *Charley's Aunt* (1892) by Brandon Thomas (1856–1914), and *What the Butler Saw* (wr. 1967, perf. 1969) by Joe Orton (1933–67); current *farceurs* include Michael Frayn (b.1933), Alan Ayckbourn (b.1939), and Terry Johnson (b.1955).

Finally, two more general tendencies. From the eighteenth century the *forestage* (140 >) diminished, and as plays were increasingly framed by the proscenium arch the possibilities of realistic staging began to be explored in various ways. The great actor-manager David Garrick deployed theatre-designer Philippe Jacques de Loutherbourg (1740–1812) in the 1770s (194 >), and by the mid-nineteenth century pictorial staging was considered very important, an aesthetic which further encouraged the growth of proscenium-arch theatres. In the 1850s Charles Kean (1811–68) was noted for meticulous research into classical plays, and his desire for historically accurate settings anticipated the flawed but very influential attempts from the 1880s by William Poel (1852–1934) and his Elizabethan Stage Society to return Shakespeare to Jacobethan performance conditions (195 >). By the end of the century some productions showed excessive concern for pictorialism: Herbert Beerbohm Tree (1853–1917) had a particular reputation for extravagant Shakespeare—his *Dream* (1900) boasted a forest-floor of real grass with live rabbits.

The influence of Eugène Scribe (1791–1861) filtered through to England from France after 1850. Credited with inventing the *well-made play* (*pièce bien faite*), Scribe devised plots which had a coherence and causality missing from melodrama and which worked to maximize suspense: they began with exposition and progressed through crises and complications to reach logical, plausible endings. Each act closed with a climax, each scene contributed to the overall plot, and the dénouement resolved all narrative threads. Often belittled as formulaic and unartistic, Scribe had an influence on subsequent generations of playwrights that is clear in the work of Ibsen, Oscar Wilde (1854–1900), and Shaw; the work of David Hare (b.1947) is often well made in the ways Scribe championed.

10

Social genres:
political theatre, agit-prop, documentary drama, and epic drama

social [. . .] Concerned with, interested in, the constitution of society
and the problems presented by this. (*OED2*)

All plays are implicitly political by virtue of the subject-matter, form,
and linguistic registers they contain, and the audience for whom they
are intended; all productions are implicitly political because the
resources they consume are denied to another play, company, and
space. Plays may also explicitly deal with governmental policy, as the
anti-apartheid play *Siswe Bansi is Dead* (1972) by Athol Fugard
(b.1932) and the socialist plays *Maydays* (1983) and *The Shape of the
Table* (1990) by David Edgar (b.1948) do. An author may use explicit
politics to cover implicit ones, as Miller's *The Crucible* (1953) explicitly
deals with superstitious seventeenth-century witch-hunts but implicitly concerns anti-communist witch-hunts led by Joseph McCarthy
(1909–57). A director's interpretation can make an implicitly political
play explicit, or impose an agenda different from anything the playwright intended: Baz Luhrmann's filmed *Romeo and Juliet* (1996) maps
Shakespeare on to gang-rivalry in modern California; Richard
Loncraine's *Richard III* (1995) uses an imaginary 1930s British fascist
dictatorship. Performance at a specific location before a specific audience generates additional layers of political meaning: a new play by a
British or Irish writer performed at the RNT or *Royal Court*, for
example, is automatically viewed as representative of the nation's
drama, but a new play premièring in a local arts centre has very
different political resonances.

This chapter concerns genres which deal <u>explicitly</u> with politics, overtly challenging the social status quo and promoting alternative agendas. Modern political drama is intimately connected with left-wing ideologies, and has roots in Ibsen and his late-nineteenth-century imitators. Ibsen's theatrical projects in the 1880s–90s drew on experiments in realism already evident on stage (as in the novel) and the post-Darwinian[1] theories of Émile Zola (1840–1902), who argued that human behaviour was conditioned by heredity and genetics as well as environmental factors such as poverty, class, and social prejudice, and that art should represent the interconnectedness of an individual and a social situation. Ibsen's *A Doll's House* (1879) and *Ghosts* (1881) exposed that relationship so effectively that most mainstream European theatre has since been strongly preoccupied with *psychological realism*.

Ibsen's *Naturalism*, predicated on realist sets and naturalistic acting, makes his plays difficult to label generically: they borrow character-types and situations from melodrama but are well made, and reject the conventional morality of both genres. In *A Doll's House* Nora is recognizably a stock ideal mother/wife, her husband Torvald a stiff, 'principled' patriarch, and Krogstad a villain who threatens their domestic stability; but when Nora chooses to leave her husband and children, rejecting ideologies of domestic servitude and oppression to go in search of education, financial independence, and self-fulfilment, she breaks the mould of stock-character and the dominant social construction of middle-class women in late-nineteenth-century Europe. The way she breaks her mould was also new: she gives a long, reasoned, and highly articulate explanation for her decision, mapping her psychological profile in great detail and describing her journey as a series of socially conditioned responses to environment. This display of cause-and-effect, the provision of a realistic milieu and psychological *throughline* for Nora, are now elements we take for granted in most realist (including television) drama; otherwise we could not be dissatisfied by 'failure' to deliver them nor describe characters or plotlines as 'unconvincing'.

Considered morally and politically inflammatory for their time,

---

[1] Charles Darwin (1809–82), published *On the Origin of the Species by Means of Natural Selection* in 1859, arguing, against the orthodoxies of the time, that the origins of man and other species were natural and not divine.

both *A Doll's House* and *Ghosts* caused sensations throughout Europe, and in London predictably fell foul of censorship (208 >), the Lord Chamberlain refusing a performance-licence; London premières therefore took place in small, private *theatre-clubs*, which in the 1880s–90s became a customary way of evading the law. Ibsen's plays provided a model for a 'literary' drama about contemporary issues, but demonstrated potential as vehicles for political protest, and it was not long before playwrights with socialist agendas began to experiment in similar vein: Englishmen Harley Granville Barker (1877–1946), H. A. Jones, and Pinero, American Elizabeth Robins (1862–1952), and Anglo-Irishmen Shaw and Wilde, among many others, owed much to Ibsenite Naturalism, and came to form a late-nineteenth- and early-twentieth-century theatrical *avant garde*.

The political impact of Ibsenite Naturalism was heightened by the ways his plays and those he influenced combined realist sets with new levels of naturalistic acting. A requirement for the separation of stage and audience became all but absolute, and *fourth-wall* productions the norm: spectators watched actions unfolding independently of them-selves, actors referred only to the world of the play and sought no interaction with spectators, sets ceased to be spectacular, designers aimed for a post-photographic quality of reproduction, creating detailed middle-class interiors (often drawing-rooms, hence *drawing-room drama*), and audiences looked upon copies of the world in which they lived. Playwrights emphasized the importance of realist sets with detailed stage-directions (Shaw's were notoriously lengthy) and actors had to find a style matching the sophisticated dialogue of Naturalist drama and true to the interest in individual psychology rather than stock-characters. In London Shaw and Granville Barker helped actors to (re-)train, particularly at the Royal Court, but the major develop-ment was in Moscow where Stanislavski sought to help actors play Chekhov's (post-)Naturalist rôles. He developed the first systematic actor-training, encouraging a style that looked unstudied and enabled actors to seem immersed in their character 'for real', as though rôle and actor were one.

After 1914–18 the socialist struggle against bourgeois capitalism intensified throughout Europe and developed mass support. Despite the General Strike (1926) and the Jarrow March (1936) extreme tumult was averted in England, but revolutionary activities shook other European countries; the most direct form of political theatre, *agit-prop* (agitation-propaganda), emerged in the Soviet Union after the 1917 revolution and spread to Germany in 1918–33. It grew from the working-class struggle for a socialist state as an instrument to raise spectators' (workers') consciousness of a particular political/social situation and promote Marxist ideology and mass protest against capitalism.[2] In England as abroad, workers' theatre-groups, usually affiliated either to the Labour Party (founded 1900) or the British Communist Party (founded 1920), practised agit-prop in the 1920s–30s, taking theatre directly to audiences by playing in community halls, factories, or any available space. Equating theatrical illusion with capitalist conspiracy, they operated without stage or curtain and often without props. Agit-prop shows were mobile and followed an easily adaptable formula, a revue format with songs, sketches, mono-logues, gags, improvization, and *living newspapers*: its first purpose was propaganda and it aimed for maximum audience participation. Agit-prop faded in 1930s England but returned in the 1960s–70s via left-wing protest-movements; it has been important in parts of India, particularly Bengal (where the Communist Party is a major force) and Tamil Nadu (where nationalist politics dominate).

The political turmoil in Russia and Germany in the 1920s–30s also generated experiments in *documentary drama* (*docudrama*), plays con-taining news reports, manifestos, testimonials, court hearings, etc. (and subsequently film or video of real events), selected, edited, and assembled by a writer or writing-team to present and construe a cur-rent issue of particular political sensitivity. Such plays may be wholly assembled from documents or partly fictional, and frequently adopt the form of a trial or inquiry to cite otherwise disconnected evidence. In 1920s Berlin Erwin Piscator (1893–1966) sought to give accounts of modern political events from a communist point of view: initially he hired teams of writers to research political subjects, assemble docu-ments, and create fictional narratives; in the 1960s he concentrated on plays by single authors, famously directing *The Representative* (1963) by Rolf Hochhuth (b.1931), an indictment of Vatican

---

[2] Karl Marx (1818–83) argued in *Das Kapital* (1867) that diminishing numbers of capitalists were exploiting the rewards of improved industrial methods at the expense of an increasingly dependent and wretched labouring-class. His remedy was the abolition of private property by victory in the class war.

complicity in the *Sho'ah*, and *The Investigation* (1965) by Peter Weiss (1916–82), a digest of the 'Auschwitz Trial' in Frankfurt (1963–65). Piscator's early experiments used new technology to strengthen the political message, deploying film footage, projections of still images or banks of relevant information, treadmills, revolving platforms, and multi-layered sets.

Docudrama rejects a theatre of pure fiction as politically ineffectual, and exposes the manipulation of events by foregrounding the act of manipulating data itself. In England Peter Brook (b.1925) controversially explored the genre in *US* (RSC, 1969), criticizing the US invasion of Vietnam, and Richard Norton-Taylor (b.1944) recently raised its profile with *The Colour of Justice* (1998, televised 1999), based on transcripts of a public inquiry into the unsolved racist murder in 1993 of Stephen Lawrence. Documentary drama can be potent, and sometimes the threat of performance is perceived as too great: *Theresa* (1990) by Julia Pascal (b.1949), about collaboration with Nazism in the Channel Islands in 1940–5, is banned in Guernsey to this day (212 >).

The most influential political genre since 1945 has undoubtedly been *epic theatre*, primarily the creation of Bertolt Brecht (1898–1956) though the term was borrowed from Piscator. Brecht spent his life evolving a theory and practice of theatre as a forum for political ideas: as a German his own politics were rooted in opposition to Fascism and a belief in Communism as a way of thwarting Hitler—he spent 16 years (1933–49) in exile and his plays, like all work by anti-fascist artists, were in Germany classified as 'degenerate' and banned. He developed epic drama in reaction to the dominance of well-made plays and naturalistic acting-styles; the well-made play, he argued, was 'Aristotelian', bourgeois in content and form, addressed only the middle classes, and invested in preserving the status quo (even if it criticized it). He questioned the tragic qualities of Ibsen's Hedda Gabler and Pinero's Mrs Ebbsmith, seeing them as representing decadent self-indulgence in a world of capitalist privilege; their 'tragedies' depended on individual entrapment by social circumstances, but unlike Nora's in *A Doll's House* bowed to prejudices and offered no alternative course of action. Brecht aimed to appeal to less privileged classes, treating contemporary issues such as war, stock-markets, poverty, unemployment, and corruption in high places; most importantly, as a communist he was interested in representing the possibility of changing society to politicize his spectators <u>and his actors</u>. Brecht wanted what he called 'a scientific theatre for a scientific age', plays that represent human beings as dynamic and able to make informed decisions about their lives: he places his characters in certain social situations from which they either learn, become responsible, and begin a process of social change (Andrea in *Life of Galileo*, 1943), or do not learn, do not become responsible, and do nothing to alter the status quo (Mother Courage in *Mother Courage and her Children*, wr. 1941, perf. 1950). The most obviously didactic and Communist of his plays are the *Lehrstücke* ('learning plays') such as *He Who Says Yes, He Who Says No* (1930), short works designed to teach amateurs moral and political lessons through participation in performance. Brecht was adamant that *Lehrstücke* were only to be used in schools and factories, not performed in established theatres or used as anything but pedagogical exercises.

The main objective of Brecht's epic theatre was to awaken spectators' intellectual faculties, making them question events on stage and think about alternative actions. Nineteenth-century plays and performance styles had focused on spectators' emotional rather than intellectual responses, depending on audience empathy with 'characters' and emotional involvement in plots. Brecht decided he must change the audiences' attitudes to the material they were viewing, saw that to do it he should interrupt their identification with the play as much as possible, and developed the theory and practice of *alienation* (*Verfremdung*). Simply put, the alienation effect (*Verfremdungseffekt*) is a tool-kit of distancing devices deployed to interrupt a spectator's process of identification with plot and character, encoded in plays as strategies which seek to force a spectator to concentrate not on <u>what</u> the story is but on <u>how</u> it is told and what the consequences of an action may be. Thus epic theatre concentrates on narrating action rather than allowing spectators to become immersed in events, and the form of epic plays does not rely on well-made plot-devices of conflict, tension, and resolution—linear action—but on *montage*, an assembled series of scenes each complete in itself. Plot is deprivileged and frequently told in advance in brief descriptions of forthcoming action at the beginning of scenes:

Spring 1624. The Swedish Commander-in-Chief Count Oxenstierna is raising troops in Dalecarlia for the Polish campaign. The canteen woman Anna Fierling, known as Mother Courage, loses one son.[3]

In performance such scene-descriptions are often recited by an actor and/or projected or written on placards. The distance between actor and character is maintained through emphasis on action, not psychology, and characters break the fourth wall by introducing themselves or being introduced in deliberately metatheatrical ways—for example the Prologue in *The Resistible Rise of Arturo Ui* (wr. 1941, perf. 1958), the title itself operating as a brilliant alienation-device.[4] Characters address audiences directly, narrate actions, summarize events, break into song, subvert situations, and expose other characters through unexpected decisions or comic japes (for example, soldier Schweyk in *Schweyk in the Second World War* (wr. 1941–3, perf. 1957), who encounters Hitler in a snowstorm fleeing his own orders to march on Stalingrad).[5] Brecht's 'characters' constantly refer to their social rôles and to a social hierarchy: a clear example is Shen Teh in *The Good Person of Szechwan* (1943), who plays a dual rôle as an exploited, penniless female prostitute and a businessman who prospers through ruthless egoism in a system which recognizes and rewards greed.[6] Performatively, Brecht's epic plays required a new kind of actor- and director-training, but also a different creative response from composers, singers, designers, *lighting-technicians*, and *set-builders*, all instructed to exploit alienation to its full theatrical potential. The influence of epic theatre remains significant, and a generation of political playwrights in the 1960s–70s experimented with it, including Edward Bond (b.1934), Caryl Churchill (b.1938), Hare, and Edgar.

Since the 1960s, and especially since the end of English theatre censorship in 1968 and the abrupt disintegration of communism in Eastern Europe since 1989, European playwrights have tended to address politics not in general but in relation to specific constituencies, reflecting a growing pan-European sense of different national, regional, cultural, and social identities. *Issue-plays*, which treat a matter in relation to a specific audience (feminist, gay, lesbian, black,

[3] Brecht, *Plays 5*, p. 109.
[4] Brecht, *Plays 6*, pp. 117–19.
[5] Brecht, *Plays 7*, pp. 207–9.
[6] Brecht, *Plays 6*, pp. 3–111.

homeless, prisoners) were common in the 1970s–80s, and in some countries AIDS-plays remain vital in educating sexual behaviour and challenging bigotry against HIV+; *community-plays*, in which a community participates in a play written specifically for (and sometimes by) itself, have also been important. Yet many mainstream successes described as 'political' are only narrowly so—consider, for example, Hare's *The Secret Rapture* (1988), hailed as 'feminist' but unenlightened in its gender politics, or the narrow focus of *Oleanna* (1992) by David Mamet (b.1947), hailed as a radical treatment of sexual harassment. *Utopian theatre* promoting a specific political ideology as a panacea all but disappeared in Western Europe in the 1990s, submerged by declining funding and the consequent need for risk-free and trendily commercial plays, and marginalized by a growing general disillusionment with all politicians and organized politics. There has been a notable use of theatrical techniques by some protest organizations, particularly Greenpeace, but the most coherent radical theatre of recent times has come from Brazilian playwright-director and theorist Augusto Boal (b.1931), who after imprisonment and in exile invented the genres of *forum theatre*, a mode of community argument and self-determination, and *invisible theatre*, which permits intervention in the play by unsuspecting spectators.

11

The impact of technology:
light, sound, radio- and TV-plays, and film-genres

The history of stage-lighting predates electricity. Renaissance dialogue often describes the quality of light to compensate for effects that could not be controlled: Kent in *King Lear* tells Oswald, "Draw you rogue, for though it be night, yet the Moone shines, Ile make a sop oth' Moonshine of you" (2.2.30–2), and Mooneshine in the inset 'Pyramus and Thisbe' in *Dream* is an extended joke on necessity. Torches and 'tapers' (candles), frequently referred to in stage-directions and dialogue, symbolically represent night as well as adding atmosphere, and emphasize what those in the theatrical world can and can't see or hear, as in Paris's tense nocturnal arrival at Juliet's tomb:

> *Par.* Give me thy Torch Boy, hence, and stand aloft,
> Yet put it out, for I would not be seene :
> Under yond young Trees lay thee all along,
> Holding thy eare close to the hollow ground,
> So shall no foot upon the Churchyard tread,
> Being loose, unfirme with digging up of Graves,
> But thou shalt heare it: whistle then to me   (5.3.1–7)

Hamlet opens with a jumpy exchange between sentries who can't see each other in the dark, creating an eerie atmosphere for the entrance of the ghost, and Lady Macbeth's sleep-walking scene (5.1.) exploits the candle she holds as a symbol of stricken conscience and failing spirit.

   Once theatrical performance moved into roofed buildings lighting became increasingly sophisticated, including the use of chandeliers, *footlights* (at the actors' feet), and coloured glass or diffusion through water to produce *washes* of light, but depended on candles and oil-lamps until the nineteenth century, when change became rapid. In 1803 the Lyceum Theatre, London, demonstrated *gaslight*, and like the Chestnut Street Theatre, Philadelphia, had fully installed gas-lighting by 1817: gas-lamps intensified the quality of light and were easier to mount above the stage, but like oil-lamps smelled and were a serious fire-hazard. *Limelight*, invented in 1826, was made by heating lime in an oxyhydrogen flame, and with a hand-operated spotlight produced intense beams and precise spots of light; in 1879 the California Theatre, San Francisco, opened with electric lighting, followed in 1881 by the Savoy Theatre, London. Electricity provided even brighter light, was much safer, did not smell, and did not create such oppressively hot working-conditions; rapidly installed in theatres across Europe and America, electric lighting was standard by 1914. *Dimming* and *fading* became possible, as did subtler colouring. For many years equipment was extremely bulky and vast technical teams were needed; but by the late twentieth century computerized *lighting-boards* enabled multiple settings of composition, intensity, and colour to be stored as a *lighting-plan*, one person in the *lighting-box* controlling a complex show.

Lighting is not in itself generic, but an electrified theatre affects all expectations and some modern playwrights have given stage-lighting a rôle in their work at least as significant as that of words. Beckett was exact about the quality, intensity, and timing of *fade-up*, *fade-out*, and *blackout* in many of his plays: in *Not I* (1972) only the actor's mouth and an auditor are visible; in *Play* (1963) a spotlight provokes speech as it relentlessly moves between three actors' faces; and in *Catastrophe* (1982) the lighting-technician Luke is the only character given a name and the rôle of light in creating the final image is crucial.[1] The last scene of the notoriously disturbing *Blasted* (1995) by Sarah Kane (1971–2000) has eight stage-directions in two pages specifying '*Darkness. Light.*' before a final blackout.[2] In the farce *Black Comedy* (1965) Peter Shaffer (b.1926) reverses the light/dark conventions in theatre, representing a theatrical world in the midst of an electricity-cut while the audience watch in full light.

---

[1] Beckett, *Complete Dramatic Works*, pp. 305–20, 373–83, 455–61.
[2] Kane, *Complete Plays*, pp. 59–60.

Electricity also revolutionized the *amplification* and recording of sound, enabling drama as much as records and music. Beckett explored the dramatic possibilities of the tape-recorder in *Krapp's Last Tape* (1958), a *monologue* which works as a one-man dialogue, recordings narrating fragments of Krapp's past as Krapp himself acts as editor:

> [. . .] clear to me at last that the dark I have always struggled to keep under is in reality my most—[KRAPP *curses, switches off, winds tape forward, switches on again*]—unshatterable association until my dissolution of storm and night with the light of the understanding and the fire— [KRAPP *curses louder, switches off, winds tape forward, switches on again*]—my face in her breasts and my hand on her. We lay there without moving. But under us all moved, and moved us, gently, up and down, and from side to side.[3]

Beckett also used the recorded voice in *Rockaby* (1980) and the microphone in *What Where* (1983); the microphone is often associated with representations of absolute power, and Brecht in *The Resistible Rise of Arturo Ui* (wr. 1941, perf. 1958), like Edgar in *Albert Speer* (2000), connects it unequivocally with Fascism.[4] The French playwright Marguerite Duras (1914–96) experimented radically with sound in *India Song* (wr. 1972, pub. French 1973, English 1976), pushing the idea of theatrical *oversound* to new limits in a mesmeric piece using (as a film might) prolonged recorded *voice-over* as *soundtrack* to stage-action, so detaching verbal narration from actors and privileging movement over speech.[5] Duras was *commissioned* by Peter Hall for the NT, who then baulked; she rewrote the piece as a film, released in 1975, and the stage-première was not until 1993. Directors have also taken advantage of acoustic techniques: at the start of his 1993 RNT production of *Machinal* (1928) by Sophie Treadwell (1885–1970), Daldry deafened the audience with the amplified sound of the *safety-curtain* being raised as a prelude to the depiction of a woman reduced to mere automaton in a terrifyingly mechanized world.[6] Actors can be *miked* for effect or of necessity: in Peter Hall's 1996 RNT production of *Oedipus* adapted by Ranjit Bolt (b.1959)

---

3 Beckett, *Complete Dramatic Works*, p. 220.
4 Brecht, *Plays 6*, pp. 208–9; Edgar, *Albert Speer*, I.9.I, p. 56.
5 Duras, *Four Plays*, pp. 119–83.
6 See Lesser, *A Director Calls*, pp. 56–8.

masks so muffled actors' voices that microphones were fitted inside them.[7]

Mass media have also created their own genres. Radio-broadcasting and formative experiments with *radio-plays* began in earnest after 1918: the power of a radio-play lies in the imaginative hold it can claim over listeners who conjure up their own visuals to match word and sound; its extraordinary potency was demonstrated in 1938 when CBS transmitted an adaptation by Orson Welles (1915–85) of H. G. Wells's novel *The War of the Worlds* (1899).[8] The dramatization narrated an invasion by Martians as if it were happening and thousands, believing it to be a news report, fled their homes in panic. Even now, with radio supposedly declining, BBC Radio remains a major commissioner of drama, vital to many younger writers, but established stage-playwrights who continue to write for radio find their work is barely mentioned by the press, and generally only authors in the *high canon* (Beckett, Pinter, Stoppard, Churchill) have radio-plays published.

The pragmatics of staging a play impose visual limitations on locations, time-zones, and the inner-worlds of characters, but radio can exploit these things to the full. Its advantages are well understood in *Educating Rita* (1980) by Willy Russell (b.1947), in Rita's one-line essay on how to resolve the staging difficulties of Ibsen's *Peer Gynt*: "Do it on the radio".[9] The dead can mix with the living, minds can be inhabited, and minute details of myriad lives and places narrated, as in *Under Milk Wood* (broadcast 1954) by Dylan Thomas (1914–53), which he called "a play for voices". With great lyrical intensity he explores the music of different voices, sounds, and fragmentary narratives, creating a vivid impression of one day in a Welsh seaside-town. Dependent on poetic logic and generating different moods with varied sounds, *Under Milk Wood* demands to be heard rather than read:[10]

---

[7] See Peter Reynolds, *Unmasking Oedipus* (London: RNT Publications, 1996), p. 19.

[8] Variously available on audio-cassette and CD (e.g. Hodder Headline Audiobooks HH129).

[9] Russell, *Educating Rita and Others*, p. 192.

[10] Several recordings are available on audio-cassette, notably one with Thomas and the original cast (HarperCollins Audiobooks HCA46), and a 1963 BBC version starring Richard Burton (BBC Radio Collection ZBBC1755).

FIRST DROWNED
Remember me, Captain?

CAPTAIN CAT
You're Dancing Williams!

FIRST DROWNED
I lost my step in Nantucket.

SECOND DROWNED
Do you see me, Captain? the white bone talking?
I'm Tom-Fred the donkeyman . . . We shared the
same girl once . . . her name was Mrs Probert . . .

WOMAN'S VOICE
Rosie Probert, thirty three Duck Lane. Come on up,
boys, I'm dead.

THIRD DROWNED
Hold me, Captain, I'm Jonah Jarvis, come to a bad
end, very enjoyable . . . [11]

Beckett too explored inner states, merging the internal and external worlds of his characters, and mixing landscapes of memory and of the present in *All That Fall* (1956) and *Embers* (1959). Stoppard, conversely, shows a fascination with the external world, mapping space through sound in *Albert's Bridge* (1965) by representing the different positions of four men painting a bridge through loudness or softness of speech. Plays can appear in both stage- and radio-versions, and it can be instructive to compare texts: in the radio-version of Pinter's *A Slight Ache* (1959) the mute match-seller is ambiguous, possibly only a construct of other characters' imaginations, but in the stage-version (1961) he is cast and a realm of ambiguity that radio can utilize is lost. The lesson works both ways, for perhaps the greatest weakness of radio-drama relative to the stage is that on radio even a pause can be taken not as silence but as *dead air*, and the rich sound-effects of radio reflect a necessity for constant noise.

In the 1940s–50s *television-drama* was performed 'live' in the studio, and so tended to remain much like stage-plays; since the invention of video-tape in 1958 it has developed very successfully in sophisticated forms, latterly boosted by the develoment of a retail-market for video. *Television-plays* had shown *ratings* power in America with *Marty* (1953) by Paddy Chayevsky (1923–81), about a butcher longing for love, and

---

[11] Thomas, *Under Milk Wood*, pp. 4–5.

the tense *Twelve Angry Men* (1954) by Reginald Rose (b.1920), depicting an all-white jury forced to decide on the life or death of a non-white defendant. In the US 'Hallmark Hall of Fame' (NBC 1952–79, CBS 1980–) and 'Armchair Theatre' (ABC, 1957–) sponsored much new writing; in the UK the BBC developed a *slot* for hard-hitting television plays from 1964 with 'The Wednesday Play' (from 1970 'Play for Today'). Many established theatre-writers were attracted to TV; others made names specifically through TV-drama, including Jeremy Sandford (b.1930) who had a notable success with *Cathy Come Home* (1966), David Mercer (1928–80), and Alan Plater (b.1935). Drama *series* have proved popular, from *costume-dramas* such as *Elizabeth R.* (1971), six plays about the life and death of Elizabeth I by different authors but with a shared cast, to police and detective series such as *The Bill* and *Murder She Wrote*, sci-fi series such as *Star Trek* (first broadcast 1966), and *The X-Files*. Adaptations of novels also enjoy immense success, especially costume-dramas from works by Jane Austen and Charles Dickens, and crime-drama from novels by Colin Dexter (b.1930, Morse), P. D. James (b.1920, Dalgliesh), and Ruth Rendell (b.1930, Wexford); there has also been much first-rate crime-writing specifically for TV, often by teams of script-writers in such series as *Hill Street Blues, NYPD Blue*, and *Homicide: Life on the Street*, but few scripts are published, and except in courses devoted to TV-writing little serious attention is paid.

Film and television monologues have found a large print-market: *Talking Heads* (broadcast 1988, staged 1992) by Alan Bennett (b.1934) is a text used by many schools, and *Swimming to Cambodia* (perf. and pub. 1985, filmed 1986) by Spalding Gray (b.1941) is also popular; but Hare's *Via Dolorosa* (perf. 1997, broadcast 1999) highlighted the problems of filming a stage-show. In a class of his own, Dennis Potter (1935–94) wrote strikingly original TV-drama, adapting his knowledge of stage-musicals to produce startling anti-naturalist work epitomized in *Pennies from Heaven* (1978). Potter experimented vigorously—in *Blue Remembered Hills* (1979) all rôles are children played by adults—and *The Singing Detective* (1986) gained international recognition:

> From Marlow's point of view the medical team beams down at him in a wholly unnatural, hallucinatory fashion. They repeat themselves, each with a click of the fingers.

CONSULTANT: Barbiturate!

REGISTRAR: Antidepressants!

VISITING DOCTOR: Valium!

REGISTRAR: And Librium!

As Fred Waring's Pennsylvanians' music crashes in, the lighting switches to vaudeville colours. Music: 'Dry Bones'.

   The consultant and his team lip-sync to the zestful vocals, complete with clicking dry-bone sounds and bouncy music, whereas the rest of the ward (initially) carries on unaffected, unconcerned.[12]

This technique was extended in *Karaoke* and *Cold Lazarus* (both broadcast 1996) and greatly influences advertising, but the major modern phenomenon of TV-drama is *soap operas*, some enjoying international audiences of hundreds of millions. But again, while videos or novelizations may be for sale scripts are rarely available or studied.

   Scripts of TV-drama and films <u>are</u> increasingly available to buy, but readers should treat with caution texts which are not true *shooting-scripts* and read more like novels. The main difference between reading a script for film or TV and a play for theatre is that screen-writers specify visual narratives in much more detail, and may use technical terminology for camera-angles and shots (*point-of-view, close-up, long-shot*).[13] Cinematic possibilities, especially close-up and voice-over, have enormous consequences for actors (who must control facial expression with great precision), casting (same-age same-gender becomes all but obligatory), and dialogue (long speeches are much rarer than in stage-plays, except in voice-over), and must be imaginatively allowed for by readers. The difficulties in reading such drama are illustrated by Hare's *Licking Hitler* (broadcast and pub. 1978): the first spoken words come in scene 3, headed "INT. CORRIDOR. DAY":

ARCHIE: (VO) The question of Hess.
   (*Pause.*)
   Nobody really believes that Hess flew to Britain on the Führer's instructions. Hess flew to Britain for one simple reason; because he's a criminal lunatic.
   (*The camera pans slowly round to a bare passage leading down to the servants' quarters. A few hunting and military pictures hang at random on the*

12 Potter, *The Singing Detective*, pp. 28–9.
13 For a detailed glossary see Thompson and Bordwell, *Film History*, pp. 819–24.

cream walls. At the bottom of the passage the sun shines brilliantly through the glass panes of the closed door of the gun room, from which ARCHIE'S *voice is coming.*)
Now what is frightening about Hess is not what he has done. It is the fact he once found his way so easily into Hitler's confidence. As loyal Germans we have to face the fact that Adolf Hitler chooses to surround himself with fools, arse-lickers, time-servers, traitors, megalomaniacs . . . and men who wish to rape their own mothers.[14]

Only in the next scene, when Archie is first <u>seen</u>, do readers learn that he "*is in his late twenties but already looks much more mature; squat, powerful, stocky, a Clydesider with a very precise manner*": but a viewer would know him for a 'Clydesider', a working-class Glaswegian, as soon as his voice-over started. The shock-opening turns largely on the confusion of <u>hearing</u> a powerfully Scottish voice saying "As loyal Germans we . . . ", but first-time readers can experience it only in constructed retrospect. In general, visual narratives and/or sound-track may be far more eloquent than any dialogue, and as a rule filmgoers are more arrested by action-sequences than lengthy conversations, though viewers of TV-drama tolerate a slower pace.

Besides these techno-specific genres (and the political and musical genres already discussed) twentieth-century playwriting was not generically innovative. Rather, novels and films were overwhelmingly the engines of genre, and the rich variety of new genres they generated have been borrowed and quoted in stage-plays since the 1920s. We have no space to go into detail, but the abundant novel and film genres and the way they have influenced playwrights and directors must be taken into account by all consumers of modern drama. Stoppard's *The Real Inspector Hound* (1968) borrows from the crime-novels, stage-plays, and film-adaptations of Agatha Christie (1891–1976), and Daldry's production of Priestley's *An Inspector Calls* fashions itself on cinematic stereotypes of the detective. The stage-play *Mojo* (1995) by Jez Butterworth (b.1969) owes a clear debt to the *gangster-movies* of Quentin Tarantino (b. 1963), as does *Real Classy Affair* (1998) by Nick Grosso (b.1968). *Masterpieces* (1983) by Sarah Daniels (b.1957) is influenced by popular *court-room drama* on TV and film. The war-plays *Dingo* (wr. 1961, perf. 1967), *H* (1969), and *Jingo* (1975) by Charles Wood (b.1933) owe much to the tradition of British war-films, with

[14] Hare, *History Plays*, p. 93.

which Wood's controversial Falklands TV-play *Tumbledown* (1988) engages directly. Peter Shaffer's *Equus* (1973) draws on Hollywood psychodrama; *Sleuth* (1970) by Anthony Shaffer (b.1926) on Hitchcock's thrillers in general, and *Her Aching Heart* (1990) by Bryony Lavery (b.1947) specifically on *Rebecca* (1940); and the notorious *Shopping and Fucking* (1996) by Mark Ravenhill (b.1966) adds obscenity to British soap opera. The dependence of westerns on landscape and horses makes them hard to stage naturalistically, but they turn up as musicals, including *Seven Brides for Seven Brothers* (1954), a version of the rape of the Sabine Women, and *Annie Get Your Gun* (1946), a *barn-stormer* by Irving Berlin (1888–1989). Even science-fiction, whose locations and special effects make staging a serious problem, has been borrowed: *R.U.R.* (*Rossum's Universal Robots*, 1921) by Karel Čapek (1890–1938) is the source of the word 'robot'; and Ayckbourn's *Henceforward* (1987) has a whole battery of high-tech sound-recording and video-equipment on stage, two characters (Lupus, Young Geain) who appear only on video-screens, and a female robot-protagonist (Nan 300F). These genres may govern whole plays, or be invoked only in particular scenes or by specific characters; they also influence actors and directors and in any modern play (or production) any film- or TV-genre, from westerns to weather-reports, may be momently or lengthily invoked and bring with it all its attendant expectations.

The traffic is not one-way. Film was at first thought a way of recording stage-drama, and film-archives (increasingly available on video) offer a rich education in the acting-styles of every period since the 1890s: to compare, for example, the films of Beerbohm Tree as King John (1899), Richard Burton (1925–84) as Hamlet (1964), and Ian McKellen (b.1939) as Macbeth (1978) is a revelation.[15] Many plays have been filmed directly (rather than on stage), an immensely valuable resource, especially for those with limited access to theatre: but great care is needed, and one must be respectful of film as film, a medium quite other than stage-performance. Text is usually heavily cut, both for length and because visual images can be substituted for description; plot may be simplified or altered; and sequence will commonly be rearranged: there is no more point in requiring a film to be 'faithful' to a stage-text than in expecting a stage-production to

---

[15] All video details are given in the Bibliography.

manage cinematic special-effects. A film is an <u>alternative</u> to stage-production, but neither an equivalent nor a substitute, and readers or viewers who as critics forget that will rapidly go far astray. Modern stage-plays have also been filmed, including *Mojo, Equus, Sleuth*, and most recently *East is East* (perf. 1997, filmed 1999) by Ayub Khan-Din (b.1963), *The Winter Guest* (perf. 1995, filmed 1997) by Sharman Macdonald (b.1951), and *The Rise and Fall of Little Voice* (perf. 1992, filmed 1998) by Jim Cartwright (b.1958). Again, such films are a resource for anyone reading or teaching those plays, and for students familiar with film but not theatre may be a vital way into text, but they cannot and do not try to reproduce stage-performance and may serve as much to blind readers to stage-possibilities as to entice them by bringing texts alive.

Finally, mod cons feature in many plays. TVs became a popular prop in domestic scenes, and in the 1970s–80s fashionable avant-garde directors such as Peter Sellars (b.1957) included them in productions of opera and classical plays.[16] Terry Johnson has a chilling scene in *Imagine Drowning* (1991) in which a murderer's recorded confession is played back on video-tape. Ravenhill's *Faust (Faust is Dead)* (1997) has one scene set on the David Letterman Show (2), two involving a camcorder (4, 10), and one with computer image-editing (14). The favourite, though, is telephones, which since their invention have provided a way of relaying unexpected information or vital parts of the plot set-up. The radio-play *Cigarettes and Chocolate* (1988) by Anthony Minghella (b.1955) famously starts with a long sequence of taped answer-phone messages, building up the anticipation of hearing Gemma, the recipient; but when she does speak she announces her decision to stop talking, 'like suicide in a way',[17] and subsequently remains silent in company until the very end, while others continue to converse, phone, and leave messages around her. *Separation* (1987) by Tom Kempinski (b.1938) concerns a writer who conducts a long-distance relationship by telephone, but in thrillers and crime-dramas telephones are more often a stock-prop, as parodied by the housekeeper in Stoppard's *The Real Inspector Hound*:

[16] On his 15-TV *Merchant of Venice* (1994) see Peter Holland, *English Shakespeares: Shakespeare on the English stage in the 1990s* (Cambridge: Cambridge University Press, 1997), pp. 257–9.

[17] Minghella, *Plays 2*, p. 8.

(*The phone rings.* MRS DRUDGE *seems to have been waiting for it to do so and for the last few seconds has been dusting it with an intense concentration. She snatches it up.*)

MRS DRUDGE (*into phone*): Hello, the drawing-room of Lady Muldoon's country residence one morning in early spring? . . . Hello!—the draw— Who? Who did you wish to speak to? I'm afraid there is no one of that name here, this is all very mysterious and I'm sure it's leading up to something [. . .][18]

Unsurprisingly the telecommunications revolution has been easily absorbed: Ravenhill's *Shopping and Fucking* specifies mobile phones (sc.10), and Marber's *Closer* has a seduction-scene making clever use of e-mail, the actors typing at computer-keyboards while their messages to one another appear on a large screen above them (1.3). Technology is now notably represented without the anxieties that attended it in the early-twentieth century, visible in Čapek's *R.U.R.* and Chaplin's *Modern Times* (1936), the expectations it arouses changing as its influence on genre evolves.

[18] Stoppard, *Plays 1*, p. 11.

III

DEFINING ARCHITECTURES

Architecture, of all the arts, is the one which acts the most slowly, but the most surely on the soul.

Ernest Dimnet, What We Live By (1932)

12

The study

A written play-text must be written somewhere. One such space is evoked in Jonson's 'An Execration upon Vulcan', written after fire destroyed his rooms and books in November 1623; the poem is a partial inventory both of his own books and of his mental furniture, suggesting the range of sources on which he drew. He mentions verse and prose romances, tales of adventure that many of his characters know and admire or scorn, the Talmud and Koran, classical works and translations, his own *English Grammar*, some poems, and a substantial work-in-progress about Henry V; books in Latin, Greek, and Hebrew borrowed from three notable scholars, Richard Carew (1555–1620), Robert Cotton (1571–1631), and John Selden (1584–1654), may have been among those destroyed. Worst of all, Jonson lost "twice twelve years' stored-up humanity":[1] commonplace-books filled with observations, jottings, and quotations gathered from his reading. Many authors compile such personal and irreplaceable note-books to draw on in their own writing, and to lose an accumulated set of them was a terrible blow.

Jonson was one of the great classicists of his time, an assured reader in Latin, Greek, and Hebrew as well as English and probably at least one Romance language; however professional an actor, developing styles and stage-business with other actors, he was also a proud and learned writer whose plays embody great knowledge of and respect for classical plays and Aristotle. Plautus and Seneca offered models to which he sometimes closely adhered, and some plays in his folio *Works* (1616) have *marginalia* and notes (e.g. identifying the sources of Latin tags in the dialogue) which may interest readers but are not

---

[1] Ian Donaldson, ed., *Ben Jonson* (Oxford and New York: Oxford University Press, 1985 [Oxford Authors]), p. 367 (l. 101).

performable. All playwrights are influenced by the plays they know, and if TV and modern travel have made direct encounters with the performance of other cultures a common experience, the reading of texts remains a vital resource and a principal means of access to lost performance cultures—so it is not surprising that knowledge of languages is common in theatre. Jonson's degree of scholarship is rare (though Tony Harrison and Wole Soyinka are also notable classicists), but Shakespeare too could read Latin, modelling *Errors* closely on Plautus and regularly raiding Ovid. He was content to base his Histories on the *Chronicles* of Raphael Holinshed (*c*.1529–80), and most of his Roman material on the great translation of Plutarch by Thomas North (*c*.1535–1601), but took comedic plots from French and Italian sources and could probably read both languages.

At particular times foreign models have achieved particular influence—classical plays in the Renaissance, French well-made plays in the nineteenth century—but a general polylingualism remains common today, one obvious index being the frequency with which playwrights (and in continental Europe and the USA, *dramaturgs*) also work as play-translators: Beckett from French, Stoppard from German (he also speaks Czech), Harrison from Greek and French (he also speaks Hausa and Czech), Martin Crimp (b.1956) and Christopher Hampton (b.1946) from French, Lee Hall (b.1966) from German and Italian, Timberlake Wertenbaker (b.1951) from French, Greek, and Italian, and so on. Conversely, playwrights who cannot read a language can access works in that language only in translation, and are at the mercy of translators who may lack dramatic skill. In every case one must as a reader ponder what languages and drama playwrights know, and whose influences they reveal.

Both Jonson and Shakespeare also undertook specific research, as of the strange alchemical terms spouted by Subtle in *The Alchemist*, or the sequence of commands needed to steer a ship off a lee shore in *The Tempest*. Such research varies enormously, but almost all playwrights undertake it in some way; if Shakespeare was careless about geography, famously giving Bohemia a sea-coast in *The Winters Tale* (*c*.1610), he was careful to get the nautical terms in the first scene of *The Tempest* right, to make it clear the ship splits only because Prospero's magical storm is too powerful even for experienced and well-drilled sailors to resist. With the rise of the well-made play and dramatic realism a general requirement for accurate *period-detail* also began to develop: Elizabethans did not care about historically accurate costume, but in the mid-nineteenth century Charles Kean (1811–68) began to explore the use of realistic historical costume, and the producers of *Shakespeare in Love* (1997), like all modern purveyors of costume-drama, were deeply concerned to make costume and details plausibly accurate and free of gross *anachronism*. Though the responsibility of producers, a requirement for accurate period-detail demands work from authors; and modern issue-plays and docudramas demand comprehensive research. For a playwright like Norton-Taylor, shaping transcripts of public inquiries into a dramatic form and genre that privilege fact and eschew theatrical fiction, the business of playwriting is grounded in a deskbound confrontation with researched material.

It is of course true that research takes forms other than reading. Many experienced playwrights are sharply aware of the theatre-spaces for which and the actors for whom they write, and get to know spaces, audiences, actors, and styles as necessary beforehand. They tend to be inveterate playgoers themselves: in the case of *Commedia dell'Arte*, for example, an obvious influence on Shakespeare, there were few written sources he <u>could</u> have consulted and his knowledge probably derived from seeing and talking to performers, experiences he could have discussed with his fellow-actors in the King's Men—who could have seen *Commedia* for themselves. Professional actors also store memories of the acting they do and see: Robert Armin (c.1558–1615), probably the Fool in the first production of *King Lear* opposite someone's Edgar/Poor Tom o' Bedlam, later wrote a play himself, *The History of the two Maids of More-clacke* (1608), which features a Bedlam-beggar. Actor-training now includes a considerable variety of practice and theory, and it is always worth checking *programmes* to see where actors and directors trained and what kind/s of theatre they have worked in—which often explains the particular strengths and weaknesses of a production.[2] In many current models of theatre actors and directors are actively required to research other works by the playwright (and earlier productions of the play) they are performing, as well as

[2] This information is usually given in the company biographies towards the back of the programme; the various UK drama-schools are detailed in Fenner, ed., *The Actor's Handbook*.

anything else that might help their work. With highly naturalistic acting the norm for film and TV the forms of research have greatly expanded, and may include extended visits to particular milieux employed in a script.

In short, for both writers and performers the study, a place of books (and now of the Web), <u>and the act of study</u>, however undertaken, are necessary adjuncts to their art, and no reader of drama can afford to ignore what writers and performers may have known and drawn upon; any more than they can afford to ignore in reading the limitations of their own knowledge, and the possibility of expanding it with study undertaken for themselves.

13

Rehearsal and administrative spaces

Rehearsal has long been mystified and academically neglected, but since 1900 has increasingly been recognized both as a process in its own right and as a vital component of performance deserving study.[1] It is easy to assume that rehearsals use the stage itself, but commercial stages are usually occupied by another play/set during the *rehearsal-period* of a new production, access may be impossible until just before opening, and many companies now use whatever adequate space is most easily (and cheaply) rentable. But already the difficulty of generalizing is apparent, for this assumes a distinct theatre and company, substantial sets, and an extended rehearsal-period, variation in any of which must affect rehearsal-processes. The nature of rehearsal in earlier times, moreover, is largely obscure, and detail is rare: for play-readers the important thing is never to forget that the nature and duration of rehearsal has varied historically, for playwrights always write for the theatre they know and rehearsal-practice affects that theatre.

Shakespearean texts, for example, are easy to learn fast, because the lines are usually balanced with antitheses, parallel clauses, etc., so that, as actor Tim Pigott Smith (b.1946) says, 'when you know one half, you know the other'; a dense, circling text like Beckett's *Not I*, though shorter than many Shakespearean rôles, is murder to learn and deliver,[2] demanding lengthy rehearsal much as its staging demands a spotlight. Prescribed action also varies with rehearsal-

---

[1] See Johnstone, *Impro*; M. Rostain, '*The Tragedy of Carmen* : A Rehearsal Log' and Charles Marowicz, '*Lear* Log', both in Williams, *Peter Brook*; Stafford-Clark, *Letters to George* (1997); and Giannachi and Luckhurst, eds, *On Directing*.

[2] See Whitelaw, . . . *Who He?*; the play was written for Whitelaw to perform.

practice: Shakespeare was content with minimal stage-directions because he could trust his fellow-actors to know how to do a fight, a sad parting, or an inset-play, and simplified their task by including some instructions in the dialogue—actors playing Volumnia in *Coriolanus* (1608) need only listen to themselves at 5.3.169 ("Down Ladies: let us shame him with our knees")[3] to know they must kneel. Restoration playwrights concerned to articulate forestage against *scenic stage* (140 >), nineteenth-century playwrights concerned with spectacular staging, and twentieth-century playwrights concerned with delivery as part of a throughline will all provide more and other stage-directions than a Renaissance playwright would have thought reasonable or useful.

In classical Athens the rehearsal of choruses was the responsibility of the *choregos*, a wealthy citizen who financed the production, but authors probably rehearsed actors and brought actors and chorus together. Little is known, but the distinction of actor- and chorus-rehearsal was possible because in performance they used different areas of the space (131 >), and would have reflected chorus-members' relative lack of experience, the demands of choric delivery and dance, and any special techniques needed by particular actors (*deus ex machina* entrances, for example).

Jacobethan rehearsal-practice is equally little known in detail, but there is enough evidence to draw some conclusions. The account-books of Philip Henslowe (*c.*1550–1616), leaseholder of the Rose and later the Fortune, show that in *season* the Lord Admiral's Men performed a different play each day, six plays per week; on average, one was new, one or two had been performed the previous week, and the rest were revivals from previous seasons or earlier in a current season. Some pre-season preparation could have been done, but extended rehearsal-periods for each new play would have been impossible; and on the evidence of command-performances the major companies could do any play they had ever done at short notice. The players arriving at Elsinore readily accept Hamlet's request to perform *The Murder of Gonzago* (plus additions) the following evening, and the implication (supported by the Player-King) is that leading actors knew tens of rôles, and once a play had bedded down in their *repertoire*

---

[3] shame him with] shame him shame him with F.

needed only a read-through and perhaps a walk-through to prepare a performance.

Such actors develop their own performances, but with longer, more complex scripts the scope actors were allowed came under pressure, and the need for some coherent and directed rehearsal grew. The chaotic picture in *Dream*, actors using a "greene plot" and "hauthorne brake" (3.1.3–4), is patently a send-up, like the resulting performance of *Pyramus and Thisbe*, but testifies to a pragmatic flexibility that should be kept in mind. The players at Elsinore, far more professional, are equally adaptable, but Hamlet famously commands in his critique of acting that they:

> let those that play your Clownes, speake no more then is set downe for them. For there be of them, that will themselves laugh, to set on some quantitie of barren Spectators to laugh too, though in the meane time, some necessary Question of the Play be then to be considered: that's Villanous, & shewes a most pittiful Ambition in the Foole that uses it.

(3.2.38–45)

Like all Shakespeare's metatheatre this is alive with intellectual fun, and cannot be taken as a simple expression of his own views, but nevertheless points to the possibility of interpretative control exercised in rehearsal. Shakespeare was unusual in his day in scripting clown-rôles relatively heavily, but also scripted a part for a dog (Crab in *Two Gentlemen of Verona*) and cannot have had much hope that his canine player would curb its "pittiful Ambition" or heed instructions in rehearsal. Hamlet's stress on rehearsal led John Gielgud (1904–2000), directing Burton on Broadway in 1964, to conceive his whole production as a rehearsal, partly to free Burton from any preconception of 'how Hamlet should be'.[4]

A similar ambivalence is revealed by Lord Letoy in *The Antipodes* (1638) by Richard Brome (*c*.1590–1652); he tells the actor Byplay that he is "incorrigible, and / Take license to your selfe, to add unto / Your parts, your owne free fancy; and sometimes / To alter, or diminish what the writer / With care and skill compos'd" (D3v, 2.2.39–43); but speaking to another about Byplay Letoy is far more positive:

---

[4] The show is available on video; details in the Bibliography.

Let. Well Sir my Actors
Are all in readiness; and I thinke all perfect,
But one, that never will be perfect in a thing
He studies; yet he makes such shifts extempore,
(Knowing the purpose what he is to speak to)
That he moves mirth in me 'bove all the rest.
For I am none of those Poeticke furies,
That threats the Actors life, in a whole play,
That addes a sillable, or takes away.
If he can fribble through, and move delight
In others, I am pleased   (D2v; 2.1.14–24)[5]

Byplay is a theatrical term, usually wordless action carried on aside and distinct from the main business, so it is likely this Byplay is addicted to "shifts extempore" in more than speech. A theatre-practice celebrating such shifts and tolerant of *fribbling*, confident in actors' capacities to say the right sort of thing in their own words, probably has stock-characters, performs for a culture in which author-ship is not privileged, and thinks rehearsal a luxury: conditions which prevailed until the later nineteenth century.

Restoration and eighteenth-century rehearsal-practices are only beginning to be studied and the evidence of plays featuring rehearsals, notably Buckingham's *The Rehearsal* and Sheridan's *The Critic*, is made problematic by their comedy and burlesque. Several recent plays, including Wertenbaker's *Our Country's Good* (1988), *Playhouse Creatures* (1993) by April de Angelis (b.1960), and *Cressida* (2000) by Nicholas Wright (b.1940) imagine Restoration and eighteenth-century rehearsal to excellent dramatic effect, but it is not history. It seems clear that as runs grew longer, the scenic stage became dominant, and sets became more elaborate and technically complex, a longer rehearsal-period became normal. So much is com-mon sense, but caution is needed: early twentieth-century *repertory theatre* normally allowed only a week for rehearsal, during which the cast were performing another play in the evenings. Real change seems specifically associated with Ibsenite Naturalism, the consequent shift in actor-training driven by the need to find new styles for psycho-logically realist rôles, and the emergence of the director as controller of an interpretation by which actors must abide.

Rehearsal-time today depends largely on funding: in contemporary

---

[5] Richard Brome, *The Antipodes* (London: J. Okes, 1640).

British and American theatre rehearsal-periods of three to four weeks are normal, but in German theatre, with far more subsidy, rehearsals lasting several months are not uncommon, and in Soviet Russia, with full subsidy, one *King Lear* took two years to reach the stage. Within each system the nature of rehearsals varies enormously, from company *warm-up* or *trust exercises* to *blocking*, improvization, and intensive individual work on single speeches, and is generally at a director's discretion. There is no ideal or necessary way of rehearsing; many different modes have strengths to exploit and weaknesses to avoid: but there is in commercial and semi-funded theatre a financial problem with anything needing 'longer than normal' rehearsals, and major projects in masked theatre (Harrison's *Oresteia*) or extended works like the play-cycles *The Greeks* (1980) and *Tantalus* (2000) by John Barton (b.1928), are *de facto* restricted to *flagship* theatres/ companies which can fund the necessary rehearsals. Purpose-built *rehearsal-rooms* are beautifully functional and safe, with sprung floors, padding, mirrors, video- or CCTV-equipment, a *mock-up* of the associated stage, etc., but similarly restricted to generously funded modern *theatre-complexes*.

Much can be told from the administrative spaces associated with a theatre. Storage space for costumes, props, scripts, etc. has always been necessary, but the *stoa* (131 >) and *tiring-house* (135–6 >) were direct adjuncts to the stage and did not imply any company-remit beyond performance. As theatre became more broadly established and fiercely competitive, playwriting commoner, sets more elaborate or technical, and financial accountability a greater legal concern, administrative space became needed for managers, play-readers, and other functionaries, and was generally provided to some degree in most proscenium-arch theatres. With the exclusion of off-stage actors from a stage-area increasingly filled with scenery and *stage-hands* (205 >), an assembly-room was needed where actors could wait, known since *c.*1700 as *green-rooms* from the colour they were traditionally painted. The emergence of star-actor(-manager)s led to the provision of individual *dressing-rooms*.

Major change, most obviously embodied in flagship theatre-complexes like the RNT, came in the wake of Brecht's functional reconception and didactic structuring of the *Berliner Ensemble* as a political theatre-machine. An educational remit for actors and audience requires a print- and/or film-library, study space, and a programme department; a remit to educate young writers requires a literary manager and staff; public popularity demands assorted public facilities; and the whole massive organization needs a management team who themselves need space. The net result is that writing for, say, the RNT is a wholly different business than writing for the Bush, a *pub-theatre* specializing in new plays, and in comparing a play like Hare's *The Secret Rapture*, written for the RNT, with another treatment of family dysfunction, *Not Fade Away* (1993) by Richard Cameron (b.1948),[6] written for the Bush, it is well to keep the whole of those theatre buildings in mind.

Finally, there is the remarkable case of Alan Ayckbourn, who designed and runs his own theatre-complex, the Stephen Joseph Theatre in Scarborough. He specifically required his green-room to be central and to contain common kitchen-facilities, so that all his theatre-staff, whether actors or cleaners, use it and meet one another every day; he also required a glassed viewing-room to overlook the rehearsal-room, again open to all staff (and others by prior arrangement) who are encouraged to observe rehearsals and learn about the evolution of a play. Many directors, especially in the UK, are fiercely territorial about rehearsal privacy, some resenting even the presences of author, dramaturg (186–92 >), and artistic director, so for Ayckbourn not simply to welcome but architecturally to facilitate the observation and criticism of rehearsals suggests strong convictions. It is for his own theatre that he primarily writes, and the conditions encoded in its architecture offer a fascinating insight into his plays, suggesting a sharper satirical edge to his observations of class-consciousness and social snobbery than the usual reading of him as a bourgeois farceur allows.

[6] In Bradwell, ed., *The Bush Theatre Book*.

14

The stage and auditorium

Space is neither neutral nor passive. Any given spatial relation of audience to performers limits some and enables other possibilities, and the processes whereby the costs of space and architecture, limits of technology and finance, and (imagined) needs of performance interact to determine the material forms of stages are highly complex—compare the state-funded building of a flagship theatre (*Kennedy Center*, NT), the charitably funded construction of Globe III, and the privately funded conversion of a pre-existing space into a *black hole*, all of which coexist. You must, therefore, understand the summary descriptions and figures that follow only as guides to period archetypes, done as best we can and evidence allows but inevitably partial and contingent.

However, two theoretical distinctions illuminatingly apply throughout.[1] The first is between theatre-space and *theatrical space*: theatre-space is fixed material structure, whether natural rock, streetscape, or walls and bolted chairs; theatrical space is created in performance, and though in one sense dependent on and contained by theatre-space, is in others anything but. Theatre-space is fixed once a performance-location is chosen; but theatrical space, if encoded in elements of text and *mise-en-scène*, is generated by body and voice: if an actor in performance stands by a real wall and, asked if X is coming, peers straight at the wall as if into the distance before replying, for theatrical purposes that wall is for the moment not there. It remains in theatre-space but not theatrical space, which becomes Rome, a blasted heath, or a drawing-room as performance requires.

The second distinction is between *theatrical space-within* and *theatrical space-without*: theatrical space-within is what spectators see,

[1] These distinctions are variously made: we follow the terminology developed in Scolnicov, *Woman's Theatrical Space*.

theatrical space-without that which is unseen but implicit in performance, whether the next room or a distant city named in dialogue. Within/without corresponds to on-stage/off-stage, but those terms apply to theatre-space: an actor who has 'died' may be off-stage but not necessarily in theatrical space-without—Hamlet's father is, adding Purgatory to the many locations comprising the theatrical space-without of *Hamlet*, but Mercutio (in *Romeo*) is not; people merely reported (Ragozine in *Measure*, Godot in *Waiting for Godot*) occupy theatrical space-without but are never either on- or off-stage. There may also be a *gendered* distinction between theatrical spaces-within and -without, if (in a sexist culture) one is made to represent private/domestic space 'proper' to women and the other public/civic space where men dominate; the natural articulation of theatre-space between places for actors and spectators will also be gendered if women are prevented from acting or spectating.

Our concern here is to catalogue theatre-spaces from classical amphitheatres to contemporary studio-theatres, and our figures and commentaries describe and provide a vocabulary. Any theatre-space influences the theatrical spaces of plays written for it, and we include where appropriate brief accounts of how a particular play or scene could be performed in a space.

A. Classical Amphitheatres

The simplest notion of acting plays requires a visible platform and a means for actors to enter/exit, and basic stages (*phylakes*) were used throughout the classical period; but the great *amphitheatres*[2] like those at Athens and Epidauros were 230–330 + ft (70–100 + m) on the longest axis and vastly more complex. (See Figure 1.) Though they are often depicted as circular, archaeology suggests asymmetry was usual. The façade (*skênê* → 'scene') represented the outer wall of a building entered through a central door, a threshold between an unseen space of home and hearth (*oikos* → 'economy') generally associated with the feminine, and a seen space of city and people (*polis* → 'political', 'metropolis') generally associated with the masculine. A wheeled platform (*ekkyklêma*) allowed objects or tableaux to be thrust out from the

---

[2] Greek *amphi*, 'of both kinds, on both sides', + *theatron*, 'place for viewing'.

Figure 1: The classical amphitheatre

door. Behind the *skênê* was a colonnaded walkway (*stoa*) separating the stage-area from abutting precincts and perhaps serving as a backstage-area to store masks etc.

The side exits (*eisodoi*) were conceptually polarized, one to/from far-away places (overseas, battlefields), the other to/from nearby places (houses, fields); the 'near' *eisodos* may have been wider than the 'far' one to permit processional entrances and both developed into wings (*paraskênia*) projecting beyond the *skênê*. The acting-area was divided between a rectangular stage immediately in front of the *skênê* for actors, and a circular *orchêstra* (lit. 'place of dancing') for the chorus. Theatrical space-within usually represents a public space, such as a paved area before a palace; its *command-point* (where action/audition could be dominated) was marked by a navel or upright stone (*omphalos, thymêle*) which perhaps served as an altar. Actors could use the top of the *skênê* when playing watchmen or gods and a crane (*mêchanê* → 'mechanism', 'machine', 'Meccano') for flying entrances in *deus ex machina* endings, but there is much debate about on-stage constructions: all would have been wooden, perhaps temporary, and no direct evidence survives. The use of back-drops (*skênographia* → 'scenography'), painted directly on to the *skênê* or a cloth *back-drop* hung in front of it is probable, but no detail survives.

In the *theatron* (lit. 'place of viewing', → 'theatre') semi-circular tiered seating gave clear *sight-lines* and made for the excellent acoustics necessary for masked acting (the lack of side walls explains the requirement for actors always to face the audience). Capacities ranged from 1,000–2,000 to 20,000 + , the largest alleged audience of *c*.30,000 implying a gathering of all adult male Athenian citizens; there were 'seats of honour', but tiered seating (made accessible by division into wedges) makes for equality of audience-members and ticketing was introduced in the 440s–30s BCE to regulate seat allocation. The composition of the audience is unknown, but if restricted to men implies a continuity of audience and (civic, 'masculine') *polis* mapped on to the theatrical space-within, but a relatively greater disjunction at the *skênê*, concealing the (private, 'feminine') *oikos*; amphitheatres were also located within temple complexes, the entire theatre-space forming one part of a highly articulated sacred space imposing a common identity on audiences and performers. They were also in their nature open, places of publicity and commonality rather than of privacy and individuality.

Despite the uncertainties the fundamental relations of surviving texts to the space is clear: in *Agamemnon*, for example, the *skênê* is the wall of Agamemnon's and Clytemnestra's palace in Argos; he returns from Troy with Cassandra, entering via the 'far' *eisodos*, while the Chorus (twelve Elders of Argos) and Aegisthus (Clytemnestra's lover) use the 'near' *eisodos*; and though Agamemnon triumphantly dominates the *polis* the main action is his disappearance into the *oikos*, where Clytemnestra invisibly but audibly kills him to avenge their daughter Iphigenia (whom he sacrificed before departing a decade ago). His and Cassandra's bodies are then displayed to the *polis* on the *ekkyklêma*, and the reaction of Chorus (and audience) sets the scene for the next play in the trilogy (*Choephori*) in which he is avenged.

B. New Comic and Roman Theatres

Between the Greek amphitheatres (fifth and fourth centuries BCE) and the Theatre of Pompey in Rome (55 BCE), a period textually dominated by Menander, Plautus, and Terence, only temporary wooden stages were built and no direct evidence survives. What is known is inferred from prose and dramatic texts (which seem broadly consistent in the stage-design they assume) and from illustrations in mosaic or fresco and on decorated pottery.

A wooden stage (*scaena*) was backed by a façade (*frons scaenae*) with three doors and perhaps windows; the middle door might be larger and/or distinguished by a portico with a small roof (*vestibulum*). There were paired side exits like *eisodoi*, leading to particular named but unseen locations. The three doors were conceived in theatrical space as the front doors of adjacent dwellings or shops; the area immediately in front of them was the *platea* or *via* (= street), and theatrical space-without commonly included a back-alley (*angiportum*) whereby characters could 'go next door'.

The persistently political rather than religious function of Roman theatre-practice made audience-control primary. The provision of entertainments of all kinds was a major political issue, and rapid socio-political changes following the Roman victory over Carthage in 201 BCE saw the emergence of celebrity actors linked to lawyers and orators[3] and a civic anti-theatricalism which prevented the building of stone theatres until the last years of the Roman Republic. That restriction was voided by Pompey the Great in 55 BCE, and his enormous theatre was a political machine despite the inclusion of a temple within the complex. The design developed that of the temporary theatres on a gigantic scale: the *scaena* was 300 ft (92 m) wide, the *frons scaenae* three stories high, richly inset with openings and columns across its entire width, and extended by wings connected to a colonnaded *gallery* (*versurae*) running around both sides of the auditorium to the temple facing the stage; the wings supported a linen awning (*vela*) which shaded (part of) the audience. Capacity was *c*.17,500, and the complex included a political assembly-room (*curia*) and behind the *scaena* a 600 ft (184 m) park (*Porticus Pompeii*) to relax in between performances.

The whole building was free-standing so that access could be screened and audiences marshalled. An orchestral area in front of the *scaena* probably offered privileged seating, and all seating arranged audiences hierarchically into socio-political categories; programmes included athletics, music, gladiatorial combats, and animal shows which probably used the orchestral area, though plays may have been restricted to the *scaena*. Other than Senecan tragedy, little new drama was written after *c*.100 BCE, but both tragedy and comedy remained

---

[3] Notably Quintus Roscius Gallus (131–62 BCE) and Clodius Aesopus (?d.50 BCE).

sufficiently vigorous to develop a new tragedic mask with an elong-ated forehead (*onkos*), and distinct stylized footwear—for tragedy the *cothurnus*, a high-soled shoe producing an awkward walk, and for comedy the *soccus* (→ 'sock'), a light and agile slipper. But plays could not compete politically with lavish spectacles of human and animal death, and never had in Rome the civic and sacred rôle fundamental to Athenian drama.

Yet where there were theatres there were also dramatic perform-ances, however relatively unimportant, and the Theatre of Pompey remained in continuous use for over five hundred years, a model for hundreds of theatres built across the empire by Caesars from Julius onward. Though smaller, these theatres had an average capacity of several thousand carefully arranged spectators; the *frons scaenae* was sufficiently large and solid to allow an upper-floor/balcony (*distegia*), and the *scaena* sufficiently raised to allow the introduction of a stage-trap into wooden stage-boards. Complex scenic-machinery developed, including *scaenae ductiles*, painted images set into the *frons scaena* which could be *discovered* with small curtains (*siparia*), and *scaenae versatiles*, rotatable boards or cloth with different images on each side: tragedy, comedy, and satire probably had particular con-ventional scenes of palaces, streets, and landscape, amounting to *gen-eric décor*, but *scaenae ductiles* and *versatiles* imply the possibility of scene changes <u>during</u> performance. There was also a large curtain (*aulaeum*) which could cover (most of) the *frons scaena*.

Variable scenery and the mass production of Roman theatres sug-gest major development, but political tensions, imperial decline, and the hostility of the emergent Christian Church to 'pagan' art restricted the dramatic legacy of Rome until the Renaissance. Revivals of classical comedy and tragedy continued until their Christian sup-pression in the seventh century CE; lesser dramatic entertainments and spectacles evolved into the mediaeval traditions of travelling players and entertainers.

C. Mediaeval Platform-Stages and Pageant-Wagons

Any demarcated area large enough to permit movement and visible from a surrounding area can be a stage, and the simplest constructed stages, little more than a table in a space, are called *platform-stages*. If one side is near a wall or provided with a back-drop the restriction of sight-lines to a semi-circle provides a front/rear orientation, but platform-stages, especially if temporary or mobile, have no equivalent to the *skênê* or *frons scaenae* and a theatre-space which may vary from performance to performance. The configurations of theatrical space-within are highly labile, but in Mysteries and Moralities drew stability from the sacred and civic contexts of performance and the annual repetition of substantially similar linked texts with recurrent rôles.

Audiences for civic processions are widely extended in space and discontinuous, unified far more by a shared knowledge of the (sacred) meaning of the performance than any aspect of stage-design; for performances in public squares an audience becomes more concentrated and its sight-lines more focused, a process sharply accelerated if the platform-stage is placed at one end of a rectangular room. Should a dining-hall be used, with a high-table daïs as (or supporting) a platform-stage, a social distinction of auditorium and stage is incorporated, and when such halls also have a gallery for minstrels or spectators a further vertical elevation in the theatre-space and potentially the theatrical space-within.[4] The simplicity of platform-stages allows great freedom of acting but severely restricts the quality of spectacle, the complexity and duration of audition that can be sustained, and the quality, complexity, and length of plays predicated on their use for performance.

D. Jacobethan Amphitheatres

Though probably reflecting earlier sixteenth-century use of three-sided, galleried inn-yards for touring-performances, Elizabethan amphitheatrical design was influenced by recovered classical texts, particularly the *De Architectura* (*c*.40 BCE) of Vitruvius (dates unknown), first printed in 1486. Two basic Roman features recur, the *frons scaenae*, now the *tiring-house wall*, and the left/centre/right exits, but incorporation into the overall design of a multi-level *tiring-house* and stacked encircling galleries give Jacobethan amphitheatres a strong vertical axis. (See Figures 2 and 3.) The ground floor of the tiring-house provided a *within*, from which voices could call; the first

---

[4] See Alan H. Nelson, *Early Cambridge Theatres: college, university, and town stages, 1464–1720* (Cambridge: Cambridge University Press, 1994).

Figure 2: The Jacobethan amphitheatre (1)

floor provided an *above* (for castle-battlements and high windows, for example), but may also have housed musicians and the highest-priced *box-seats*; scripts, costumes, and props were stored there, and on the highest level were the *thunder-run* (a metal-lined wooden trough down which cannon-balls were rolled) and a platform from which performances were trumpeted and a small cannon could fire blanks. The tiring-house also provided access to the *Heavens*, a painted roof over the 'rear' part of the stage from which gods or other flying beings (e.g. Ariel) could be lowered.

The left/right exits were paired, but the central double-width curtained opening, the *discovery-space*, was distinct: its curtains could discover a tableau, or conceal large props (beds or thrones) before they were pushed on-stage; the double-width allowed processional entrances/exits (e.g. the soldiers carrying Hamlet's body), which made it the favoured route for rulers, etc. to make *authority-entrances*, arresting the action. Thus in *Romeo* 1.1 Montagues might enter left and Capulets right, mix in fighting, and at the Duke's entrance via the discovery-space re-polarize—a visual presentation of their enmity and

Figure 3: The Jacobethan amphitheatre (2)

the Duke's authority (cf. the vertical separation from Juliet which Romeo closes by climbing up to her). The discovery-space was also the favoured entrance for Fools, who might initially peep through the curtains;[5] and could serve uncurtained as Prospero's cell, a mini-stage around which inset-performances could be articulated, etc.

The stage, at Globe II 43 × 27 ft (13 × 8 m), was flat, and the command-point close to the 'front', near the geometrical centre of the polygon formed by the theatre-walls (c.100 ft/30 m in diameter). The pillars supporting the Heavens could 'conceal' eavesdroppers, or do duty as trees, posts, etc. as required. The stage-trap, let into the stage-boards centre-'front', gave access to the under-stage, sometimes dubbed the *Hell*, which allowed sudden dis/appearances and other special effects, as well as the ready provision of graves, pits, etc. There seems to have been some use of generic décor, particularly draped black cloth for tragedy, but how widely such techniques were used is uncertain.

Performances were by daylight, beginning at 2 p.m. Most audience-

---

[5] See the frontispiece to Francis Kirkman, *The Wits* (1662), reproduced in, e.g., *Riverside Shakespeare*, plate 10 (following p. 490).

members paid one penny to stand in the *pit*, pressing against the stage on three sides; those who wished could pay extra pennies for seating in the *first, second,* or *third galleries*, or most expensively in boxes adjacent to the stage and in the tiring-house. The presence of many audience-members on three sides (capacity was 2,000–3,000), and of some on the fourth side, limits any simple stage-front/-rear distinction, and the physically and vocally mobile acting necessary to quieten and dominate such a dense, encirling, and secular audience corresponds with the intense metatheatricality and unmasked acting of Jacobethan plays. When Jaques, standing near the command-point of Globe II, said "All the world's a stage, / And all the men and women, meerely Players"[6] the audience understood at many levels the manner of their implication in the action.

E. Jacobethan Private and Hall-Theatres and Masquing-Houses

Jacobethan companies also performed on much simpler stages, in public (when touring) and in command-performances (as at court); some texts (e.g. Marlowe's *Doctor Faustus*) survive in amphitheatrical and touring versions. From at least the 1580s some children's companies performed in roofed halls; and from *c.*1600 at least one *hall-theatre*, the *Blackfriars*, seems to have had a stage and tiring-house structure similar to that of the amphitheatres (but presumably truncated above the Heaven, necessary for wire-descents, for example).

Stage-architecture was similar in hall-theatres and amphitheatres, but the relations of stage and actors to audience were not. Even if the stage was against a long wall a much greater proportion of the audience spectated from the 'front'; while there may have been a single gallery most were seated on benches in a space more like modern *stalls* than the pit, with the best seats closest to the stage. Hall-theatres had smaller capacities (?*c.*800), cost more to attend, sixpence or one shilling (= 12 pence), and had more élite audiences. A roof made torches and candles necessary, and replacing daylight with fire-light began profoundly to change the nature of acting, the practice of mimesis,

---

6 *As You Like It* 2.7.139–40; the motto *Totus mundus agit histrionem* (All the world's a stage) may have been displayed outside and/or inside Globe I and II.

and the efficacy of illusion; it also enabled evening shows. The King's Men gained use of the Blackfriars in 1608, and Shakespeare's late plays (especially *Pericles, Winter's Tale,* and *Tempest*), filled with intense silences and spectacles, are associated with his exploration of a new theatre-space.

A more formal but related development is evident in masques with the introduction by Inigo Jones of Italian perspectival scenery and eventually of theatres reflecting early Italian opera houses. The Roman *frons scaenae* had used painted columns, windows, etc. and inset curtained or rotatable panels; the new technique used painted *flats* or *wings* angled in rows and perspectival back-drops or *shutters,* paired flats extending across the width of the stage, which generated a sense of stage depth but greatly narrowed the area from which satisfactory viewing was possible. A painted arch may sometimes have been used to frame that view, and such framing is implicit in perspectival illusion. With court resources available and court taste to be sated elaborate machinery developed, allowing rapid changes of illusory scene (multiple or rotating flats and back-drops) and spectacular effects; substantial resources were devoted, successively, (1) to converting the Whitehall Banqueting House (1608) and the Cockpit (1611); (2) to building a new Banqueting House[7] (1621–2); (3) to rebuilding the Cockpit as the Cockpit-in-Court (1629–30); and (4) to building a new *masquing-house*[8] (1637–8). The advantages of each space varied—the Cockpits had raked seating but stages too shallow for much use of perspective—but the new Banqueting House, a magnificent double-cube measuring $110 \times 55 \times 55$ ft ($34 \times 17 \times 17$ m) with a stage at one end (40×27–40 ft, raised 6 ft; 12×9–12 m, raised 2 m) and galleries, combined perspectival scenery with features of the tiring-house and anticipated the capacities of Restoration theatres, not least in offering expensive spectacle to restricted audiences. Over the period as a whole theatres moved from down-market east to south to up-market central and west London, beginning a social narrowing of audience composition still evident in mainstream English theatre today.

---

[7] The old one burnt down, 12 January 1619.

[8] It replaced the Banqueting Hall, from which performances were banned in 1635 in case new ceiling-paintings by Rubens were damaged by candle-smoke.

F. Restoration and Augustan Theatres

The closing of the theatres during the years 1642–60 fractured theatre-practices: some performance continued, and some personnel active before 1642 returned after 1660; amphitheatres and hall-stages were demolished (and could not in any case accommodate perspectival scenery). Gibbon's Tennis-Court in Vere Street was converted in 1660 but proved limiting, and new theatres were built with perspective in mind: in Lincoln's Inn Fields (1661); the Theatre Royal, Bridges Street (1663, burnt 1672); the Duke's Theatre, Dorset Garden (1671); the Theatre Royal, Drury Lane (1674), designed by Christopher Wren (1632–1723); the Queen's Theatre, Haymarket (1705), designed by playwright-architect John Vanbrugh (1664–1726); an expanded Lincoln's Inn Fields (1727); and the Theatre Royal, Covent Garden (1732).

None survives (though theatres remain on the Drury Lane, Haymarket, and Covent Garden sites), but surviving plans and accounts show that all had a *proscenium wall* dividing the building and pierced by a proscenium arch, which was curtained. (See Figure 4.) Spectators were restricted to one side of the proscenium wall, but the stage was not: behind the wall was the *scenic stage* (*scene* in stage-directions), about 20 ft (6 m) deep and perhaps raked, equipped with flats and shutters, a stage-trap, and other machinery; in front of the wall was the *forestage*, probably flat, bare, of about the same depth, and

Figure 4: The Restoration theatre

extending to abut the galleries and boxes which encircled the auditorium. Exits/entrances could be made to/from the scenic stage between the flats (= 'from the wings'), and to/from the forestage through the proscenium arch or via one or more *proscenium doors* between the boxes abutting the forestage. A *prompter's-box* may also have been incorporated, but evidence from before *c*.1800 is scant, and actors may have continued to use a *prompt-corner*.

Without a permanent within or above the articulation of scenic stage against forestage became critical. The kinds of acting required for scenic stage (amid scenery) and forestage (amid the audience) were in some ways distinct: both tragedy and comedy used both parts of the stage and stage-directions often indicate movement between them, but the requirement for actors to move from scenic stage to forestage is more frequent in comedy and it seems likely that comedic acting utilized the unframed metatheatricality generated by forestage interaction with the audience, while tragedic acting utilized the greater distance, relative isolation from the audience, and framed pictoriality of the scenic stage—as Peter Holland puts it, "The pressure of the conventions makes the scenery an environment for tragedy but a back-drop for comedy".[9] In keeping, comedies tend to be set in London, often using scenes of public parks and meeting-places familiar to the audiences as well as of private interiors, but tragedies tend to be set abroad, often in exotic locations, and use exterior scenes that might reflect the 'real' appearance of, say, (particular buildings in) Venice or Granada or might be fantastical. There was no generally consistent mapping of theatrical space-within on to theatre-space comparable to the classical *oikos* and *polis* or Jacobethan amphitheatrical practice, but scenes and scenic stage/forestage movement of actors can usually be worked out from scene-headings and stage-directions.

The auditorium was highly articulated. Theatres designed to allow opera or musical drama had to provide a place for musicians, the *orchestra-pit*, but all used the (rest of the) pit for seating. That and the first gallery were used by a mixed audience including fashionable beaux and prostitutes, those who came as much to be seen as to see; admission was 2 shillings and 6 pence (2*s*.6*d*.); the *Royal Box* and

---

[9] Holland, *The Ornament of Action*, p. 38.

other boxes were used by the aristocratic and wealthy (4s.); the *middle-gallery* by citizens, their wives, and independent tradesmen (1s.6d.); and the *upper-gallery* by servants, their wives, and working-men (1s.). Capacities may have been up to 1,400 but audiences of *c*.500 seem to have been usual. There is good evidence of a relatively élite group of regular theatre-goers, including Charles II, the first English monarch to attend public theatres, which perhaps amounted to a *côterie audience* and certainly suggests that the percentage of London's population attending the theatre had declined since *c*.1600, narrowing socially as well as becoming firmly hierarchized within the auditorium. This fits with the increasingly up-market (west-central) environs of the theatres, sharply accentuated in the replanning and development of London after the Great Fire of 1666.

G. Nineteenth-Century Proscenium-Arch Theatres

From 1660 to *c*.1900 London theatre-building was more or less continuous, driven by the proliferation of legitimate and illegitimate theatre and the frequency of theatre fires (especially after the introduction of gas-lighting). Design evolution was also continuous, with existing theatres frequently being adapted or refitted, but the most important trend was the progressive disappearance of the forestage: retreating from the boxes to become a *thrust-stage* sticking out like a tongue into the auditorium, flattening back against the proscenium wall to become an *apron-stage*, until a physical separation of actors and audience was achieved and theatrical space-within was visible only through the proscenium arch. (See Figure 5.) Over the same period acting styles retreated from all *extra-dramatic* and direct address to the audience, and élite theatre became increasingly dominated (as in many ways English theatre still is) by a combination of pictorial illusion and naturalistic acting.

The proscenium-arch stage expanded rather than altered the scenic stage. To accommodate the whole of the action stage-depth from proscenium to back wall increased considerably; but perspectival flats and back-drops were still used, and in later theatres could rise out-of-sight above the stage (into the *flies*) as well as slide out-of-sight to the sides (into the wings). Greater depth permitted sharper raking (hence *up-* and *downstage*) to assist perspectival illusion; variable raking and

Figure 5: The nineteenth-century proscenium-arch theatre

devices such as *revolves* and elaborate or mechanized stage-traps became possible. The prompter's-box was fully incorporated into the understage area, usually centre-front with a small hood to conceal the prompter's head from the audience. Two variants of the set also developed: in the 1840s the *Cyclorama*, a painted surface curved like a giant semi-cylinder encircling the stage from one side of the proscenium arch to the other; and later in the nineteenth-century the *box-set*, comprising side- and rear-walls plus partial roof, placed like an open box on its side against the proscenium arch. Normal for drawing-room drama, the box-set logically implies the fourth wall, an imaginary 'sheet of glass' filling the proscenium arch which for audiences is transparent but for naturalistic actors 'seals' the theatrical space-within that characters inhabit. In *A Doll's House* one wall of Torvald's and Nora's home becomes the fourth wall of the theatre in which it is being played; the play has few *soliloquies* (all naturalistic) among its *colloquy*, no asides, and no extra-dramatic address (e.g. prologues and *epilogues*), leaving Torvald and Nora to 'live through' (not 'enact') the break-up of their marriage while audiences 'secretly' observe it all happening.

In most auditoria terminology changed more than fundamental

design. The pit became the stalls, and the first, middle-, and upper-galleries the *dress-circle* (for which evening-clothes were expected), *circle*, and *upper-circle* (also known as the *gods*, probably because one looks down from great height on a distant stage). The only major development began with the opera house in Bayreuth, completed in 1876 at the behest of Richard Wagner (1813–83), where pit and galleries were replaced by a raked fan of seats, a design with excellent sight-lines recalling classical amphitheatres which has influenced some twentieth-century theatres. With electricity and its consequent technologies lighting- and *sound-boxes* from which to control the scene were often placed in the auditorium to allow technicians to monitor what the audience sees/hears; and the almost universal modern practice of dimming house-lights during performance began to develop. The foyer, between street-doors and auditorium, gradually expanded to include the facilities standard today (toilets, bars, restaurants, kiosks).

H. **Modern Studio-Theatres**

Popular theatre (including music-hall and pantomime) never had much truck with realist fourth-wall sets, and from at least the 1890s, when William Poel began experimentally to 'reconstruct' Jacobethan stagings of Shakespeare, the restrictions of proscenium-arch theatres and naturalistic acting have been more or less appreciated. The financial challenge of cinema and subsequently TV has encouraged smaller theatres in which many kinds of drama can be successfully staged; similar concerns attend the university theatre-spaces required by the enormous rise in student numbers and drama degrees. Since 1945, and especially with the growth of *fringe theatre* and *off-(off-)Broadway* since the 1960s, a pragmatic, minimalist approach has prevailed, resulting in theatres without a proscenium wall and with reconfigurable seating.

The general term is *studio-theatres*, which at their simplest—largeish rooms, usually rectangular, draped all around with black (or white) curtains—are also known as black holes, *white holes*, or (if above bars) pub-theatres.[10] The lighting-rig is centrally suspended from

---

[10] 'Pub' is short for 'public house', a commercial bar.

scaffolding and any part of the floor can become the 'stage', though the location of doors and power-points may make one orientation more attractive than others. Seating, banked on rostra to maintain sight-lines, can be arranged to replicate the physical concentration of audiences in proscenium-arch theatres (Figure 6a); *in the round*, encircling the acting-space (Figure 6b); to create a traverse-stage with

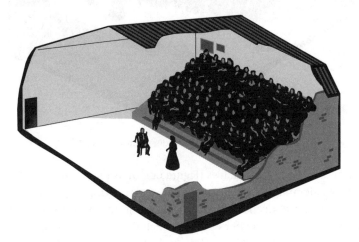

Figure 6a: The modern studio-theatre (concentrated seating)

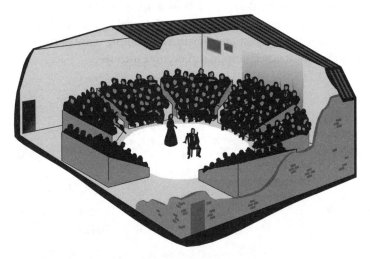

Figure 6b: The modern studio-theatre (in the round)

Figure 6c: The modern studio-theatre (traverse)

the audience in facing halves (Figure 6c); or as may be desired. Both naturalistic and self-aware (Brechtian, epic) acting is possible. The only limits are ingenuity, public safety (e.g. the need for adequate fire-exits), and the smallness of most such theatres, which (like financial restraint) limits the possible size of cast and scope of action. Studio-theatres (like platform-stages) in one sense offer playwrights and actors great freedom, as well as a space which can in theory accommodate any play written for any space, but in reading plays written specifically for studio-theatres a troubling sense of constraint and stifled theatrical ambition can become intrusive.

15

The spaces of the book trade: the scriptorium, printshop, publishing house, bookshop, and library

Behind every performance are the spaces of study, rehearsal, and stage, and behind every book are one or more spaces of the book-trade. Before printing texts were hand-copied, and hands had to be trained. *Scriptoria*, usually in monasteries, copied sacred or approved texts—the basis of church control over what people read; reading was itself a restricted skill. The growth of international commerce extended literacy and guilds probably helped prepare scripts for actors in medieval play-cycles, but had no interest in producing multiple copies for wider distribution.

Printing reached Europe in the fifteenth century. Its advantages were evident and its dissemination rapid, but cost was extremely high: metal type had to be designed and cast in huge quantities, and composition (setting type), *imposition* (creating pages), and *presswork* (printing pages) were skilled, time-consuming tasks.[1] Compositors needed clear *copy* from which to set, so professional scribes remained both an essential part of printing and a viable alternative means of text production until the late-nineteenth- or twentieth-century inventions of typewriters, carbon-paper, photocopiers, and word-processors. For actors the major consequence was the normal provision for learning lines of a cue-script, not a complete play-text (of which there might be only one copy, the Book): and actors beginning

---

[1] See Gaskell, *New Introduction to Bibliography*.

rehearsals knowing only their own rôle in any detail are *de facto* invited to make a greater contribution to a production than actors who repeatedly read a complete text which awaits their enactment. Cue-script actors are more likely to make interventions recorded in the Book; if a play was sold to a printer the Book often provided the copy, allowing actors' additions (or cuts) to mingle on the page with the author's initial text: so in reading texts derived from company Books the possibility of others' contributions must be borne in mind.

Commercial issues also restrict text production. Elizabethan printers had some legal protection from piracy, but theatre-companies could maintain exclusive rights to plays they purchased from authors only by restricting availability of the text. This explains the theory of 'bad' quartos, plays stolen from companies by actors who dictated them to printers, but also partly explains the relatively small number of Jacobethan plays that survive: about 375 play-texts written in the years 1576–1642 are known, but perhaps ten times as many were acted and have perished, including at least two by Shake-speare and five by Jonson. Piracy could encourage a company to sell their play to a printer, and, if the pirating company made additions, generate a distinct text—there is an *induction* by John Webster (*c.*1580–*c.*1625) to *The Malcontent* (1604) by John Marston (1576–1634), explaining its theft from the Children of the Chapel Royal; companies in financial straits might resort to selling plays, as the Lord Chamberlain's Men did in the years 1597–1600: but prevailing conditions generally discouraged the printing of plays, and restricted the survival of play-texts—one of many filters narrowing the range of drama it is possible to read.

Nor has it ever been assumed that a play should be printed simply because it has been performed, nor that if printed it should remain in print. Quartos were to Jacobethans somewhat as paperbacks are to us: pocket-sized and produced to very variable standards, books to read and pass on or sell rather than permanent works for the shelf—especially if play-texts, drama being an ephemeral form with little literary standing. The extent of that attitude can be gauged from the reaction in 1616 to Jonson's publication of his *Works* in folio, a format hitherto restricted to the Bible, theology, classical translation, and other élite scholarship: Jonson deliberately claimed for his vernacular drama and poetry the status of classical work; his contemporaries scorned his presumption as readers today might a leather-bound set of comics. His radical agenda led him to exclude his comedies of the mid–1590s, presumably as juvenilia, and they are lost; but in 1623 the folio model was followed by John Heminges (d.1630) and Henry Condell (*c*.1562–1627) for *Mr. William Shakespeares Comedies, Histories, & Tragedies. Published according to the True Originall Copies*, and while it took time the prestige of that volume marks a significant change in the attitude to printing and reading plays.

1 has its problems, however. Though produced to a high standard errors are inevitable in such a large book (every single letter, mark, and space was created by a small piece of metal stood upright in a tray), and as in Jonson's folio (though for other reasons) some plays were omitted: two are lost (*Love's Labours Won, Cardenio*), two or three survive (*Pericles*, the collaborative *Two Noble Kinsmen*, the disputed *Edward III*) with a fragment (*Sir Thomas More*). Possible incompleteness creates a *Shakespeare apocrypha*, anonymous plays at one time or another attributed to him,[2] but the *canon* established by F has endured and the plays it excluded continue to suffer relative academic and performative neglect.[3] F also poses a textual issue concerning Ralph Crane (d.1626 +), a scribe whose distinctive habits mark five (perhaps seven) F-texts:[4] retained by Heminge and Condell to produce *fair-copy* for the printer, Crane's job was to clarify and organize the copy he was given, probably company Books but perhaps Shakespeare's foul papers, and in so doing he became Shakespeare's first editor. Accustomed to liturgical practice and trained in court-reporting, Crane produced copy that was for actors as much as readers: his punctuation, for example, is often *elocutionary* (guiding voice) rather than *syntactical* (indicating syntax), and in phrases such as "thy tongue, and heart" or "to inforce, or qualifie the Lawes"

[2] The major contenders, printed in F3 (1663), are *The London Prodigall; Thomas, Lord Cromwell; Sir John Oldcastle; The Puritan Widow; A Yorkshire Tragedy*; and *Locrine*; cases have also been made for Shakespeare's hand in *The Troublesome Reign of King John, The Famous Victories of Henry V, Faire Em, The Merry Devil of Edmonton, Mucedorus, The Birth of Merlin*, and *Arden of Faversham*. Analysis indicates that none is his, but debate has not quite died.

[3] For a recent discussion see Richard Proudfoot, *Shakespeare: Text, Stage, & Canon* (London: Arden Shakespeare, 2001).

[4] The five are *Tempest, Two Gentlemen of Verona, Merry Wives of Windsor, Measure, for Measure*, and *Winters Tale; Othello* has recently been added to the list, and *Cymbeline* suggested.

(*Measure* 1.1.45, 65) the medial commas do not indicate logical pauses ('thy tongue [PAUSE] and heart'/'to inforce [PAUSE] or qualifie') but emphasis on the following word ('thy tongue AND heart'/'to inforce OR qualifie'). Editors usually remove Crane's work, but in consulting F you should be aware of it as a different text and a different kind of text; as you are aware in reading a modern edition of consulting something intended more for eye and reader than ear and actor.

It is a very recent privilege to be able to assume that 1 is there to be consulted. Expensive on publication (in 1623 it cost 21 shillings, for most people several months' wages, and 252 times more than entry to the Globe), it skyrocketed in value with scarcity and Shakespeare's development as an icon; each of the surviving 228 copies is now worth at least £250,000 ($400,000). No facsimile was produced until 1862–4, and facsimiles were also expensive, so from the eighteenth-century beginnings of the editorial tradition with Rowe and Dr Johnson to the later twentieth century 1 was available only to those with money or access to library copies, for which academic credentials were increasingly necessary. Everyone else had edited texts, the variety of which (from cheap, unannotated one-volume *Complete Works* to academic multi-volume series) maps a fiercely competitive, dynamic market utterly subject at all times to the technological and financial limits of commercial publishing. In that sense every book tells a story, of careless haste or scholarly devotion, and the effects that story had on the words you read should <u>always</u> be part of your reading; but today new resources are changing the parameters. Digital photoreproductive technology has made facsimiles much cheaper, and for those with access to university libraries[5] or on-line databases[6] every page of most plays printed in England 1475–1700 is available:

---

[5] See A. W. Pollard and G. R. Redgrave, *A Short-Title Catalogue of Books Printed in England, Scotland, and Ireland and of English Books Printed Abroad 1475–1640* (2nd ed., rev., 2 vols, London: Bibliographical Society, 1976, 1986)—known as the *STC*; and Donald Wing, *Short-Title Catalogue of Books Printed in England, Scotland, Ireland, Wales, and British America and of English Books Printed in Other Countries* (2nd ed., rev., 3 vols, New York: Index Committee of the MLA/Index Society, 1951, 1972, 1982)—known as *Wing*. Both are in most university and some public libraries, and are invaluable reference-guides; all books in Pollard and Redgrave can be read on microfiche, affordable by many institutions. If you can't find them, ask: microfiche is often not on open-shelf.

[6] Try *Early English Books On-Line*, maintained by the University of Missouri.

the effects are already revolutionary; how they will affect publishing remains to be seen.

Shakespeare's status has for centuries ensured that a text has always been available, but few playwrights have been as lucky. Performative success and commercial publication are interdependent, but old plays are liable to go out of print, and if a revival occasions a reprint the text is likely to be the adapted text of the revival, not the original. Many Jacobethan and Restoration plays have become widely available to students only since 1945, and some still languish in obscurity: publishers only publish what they think they can sell, and tastes change. Augustan and Victorian audiences cared little for what they found overblown and immoral: Middleton was edited only in 1885–6, and Marston not until 1934–9; but we are no better, for among the works hardest to obtain today are eighteenth- and nineteenth-century plays once enormously popular but now thought *hack-work*, sensation-fodder unworthy of study. The introduction of machine-printing in the early nineteenth century reduced unit costs but did little to expand the range of available plays, in some ways narrowed by the growing middle-class market for 'improving' books and educational market for approved 'classics'; machine-technology contributed to a great loss of nineteenth-century plays when the *stereotype* plates used to print them were melted down for ordnance in 1914–18 and never recreated.

Besides the gradual emergence of the high canon, that group of authors from Shakespeare and Jonson to Pinter and Churchill deemed sufficiently 'important' that they 'should be taught' and available in academic editions (from university presses) and classic series (e.g. Penguin English Library, Everyman), the most important development was of specialist publishing houses and bookshops. Printers and booksellers have always specialized, some in drama: Jacob Tonson (1656–1737), for example, published Dryden, Behn, and Otway, doing much to promote the reading of their plays; and the firm of Samuel French in London now provides most late-nineteenth- to mid-twentieth-century play-texts for actors, and runs a well-known specialist theatre-bookshop. The effect of publishing-house development is clear in the centrality to contemporary British play-publishing of two firms, Methuen and Faber, responsible for almost all 'major' contemporary English and foreign-language playwrights, whose editorial decisions about what to accept are massively influential on what is read and taught. For both publishers drama is only one part of their business, and neither Methuen (now part of Reed International) nor Faber (who remain independent) is interested in work that will not sell in quantity. Smaller specialist publishers devoted to drama, notably Oberon Books and Nick Hern Books, make as much recent work available as they can, but neither has the distribution resources of Methuen or Faber, and the bookshops from which you can buy their products and libraries from which you can borrow them are relatively few.

Remember therefore that neither bookshops nor libraries (including university libraries) are in any way neutral. Both in theory help customers to obtain what they want, but customers must first know of it; having limited shelf-space, both decide what to stock as a function of estimated demand. Unless there is a strong local market (an active drama-group or university drama-department, for example) contemporary drama is likely to be underprivileged or unrepresented, a situation exacerbated by the increasing dominance of chain-bookstores with centrally determined stock-policies. Public libraries similarly have relatively little interest in hard-to-obtain, ephemeral work, and for university libraries pamphlet or paperback-only formats are discouraging;[7] the severest limitations, though, are cost and for university librarians an increasingly direct link between syllabi and purchasing. What a university makes available is now often determined by what an individual teacher requests a library to stock, and if many drama-teachers make sterling efforts to bolster and maintain library-stocks, others do not—especially in English (as distinct from drama) departments which habitually stick to a well-established historical canon and deprivilege performance, preferring to teach classic plays as literary texts.

For readers, therefore, the availability of older or contemporary non-canonical texts is a problem, and for students at universities unconcerned with drama in its own right potentially a major handicap. The difficulty of understanding Ibsen without knowledge of

---

[7] Even in libraries which stock contemporary drama and the five *deposit libraries* to which a free copy of every book published in the UK must be sent, cataloguing and shelving policy may make pamphlets, spiral-bound, or stapled books hard to find; it is always worth checking with a librarian.

melodrama, for instance, remains strongly encoded in commercial and library stocks which promote attention to *Hedda Gabler* but not *Lady Audley's Secret*. Specialist bookshops (as at flagship and larger theatres) and libraries (the Billy Rose collection at the New York Public Library, the Theatre Museum, Covent Garden) are eye-openers; but the real change in process is the appearance of internet bookshops with huge multi-sourced stocks and interactive search-engines (Amazon.com/.co.uk, bol.com) and print-on-demand publishers who are rendering the idea that a text can be 'out-of-print' obsolete. For contemporary playwrights and specialist publishers the internet is a lifeline, and for serious readers an increasingly vital resource; but it too will reveal ideologies and limitations, and no reader can afford to ignore the effects of production- and distribution-processes which enable them to read one thing but prevent them reading others they cannot buy and may not know exist.

IV

PERSONNEL IN PROCESS

I can take any empty space and call it a bare stage. A man walks across this empty space whilst someone else is watching him, and this is all that is needed for an act of theatre to be engaged.

Peter Brook, *The Empty Space* (1968)

16

Playwrights

Authorship in theatre-making is complicated. Even setting aside collective creation of performance and the question of anonymous texts, and asking only about published texts, it is often difficult to assess how many hands took part in writing and what section/s are attributable to whom. Post-Romantic readers trained on poetry tend to think writing a solitary task, but on the Jacobethan stage *collaboration* was normal: Thomas Dekker (?1570–1632), for example, contributed to at least 50 plays; 20 have survived; six are usually credited to him alone; only two or three feature in most constructions of 'the playwright Thomas Dekker'. There is also a post-Romantic tendency to valorize the author as an original creator, but few Renaissance playwrights wrote 'original' plots, preferring to treat existing stories in their own ways. Plays, generally written quite rapidly, were not thought worthy literary artefacts; playwrights had little status and often no control over publication, having sold their work outright to companies which delayed or avoided publication because they had no copyright security, making it easy for plays in the public realm to be stolen by rival performers. Selling plays to a printer was a possible source of cash, and many individual plays were printed: but no one collected their own plays before Jonson's folio dramatic and poetic *Works* in 1616 formally defined him as sole author of nine plays.[1] He showed concern for <u>readers</u> in the 1605 quarto of *Sejanus* in detailed marginalia on his classical sources; the folio embodied his desire to preserve and assert his works and in some ways set Western conceptions of the playwright on a new course.

Playwrights achieve performance by submitting a play as an

---

[1] *Every Man in, Every Man out, Cynthia's Revels, Poetaster, Sejanus, Volpone, Epicoene, Catiline,* and *The Alchemist.*

unsolicited manuscript or being commissioned to write a play. Renaissance playwrights largely wrote for particular companies, tailoring rôles for specific actors, and Henslowe's *Diaries* show that commissioning was usual. Companies commissioned, but so did nobles and royalty: John Dennis (1657–1734) and Nicholas Rowe (1674–1718) preserve an apocryphal story that Elizabeth I (having enjoyed *Henry IV*) commanded Shakespeare to show Falstaff in love, and he duly wrote *Merry Wives* in two weeks;[2] Jonson's court-masques of 1605–34 were commissioned by James I and Charles I. Companies could do as they wished with plays they owned, but some authorial control over performance could be gained through royal favour, other high connection, or, most obviously, inside influence: and many writers (including Shakespeare and Jonson) were actors before *de facto* becoming *resident-dramatists*. If like Shakespeare they were *sharers* security of income also enabled them to write fewer plays at greater leisure; but he is far more the exception than the rule.

After the Restoration the development of print- and reading-cultures enabled writers to earn from publication as well as performance. Dryden drew income as a playwright from more varied sources than Middleton, and with the growth of theatre outside London freelance playwriting became widespread in the eighteenth century and common during the nineteenth. But the need to write for star-actors continued and great actors could have many plays written for them. Betterton was renowned for Rake rôles and Thomas Southerne (1660–1746) wrote Lovemore in *The Wives' Excuse* (1691) for him, naming Betterton, not Lovemore, as speaker of the epilogue;[3] Congreve's *The Way of the World* (1700) similarly has a Prologue spoken by Betterton and an Epilogue by Mrs Bracegirdle (1671–1748), and Rowe's *Tragedy of Jane Shore* (1714) a Prologue by Robert Wilks (?1665–1732) and an Epilogue by Mrs Oldfield (1683–1730). Victorien Sardou (1831–1908) wrote *La Tosca* (1887), *Cléopâtre* (1890), and *Gismonda* (1894), and Wilde *Salomé* (1896), for Sarah Bernhardt (1844–1923), one of the most admired (and tempestuous) performers of her time.

For independent authors, however, actors can be trouble, and from

---

[2] See Schoenbaum, *Shakespeare's Lives*, p. 51.
[3] Cordner and Clayton, eds, *Four Restoration Marriage Plays*, p. 334.

the late seventeenth to the late nineteenth century playwrights, many scraping a living, frequently had to contend with actor-managers who regarded plays as display-vehicles for their own talents and thought nothing of drastically re-shaping them to suit—or requiring the author to do so. Playwrights' memoirs abound with complaints about the indignities they and their play-texts had to suffer,[4] but the power of leading actors eventually declined, and they have had virtually no say in play-selection procedures in theatres since *c.*1900 unless also Artistic Directors, like Laurence Olivier (1907–89) at the NT from 1963–73. Freed from compulsion independent playwrights have less commonly written specifically for leading actors, but they do write for actors they admire: Pinter wrote the rôles of Sarah in *The Lover* (1963), Ruth in *The Homecoming* (1965), and Anna in *Old Times* (1971) for Vivien Merchant (1929–82), and Stoppard the rôle of Henry Carr in *Travesties* (1974) for John Wood (b.1933), as well as rôles in *Arcadia* (1993) and *Indian Ink* (1995) for Felicity Kendal (b.1946). More recently, Joe Penhall (b.1967) wrote the lead in *Blue/Orange* (2000) for Bill Nighy (b.1949) and begged him to play it: Nighy agreed and the play opened at the RNT and transferred to the West End.

The rise of the playwright's status at the expense of actor-managers was gradual. The 1832 Dramatic Copyright Act recognized the playwright's rights; the 1842 Copyright Act followed; the 1911 Copyright Act gave full protection. The market for new plays increased sharply, especially with the end of the theatrical monopoly in 1842 and the subsequent proliferation of new theatres; audiences demanded new melodramas and spectacles, and playwrights capitalized. Boucicault's sensation-drama was particularly successful from the 1840s to the 1880s in London and New York, and he instituted a system of *profit-sharing* which led to playwrights' receipt of *royalties*. In the 1880s–90s the battle for literary prestige was taken up vigorously by Shaw, Granville Barker, Pinero, and Jones, who insisted that text must be privileged above all else and an actor's task was to serve it. They pressed for the wider publication of plays, campaigning for their value as texts to read as well as perform; Shaw in particular meticulously prepared texts for print, including prolific stage-directions which

---

[4] For an imagination see de Angelis, *Playhouse Creatures*, in *Plays 1*, p. 203.

made them read like novels. The opening stage-direction of *Pygmalion* is a good example:

> *Covent Garden at 11.15 p.m. Torrents of heavy summer rain. Cab whistles blowing frantically in all directions. Pedestrians running for shelter into the market and under the portico of St Paul's church, where there are already several people, among them a lady and her daughter in evening dress. They are all peering out gloomily at the rain, except one man with his back turned to the rest, who seems wholly preoccupied with a notebook in which he is writing busily.*
> *The church clock strikes the first quarter.*[5]

A final ratification of playwriting as a respectable as well as profes-sional occupation came when Gilbert was knighted in 1907 and Pinero in 1909.

Today, professional playwrights are still usually commissioned to write plays but those enjoying current popularity can take chances, writing the play they want and submitting it. Flexing their greater power, established playwrights such as Brecht, Fo, and Brian Friel (b.1929) founded their own companies to control the production of their work and distinguish themselves from the mainstream, effect-ively becoming self-commissioning. New playwrights rely on *literary agents* or send unsolicited scripts to theatres/directors specializing in new writing, but since the 1960s the *development* of new playwrights has become a significant feature of theate, including *writer-in-residence* schemes. They too found companies, as Julia Pascal (b.1949) did with Pascal Theatre Company, John Godber (b.1956) with Hull Truck, and David Greig (b.1969) with Suspect Culture. Ayckbourn, as Artistic Director of a theatre, is in the rare position of playwright-manager: the combination is often perceived by critics as debilitating creativity but his output has never let up; with 50 + plays in print he is among the world's most performed playwrights.

Such autonomy is alluring, but commissioning, even of oneself, is not just about finding a playwright to write a successful play: a par-ticular kind of play may be wanted for a particular company or a specific occasion, and prompts may be fruitful. de Angelis was com-missioned by the RSC to write a play for and about the people of her native Warwickshire; it was her first specific brief, but the idea for *A Warwickshire Testimony* (1999) came from her own research and a

[5] Shaw, *Complete Plays* (London: Odhams Press Ltd, n.d.), p. 716. The Penguin text of *Pygmalion* is slightly revised; see p. 13.

parish newsletter she might otherwise never have seen. Clean Break Theatre Company commission female playwrights to research aspects of women's prison life and write plays which speak to prisoners, ex-prisoners, and those with no experience of theatre; the brief is challenging but outstanding plays have resulted, notably *Mules* (1996) by Winsome Pinnock (b.1961) and *Yard Gal* (1998) by Rebecca Prichard (b.1971).

Plays may also be commissioned (or written independently) for particular stages or to explore spatial challenges. In the television-play *Quad* (1982) Beckett specified the measurements of the square across which four performers move in a series of precise formations; as in all his short plays space is further limited and controlled through lighting-instructions. Edgar's *Entertaining Strangers* (1985) was first written as a community-play set in St Mary's Church, Dorchester, with a cast of 180; when it was commissioned to play at the NT's Cottesloe theatre in 1987 Edgar rewrote it for an entirely different space and a cast of 30 in-house actors. Harrison wrote his extraordinary *The Kaisers of Carnuntum* (1995) for the Roman amphitheatre at Petronell/Carnuntum in Austria (where his protagonist Commodus first saw blood spilt), which functioned as a metaphor for the meeting of East and West.

The processes of writing play-texts also vary, reflecting the possibilities and demands of performance. The image of a writer sitting in a garret (reaffirmed by *Shakespeare in Love*) is limitedly true for theatre: up to a point playwrights do work alone, writing and re-writing until satisfied (or a deadline), but their apprenticeship involves learning about stage-craft and the actor's craft, and much is discovered only in the doing of the play. They may attend rehearsals, and may be required to re-write speeches or sections. The business of writing is different for everyone, dictated by theatre-space, intended audience, and time available: nineteenth-century *hack-writers* could complete a play in days; new writers who do not often have the luxury of time are forced to write quickly; Stoppard takes up to five years; Hare takes a year or two;[6] Ayckbourn takes a month off to write a play, but actually writes in a week or so, having booked a slot and chosen a title a year in advance:

6 Hare, *Writing Left-Handed*, p. 74.

I know that there's no way I'd start a play four weeks before it's due to go on. That just isn't the way I write. I know I've got to be within single figures of the opening date before there's any chance [. . .] If I get time for rethinking—I'm a really ferocious critic of my own work, I really am—I would destroy it. There's no way it would survive if it didn't have to survive just in order for there to be something there.[7]

This is a privilege which Ayckbourn has only because he runs his own theatre, and such individual pressure does not suit everyone.[8]

Since the 1950s fundamentally alternative writing-practices have increased, inspired by Brecht's collaborative-writing experiments and a desire to find ways of incorporating writers more fully into the process of making theatre. Joan Littlewood (b.1914) set up Theatre Workshop in London's East End in 1953: plays were created or honed in *workshops* with the writer, actors, and director, notably *Oh What A Lovely War!* (perf. 1963, filmed 1969). In 1973 Hare, David Aukin (b.1942), and Max Stafford-Clark (b.1941) set up Joint Stock Theatre Company, aiming to give every company-member—actor, designer, administrator, or writer—a part in the process of play-making: everyone undertook research and brought in material, much relied on improvization by actors, and this working-method produced innovative plays, including Hare's *Fanshen* (1975), *The Ragged Trousered Philanthropist* (1978) by Stephen Lowe (b.1947), and Churchill's *Cloud Nine* (1979).[9] In 1980 Elizabeth LeCompte (b.1944), Spalding Gray, Willem Dafoe (b.1955), and others founded the Wooster Group in New York, one of the most influential recent avant-garde companies; they collaboratively produce *devised* work, using sound, film, movement, text, and video. In Theatre de Complicite, founded in 1983 by Annabel Arden (b.1959), Simon McBurney (b.1957), and Marcello Magni (b.1960), writers work as part of the ensemble and material generated through improvization is assembled by the director;[10] Complicite actors are accomplished movement- and mime-artists, often trained by Jacques Lecoq, and their physical style has had a major impact on playwrights and actors in England.

For playwrights who perform, including the living writers Bennett,

[7] Watson, *Conversations with Ayckbourn*, p. 73.

[8] See Plimpton, ed., *Playwrights At Work*.

[9] See Ritchie, ed., *The Joint Stock Book*.

[10] See Giannachi and Luckhurst, *On Directing*, pp. 67–77; Luckhurst and Veltman, *On Acting*, pp. 1–8.

Steven Berkoff (b.1937), Fo, Pinter, and Sam Shepard (b.1943), the acts of performance and writing become profoundly intertwined. Some take to the stage unexpectedly: Eve Ensler (b.1960?) was so moved by her interviews with women for *The Vagina Monologues* (1996) that she decided to perform it; Hare celebrated his fiftieth birthday with a monologue, *Via Dolorosa* (1998), for self-performance in London and on Broadway—but unlike Ensler's work, performed by many actresses:

> Via Dolorosa *is* [. . .] *ideally to be performed by its author. At the outset, the lights go up and the author is found on the stage. He begins to speak.*
>
> **Author** Partly, of course, I just want to see what it's like. That's what I'm doing here. If you're wondering. The last time I acted was when I was fifteen [. . .]. The experience taught me all I needed to know. Since then, I've always tried to get Judi Dench to do this sort of thing.[11]

Critics and public alike were more curious to see Hare on stage than about the play, and the obvious limitations of his acting were tolerated as they would not have been in a professional. *Via Dolorosa* suggests an underlying crisis in Hare about the value of certain acting conventions, about "people [. . .] played by people whose profession is to pretend to be other people",[12] as though he needed to go on stage to restore his faith in playwriting. Harrison, conversely, wrote himself emphatically into the end of *The Kaisers of Carnuntum*.

> (**Tony Harrison** *enters with the amphitheatre sign and rams it into the heart of Commodus. He also carries the script of* The Kaisers of Carnuntum.)
>
> **Tony Harrison**
> At least it can be said that this sign's now right.
> A comedy and tragedy were acted here tonight.
>
> (*After two beats of silence, with a bestial shriek the bloody body of Commodus rises from the Colosseum, swinging the signpost. Tony Harrison flees, scattering the pages of the play's script to the four winds.*
>   *Commodus removes his bear-muzzle, laughs, and bows to the audience, indicating that the show is over.*)[13]

The open, aggressive, and comedic self-representation of this moment stands in considerable contrast to those Restoration prologues and epilogues "Spoken by" Betterton or Mrs Bracegirdle.

---

11 Hare, *Via Dolorosa*, p. 3.
12 Ibid., p. 3.
13 Harrison, *Plays 3*, pp. 108–9.

Finally, relationships between playwrights and <u>directors</u> are very significant once production starts, and partnerships form when a director has a particular sensitivity for or interest in a writer's work, as Peter Hall (b.1930) had for Beckett's plays or Richard Eyre (b.1943) for Hare's. Stafford-Clark's direction has been critical in helping many writers to develop their talents, including Churchill, Ravenhill, and Wertenbaker. A director can bring such luminosity to a play that their work outclasses the writing or allows it to be appreciated differently: Ian Rickson (b.1964) was vital to the reception of Kane's *Blasted* (1995) and *Cleansed* (1998); he had to contend with stage-directions presenting real difficulties of representation, including "He puts his mouth over one of **Ian's** eyes, sucks it out, bites it off, and eats it." and "He eats the baby."[14] John Dexter (1925–90) was equally critical to Peter Shaffer's successes with *The Royal Hunt of the Sun* (1964), *Black Comedy* (1965), and *Equus* (1973): 'THE MIME OF THE GREAT ASCENT', Scene VIII in *Royal Hunt*, had only a four-line opening stage-direction for Dexter to translate into a scene of extraordinary audio-visual effect:

> As OLD MARTIN describes their ordeal, the men climb the Andes. It is terrible progress: a stumbling, tortuous climb into the clouds, over ledges and giant chasms, performed to an eerie, cold music made from the thin whine of huge metal saws.[15]

Dexter's direction was a *tour de force* unmatched by other *physical theatre* in England at the time, and few directors could have met the challenges in Shaffer's texts with such brilliant stagings. Their collaboration encouraged Shaffer to push his own imagination, culminating in the astonishing theatre of *Equus*; but Dexter felt he was as much a creator of Shaffer's plays as Shaffer himself and refused to direct *Amadeus* (1979) unless given a percentage of the *box-office*, in effect demanding royalties for his direction. Shaffer and Dexter feuded bitterly, and Hall replaced Dexter as director,[16] an ugly affair highlighting the problems of attribution in theatre-making. There has been little academic thinking about writer-

[14] Kane, *Complete Plays*, pp. 50, 60.

[15] Shaffer, *Royal Hunt*, p. 37.

[16] *Peter Hall's Diaries* (ed. John Goodwin, London: Hamish Hamilton, 1983), pp. 440–7.

director relationships in the creation of plays but this is beginning to change: the collective creation of performance can only be set aside for so long.[17]

---

[17] See Nelson and Jones, *Making Plays*, and Wu, ed., *Making Plays*.

17

Directors

The rise of the director was perhaps the major phenomenon of twentieth-century theatre. Before *c*.1875–1900 the actor-manager or leading actor of a company dictated the organization of rehearsals, and a play's overall <u>artistic</u> coherence was unimportant. In the late nineteenth century perceptions began to change, influenced by the Meiningen Court Theatre productions[1] (1874–90) which featured careful choreography and emphasis on rehearsal-process; the rise of Ibsenite playwrights who demanded coherent production-values to match their cause-and-effect plays; and André Antoine (1858–1943), who from the mid–1880s mounted Naturalist productions in small, independent theatres with rigour and artistic consistency. An avant-garde desire for plays of high quality performed to high standards encouraged experiments in modern directing, and found particular fruition in the work of Shaw and Granville Barker at the Royal Court.

Unrecognized in his native England, Edward Gordon Craig (1872–1966) argued passionately for theatre-making as a creative art in *On the Art of the Theatre* (1905). Advocating productions led by artists who understood not just acting but <u>all</u> theatre-arts (including technology, lighting, design, costume, and movement), Craig forecast that "The whole renaissance of the Art of the Theatre depends upon the extent that this is realised".[2] A contemporary of Craig's, Stanislavski, worked at the Moscow Art Theatre from 1897 to 1917, establishing himself as a director of Chekhov's plays, and was the

---

[1] Based in Germany, owned by the Duke of Saxe-Meiningen, and run by Ludwig Chronegk (1837–91), the company was famed for the standard of their ensemble-work and the historical accuracy and artistic coherence of their productions. Tours of Europe stirred great interest.

[2] J. Michael Walton, ed., *Craig On Theatre* (London: Methuen, 1983), p. 69.

first to invent a rigorous system of actor-training; it has had wide international impact. The later propagation of Brecht's techniques of actor- and director-training at the Berliner Ensemble from 1949 to 1956 opened up acting- and production-styles which could explore the gap between actor and rôle.

In 1950s–60s England directors Peter Hall, John Barton, and Peter Brook successfully challenged fixed notions about how Shakespearean plays could be interpreted, paving the way for subsequent generations of experimental directors and quite different pedagogic approaches to Shakespeare. Brook's famous 1955 production of *Titus Andronicus* (1593) reclaimed a play often declared unstageable by finding symbolic ways to represent the rape and mutilation of Lavinia; a second major challenge was encoded in his publication of *The Empty Space* (1968) and radical 1970 production of *Dream*, set in an adult adventure-playground, which abandoned period-costume and -detail.[3] Barton had particular strengths in understanding how Shakespearean verse could be delivered without heavy-handed stylization, and adapted Shakespeare, reclaiming the *Henry VI* plays by fusing them with *Richard III* in the three-evening *The Wars of the Roses* (1963). The frequency with which the histories are now taught and staged owes much to Barton, still revered as a workshop-leader,[4] but the rôle of directors and the vividness of many contemporary productions poses a challenge which must be addressed.

Before and during rehearsals a director <u>has</u> to make practical decisions about <u>how</u> a play is to be done. Readers can luxuriate in ambiguities, contradictions, and intricacies embedded in play-texts without any need to 'solve' them technically, but directors must make the play and their vision of it work on stage. The ending of *Measure* leaves a reader pondering all sorts of dramatic possibilities: having reunited Isabella with the brother she thought dead and subjected her to all manner of moral torments, the Duke's last speeches, extraordinarily, contain two proposals of marriage, at 5.1.491–3 and again in the closing lines:

[3] For illustrations see Kennedy, ed., *Looking at Shakespeare*.

[4] A TV-series of workshop-films, *Playing Shakespeare*, was broadcast in 1984, and the edited scripts were subsequently published with the same title. A second series was recorded in America in 2001.

> Deere *Isabell*,
> I have a motion much imports your good,
> Whereto if you'll a willing eare incline;
> What's mine is yours, and what is yours is mine.
> So bring us to our Pallace, where wee'll show
> What's yet behinde, that meete you all should know.   (5.1.534–9)

Readers should muse on the generic complexities of such an ending and its resistance to closure, but the director has to instruct the actors playing Isabella and the Duke (and all actors on stage) how to behave, move, speak, and look. Is there at either moment a movement towards each other, implying mutual satisfaction at the thought of marriage? Does the Duke move and Isabella stay still, or vice versa? Is Isabella shocked, disapproving, angry, resentful, demure, or none of these? How long has the Duke harboured such thoughts? and has he perversely been testing a future bride? Is the Duke to be believed or is this another manipulation? Is Isabella in any position to refuse, being of lower rank and the Duke's subject? There are many more questions encoded in the scene, and directors make choices in relation to decisions made throughout the play and their overall interpretation: one may choose to unite the pair and override the ambiguity of the text; another to instruct actors to give their lines without emotional colour and stay frozen to the spot, then go to stage-blackout; a third to undercut an apparent union, perhaps by bringing out the Duke's relish in his own power or with an expression of disdain (however slight) from Isabella. In each case that is their right, and no case is, or should be thought, or can be, 'definitively' correct or foolishly 'unfaithful'; any approach prescribing an ambiguous stage-ending is as mistaken as one prescribing a certain reading of the textual ending.

Such moments occur constantly. In *Richard III* (1.2) Richard cynically woos Anne over the corpse of the husband he has murdered: the scene is chilling and grotesquely comical, for within 200 lines Anne expresses her loathing of Richard yet agrees to marry him and wear the ring he produces. The stage-business with the ring is conveyed in three lines:

> [*Rich.*] Vouchsafe to weare this Ring.
> [*An.* To take is not to give.]
> *Rich.* Looke how my Ring incompasseth thy Finger,   (1.2.200–2)[5]

---

[5] The crotcheted speech-prefix and line, omitted in F1, are supplied from Q1 (1597).

The gestures of giving and taking are very significant, and the director has to decide whether Anne holds out her hand or Richard takes it: any such gesture is a submission on Anne's part and an act of manipulation on Richard's, but the range of emotional resonances which can be explored in the simple giving and taking of an object is considerable. For the actor playing Anne the extremes of emotion explored are difficult to chart and the director has to try and steer a constructive practical route to their physicalization. Similar considerations apply to many rôles, and are as intense in, say, Ibsen, O'Neill, and Churchill as in Shakespeare.

Directors of classical texts frequently try to offer new ways of seeing a play, but the gift for innovation is rare and received ideas about the meanings of actions, characters, and speeches can greatly inhibit fresh inquiry, as Jonathan Miller has pointed out:

> When a director approaches a play like *Hamlet* or *The Merchant of Venice*, the initial reaction is, in many instances, not determined by a positive view of a particular character but by a desire to overthrow a tired interpretation. The role of precedent is very strong, and there is a tendency for performances to clone. Actors, and directors, like to preserve their originality and would feel very offended if anyone accused them of going by prototype, but I think there is a conspiracy in the theatre to perpetuate certain prototypes in the belief that they contain the secret truths of the characters in question. This collusion between actors and directors is broken only by successful innovation which interrupts the prevailing mode.[6]

Conventionally, Ophelia is played as weak and simpering, but though abused and powerless she may be played with rebellious characteristics; as Helena Bonham Carter (b.1966) showed in the film-*Hamlet* (1990) by Franco Zeffirelli (b.1923) there can certainly be method, and more, in her madness. Similarly, the convention of playing Hamlet as a Romantic contemplative is powerfully received (particularly in 'To be or not to be', 3.1.55–89), but ignores the metatheatricality of the text and Hamlet's potentially self-conscious playing to those perhaps spying on him. Miller argues that directors must be aware of what he calls a play's *afterlife*, the possibility of interpretative evolution and successive re-creations of a work within different cultures at different

---

[6] Miller, *Subsequent Performances*, p. 109.

times,[7] and promotes the director's imaginative interpretation of a work over the historical *reconstruction* of plays. Brook, similarly, pleads in *The Empty Space* for 'living theatre' in place of 'Deadly Theatre' which "approaches the classics from the viewpoint that somewhere, someone has found out and defined how the play should be done".[8]

New plays require as much engagement in extracting meanings from text as classics. Early in his career Miller found it as hard to direct living authors as dead ones: directing *The Old Glory* (1964) by Robert Lowell, a major poet who made several forays into theatre, he made "long and often very intrusive inquiries" into Lowell's intentions but never got precise answers:

> In fact, in this particular case, it was the other way round. [Lowell] was constantly surprised to find that in the process of rehearsal meanings with which he was unacquainted were disclosed by his own play.[9]

Lowell's discoveries in rehearsal are the usual experience of writers who see ideas and images in their heads given physical shape. His subsequent *Prometheus Bound* (1967) demanded imaginative flights of staging, and he was happy for Miller to make radical visual suggestions. But when Miller directed *The Freeway* (1974) by Peter Nichols (b.1927) the play's social realism demanded a different approach: Nichols was intolerant of interpretations other than his own, Miller felt confined rather than supported by his presence at rehearsals, and the show was not a success.[10] The director's art is distinct from the playwright's, which Nichols did not adequately appreciate.

Every rehearsal-process is a unique journey into the unknown, and directors have to structure rehearsals round the strengths and weaknesses of their actors, allowing room for creative play and problem-solving. Different directors perceive their rôles differently: David Glass (b.1957) sees himself as a mobilizer and facilitator of actors who keeps everyone focused on a shared vision of the performance; Simon McBurney is concerned most with releasing actors' creativity; Katie Mitchell (b.1964) sees herself as a research-leader of a team of actors

---

[7] Miller, *Subsequent Performances*, p. 23.
[8] Brook, *The Empty Space*, p. 17.
[9] Miller, *Subsequent Performances*, p. 81.
[10] Ibid., p. 85.

exploring a text.[11] Every director has personal techniques of working with actors, but needs to be alive to serendipitous discovery: Mitchell works with Stanislavskian rigour and explores the meaning of every word, requiring actors to have a detailed psychological profile of their character and to imagine and improvize scenes not in the play; Pinter refuses psychological exposition in directing his plays, limiting himself to technical instructions to do with action and vocal pitch, so actors cannot know with certainty why their characters do and say the things they do.[12] Berkoff is similarly uninterested in character-study, running rehearsals as a master-class to teach his actors the precise mime-actions he requires.[13] Beckett directed with meticulous attention to technicalities, such as the length of a silence or pause, the precise movement of an actor's hand or foot, and the intonation of single words: plot and narrative are not driving forces in his work, and as a director he was not concerned with meeting audiences' or actors' expectations. Billie Whitelaw asked Beckett just one question about character during the time they spent rehearsing various plays together, about May in *Footfalls* (1976):

'*Am I dead?*'
He thought for a second, then said: 'Well, let's just say *you're not quite there.*'[14]

There were actors who found the physical demands of acting in Beckett's plays too brutalizing. The stereotypical image of the auto-cratic director who bullies a cast is no myth, and most actors have at least one horror-story to recount. Playwrights, fascinated by the power directors wield, have certainly written them into plays. Pirandello created a furore when *Six Characters in Search of An Author* (1921) was first shown in Rome: six imagined but incomplete characters in an author's mind gate-crash rehearsals of another play and demand that their own stories be directed to completion; the Director (or Producer as they were then frequently called) struggles against anarchy, proclaiming all will be resolved, but the fictional figures prove beyond his control. In *The Plebeians Rehearse The Uprising* (1966) Günter Grass (b.1927) represents Brecht as a committed communist in his writing

---

11 Giannachi and Luckhurst, eds, *On Directing*, pp. 43, 74, 96.
12 Luckhurst and Veltman, eds, *On Acting*, pp. 148–9.
13 Ibid., p. 82.
14 Whitelaw, . . . *Who He?*, p. 143.

and directing, but afraid to become an activist supporter of workers' rights. The Director in Beckett's *Catastrophe* (1982) is represented as a grotesque dictator, intent on realizing his own vision at the expense of the actor whom he never bothers to address directly and obviously regards as sub-human.[15]

Whatever the ambiguities of the function, much theatre has become director led since the 1960s. Brook, one of the foremost directors in Europe, left England in 1970 to work in France because he felt an English distrust of experimentation for its own sake was inhibiting him, and with help from Jean-Louis Barrault established the International Centre of Theatre Research, now based at the Bouffe du Nord in Paris. Warner has acquired an international reputation for her bold productions of classic texts and repeated direction of actor Fiona Shaw (b.1958). Stein became famous for productions at the Berlin Schaubühne carefully researched by both cast and production staff with social, political, and artistic findings fed into a lengthy rehearsal-period. Mnouchkine is renowned for her collaborative devised productions in Paris. Robert Wilson (b.1941) has a reputation for mesmerizing shows full of striking visual and aural effects. To imagine in reading the sort of thing that Brook, Warner, or any favourite director might do with the play in hand is enjoyable, and a useful way of forcing thought about variant stagings; but any reader who hopes to relate productions to texts, whether classic or contemporary, and all students using performance-evidence as part of textually based criticism, must assess the directors who shape the performances they see and hear.

---

[15] The title is ironic, for a *catastrophe* (lit. 'sudden turn') is in theatre the stroke that precipitates the dénouement, particularly but not exclusively in tragedy; and this director's catastrophe is not what he thinks.

18

Actors

Acting is an ancient art, but the skills attributed to its craft are culturally and historically specific. Over the centuries there have been many notable actors in the West: we select a few as stars of their times to emphasize the importance of thinking about and (if possible) researching an actor's conditions of work, personality, particular skills, reputation for certain kinds of rôles or forms of audience-interaction, and responsibility for *creating* particular rôles.

The invention of acting in the later sixth century BCE is credited to Thespis, who first created a rôle with a distinct narrative for a solo-actor to speak alongside the chorus. Ancient Greek actors were men trained in the use of masks covering the entire head, delivery of verse and song, and dance. The demand and range of *voice-work* for tragedic actors was high, as the same actors appeared in all four plays presented by a tragedian in a single day. Comedic actors were probably trained with greater physicality, but little is known of performance-styles. The other great name surviving from classical antiquity is that of Roscius, who did much to enhance the status of the actor and was admired for his virtuosity both in tragedy and the comedies of Plautus and Terence: *Roscius* subsequently became a praise-name for an actor combining consistently high quality with generic versatility.

Before the late sixteenth century the terms *player* or *comedian* were in common use and 'actor' merely denoted "one who acts, performs any action or takes part in any affair; a doer" (*OED2*, p. 3). The first specifically theatrical use is in *The Defence of Poesie* (wr. *c.*1581, pub. 1595) by Philip Sidney (1554–86) where it acquires the modern sense, "one who personates a character, or acts a part; a stage player or dramatic performer" (*OED2*, **3**). It is significant that actor came into theatrical use at a time when acting-style was metatheatrical, self-consciously playing with the fictiveness of rôles; *personation* also began to be used to describe what some actors were doing, and distinguished a new art of individual characterization from a traditional style of *oratory*.[1]

Personation was the strength of Richard Burbage[2] (*c*.1568–1619), credited as the first great English actor and the leading player with the Chamberlain's/King's Men from 1594 until his death. He created the rôles of Ferdinand in Webster's *The Dutchesse of Malfy* (1614) and Richard III, was the first adult to play Malevole in Marston's *The Malcontent* (1604), and probably created Romeo, Richard II, Prince Hal/Henry V, Benedick, Hamlet, Othello, Duke Vincentio, Lear, Macbeth, Anthony, Coriolanus, and Leontes (probably all written specifically for him). Burbage was admired for his rhetorical gifts, persuasive actions, and especially his ability to bring consistency and coherence to a rôle: Richard Flecknoe (?d.1678) makes clear that by comparison much acting was rough and less sustained:

> we may say, that he was a delightful *Proteus*, so wholly transforming himself into his Part, and putting off himself with his Cloathes, as he never (not so much as in the Tyring-house) assum'd himself again until the Play was done: there being as much difference betwixt him and one of our common Actors, as between a Balladsinger who onely mouths it, and an excellent Singer [. . .] He had all the parts of an excellent Orator, (animating his words with speaking, and Speech with Action) his Auditors being never more delighted then when he spoke, nor more sorry then when he held his peace;[3]

Burbage's rival, Edward Alleyn[4] (1566–1626), built a reputation in plays by Kyd, Marlowe, Robert Greene (1558–92), Dekker, and Chapman at the Rose and Fortune theatres; his rhetorical skills were of the old school of oratory, and Hamlet's instructions to the players, probably spoken by Burbage, may have been intended to mock Alleyn and other actors of his ilk:

> Speake the Speech, I pray you, as I pronounc'd it to you trippingly on the Tongue : But if you mouth it, as many of your Players do, I had as live the

---

[1] Gurr, *Shakespearean Stage 1574–1642*, pp. 99–100.

[2] For a portrait see *Riverside Shakespeare*, plate 12.

[3] Richard Flecknoe, 'A Short Discourse of the English Stage' (1664), p. 6, in David Womersley, ed., *Augustan Critical Writing* (Harmondsworth: Penguin, 1997), pp. 3–7.

[4] *Riverside Shakespeare*, plate 11.

Town-Cryer had spoke my Lines : Nor do not saw the Ayre too much [with] your hand thus, but use all gently [. . .] Be not too tame neyther : but let your owne Discretion be your Tutor. Sute the Action to the Word, the Word to the Action, with this speciall observance : That you ore-stop not the modestie of Nature ; for any thing so over-done is fro[m] the purpose of Playing, whose end both at the first and now, was and is, to hold as 'twer the Mirrour up to Nature ; to shew Vertue her owne Feature, Scorne her owne Image, and the verie Age and Bodie of the Time, his forme and pressure. [. . .] Oh, there bee Players that I have seene play [. . .] have so strutted and bellowed, that I have thought some of Nature's Jouerney-men had made men, and not made them well, they imitated Humanity so abhominably.[5]

(3.2.1–35)

Hamlet sees power in restraint and moderation, recommending a sub-tle range in speech and physicality; 'bellowing' and 'strutting' destroy effect and strangle the play. Alleyn was an admired musician, which suggests some subtlety, and if he did bellow and strut it harmed nei-ther his reputation nor success. Actors had little social status, but Alleyn and Burbage (like Shakespeare) died richer than they were born, and Alleyn (greatly enriched by a business partnership with Henslowe, whose step-daughter he married)[6] made lasting use of his money to found the College of God's Gift at Dulwich, where his papers are deposited.

The great comedic entertainers, especially *clowns*, were vital crowd-pleasers in Renaissance theatre, and Shakespeare's clown- and Fool-rôles developed in tandem with specific actors' talents. The most influential figure of the age was Richard Tarlton (d.1588), legendary for his extemporization and musical skills, a favourite with Queen Elizabeth until political joking gave offence.[7] Hamlet's remarks about Yorick ("a fellow of infinite Jest;of most excellent fancy", 5.1.184) and the Fool in *Lear* may be remembrances of Tarlton, who had some part in training both William Kemp (?d.1605) and Robert Armin

---

[5] "ore-stop" is usually emended to 'overstep', but Hamlet refers elsewhere to the 'stops' of a recorder (3.2.360, 365), and the word also meant the marks of punctuation which signal syntactical closure or require a pause in delivery. The spelling 'abhominably' reflects a false etymology or pun, *ab* + *homin-*, meaning 'inhuman'.

[6] His second wife was Constance Donne, daughter of the poet-cleric.

[7] *Riverside Shakespeare*, plate 12.

(c.1568–1615), successively principal clowns of the Chamberlain's/ King's Men.[8] Kemp was also a brilliant improviser, dancer, and physical comedian, like Tarlton played rustic clowns, and probably created Dogberry (*Much Ado*), Bottom (*Dream*), and Falstaff; he was particularly famous for *jigs*, pendant scenes performed after a play, and may have left the company in 1599 because of a decision to discontinue jigging at the new Globe.[9] It is often said that Shakespeare's Fool-rôles change with Armin's arrival, from rustic clowns and malapropizing constables based on Tartaglia to the wise, musical Fools exemplified by Feste in *Twelfth Night*, the Fool in *Lear*, and Autolycus in *Winter's Tale*, but the claim is overstated. Elbow in *Measure* is clearly a Tartaglia-type, someone had to play the 'Kemp-rôles' in revivals, and Armin probably created Jaques rather than Touchstone (*As You Like It*), as well as Thersites (*Troilus*), Menenius (*Coriolanus*), Cloten (*Cymbeline*), Stephano or Caliban (*Tempest*), and Drugger in Jonson's *Alchemist*.[10] Any kind of one-for-one swap is too crude, but it does seem that writing for Armin (a skilled musician and acute observer who wrote on Fools and was a playwright himself) prompted Shakespeare to think deeply about Fools, and that the Fool-rôles he wrote after 1599 are more musical, variably sophisticated, and liable to melancholy than those written for Kemp.

Boy-actors playing female rôles and boys employed by the children's companies also commanded respect on the Jacobethan stage. Records of boy-choristers acting in occasional plays date to the fourteenth century, but in 1575–6 the Boys of St Paul's acquired their own private theatre (exact location unknown) and the Children of the Chapel Royal the first Blackfriars theatre. John Lyly (c.1553–1606) was engaged by both companies from 1582 to 1590 and the quality of his writing forced performers to new heights. The first decade of the seventeenth century saw the zenith of the children's companies, when Dekker, Marston, Chapman, Middleton, and Beaumont all wrote for them and they posed a genuine threat to their adult rivals. Parts written for boys often demanded virtuoso skills of rhetorical delivery, few concessions being made to age and experience: outside

---

[8] *Riverside Shakespeare*, plate 11.

[9] See Wiles, *Shakespeare's Clown*, pp. 46–8.

[10] Ibid., chap. 10. Armin was famously short, and was once apprenticed to a goldsmith, which explains some lines if he played the speaker/interlocutor.

school-plays modern child-actors usually play only children,[11] but Jacobethan boys played Vices, tragic protagonists, heroic leaders, and rôles full of sexual innuendo in plays that explore politics, intrigue, and corruption as acutely as anything written for adult actors. Solomon Pavy (1590–1603) was renowned before he died, having appeared in Jonson's *Cynthia's Revels* (1600) and *Poetaster* (1601) and been widely praised for his aptitude for playing old men. Another prodigy, Nathan Field (1587–*c*.1620), shone in Chapman's *Bussy d'Ambois* (1604) and made a name for flamboyant acting which he sustained in a successful adult career.[12] The names of boys who played with adult companies are mostly lost, but it seems likely that Shakespeare twice had an exceptional boy for whom he wrote: in *c*.1598–1602 one skilled at comedic younger women and metatheatre, who created Beatrice (*Much Ado*), Portia (*Merchant*), Rosalind (*As You Like It*), Viola (*Twelfth Night*), and perhaps Ophelia (*Hamlet*) and Cressida (*Troilus*); and in *c*.1606–10 one skilled at tragic older women, who created Lady Macbeth, the Countess of Roussillon (*All's Well*), Cleopatra, Volumnia (*Coriolanus*), and Hermione (*Winter's Tale*).

In Restoration drama, especially comedy, acting-styles were much affected by the proximity of actor to audience, the forestage giving a directness of contact which actors acknowledged in playing and which generated an acting culture relying heavily on personality-cults, beginning the dominance of actor-managers. Restoration audiences became sophisticated readers of how personality mediated rôle-playing. Leading actors owned and kept their parts until death, when they were redistributed, a practice upheld morally rather than legally but respected by actors and managements alike; Betterton's legacy, for example, included 11 bundles of plays and parts.[13] Ownership of parts meant actors were associated exclusively with specific rôles and particular playwrights: casting toyed with audiences' expectations; specific actors are also referred to or described in play-texts more often than before.[14]

[11] The great exception is *Bugsy Malone* (dir. Alan Parker, 1976), well worth watching (with a sharp eye on one's own reactions to the all-child cast) whenever reading a play written for children's companies. Potter's *Blue Remembered Hills* (1978) disturbingly reverses the trope, using an all-adult cast to play child-rôles. An all-child *Dream* (dir. Christine Edzand, 2001) has just been released.

[12] *Riverside Shakespeare*, plate 11.

[13] See Holland, *The Ornament of Action*, p. 65.

[14] Ibid., pp. 63–4.

The advent of female actors on the London stage in 1660 brought a different consciousness of sexualities to acting and spectatorship, and female rôles and bodies were fully exploited by playwrights. Nell Gywnn was as famed for her looks and sexual libertinism as for stage-appearances, and continued to act while Charles II's lover in the 1670s: her comedic acting was held to be deft and vibrant, her trage-dic acting not a forté, but the audience's knowledge of her private life was assumed in the performance of Dryden's *Tyrannick Love* (1669). She played the morally irreproachable Valeria and spoke a mock-epitaph for herself: "Here *Nelly* lies, who, though she liv'd a Slater'n, / Yet dy'd a Princess, acting in S. *Cathar'n*".[15] *Breeches parts*, women playing male rôles, became a feature of comedy, Anne Bracegirdle (1671–1748) becoming a favourite, followed by Peg Woffington (?1714–60), who made a reputation in 1740 as Sir Harry Wildair in *The Constant Couple* (1699) by George Farquhar (1677–1707); they remained popular in the Victorian age and survive today in the Prin-cipal Boy of pantomime. *Cross-casting* is also sometimes used in Shakespeare: Bernhardt's Hamlet (1900) was internationally renowned; more recently Fiona Shaw played Richard II (RNT, 1995) and Kathryn Hunter (b.1958) King Lear (Haymarket, Leicester/Young Vic, 1997).

The style for Restoration tragedy, more dependent on the scenic stage and requiring self-conscious placement against perspectival scenery, followed precise gestural indices influenced by traditions of oratory:

> The links of oratory and acting are shown by Bulwer's frontispiece to *Chironomia* [1644] (subtitled 'The Art of Manuall Rhetorique') which shows Roscius the actor with Demosthenes. The style of movement in tragic acting was stiff, representative of a limited range of practicable emotions with no gradations in between—though there do appear to have been exceptions, particularly Betterton's significantly more restrained style. The vocal technique owed much to the style of preaching and canting. The voice was used musically with a whining, nasal tone that must have risked droning monotony.[16]

---

[15] *The Works of John Dryden*, vol. 10 (ed. M. E. Novak, Berkeley, Los Angeles, and London: University of California Press, 1970), p. 193; Novak includes a wonderful picture of "Nell Gwyn Rising from the Dead to Speak the Epilogue".

[16] Holland, *Ornament of Action*, p. 60.

Betterton was noted for tempered acting without excessive 'ranting' and 'canting', common in tragedic performances. Similarly, Elizabeth Barry (c.1658–1713), who dominated tragedic female rôles from playing Monimia in Otway's *The Orphan* (1680) to 1710, had a reputation for unusual discipline and moving audiences to tears.

In the eighteenth and early nineteenth centuries acting conventions and *lines of business* changed in response to concerns with sentiment. Leading actors (and spectators) were expected to possess and demonstrate 'sensibility'—capacity for refined emotion, facility to feel moved by the pathetic in literature and art, and especially compassion for others' suffering.[17] Garrick, who dominated London theatre as actor and manager from the mid–1740s to his last performance in 1776, was unmatched in brilliance, virtuosity, and range, affecting audiences profoundly: though the practice may have existed before him, he became master of the *start*, a moment when his character perceived something and responded with intense emotion—horror, surprise, grief, triumph, or despair. His starts became legendary, and Georg Lichtenberg, a German tourist, described the moment at which Garrick-as-Hamlet sees his father's ghost:

> Garrick turns sharply and at the same moment staggers back two or three paces with his knees giving way under him; his hat falls to the ground and both his arms, especially the left, are stretched out nearly to their full length, with the hands as high as the head, the right arm more bent and the hand lower, and the fingers apart; his mouth is open: thus he stands rooted to the spot, with legs apart, but no loss of dignity, supported by his friends, who are better acquainted with the apparition and fear lest he should collapse.[18]

Edmund Kean (1789–1833), the foremost Romantic actor, developed Garrick's starts and came to be a master of *points*—a gesture, posture, or shift in voice-pitch marking a climactic moment in a speech, rôle, or dramatic situation—and his extraordinary ability to make sudden *transitions* in mood and emotion had much to do with prowess at points. Samuel Taylor Coleridge (1772–1834) wrote of his "rapid descents from the hyper-tragic to the infra-colloquial [. . .] To see him act,

---

[17] See Taylor, *Players and Performances*.
[18] *Whitehall Evening Post*, 17 March 1779, in Taylor, *Players and Performances*, p. 31.

is like reading Shakespeare by flashes of lightning";[19] William Hazlitt (1778–1830) gave a thoughtful account of his acting-style:

> he sometimes failed from an exuberance of manner, and dissipated the impression of the general character by the variety of his resources. To be complete, his delineation of it should have more solidity, depth, sustained and impassioned feeling, with somewhat less brilliancy, with fewer glancing lights, pointed transitions, and pantomimic evolutions. [. . .] If Mr. Kean does not entirely succeed in concentrating all the lines of character, as drawn by Shakespear, he gives an animation, vigour, and relief to the part which we have not seen equalled. He is more refined than Cooke; more bold, varied, and original than Kemble in the same character. [. . .] The frequent and rapid transition of his voice from the expression of the fiercest passion to the most familiar tones of conversation was that which gave a peculiar grace of novelty to his acting on his first appearance.[20]

If Kean's genius was erratic, his acting-style spawned many imitators: points and transitions were a feature in classics and melodrama, and in popular melodrama actors self-consciously exhibited their mastery of gesture and attitude. His life and style were celebrated by Alexandre Dumas *père* (1802–70) in the stage-play *Kean* (1836), adapted by Jean-Paul Sartre (1905–80) in 1954, and revived in English translation in 1989 with Derek Jacobi (b.1938) in the title-rôle. But points did not suit Ibsenite playwrights, and by the 1890s Shaw was complaining that actors who insisted on them disrupted the flow of the play in an absurd and exaggerated fashion.[21]

If Kean was the critical measure for male actors for much of the Victorian era, Sarah Siddons (1755–1831) was the equivalent for female actors though her style was the opposite of Kean's. Siddons, like her eldest brother John Philip Kemble (1757–1823), anticipated a Stanislavskian idea of throughline, mapping the emotional intensity of her performances with great care, building up to climaxes, concentrating on the coherent presentation of a rôle, and creating a character in the psychologized, novelistic sense. Her playing of Lady

---

[19] R. A. Foakes, ed., *Coleridge's Criticism of Shakespeare: A Selection* (London: The Athlone Press, 1989), pp. 184–5.

[20] William Hazlitt, *Characters of Shakespear's Plays* (London: J. M. Dent, 1906 [Everyman]), pp. 173–5.

[21] G. B. Shaw, *Our Theatre in the Nineties* (1932; 3 vols, London: Constable and Co., 1948), III.124, 132.

Macbeth from 1794 made her a legend; her portrait was painted by Reynolds and Gainsborough. Younger brothers Stephen (1758–1822) and Charles (1775–1854) also acted, as did Charles's daughter Fanny (1809–93), and such acting dynasties marked the nineteenth century. Kean's was extended by his son Charles (1811–68), a wooden actor but very successful manager of the Princess's Theatre, 1850–9, noted for the meticulous historical accuracy of his sets for classical plays and use of focused limelight. The great later name was Terry, including Benjamin (1818–96), his wife Sarah Ballard (1817–92), and five children:[22] the outstanding figure was Ellen (1847–1928), who from 1878 to 1898 played opposite the great Henry Irving (1838–1905) at the Lyceum, and as Lady Macbeth in 1888 inspired a famous portrait by Sargent. In 1903 she celebrated half a century on stage with a Drury Lane *matinée* in which 22 Terries appeared, and in 1925 became a Dame (the female equivalent of knighthood). Her children by theatre-designer and architect E. W. Godwin (1833–86) were the pioneering director Edith Craig (1869–1947) and designer Edward Gordon Craig; John Gielgud was her great-nephew. In America the equivalent dynasty, fusing stage- and screen-work, was the Barrymores,[23] who collectively inspired a popular Broadway comedy, *The Royal Family* (1927) by George S. Kaufman (1889–1961) and Edna Ferber (1885–1968). The children of John Barrymore (1882–1942), Diana (1921–60) and John Jr (b.1932), both had troubled acting careers, and his granddaughter Drew (b.1975), catapulted to child-stardom in Spielberg's *E.T.* (1982), continues to attract headlines.

The importance of dynasties lies partly in the power they wield in their heydays and the rôles written for and about them, individually or collectively, but also in the way they preserve and transmit acting-styles and particular ways of interpreting major rôles over generations. Irving, knighted in 1895 and manager of the Lyceum Theatre 1878–98, was the most popular actor of his time, a showman who dominated productions with melodramatic over-acting condemned as heavy-handed and self-promoting by the avant garde. He loved the externals of rôle-playing, and was a skilled make-up artist, like his

[22] Kate (1844–1924), Ellen, Marion (1856–1930), Florence (1855–96), and Fred (1863–1933).

[23] Maurice (1847–1905), his wife Georgina Drew (1856–92), and children Lionel (1878–1954), Ethel (1879–1959), and John.

major rival Beerbohm Tree, manager of His/Her Majesty's Theatre 1897–1915, founder of the *Royal Academy of Dramatic Art* (RADA) in 1904, knighted in 1907, and a showman of the same stamp. In both men's stage-work the influence of Garrick and Edmund Kean spilled into the early twentieth century. The post-Ibsenite dominance of psychological realism and autocratic directors, with the influence of film and TV, made Gielgud's style of necessity very different, but modern as he could be he too preserved a flavour of styles now lost, as his reputation for fine delivery, outstanding verse-speaking, and elegant posture suggests.[24]

Special mention should be made of Laurence Olivier, known for his physical characterizations and energy. In 1935 he and Gielgud created a great stir by swapping the rôles of Romeo and Mercutio midway through a run. Like Gielgud, Olivier showed extraordinary versatility, acting in classics and plays by Osborne and Pinter, and adapting his skills to film; he directed the stunning 1944 film of *Henry V* (about victory in France) premièred on the evening of the D-Day landings in Normandy, was the first Director of the NT (1963–73), and in 1970 became the first actor to be ennobled. In addition to many film-performances a fair amount of his stage-work is available on video, and his physical force is evident in his last great performance, Lear in a 1983 TV-film: he reputedly had to be dissuaded from stripping completely in the storm scenes, but baring much of his ageing body brought to the rôle a memorable vulnerability combining Lear's old age and infantile anger.

The training function of dynasties and on-the-job apprenticeships has since *c.*1900 largely been replaced by more formal training,[25] a major preoccupation of twentieth-century and contemporary theatre-practitioners. The impact of Stanislavski's coherent theory of actor-training at the Moscow Art Theatre in 1898–1924, which he called *the System*, has been profound: his influence was felt slowly in

[24] Recordings of Gielgud and some earlier actors, including Tree and Irving, are available on, e.g., *Great Shakespeareans: Recordings 1890–1937* (Pavilion Records/Pearl CD 9465, 1990) and *Great Historical Shakespeare Recordings* (Naxos AudioBooks NA220014, 2000). Gielgud can also be heard on film in Peter Greenaway's *Prospero's Books* (1991) and as the butler Hobson in *Arthur* (1981); see also the extensive obituaries in the UK broadsheet press, 23 May 2000.

[25] Early experience as *extras* (principally in film) and *understudies* (principally on stage) continues to be important.

the UK, but his pupil Richard Boleslavski (1887–1937) had an immediate impact in the US as a teacher, and with Maria Ouspenskaya (1876–1949) co-founded the American Laboratory Theatre (1923-30). Stanislavski provided actors with a method of breaking-down play-texts into *units* and *objectives*, and of mapping and analysing psychological motivation and *subtext*—methods used by many actors and directors today. He also trained actors to build-up *affective memory*, an emotional repository to draw on to give impetus and psychological meaning to their physical and vocal expression.[26] He developed his System working with (post-)Naturalist plays in the early twentieth century: modern familiarity with Freudian psychology can lead to a retrospective imposition of his ideas on to plays from earlier times, which may help actors but can seriously mislead readers. Rôles written as psychologically realist need to be thought of as such; those written otherwise must be thought of otherwise: a good example is Anne Frankford in Heywood's *A Woman Killed with Kindness* (*c.*1605), an apparently pious, faithful, and happy wife who when propositioned by an obvious villain called Wendoll vigorously refuses then promptly agrees. To ask what secret causes lead her to such abrupt adultery is like asking a corner-piece of Lego why it wants to turn a right-angle: Heywood provides neither explanation nor any room for explanation, but merely deploys an 'adultery-shaped piece' and moves on to his central interest: what happens when her husband finds out. To play Anne Frankford with psychological realism, as Saskia Reeves (b.1960?) did in Mitchell's 1991 RSC production, is to run a serious risk of incoherence at the moment of Anne's surrender to Wendoll, confusing *dramatic motivation*, what an actor has to make a rôle do in a given scene (in this case resist and then capitulate), with post-Freudian ideas of coherent psychological narrative. Shakespeare was more interested in psychology than Heywood but needs great caution, especially in the comedies: the repentance of Duke Frederic in *As You Like It*, who marching with his army met "an old Religious man, / [and] After some question with him, was converted / Both from his enterprize, and from the world" (5.4.160–2) is pointedly implausible (if very much as we like it), and rôles like Leontes in *Winter's Tale* are also hard to psychologize persuasively.

---

[26] The clearest account of the System is Benedetti, *Stanislavski & The Actor*.

Stanislavski's approach has been the major influence on American actor-training for film. Film-actors work in short, intense bursts to camera, usually out of narrative sequence, and must be able to step 'into character' at will and at any point in the plot. The possibility of retakes means that neither *drying* (forgetting lines) nor *corpsing* (inappropriate laughter which 'kills' the rôle being presented) are problems. A famous disciple of Stanislavski's, Lee Strasberg (1901–82), Artistic Director of the *Actors' Studio* 1951–82, was the leading exponent of *the Method* (often mistaken for Stanislavski's System), which stresses the need to feel emotions 'for real' in order to be able to play a part convincingly. Many of Strasberg's pupils are well known, and the *realization* of Stanley by Marlon Brando (b.1924) in the film by Elia Kazan (b.1909) of Williams's *A Streetcar Named Desire* (1951) was famously attributed to the Method; Dustin Hoffmann (b.1937) has spoken of his debt to Strasberg, as has Al Pacino (b.1940), appointed co-president of the Actors' Studio in 2000. The Method has always been controversial: its critics accuse it of encouraging emotional indulgence at the expense of technique and of being potentially damaging to actors forced in workshops to relive memories of traumata—a claim fuelled by Strasberg's infamous treatment of Marilyn Monroe (1926–62); its defenders reject both charges, pointing to the talents it has enhanced. Some actors certainly take the Method to extremes, believing they <u>must</u> temporarily live out the life of a character to prepare for a stage-play or film.

Acting is now a very competitive profession; *auditioning* for drama schools requires prior training and stamina, while actors with a limited range of skills have difficulties avoiding *typecasting*. Forms of actor-training which work in opposition to Stanislavski privilege the actor's body/voice over psychology, and since the 1960s have fuelled interest in different approaches to theatre. Meyerhold was an early progenitor of physical theatre: he worked with Stanislavski for a time but set up an experimental studio at the MAT to develop his own physical method, *bio-mechanics*; there and elsewhere, from 1905 to 1930 he trained actors to suppress emotion in performance and concentrated on developing highly disciplined, almost gymnastic exercises. His influence in Russia has been profound since the 1950s, but in Western Europe he is a comparatively recent 'discovery', and by far the greater influence has been the Pole Jerzy Grotowski (1933–99), whose *Theatre Laboratory* (founded 1965) inspired a generation of post-1960s practitioners excited by an uncompromising insistence on performers rather than writers or directors. Grotowski stressed gymnastics, acrobatics, yoga, and pantomime as means for actors to reach maximal empowerment, and his book *Towards A Poor Theatre* (1968) led many would-be actors to found their own small companies and begin experimenting for themselves. Current understanding of physical theatre can be said to be based on Grotowski, though in Britain the leading actors of contemporary physical theatre mostly trained with Lecoq in France, where the work of Étienne-Marcel Decroux (1898–1991), particularly a grammar of physical expression he called *mime corporel* (physical mime), influenced pupils including Barrault and Marceau.

Interest in actor-training methods across Europe and around the world has been spurred by the end of the Cold War and the East/West division. Both in Europe and America it is now possible to take courses and workshops in *Noh theatre, Kathakali*, martial arts, mime, Boal's forum theatre, *shadow-theatre*, and many other disciplines.[27] In England the influence of more conservative schools, notably RADA, continues to be strong, but physicalizing rather than psychologizing approaches to Shakespeare are developing rapidly, boosted by the success of companies like Theatre de Complicite and Northern Broadsides, and by non-textual interest in seeing Shakespeare performed in translation.[28] For all theatre-goers an unparalleled variety of performances is available, especially for those willing to explore fringe theatre in London and off-off-Broadway in New York—but not everybody wants something new, and the RSC has experienced hostility to self-consciously modern productions of Shakespeare from tourist audiences expecting the more conservative styles which made its name. For theatre-goers who are also play-readers there is above all a constant education in the possibilities of staging, but also the simple necessity in reading a text such as Complicite's *Street of Crocodiles* (1992) of understanding the concerns and styles of the actors who created it.

[27] See Phillip B. Zarrilli, ed., *Acting (Re)Considered* (London: Routledge, 1995), and Jane Milling and Graham Ley, *Modern Theories of Performance* (Basingstoke: Palgrave, 2001).

[28] See Dennis Kennedy, ed., *Foreign Shakespeare: Contemporary Performance* (Cambridge: Cambridge University Press, 1993).

19

Dramaturgs and literary managers

A dramaturg is literally a drama-worker or -maker, from Greek *drama* + ἐργον, *ergon*, 'work', and in antiquity probably incorporated the modern ideas of playwright <u>and</u> director. The earliest English use of the word is in 1787, shortly after the tenure of G. E. Lessing, the first official modern dramaturg, at the German National Theatre, Hamburg, 1767–9. Lessing's collection of theatre-criticism, *Hamburg-ische Dramaturgie* (1768–9),[1] roused considerable interest, and the word *dramaturgy*, 'the structural composition of a drama' and 'a collection of writings about drama' as well as 'the activity of a dramaturg', followed in 1801.

Lessing is a major figure in European theatre-history but the British have been slow to realize it. His controversial appointment as drama-turg was conceived as part of a campaign to advocate a national German drama (not then established), and his helmsmanship was seen as crucial to success—a radical experiment aiming to harness his abilities not just as a leading playwright but also as a formidable Enlightenment thinker and essayist. He was appointed to write plays for the company and be a resident performance-<u>critic</u>, writing about company-plays and -actors for a leading Hamburg newspaper. The theatre-directorate saw value in demystifying theatre-processes and exposing their work to public scrutiny, hoping that Lessing's criticism would encourage self-evaluation and improvement among company-members and stimulate public interest in theatre-theory and -practice. But the idea of a National Theatre promoting a national German drama was premature, and Lessing found the rôle impossible:

---

[1] For a selection see Lessing, *Selected Prose Works* (ed. E. Bell, trans. E. C. Beasley and Helen Zimmern, London: George Bell & Sons, 1879).

he could not write plays at the pace required, an insurrection by actors forced him to stop writing critically about their performances, and, denied involvement in play-selection procedures, he was reduced to delivering scholarly analyses of plays or dramatic theory to his newspaper-editors.[2] Despite the failure of the enterprise, the impact of Lessing's post and criticism on the development of theatre-practice in Central and Eastern Europe was profound. *Theatre-managers* were quick to see the benefits of linking theory to practice and of having a functionary to educate public taste; other volumes of criticism by dramaturgs soon appeared, including the *Wienerische Dramaturgie* (1775) and *Neue Hamburgische Dramaturgie* (1791); and by the later nineteenth century the dramaturg's position in mainstream Central and East European theatre was secure. In some cases there was a *Chefdramaturg*, responsible for advising managers on artistic repertoire and liaison between playwrights and management and public and theatre, and a subordinate dramaturg, principally a play-reader.

In England Lessing's influence showed later, in the campaign to promote the building of a National Theatre by William Archer (1856–1924) and Granville Barker. In their *Scheme and Estimates for a National Theatre* (1907, k.a. the *Blue Book*) they invented a job description for a literary manager conceived as a central functionary, a literary specialist and playreader vital to artistic decision-making:

> *The Literary Manager*, an official answering to the German Dramaturg. His duties should be to weed out new plays [. . .]; to suggest plays for revival and arrange them for the stage; to follow the dramatic movement in foreign countries, and to suggest foreign plays suitable for production; to consult with the scene painter, producers, &c., on questions of archæology, costume and local colour.[3]

Archer and Barker placed the Literary Manager second in the hierarchy after the theatre director, privileging play-reading and -selection procedures, but while it was to be a literary-critical rôle requiring playwriting skills and knowledge of production they did not pursue the idea of the in-house critic for a company of actors. Barker further

---

[2] See J. D. Robertson, *Lessing's Dramatic Theory* (Cambridge: Cambridge University Press, 1939); F. J. Lamport, *Lessing and the Drama* (Oxford: Clarendon Press, 1981), pp. 123–57.

[3] William Archer and Harley Granville Barker, *Scheme and Estimates for a National Theatre* (London: Duckworth and Co., 1907), pp. 12–13.

developed his ideas of literary management in *The Exemplary Theatre* (1922), emphasizing the importance of play-reading and -selection for all theatres and expressing admiration for continental dramaturgical models; his blueprint greatly influenced the practice of Kenneth Tynan (1927–80), the first officially appointed Literary Manager in England (NT, 1963–73), and the current practices of literary managers in Britain are often unconsciously informed by Barker's thinking.

Both dramaturgs and literary managers, however, remain peculiarly invisible in Britain despite many official appointments since the 1960s. Playwrights, actors, and directors often express confusion about the exact nature of their functions, and the general public are largely unaware of their existence. The reasons relate to received ideas about theatre-making and long-standing cultural prejudices which insist theatre is predominantly entertainment, not for intellectual and artistic enlightenment. The fact that the functions of play-reading, play-selection, planning artistic policy, and play-development do not gain more prominence in British theatre-history (and even now are scarcely debated) is strange in relation both to the US and the continent. In Central and Eastern Europe mainstream theatre would be unthinkable without dramaturgs; in the US there are now over forty higher-education courses offering degrees or modules in dramaturgy (including the Yale School of Dramaturgy), placements and posts for dramaturgs in theatres across the country, and no sense that either the word or the work is alien.

The significant twentieth-century spread of dramaturgs across Western Europe and the US was the direct result of Brecht's theory and practice. Brecht evolved his ideas about dramaturgs and dramaturgy throughout his life, but it was only in running his own company, the Berliner Ensemble, 1949–56, that he could put training-schemes into practice and experiment on a grand scale. Brecht's radical reinterpretation of the traditional dramaturg's rôle was to bring them out of isolation in their offices and on to the stage as a critical part of theatre-making, a move carefully dramatized and explained in his *Messingkauf Dialogues* (1939–55),[4] which outlines his ideal

---

[4] Bertolt Brecht, *The Messingkauf Dialogues* (trans. John Willett, London: Methuen, 1965); this is an edited selection only.

dramaturg as the epitome of overlapping theory and practice. His ideal was a specialist in epic theatre and theatre-history who could structure and write epic plays, adapt plays to epic style, and critique rehearsal-processes and performance. He knew that no one person could combine these skills, and employed a team of dramaturgs whom he trained in specific tasks, but—crucially—did not differentiate between training for dramaturgs and directors, adamant that to be either required knowledge of both disciplines. Brecht's dramaturgs were principally trained as researchers, archivists, playwrights, and critics: they had responsibility for educating the public through programmes, lectures, visits to factories and schools, and the organization of amateur performances of epic plays; their critical training focused on observing actors in rehearsal and writing *Notate*. These were technically detailed notes which recorded the processes of performance and were used to give critical feedback to actors, designers, and backstage-crew before being archived. A significant part of trainees' time was spent composing the *Modellbuch* (model-book) of a production, which gave a detailed photographic record of performance and was a visual aid to understanding Brecht's acting and directing techniques.

Dramaturg/director partnerships became the norm at the Berliner Ensemble. Volker Canaris remarks:

> The dramaturg became the director's most important theoretical collaborator. Dramaturgy in Brecht's sense comprises the entire conceptual preparation of a production from its inception to its realisation. Accordingly it is the task of dramaturgy to clarify the political and historical, as well as the aesthetic and formal aspects of a play.[5]

This model of dramaturg and director working together, the dramaturg acting as researcher, textual consultant, and diplomatic critic of process, has spread across Europe and the US; in the 1970s such dramaturgs acquired the specific title of *production dramaturgs*, who undertook *production dramaturgy*. In Britain production dramaturgs are rare, though the RSC partnership of Katie Mitchell and Ed Kemp (b.1965) on *The Mysteries* (1996) gave them a higher profile. English directors generally see them as direct threats to their power and view the

---

[5] Volker Canaris, 'Style and the Director' (trans. Claudia Rosoux), in Ronald Hayman, ed., *The German Theatre* (London: Oswald Wolf, 1975), pp. 250–1.

critical practices a dramaturg inevitably brings to a production with an intense, irrational fear that they will somehow interrupt or censor creativity. In truth, prejudice about Brecht's communism continues to taint the English reception of his work and understanding of his practices.

Since the 1960s and Tynan's appointment at the NT the number of dramaturgs and literary managers working in Britain has grown at an unprecedented rate. Tynan's tenure as Literary Manager was far from easy and has been overshadowed by adulation of Laurence Olivier, the Artistic Director. Tynan's writings reveal his own initial and others' determined underestimation of the work involved in reading and commissioning plays, liaising with playwrights, writing pro- grammes, and trying to keep abreast of developments elsewhere; despite his protests very little was done to relieve an extraordinary workload that contributed to his early death.[6] He saw himself as a theatre-maker and production dramaturg, but had a fracas with George Devine over Beckett's *Play* (1964), was banned from attending rehearsals by Olivier[7], and though he proved an invaluable produc- tion dramaturg for John Dexter on Shaffer's *Black Comedy* (1965) withdrew from critical involvement in rehearsals because of time- pressure and resentments from actors. His leftist politics, flamboyant personality, and desire to promote the controversial grated badly with the NT Board, and he was eventually forced out in 1973. Olivier, how- ever, was wholly reliant on Tynan's artistic judgement and knack for discovering new talents: without him the NT's first decade would have been infinitely less sparkling, and whatever he may have felt about his own achievements he remains an inspiration for literary managers today.

There are currently (mid–2001) 31 literary managers employed in England, nine working full-time and 22 part-time; that 23 are in Lon- don highlights biased funding-structures. Literary managers are gen- erally based in theatres (a few are employed by companies without permanent bases) and are responsible for advising the artistic director on repertoire, reading and commissioning plays, liaising with play- wrights, and organizing contracts. They usually attend run-throughs

[6] See Kenneth Tynan, *Letters* (ed. Kathleen Tynan, London: Weidenfeld & Nicol- son, 1994), pp. 312–13.

[7] Ibid., pp. 292–4.

in the week before the show opens to give private feedback to the director, and occasionally trouble-shoot if a production encounters problems (they may be asked to cut or advise on re-structuring, especially if a playwright is inexperienced). The rise in literary managers is linked to intense interest in new plays, the growth of the Fringe and of small spaces in which to stage new work, and (especially since the end of censorship in 1968) the desire to do away with grand narratives and produce the work of playwrights from different political constituencies. Appointments of literary managers occur in companies or theatres where a policy decision has been made to promote new writing: the Royal Court, NT, Bush, Gate, and Soho theatres in London, Birmingham Rep, the Manchester Royal Exchange, and Ayckbourn's Stephen Joseph Theatre.

It is difficult to assess the numbers of dramaturgs working in Britain because most work on a short-term, project-basis and are not continuously employed as dramaturgs—but the figure must be well over 100. They are predominantly *development dramaturgs*, who work with inexperienced playwrights and help them develop their gifts through discussion, reading drafts and giving critical feedback, and in some cases attending rehearsals. They often assume the title of 'writing tutor' or 'mentor', and are generally experienced playwrights or directors. Besides their work in mainstream theatres such as the NT and Royal Court, they have since the 1980s frequently been employed by theatre-groups promoting minority voices: Black and Asian writers, women, the disabled, and the young disadvantaged. *Regional new writing organizations* (which sprang up in the 1980s in response to the needs of new playwrights outside London) also regularly employ dramaturgs to workshop new plays and be on hand during rehearsals. *Development dramaturgy* is much in demand and continues to spawn new initiatives.

Production dramaturgy has recently received a negative press because of the rumpus over Peter Hall's employment of Colin Teevan (b.1968) as dramaturg on John Barton's play-cycle *Tantalus* (2000). Hall's requested cuts from Teevan, not Barton, and Teevan's re-writing of sections caused Barton to disown the production and publish his own text independently. Dramaturgs are ascendant in Britain and connected not just with new writing but also with a belated concern for critical input into shows and companies; their appointments also reflect an increasing interest in research and documenting process and performance. Courses to train literary managers and dramaturgs have started at Queen Margaret College, Edinburgh; Goldsmiths' College and the Central School of Speech and Drama, London; and at the University of Birmingham.

20

Designers

Theatregoers now usually expect productions to have an overall design aesthetic incorporating every element of design, but this is a relatively recent development. Nothing certain is known about classical or mediaeval design, and the earliest extant performance-sketch, of *Titus Andronicus* in *c.*1595 (*Riverside Shakespeare*, plate 9), shows mixed contemporary (late Elizabethan) and *emblematic costume*. Jacobethan private theatre, however, became another matter: in the hands of Inigo Jones, the first celebrated designer in England, court-masques from 1605 to 1642 offered élite audiences new experiences of spectacle, full of ingenious mechanics, perspectival scenery, and extraordinary lighting-effects achieved by placing candles behind gauzy fabrics and tinted liquids. Jones's designs visually embodied symbolic meaning; his audiences read design as visual text; and he progressed from static scenes to stages that rose and fell, striving for harmony of music, picture, and movement.[1] He also combined painted design with concern for costumes and some props, but in this was far ahead of his time.

In Restoration theatres influenced by Jones perspectival scenery mounted on wings and shutters was normal, but *scene-painters* could not achieve good perspectival effects from every angle (the best was from the Royal Box), scenery was expensive, and the choice of scenes in a new play or opera could be governed by the scenery available. Restoration playwrights nevertheless provided far more stage-directions about scenes than their predecessors, incorporating scenery into composition by using tensions and contrasts manifested by locale to parallel or clash with dramatic action. Of Etherege's *She Would If She Could* (1668) Peter Holland argues:

---

[1] See John Peacock, *The Stage Designs of Inigo Jones: The European Context* (Cambridge: Cambridge University Press, 1995).

The set functions as index of place, as commentary on the action and as syntagmatic chain in ways that determine the play's course. The scenery is not simply re-emphasis of information elsewhere in the play. It is instead a device aiding the audience in their understanding of the play's meaning. It is a primary part of the perception and comprehension of the play.[2]

If scenery and sets are to work like this they must immediately convey to an audience what they represent (which tends to promote a realist approach), yet be able to be changed in performance as one scene gives way to the next (a matter for theatre-architects as much as set-designers). There is also a need to exclude anything extraneous or liable to confuse an audience's 'reading' of a design (which promotes general coherence). These are conflicting demands: real furniture, for example, may make for a more persuasive representation of an interior, but is harder to move than painted images of furniture; and in either case what constitutes coherent design? But conflicting or not, the demands for greater realism, versatility, and coherence continued, and the eighteenth and nineteenth centuries were dominated by an evolving search for better ways of combining them that took design far beyond the use of perspective to include architecture, history, and theatre-technology.

A great figure in that evolution was the Alsatian Philippe de Loutherbourg, employed by Garrick from 1771, whose mastery of romantic landscape-painting and lighting revolutionized scenic-arts at Drury Lane. His name appeared on *play-bills* as a crowd-puller, and his designs reached their height in 1779 when work on two plays by Sheridan, *The Critic* and *Wonders of Derbyshire*, was particularly praised;[3] the effects included an unusual sense of depth, partly achieved by combining *ground rows* (long, low flats) with free-standing scenery, and effective simulations of light changing with weather, time, and season. J. R. Planché (1795–1880) was celebrated for the historically accurate period-costumes he designed for Charles Kemble's *King John* (1823); he also published *The History of British Costume* (1834), an influential resource which catalysed further experiments by Charles Kean, an assiduous researcher of set and costume whose productions in the 1840s–50s visually reflected meticulously detailed reading of a play, attempting to recreate it in its period.

---

[2] Holland, *The Ornament of Action*, pp. 53–4; see also pp. 36, 38, and 45.

[3] Sheridan, *The School for Scandal and Other Plays*, pp. xxxvii–xlv.

By that time, however, design, and a rapidly developing technical ability to generate astonishing visual and mechanical effects, had become tyrants to theatre, rather than its servants; in the sensation-dramas that depended on their stagings of shipwrecks and train-crashes it was common for the set to be applauded as soon as the curtain rose.

Reaction against such tyranny was inevitable, but took a wide variety of forms, and still had to deal with the combined demands for greater realism, versatility, and coherence. One form, promoted alike by concerns with historical accuracy, fourth-wall illusion, and Ibsen-ite social commentary, was the box-set, which became dominant in the 1880s–90s, usually as a detailed interior; such sets are still widely used, but unless mounted on a revolve are hard to change without an interval. A quite different form was the work of William Poel in the last quarter of the century, who radically extended historicist concern to stage-architecture and acting-style as part of a quest to 'recover' a Jacobethan Shakespeare from theatrical accretions and distortions, sweeping sets away in favour of 'bare-stage' productions in highly detailed costume. The 'authenticity' of his work is dubious, but his productions attracted attention, and though the twentieth century has felt free to set Shakespeare in any period a director thinks interest-ing or helpful, accuracy of period-detail (particularly costume) is now a mainstream standard. The impulse to bare stages has recurred in various ways, including in Brecht, Peter Brook's 'empty space', studio-theatres, and the building of Globe III.

The most complex developments, however, were in reaction to realism itself as a primary aim and requirement of design. Aurélien Lugné-Poe (1869–1940), who ran the Théâtre de l'Œuvre in Paris from 1893 to 1929, and Russian playwrights Andrei Bely (1880–1934) and Aleksandr Blok (1880–1921), used *Symbolist* décor which was stylized and abstract; dialogue was intoned non-naturalistically, and visual and formal emphasis was placed on generating atmos-phere not expounding plot. There was also a blunt refusal by some to be limited by reality in any form: *A Dream Play* (1901) by August Strindberg (1849–1912) is a sequence of disconnected, symbolic, satirical, energetic, and often very funny scenes which represent the evolving illogic of dream-experience. Strindberg's stage-directions include:

A background of banks of cloud like crumbling slate mountains, with ruined castles and fortresses. The constellations of Leo, Virgo and Libra are visible. Between them shining brightly, is the planet Jupiter. INDRA'S DAUGHTER *is standing on the topmost cloud.*

The backcloth now shows a forest of gigantic hollyhocks in bloom—white, pink, purple, sulphur-yellow, violet. Above them can be seen the gilded roof of a castle, topped by a flower-bud shaped like a crown. Beneath the walls of the castle piles of straw are spread, covering the manure removed from the stables. The wings, which remain the same through the play, are stylized wall-paintings which simultaneously represent interiors, exteriors and landscape.

A shore by the Mediterranean. Downstage left is a white wall, with orange trees in fruit visible over the top of it. Upstage, villas and a terraced casino. Right, a big pile of coal with two wheelbarrows. Upstage right, a glimpse of the blue sea.

[INDRA'S DAUGHTER] *goes into the castle. Music. The backcloth is illuminated by the burning castle, showing a wall of human faces, enquiring, grieving, despairing. As the castle burns, the bud on the roof bursts open into a giant chrysanthemum.*[4]

The script was completed in 1901, but not until 1907 could anyone work out how to stage it, and despite the many problems it was then a great success. One of the bigger problems was the failure in rehearsal of a 'magic lantern' slide-projector—but the plan to use new cinematic technology makes clear sense, and suggests Strindberg's writing might itself be read as proto-cinematic. The play's later history, however, tells another story: the great film-director Ingmar Bergman (b.1918) directed it for Swedish television in 1963, using all the resources of TV to generate impressive spectacle, but thought his production a failure and:

> In 1970 Bergman directed the play again, on stage at the Royal Theatre of Stockholm, and this time he treated it very differently. He presented it in the small studio auditorium [. . .], judiciously cut and without an interval, so that the performance lasted under two hours, and virtually without décor. [. . .] the difference was extraordinary. What had previously seemed verbose and antiquated now sprang to life. [. . .] He dispensed totally with Strindberg's elaborate stage directions [. . .][5]

The most recent Stockholm production, by Robert Wilson in 1998, cut the dialogue differently but again systematically discarded

[4] Strindberg, *Plays 2*, pp. 183, 185–6, 231, 254. The crotchets used in this edition to indicate Bergman's cuts have been omitted.

[5] Ibid., p. 173.

Strindberg's stage-directions and found in the play a magnificent visual drama of Expressionist movement, dependent on modern lighting- and audio-technology but unconnected with cinema.

Influenced by Symbolist ideas, the first great theorist of theatre-aesthetics was Edward Gordon Craig, who argued theatre must be reclaimed from the dominance of actor(-managers) and the exigencies of Naturalist playwrights. In his visionary *The Art of the Theatre* (1905) he forecast the rise of directors, pressed for theatre-making as an art rather than a purely commercial enterprise, and contended that directors needed knowledge of all theatre-crafts to produce works of artistic unity:

> The Art of the Theatre [. . .] is divided up into so many crafts: acting, scene, costume, lighting, carpentering, singing, dancing etc., that it must be realised at the commencement that ENTIRE not PART reform is needed; and it must be realised that *one* part, one craft, has a *direct* bearing upon each of the other crafts in the theatre, and that no result can come from fitful, uneven reform, but only from a systematic progression.[6]

Craig regarded actors as imperfect artistic material who could not be precisely controlled, speculating that *Übermarionetten*, human-sized string-puppets, might offer a more satisfactory aesthetic.[7] His stage-designs were very progressive, particularly *Hamlet* at the MAT (1912) for which he invented vast, movable screens that dwarfed the actors[8]—but his aesthetic was simple, a form of visual poetry: the actor's body in non-realist costume, highlighted/concealed by atmospheric lighting, moving in space uncluttered by props. Craig's genius was recognized on the continent, not in England, and his seminal place in modern theatre-design has only recently been appreciated; the same is true of Swiss theorist Adolphe Appia (1862–1928), who practised little but whose writings and sketches influenced early Modernist theatre-design in the 1920s–30s.[9]

Many earlier-twentieth-century Modernist experiments took place, particularly in continental Europe, and preoccupations with fine art

6 Walton, ed., *Craig on Theatre*, pp. 69–70 (< 166n.2).

7 Ibid., pp. 72–101.

8 Laurence Senelick, *Gordon Craig's Moscow* Hamlet: *A Reconstruction* (Westport, CT: Greenwood Press, 1982); Kennedy, *Looking at Shakespeare*, pp. 50–7.

9 See Richard C. Beacham, *Adolphe Appia: Theatre Artist* (Cambridge: Cambridge University Press, 1987).

and technology are evident. In France Jacques Copeau (1879–1949) founded the Vieux Colombier theatre in 1913, which had no proscenium arch or wings; reacting against Naturalism and directing Shakespeare and French classics in a direct, non-declamatory acting-style with simple lighting and minimal scenery, he is credited with reforming stage-practice in twentieth-century France. In Russia Aleksandr Tairov (1885–1950) founded the Moscow Kamerny theatre in 1914 and experimented with *Cubist* and *Constructivist* sets, creating assemblages of scaffolds, platforms, and steps as instruments for actors' experiments with rhythmic movement.[10] Like Craig he was primarily interested in the actor's movement in space, and any dialogue was intoned. Constructivist experiments were undertaken by Meyerhold and designer Lyubov Popova (1889–1924), culminating in 1922 with *The Magnificent Cuckold* (wr. 1921) by the Belgian Surrealist farceur Fernand Crommelynck (1888–1970): Popova interpreted the play through movement, building an intricate configuration of moving wheels in red, white, and black linked with ladders, steps, slides, and platforms. German Expressionist design was pursued by Otto Falckenberg (1873–1947), Artistic Director of the Munich Kammerspiele 1917–47, and Leopold Jessner (1878–1945), whose productions of Schiller's *Wilhelm Tell* (1919) and *Richard III* (1920) at the Berlin Staatstheater were thought model Expressionist visions.[11] In Czechoslovakia Josef Svoboda (b.1920) experimented with *Laterna Magika*, integrating live performance and multiple film-projections of the performers.[12] And in 1956 Tadeusz Kantor (1915–90) set up Cricot II in Krakow, a theatre centred on visual artists who produced striking, atmospheric designs, invented ingenious props, and used both actors and mannequins. His 1970s *Theatre of Death* experiments and ability to create memorable stage-pictures were influential, *The Dead Class* (devised 1975) making a particular impression on directors and designers.

In England radical Modernist experimentation did not take hold in the same way, but there were notable developments. The work of *Motley*[13] in the 1930s–50s astonishingly combined elegant flexibility

---

[10] See Kennedy, *Looking at Shakespeare*, pp. 93–6.

[11] See Wilhelm Hortmann, *Shakespeare on the German Stage: The Twentieth Century* (Cambridge: Cambridge University Press, 1998), pp. 52–64.

[12] See Kennedy, *Looking at Shakespeare*, pp. 220–6.

[13] Designers Elizabeth Montgomery (b.1902), Audrey Harris (k.a. Sophie Devine, 1901–66), and Margaret Harris (b.1904).

with affordability, and their design for the 1935 Olivier/Gielgud *Romeo* created a new model for Shakespeare, widely disseminated by subsequent work in New York, Stratford, and the American Shakespeare Festival in Connecticut;[14] they also had an impact on costume.[15] Costumes designed by Cecil Beaton (1904–80) were regarded as works of art and his stunning neo-classical vision in the 1950s, especially in *My Fair Lady* (1956), made him famous. In mid-century two female designers stood out: Tanya Moiseiwitsch (b.1914) began her career at the Abbey Theatre in Dublin (1935–9), and Jocelyn Herbert (b.1917) first came to prominence at the Royal Court in the 1950s. Moiseiwitsch's audacious, extravagant designs gained her international employment, and her work on *Oedipus Rex* in Ontario (1954) and *The House of Atreus* in Minneapolis (1968) secured a reputation as the world's leading mask-designer.[16] Herbert, known for spareness of design, was associated with Brechtian bare stages at the Royal Court and her more complex later designs retain a simplicity of line and spatial apprehension: notable productions include Brecht's *St Joan of the Stockyards* and *Life of Galileo* (RCT, 1964, 1980), and Harrison's *Square Rounds* (RNT, 1992). Finally, Ralph Koltai (b.1924), influenced by sculpture and architecture, is highly reputed for work with the RSC and (R)NT.

In the 1980s–90s opera has been especially innovative: artist David Hockney (b.1937) produced stunning designs for Stravinsky's *The Rake's Progress* (Glyndebourne, 1975) and *Le Rossignol* (Los Angeles Music Center, 1981), and Wagner's *Tristan and Isolde* (Metropolitan Opera, NYC, 1987); and cartoonist Gerald Scarfe (b.1936) designed disturbing sets for *Orpheus in the Underworld* (English National Opera, 1985). Richard Hudson (b.1954) favoured white boxes in *A Night at the Chinese Opera* (Kent Opera, 1987), *Mignon* (Wexford Festival, 1986), and *Manon* (Royal Northern College of Music, Manchester, 1987).[17] Most recently Julie Taymor (b.1952) shot to international fame with her remarkable mask and puppetry designs for the stage-adaptation of Disney's *The Lion King* (New York, 1997, London,

---

[14] See Kennedy, *Looking at Shakespeare*, pp. 133–40.

[15] See Motley, *Designing and Making Stage Costumes* (London: Studio Vista, 1964).

[16] See also Kennedy, *Looking at Shakespeare*, pp. 153–64.

[17] Goodwin, ed., *British Theatre Design*, pp. 112, 140, and 146–7.

1999, Tokyo, Osaka, Toronto, Los Angeles, 2000). The show is breathtaking but was lavishly funded; financial pressures have led companies including the RSC to experiment with *season-sets* (or *season-stages*), used for several plays in the same season.

The number of revivals to which design is central and the international careers enjoyed by leading designers indicate the importance of design today, and playwrights' desires to challenge designers can generate memorable productions. Ayckbourn's *Way Upstream* (1982), about a couple on a boating-holiday, required a large water-tank and a boat, reminiscent of the boating spectaculars staged at Sadler's Wells, London, in the early nineteenth century; Edgar's *Maydays* (1983) needed rapid set-changes for scenes including the Hungarian uprising, Frankfurt airport, an English university, a squat, a train, and Greenham Common;[18] and Terry Johnson's *Hysteria* (1993) required a set to distort in the last act in the *Surrealist* manner of paintings by Salvador Dalí (1904–89). Over seven pages the stage-directions include:

> **Freud** *picks up the phone. It turns into a lobster.* [. . .]
>
> *He opens the curtains. A train is hurtling across the garden towards him.* [. . .]
>
> *The clock strikes.* **Freud,** *terrified, compares his watch. The clock melts.* [. . .]
>
> *A deep dangerous, thunderous music begins, low at first, building. The edges of the room begin to soften.* [. . .]
>
> *The room continues to melt.* [. . .]
>
> *Into the room spills a nude* **Woman.** *Glittering music.* [. . .]
>
> [**Freud**] *runs to the window. She pursues him. A train whistle blows in the garden, and the curtains billow.* **Freud** *backs away from the window. The* **Woman** *tries to embrace him. He avoids her and runs to hide in the closet. Opens the door and through it topples a cadaverous, festering, half-man, half-***Corpse.** *Screeching music.* [. . .]
>
> *The* Corpse *pursues* **Freud.** *The* Woman *tries to embrace him.* Dali, *in terror, climbs on to the filing cabinet.* [. . .]
>
> *Sounds of shunting trains compete with music; a drowning cacophony. Grotesque* **Images** *appear, reminiscent of* **Dali**'s *work, but relevant to* **Freud**'s *doubts, fears, and guilts.* **Freud** *is horrified as the contents of his subconscious are spilled across the stage.*

---

[18] Goodwin, ed., *British Theatre Design,* p. 71.

More **Bodies** *appear, reminiscent of concentration camp victims, as are the antique figures being scattered by the* **Woman** *and the* **Corpse***. Distant chants from the Third Reich. Four* **Old Ladies** *appear.* [. . .]

Dali *is hit by a swan.* **Freud** *moves to the door but it is suddenly filled by a huge, crippled, faceless* **Patriarch***. He enters and towers over* Freud*. Music descends to a rumble.* [. . .]

Dali *gestures. The* **Patriarch***, the* **Woman***, the* **Corpse** *and the old* **Ladies** *all disappear. The set begins to return to normal.* [. . .]

The air-raid all-clear siren sounds. The set completes its return to normal, as do the lights.[19]

Johnson blandly observes in an introductory note that Freud's study, which he describes in detail, *"should be naturalistically rendered to contrast with the design challenge towards the end of Act Two"*,[20] and that challenge involves far more than a melting set. Telephone-lobsters, a filing-cabinet and floor that remain safe to stand on whatever happens around them, trains, scatterable antique figures, and an angry swan must all be incorporated both practically (to work) and aesthetically (to look good); but what constitutes coherence is deeply uncertain, and in many ways meaning is sought in deliberate incoherence. Credits for the Royal Court première include a designer, Mark Thompson, lighting-designer, Rick Fisher, and sound-designer, Paul Arditti, who collaborated closely to combine a powered set that could be distorted with a full range of audio-visual suggestion and illusion: the production (which transferred to the West End) was a great talking-point, but, unsurprisingly, the play has yet to be produced again from scratch.

[19] Johnson, *Plays 2*, pp. 180–6.
[20] Ibid., p. 90.

21

Production staff, stage-crew, and front-of-house

Cinema-goers usually leave as the credits roll and theatre-goers rarely trouble themselves with small-print in the programme, but without the work of scores of people professional performance would be impossible. Stage-historians need specific knowledge of theatre personnel to understand why and by whom particular decisions were made in a given theatre, and for play-readers and critics a general knowledge is a helpful defence against error. In 1927, for example, the distinguished bibliographer Ronald McKerrow (1872–1940) made "A Suggestion regarding Shakespeare's Manuscripts": some early texts have variant speech-prefixes for the same rôle,[1] and he thought the copy for such plays could never have been used as a Book (because the variation would confuse *prompters*) and must therefore have been Shakespeare's foul papers. This argument became orthodox, especially among Arden 2 editors, but practical knowledge suggests problems. The practice of fribbling suggests prompters were not always called on in Jacobethan theatres; professional prompters following delivery line-by-line do not need even to glance at the speech-prefix to hiss the next words of dialogue; in none of the 16 surviving manuscript Books from 1590 to 1635 have variant speech-prefixes been regularized. The 'need for consistency' supposed by McKerrow and his followers is felt by <u>readers</u> (whom variation does confuse), not practitioners (who see only one actor per rôle whatever the speech-prefixes). Practical theatrical knowledge would have

---

[1] The F-text of *All's Well*, for example, designates the Dowager Countess of Rossillion as 'Mother', 'Countess', 'Old Countess', 'Lady', and 'Old Lady' (*Mo.*, *Cou.*, *Ol. Cou.*, *La.*, *Ol. La.*).

prevented McKerrow's misimagination and saved years of academic error whose consequences have yet to be untangled.[2]

For convenience and safety, therefore, a catalogue of the personnel (potentially) involved in production and performance follows, excluding only those with chapters to themselves. Our accounts are of necessity summary—*company*- and *theatre-structures* vary widely over time and place, and in smaller shows many functions will be combined—so students contemplating arguments that turn on <u>any</u> of these functions are strongly advised to do specific research. Those without personal knowledge might also contact (initially in writing) someone who actually does the job, and ask them directly about their conditions of work; quite apart from academic rectitude, many essential theatre-functionaries are little appreciated and welcome courteous interest: <u>all</u> have good stories to tell.

Production Staff

A modern production process usually begins with the artistic director of a theatre/company or an independent *impresario* deciding a play will be done. Either may appoint, or themselves act as, a *producer*, and a (joint) decision is made about a director. The outstanding contemporary figure is Thelma Holt (b.1932), an actor who moved into administration at the Open Space Theatre (1969–77) and Roundhouse (1977–83) in London, became Head of Touring & Commercial Exploitation at the NT (1985–9), and founded her own company in 1990.[3] Since then Thelma Holt Ltd has produced more than 50 shows in London and elsewhere, including work by directors Yukio Ninagawa (b.1935), Robert Sturua (b.1938), and Mnouchkine, all personal favourites of Holt's; without her energetic enthusiasm theatre would be far poorer.

Before *c.*1939 directors were sometimes called 'producers' but producers have since become (as in film) chief logisticians and link to the financiers, with overall responsibility for the budget; directors have artistic control. Depending on the general funding of the theatre/company, producers may be responsible for any or all of the

---

[2] For McKerrow's text and detailed arguments see Williams, ed., *Shakespeare's Speech-Headings*.

[3] A profile appeared in the *Guardian*, 10 March 2001, *Saturday Review*, pp. 6–7.

following: links with *sponsors*, wages, hire and purchase, transport, insurance, and publicity; they usually head a large *administrative staff*. In *producing-houses* the senior staff-producer may also be known as the theatre-manager and will have overall financial responsibility for the theatre building as well as for particular productions; the term is sometimes used in *receiving-houses* for the senior financial administrator.

Producers do not generally attend rehearsals or performances (though Holt is a notable exception, aiming to attend as many as possible of both), but in everything else it is they who have the last word. Producer and director together appoint the other *creative staff*, including any/all of a *set-designer, costume-designer, lighting-designer,* and *musical director*: who in turn supervise set-builders and *set-painters, prop-makers, riggers, costumiers,* wig-makers, and musicians. They may also appoint a *casting director*, particularly for large productions with many small rôles. Specialists may also be needed: academics to help with classic plays; *voice-coaches* to help with delivery in particular spaces, accents, verse-speaking, etc.;[4] *movement-directors* are rarer but needed for stylized, unison, or choric movement, *mask-work,* and stunts. Producers are also responsible for legality and safety, ranging from negotiation with censors or certificating authorities to ensuring adequate fire-exits: in many cities fire-regulations are extremely stringent, requiring for example, if a naked flame is used, even to light a cigarette, that everything flammable (including all costumes) be treated with fire-retardant; rules are fiercely enforced by local government *fire officers*. All UK productions must also have a designated officer responsible for the *Health and Safety issues* that constantly arise from stage-fights, special effects, etc.

The producer is usually responsible for the programme, and will have one or more writer-researchers and marketing-staff (perhaps supervised by a *marketing officer*) to generate material and sell advertising-space. The absence of close-ups in theatre makes product-placement unworkable but local businesses often help in kind in return for programme-credits and publicity. The same team is commonly responsible for advertising a show with posters, *fliers*, and

---

[4] Cicely Berry (b.1926) and Patsy Rodenburg (b.1953) have earned international respect for their teaching and writing on voice-work.

media coverage throughout its run, and for developing special offers with tourist companies, etc.

In larger, flagship, and ideologically committed theatres/companies there may also be an *education officer* and *outreach staff* who work on all productions, visiting schools to arrange workshops, backstage-tours, and visits to performances. Alarm about the rising average age of theatre-audiences is making these posts more widespread; they are sometimes linked to literary management and development dramaturgy.

Stage-Crew

Stage-crew, unlike *production staff*, are required for every performance. Both theatre of illusion and realist sets require an agent of backstage control and the *stage-manager* has overall responsibility. The term dates only to 1817 but the basic function is co-extensive with theatre: Elizabethan companies had a *Book-holder*, whose primary job was presumably the security of Books and cue-scripts, but who is widely thought to have acted as stage-manager and prompter.

Stage-managers head a team of *stage-hands* who *get in, set up*, change or *strike* sets as necessary, and *get out*; if intentionally visible to the audience <u>during</u> a scene (e.g. pushing a mobile prop) they are known as *supers*. The stage-manager usually controls any/all of the prompter, light-/*sound-technicians*, and musicians; is responsible for the safety of the crew and actors in their work and keeping the backstage-area secure; and oversees the *wardrobe-* and *property-masters* who ensure that everything is to hand as needed before, and safely stored after, a show. If there are *make-up artists* and/or *dressers* to help actors prepare (and with period-costumes or non-naturalistic make-up help may be very necessary) they are probably responsible to the stage-manager, but in practice are usually granted fair independence so long as the job gets done; as are *wardrobe* staff. There will also be at least one *doorman* on the *stage-door* to keep out inquisitive or abusive members of the public and take messages for actors, crew, etc.

Front-Of-House

Theatres with regular audiences depend not only on their shows but on the quality of their patrons' experience each time they come: the responsibility of the *house-manager*. If, as is now common, catering is financially essential to the theatre there may be a catering-manager to oversee waiters, bar-staff, and perhaps concession-staff; the house-manager controls ushers, programme-sellers, box-office staff, and ambience, and may have general responsibility for cleaners, programme-sales, leaflets, and exterior displays of posters and/or neon. There are significant safety regulations to be observed whenever the doors are open, and much routine work; but the enforcement of order, the welcome of special guests or reviewers with *comps* (free tickets), and polite, efficient dealing with late or disgruntled spectators are more than enough to make a good house-manager worth a great deal; a bad one can cost even more in lost revenue.

22

Censors

Authors may write, directors conceive, and actors rehearse, but audiences may not see (nor readers buy) if a censor intervenes. Given the relatively small number of people who can see any given stage-play one might expect censors to be more interested in printed texts and broadcast media; but the power and social importance of stage-performance dictates otherwise. The history of dramatic censorship is bound up with other forms of control, and students needing specific detail should consult the appendix on 'Censorship and the Law of the Press' in the 5th (1985) edition of the *Oxford Companion to English Literature*,[1] and the excellent essay by J. R. Stephens in the revised edition of the *Cambridge Guide to Theatre* (1995).

The control of stage-performance in England was formally regulated from at least the 1550s to 1968 and falls into two main periods, under the Master of the Revels (1574–1737) and the Lord Chamberlain (1737–1968). All play-texts had to be submitted for approval and licensed for performance, and could be arbitrarily banned or cut, but the severity of enforcement and the subjects attracting the *blue pencil* varied.[2] Although overt obscenity was little tolerated before the later twentieth century blasphemy was a greater concern: no one seems to have batted an eyelid at Hamlet's "country matters", but in most surviving copies of Marston's *Malcontent* (1604) the word 'Church' in "From the publike place of much dissimulation, the Church" (sig.

---

[1] First printed in the 2nd edition (1936), and updated in 1946, 1967, and 1985, but regrettably dropped from the 6th edition (2000); a much briefer alphabetized entry is substituted.

[2] For Jacobethan detail see Janet Clare, *'Art made tongue-tied by authority': Elizabethan and Jacobean Dramatic Censorship* (2nd ed., Manchester and New York: Manchester University Press, 1999), and Annabel Patterson, *Censorship and Interpretation: The Conditions of Writing and Reading in Early Modern England* (Madison and London: University of Wisconsin Press, 1984).

B1v, 1.3.4–5) has been razor-bladed out, and an Act of 1606 forbade the use of 'God' as an oath in plays. Thereafter texts printed 'Heavens!' or 'Zounds!' (a contraction of 'God's wounds'): editors of plays published from 1606 to 1642 now often assume these to be involuntary euphemisms and replace them with 'God', and printed oaths do not necessarily prescribe the particular word used in performance, and function more as a category, [INSERT APPROPRIATE OATH HERE], evolving over time (as stage-business must also do). Restoration plays are often thoroughly indecent even in print and censorship was unusually lax, so fairly riotous performance can be imagined; but after Collier's attack on stage-profanity (1698) and the Licensing Act which transferred the censor's office to the Lord Chamberlain (1737), the state's grip tightened and was not relaxed again until the abolition of licensing in 1968. The successful control of illegitimate theatre before 1842 and of music-hall may be doubted, but Ibsen and Shaw were often refused licences, Beckett's *Endgame* (1957–8) was stripped of references to the non-existence of God, and Osborne's *A Patriot for Me* (1965) required the Royal Court temporarily to become a private club because Osborne would not agree to the cuts demanded. The main concern was sexuality—three scenes were to be cut entirely, couples talking post-coitally were not to be shown in bed together, and references to 'clap' and 'crabs' (gonorrhoea and pubic lice) were to be deleted—but the phrase "Tears of Christ!" was also singled out to be cut.[3]

Concerns about obscenity and blasphemy in performance continue, particularly among the religious, but since 1968 formal regulation of everything but pornography has been largely abandoned and the last high-profile legal challenge to UK theatre was a private prosecution of the 1983 NT production of *The Romans in Britain* by Howard Brenton (b.1942) for publicly simulating male-rape; the case collapsed. After the *Lady Chatterley trial* in 1960 'fuck' and 'cunt' could be published, and Tynan famously said 'fuck' on BBC Radio in November 1965, but under the Indecent Advertisements Act (1889) and Indecent Displays (Control) Act (1981)[4] these words cannot be

---

[3] Osborne, *Plays 3*, p. 176. For a general, partisan account of the office see John Johnston, *The Lord Chamberlain's Blue Pencil* (London, Sydney, Auckland, and Toronto: Hodder & Stoughton, 1990).

[4] The amendment followed the 1977 failure of a prosecution of a record-shop manager for displaying the Sex Pistols' album *Never Mind the Bollocks*.

used in advertising, including the display of titles. This explains the variants of Ravenhill's *Shopping and Fucking*, called *Shopping and F***ing* or simply *Shopping and* on posters and in neon:[5] the act was simulated and the word repeatedly spoken on stage, but a ticket-seller who named the play to anyone without a ticket was liable to prosecution. The fuss (calculatedly?) served as tremendous free publicity, and the title is now sometimes printed as *Shopping and F£££ing* (or 'F$$$ing').

In the US such censorship is decentralized and varies widely between urban and rural areas. Hollywood is another matter, and from 1930 to 1966 most films were subject to the *Hays Code* and approval or disapproval by the National Legion of Decency, a largely Catholic organization partly concerned to 'keep things clean' (couples on a bed must each always have one foot on the floor) but also to stifle films "which portray, approvingly, concepts rooted in philosophies attacking the Christian moral order and the supernatural destiny of man".[6] The demise of the Hays Code opened windows of opportunity, but the Supreme Court *'Filthy Words' decision* (*FCC v. Pacifica Foundation*, 98 S.Ct.3026 (1978)) produced a list of seven obscenities (shit, piss, fuck, cunt, cocksucker, motherfucker, tits) effectively banned from public broadcast on radio and TV—and thus from the scripts of radio- and TV-drama and (via commercial pressure and consequent *self-censorship*) of anything hoping for broadcast. The case was frequently and widely cited as a precedent throughout the 1980s–90s, but the proliferation of cable, satellite, digital, and subscription services seems to be leaving law behind; broadcasting, however, remains solidly conservative.

The issue of stage-nudity is specific, but in the UK and US clumsy law tends to draw together stage-copulation, in basic fuck-shows or highly theatrical erotica, and the use of stage-nudity in classical and contemporary literary drama. In the US regulation is again decentralized, and varies from full licensing to absolute prohibition. In the UK the Windmill Theatre in Piccadilly forced a famous Lord Chamberlain's ruling in 1931—'If it moves, it's rude.'—and thereafter

---

[5] See Aleks Sierz, *In-Yer-Face Theatre: British Drama Today* (London and Boston: Faber, 2001), pp. 125–6.

[6] Quoted in Eric Rhode, *A History of Cinema from its Origins to 1970* (1976; Harmondsworth: Penguin, 1979), p. 336.

became famous for the *Windmill Girls*, all but nude, who were not permitted to move while illuminated but provided rapid tableaux in flashing light; it was the only theatre to stay open throughout 1939–45. Similar conventions remained normal until 1968: since then full stripping and pole- or table-dancing has been legal, but (unusually in the EU) stage-copulation remains illegal, and hard-core pornography became legal only in 2000. Stage-nudity has become so common in drama that some theatre-schools teach 'nude performance', and is often more rote than interesting; its potential power was memorably demonstrated by the RSC in 1968 when Maggie Wright (b.1943?) as a naked devil-as-Helen-of-Troy in Marlowe's *Doctor Faustus* had Faustus deeply uncertain what to do with his hands, and by the physical-theatre group DV8 in the gender-exploring *Bound to Please* (1996), when Diana Payne-Myers (b.1927), aged 70, was the only performer to strip.

The great issue of censorship, however, is politics. Rulers of every stripe usually resent being represented on stage, and when they can simply forbid it, but before the twentieth century were usually content to suppress the performance of a particular play; many Jacobethan playwrights spent short terms in jail after such suppressions, but were also let out again. Since *c.*1900, however, totalitarian governments have banned not only plays but playwrights and performers at will. The plays of Mikhail Bulgakov (1891–1940) were allowed no performance in the Soviet Union after 1929, though he continued to work as a director. Brecht spent 16 years of his writing life (1933–49) in exile from Nazism, deprived of the German theatre for which he principally wrote, and had only seven years back in Germany before his death. Václav Havel (b.1936), the playwright-President of the Czech Republic, could only be produced abroad from 1969 to 1990, and though he continued to write his work suffered from theatre-starvation. The East-German playwright-director Heiner Müller (1929–95) was by the 1980s far more widely performed in West Germany than in his native East. But people also fight back, and the context of censorship can itself become a creative matrix. Tom Stoppard's *Cahoot's Macbeth* (1979) celebrates the *Living-Room Theatre* of Czech actors Pavel Kohout (b.1928), Pavel Landovsky (b.1936), and Vlasta Chramostova (b.1926), all banned from public theatre, who created skilfully reduced versions of classic plays for performance on demand in people's houses. On the opening night of *Othello* (1985) directed by Janet Suzman (b.1939) at the Market Theatre, Johannesburg, no one was sure if the black actor playing Othello, John Kani (b.1943), would be arrested for kissing the white actor playing Desdemona; the kiss was undoubtedly a criminal act under South African law, and that Kani was neither prevented nor arrested was a small but significant step. Boal's invisible theatre is in its very nature a protest against censorship and suppression.

Yet politics can also be the subtlest censor, hidden behind the unwritten, the delayed, the unnoticed, and the unseen. Shakespeare's history plays of *c.*1592–9 cover every English monarch from Richard II (1367–1400) to the accession of Henry VII in 1485, but he wrote no 'Henry VII' and did not co-write *Henry VIII* until *c.*1613, a decade after the death of Henry VIII's daughter Elizabeth. Even then he steered very wide of controversy, having had a serious fright in 1601 over a command-performance of *Richard II* for the Earl of Essex the night before an attempted coup; in *c.*1596 the play had caused no problems but associated with an uprising its depiction of Richard's forced abdication came perilously close to treason. All Shakespeare's plays of *c.*1601–11 are set in the distant past or are timeless, and though they continued to reflect his own times the chance to write directly about contemporary politics was denied him. Three centuries later the objections to Ibsen were not (and could not have been) to any obscenity, but to his gender-politics and criticism of social mores; the almost complete failure of the authorities to prevent the social revolution he advocated should not disguise their sustained attempt to do so. The objection to Osborne, similarly, was less to homosexuality as such than to its conjunction in *A Patriot for Me* with the love and betrayal of country, and the force of that denial can still be felt in debates about homosexuality in the armed forces.

It has ever been thus, and still is. The mainstream is most trammelled but no one is exempt, and little contemporary Western theatre is genuinely radical in its politics or presentation of politics. The popularity of *alternative comedy* and widespread disaffection with politics-as-usual suggests many theatre-goers would welcome "a bit of politics" (the catchphrase of playwright and *stand-up* Ben Elton, b.1959); but they don't get it. All the usual motives for secrecy continue to apply, and censorship is wielded as openly as it can be, affecting both the authors and every reader of this book. Lest any doubt, consider Julia Pascal's stage-play *Theresa* (1990), about a shameful episode in 1940 when Jewish residents of the Channel Islands were not evacuated to England but detained and handed over to the occupying Germans, who sent them to Auschwitz. In Guernsey, an off-shore tax-haven where arbitrary state-censorship remains legal, the play was banned for alleged obscenity and 'good riddance' pieces appeared in the local press.[7] In London it was successfully performed in a Fringe theatre but did not transfer to a larger venue, and Pascal was invited on to a nationally broadcast radio arts-programme only to be browbeaten by a host determined to avoid substantive discussion of either play or history and hot with the convictions that war-guilt was yesterday's news and Pascal's moral outrage old hat. In France, Germany, and English regional venues it was successfully toured throughout the 1990s, feeding a demand generated by word-of-mouth, yet the text was not published until 2000 and the history in question remains strongly suppressed. But the play is at last in print, and in most places no licence for performance is needed, only the desire to perform it and the abilities to secure funding, pay the copyright fees, and persuade enough people to relax their self-censorship sufficiently to attend.

---

[7] See Mary Luckhurst, 'The Case of *Theresa*: Guernsey, the Holocaust, and Theatre Censorship in the 1990s', in Irena Janicka-Swiderska, Jerzy Jarniewicz, and Adam Sumera, eds, *Jewish Themes in English and Polish Culture* (Łódz: University of Łódz Press, 2000), pp. 138–48.

23

Audiences

All plays are written for the audiences of their day, but audience research is methodologically difficult and documentation rapidly becomes scarcer the further back in history one reaches. Nevertheless, the social compositions, behaviours, and responses of playgoers at particular times are vital to understanding how a play was first received, and how its reception changes over time. Every performance has a new audience, and subjective accounts of spectating must always be treated carefully and whenever possible compared with other accounts: different venues, casts, and acting- or stage-conventions all affect reception, and a play's potential meanings can be obscured if its social contexts are not researched. Journalism is helpful in some respects, but *theatre-critics* have their own agendas, playing to their readers, and angling commentaries to fit the market-profiles of particular media. Under-researched in the past, issues of playgoing have in the last twenty years increasingly become an academic preoccupation.

The few Jacobethan records of theatre-goers provide interesting snapshots of social composition and behaviour. Gurr's *Playgoing in Shakespeare's London* (2nd ed. 1996) has useful appendices listing playgoers and references to playgoing in the years 1567–1642, which indicate a wide range of social classes among amphitheatrical audiences and that specific theatres attracted specific sections of society. Theatres were generally associated with rowdy and licentious behaviour, and actors had to contend with audience-members who came as much to socialize, conduct business, or find a prostitute as to see a play. The Fortune in Cripplegate (1600–21, 1623–42) and the Red Bull in Clerkenwell (1604–42) had reputations for attracting the most 'down-market' clientèle and crowd disturbances were frequently reported. Plays were popular entertainment, and at all public playhouses the uneducated outnumbered the educated, but both were present; entrance to the pit for those Hamlet scathingly called *groundlings* was one penny, affordable to most, while a private box might cost a shilling or more.[1] Many playgoers remarked on this social mix:

> For as we see at all the play house dores,
> When ended is the play, the daunce, and song,
> A thousand townsemen, gentlemen, and whores,
> Porters and serving-men together throng . . . [2]

Puritan sensibilities were particularly offended by the congregation of immoral social elements and condemnation of playhouses was common;[3] Henry Crosse (dates unknown) claimed in *Vertues Commonwealth* (1603) that "a Play is like a sincke in a Towne, whereunto all the filth doth runne".[4] Private playhouses, however, attracted distinctly 'up-market' audiences and were frequented by aristocratic patrons; prices were higher, acoustics better, and all customers sat, some on stage.[5] Royal command-performances and masques took place before the monarch at Court and had the smallest, highest-status audiences of all.

The convention of <u>obligatory</u> audience-silence during performance was unknown: playgoers talked among themselves as they wished, and responded to playing with booing, hissing, heckling, applause, tears, or rapt silence. A play that failed on its first night could fail altogether and in a real sense playgoers were critics with the power to destroy plays and playwrights, who often wrote prologues and epilogues flattering audiences' discernment, berating their ill-judgement, or reminding them of the difficulty of trying to please and entertain. In the prologue to *The Alchemist* Jonson wishes away "Fortune, *that favours Fooles*", telling the "*Judging* Spectators" that he desires in its place "*To th'* Author *justice*";[6] in the epilogue to *The*

---

[1] There were twelve pennies to a shilling.

[2] John Davies (1569–1626), *Epigrammes* (?1593), in Gurr, *Playgoing*, p. 217.

[3] See Jonas Barish, *The Antitheatrical Prejudice* (1981; Berkeley, Los Angeles, and London: University of California Press, 1985).

[4] Quoted in Gurr, *Playgoing*, p. 226.

[5] See Keith Sturgess, *Jacobean Private Theatre* (London: Routledge, 1987), pp. 11–26.

[6] Jonson, *The Alchemist* (London: Thomas Snodham, 1612), sig. A4v (*The Alchemist and Other Plays*, p. 215).

Tempest the actor-as-Prospero pleads for the spectators' *"Indulgence* [to] *set me free"* (Epilogue, 20); in *As You Like It* the boy-as-Rosalind's words play with the convention of writing epilogues for male rôles, and wittily appeal to the mixed audience:

> I charge you (O women) for the love you beare to men, to like as much of this Play, as please you: And I charge you (O men) for the love you beare to women (as I perceive by your simpring, none of you hates them) that betweene you, and the women, the play may please. If I were a Woman, I would kisse as many of you as had beards that pleas'd me, complexions that lik'd me, and breaths that I defi'de not: And I am sure, as many as have good beards, or good faces, or sweet breaths. will for my kind offer, when I make curt'sie, bid me farewell. *Exit.*   (Epilogue 12–23)

Many prologues and epilogues were written for specific occasions or audiences. Jonson's prologue to *Bartholmew Fayre* (pub. 1640), beginning "Your Majesty is welcome to a Fayre",[7] was not for the first performance at the Hope Theatre on 31 October 1614, but for the second the following day, at Court before James I. Webster wrote his induction to Marston's *Malcontent* for the Globe, toying with the fact that the play was written for and performed by the Children of the Chapel at the Blackfriars, where some audience-members sat on the stage, not a Globe practice: Burbage, Condell, and John Lowin (1576–1653), all sharers, are cast as themselves; a theatre-goer seats himself on stage and all become embroiled in a discussion about theatre-making and playgoing, ridiculing the Blackfriars and making in-jokes about competition between theatres.[8] Audiences also responded to particular actors: Tarlton indulged in jesting battles with individuals brave enough to take him on, could apparently outwit the most hardened joker, and on one occasion so humiliated a heckler that bystanders encouraged him to leave.[9]

The pervasive metatheatricality of Jacobethan writing also means that play-texts of the period include numerous spectators and acts of spectating: 'The Murder of Gonzago' in *Hamlet* and "the most lamentable comedy, and most cruell death of *Pyramus* and *Thisby*" in *Dream*, to name only the best-known inset-plays, require actors to play auditors as well as performers. Shakespeare repeatedly insists at

---

[7] Jonson, *Workes* (1640), sig. A3r (*The Alchemist and Other Plays*, p. 328).

[8] Marston, *The Malcontent and Other Plays*, pp. 344–7.

[9] Gurr, *Playgoing*, p. 126.

such moments that auditors must be generous: when Hippolyta complains that 'Pyramus and Thisbe' is "the silliest stuffe that ere I heard", Theseus tells her, "The best in this kind are but shadowes, and the worst are no worse, if imagination amend them. [. . .] If wee imagine no worse of them then they of themselves, they may passe for excellent men." (5.1.210–16). A wryer generosity attends the very funny incorporation of the grocer, his wife, and her servant-boy Rafe into Beaumont's *The Knight of the Burning Pestle* (perf. 1607, pub. 1613):[10] as one play begins the grocer invades the stage demanding another, for which Rafe is volunteered to play the lead, and both plays then run in tandem amid burgeoning confusion. It was written for the Children of the Chapel at the Blackfriars, and one part of the joke is presumably that no audience-member could so successfully have bullied the adult actors at the Globe; but another part is that the grocer, given the kind of play he wants, has come to the wrong theatre, and the whole may be at the expense of those spectators who at the Blackfriars were allowed to sit on stage but may nevertheless have been unwelcome there. Jonson's curious *Grex figures* in *Every Man Out of His Humour* (perf. 1599, pub. 1600), Mitis and Cordatus, are rather like Waldo and Stadtler in *The Muppet Show*, polemical auditors not directly involved in the action and in the case of Mitis prone to complaint. A still more complex representation of spectating is in Kyd's *Spanish Tragedy* (c.1589),[11] where the action is watched throughout by the ghost of Andrea and a personification of Revenge; the inset-performances, particularly in 4.4 (where the Spanish King and his train watch a play), encode layers of spectatorship in a Chinese-box effect: playgoers watch two spectating audiences, a play-within-a-play-within-a-play, and death for Hieronimo at the end is only a prelude to hearing performances by Orpheus in Elysium (4.5.23). Great caution is needed with all dramatized audiences (as with dramatized rehearsal) but they bring the subtleties of Renaissance metatheatre to vigorous life.

After the Restoration the social rituals of spectating became self-conscious in a different way. The advent of female actors brought a new frisson to spectating: lack of skill was overlooked if the woman was attractive—"to the Theatre and there saw *Argalus and Parthenia;*

10 In Kinney, ed., *Renaissance Drama.*
11 In Kinney, ed., *Renaissance Drama.*

where a woman acted Parthenia and came afterward on the Stage in man's clothes, and had the best legs that ever I saw; and I was very well pleased with it"[12]—and theatre became a major social focus for those 'in society', a place to be talked about and seen. Comedic actors could observe individual spectators and with some patrons still seated on the stage and in boxes above it the spectacle on offer was not confined to the play, as Vanbrugh shows in *The Provok'd Wife* (1697):

> *Lady B.* Why then I confess, That I love to sit in the Fore-Front of a Box. For if one sits behind, there's two Acts gone perhaps, before one's found out. And when I am there, if I perceive the men whispering and looking upon me, you must know I cannot for my Life forbear thinking they talk to my Advantage. And that sets a Thousand little tickling Vanities on foot————[. . .] I watch with impatience for the next Jest in the Play, that I may laugh and show my white Teeth. If the Poet has been dull, and the Jest be long a coming, I pretend to whisper one to my Friend, and from thence fall into a little short Discourse, in which I take Occasion to show my Face in all Humours, Brisk, Pleas'd, Serious, Melancholy, Languishing;————[13]

Many Restoration playgoers, however, were well-informed and regular visitors versed in the latest theatrical events; improvements in printing and distribution meant that they were also avid readers of plays. Samuel Pepys (1633–1703) was more likely of an evening to be at the theatre than anywhere else: his famous *Diary* records several trips a week, often with his wife, and occasions when she went with other female friends.[14] Repeat visits to a show were common, and poor acting or plays did little to diminish enthusiasm.

Playgoing as a passion and way of life produces strong theatre, but also spectators who can be boisterous in their praise or criticism: audiences vented feelings strongly during and after performances, often causing disturbances; drunkenness continued to be a problem; and in the larger theatres of the eighteenth and nineteenth centuries

---

[12] *The Diary of Samuel Pepys* (ed. R. C. Latham and W. Matthews, 11 vols, London: HarperCollins, 1995), II.203 (28 Oct. 1661). *Argalus and Parthenia* (pub. 1639) was a romantic pastoral by Henry Glapthorne (1610–43?).

[13] John Vanbrugh, *The Provok'd Wife* (London: J. O., 1697), G1r (3.3.54–66; Cordner, ed., *Four Comedies*, p. 201).

[14] There are excellent essays on 'Plays' (by Richard Luckett) and 'Theatre' (by Peter Holland) in the *Companion* (vol. X) to the monumental Latham and Matthews edition of Pepys (< n.12).

audience-control was a significant issue. Serious disturbances occurred in 1755 and 1759, and in 1763 there were riots at Drury Lane when Garrick tried to curb spectators' abuses by abolishing half-price admission after the third act of a play; he was forced to submit to the rioters' demands, but they went on to make a massed attack on Covent Garden. The prevalent attitude is caught in a story about Garrick and Dr Johnson:

> The Doctor was accustomed to talk very loudly at the play upon divers subjects, even when his friend, Garrick, was electrifying the house with his most wonderful scenes, and the worst of it was that he usually sat in one of the stage boxes: the actor remonstrated with him one night after the representation, and complained that the talking 'disturbed his feelings': 'Pshaw! David,' replied the critic, *'Punch has no feelings.'*[15]

Wearied by mob-rule, and convinced that the audience-culture made actors' lives intolerable, Garrick left the country for two years, but later won the long-standing battle to remove audience-members from the stage and began the process of distancing actor from audience. When the 'Old Price riots' broke out at the reopening of Covent Garden on 18 September 1809, customers objecting to a new design incorporating many more private boxes and higher prices on all seats, manager John Philip Kemble refused to listen to the rioters' demands: ugly confrontations continued for 66 nights, the longest-running theatre disorder in history, and police, theatre-management, and Government were all harshly criticised in the press for their intractability.[16]

Charles Lamb (1775–1834) felt the lash with which many playwrights had to contend when an afterpiece he wrote failed. In his essay 'On the Custom of Hissing at the Theatres' (1811) Lamb expressed shock at the barbarous roar of playgoers and pleaded for moderation:

> I was found guilty of constructing an afterpiece, and was *damned*. [. . .] I could not help asking what great crime of great moral turpitude I had

---

[15] Leigh Hunt, 'Mrs. Siddons', in *Critical Essays on the Performers of the London Theatres* (1807); reprinted in A. C. Ward, ed., *Specimens of English Dramatic Criticism XVII–XX Centuries* (London, New York, and Toronto: Oxford University Press, 1945 [World's Classics]), p. 84.

[16] See Marc Baer, *Theatre and Disorder in Late Georgian London* (Oxford: Clarendon Press, 1992).

committed; for every man about me seemed to feel the offence as personal to himself, as something which public interest and private feelings alike called upon him in the strongest possible manner to stigmatize with infamy.[17]

The trauma contributed to Lamb's withdrawal from playwriting in favour of sporadic but influential criticism marked by an ambiguity about theatre and (despite the brilliance of some textual analyses) a conviction that Shakespeare exceeded the capacities of the stage and was all the better for doing so. Lamb should have been better able to cope, but the boisterousness of audiences helps to explain the over-refined Romantic (and later critical) insistence on reading Shakespeare as closet-drama, an immortal poet rather than a vulgar showman.

Audiences also of course reacted with delight and admiration. Melodrama extracted gasps of sympathy and shrieks of horror, actors knew how to wring maximum effect, and spectacular sets provoked spontaneous cheers and applause. But a concern with controlling disorderly behaviour began to show in theatre-architecture, particularly the retreat of stages behind the proscenium arch, and in pricing. In larger theatres audiences were divided into social strata through the construction of separate pay-booths, entrances, exits, and bars; and from the 1860s price increases, excluding poorer theatre-goers, mark competing claims of respectability between theatres. The first darkenings of the auditorium in 1882 and 1892, for Wagner's four-opera cycle *The Ring of the Nibelungs* (*Der Ring des Nibelungen*, wr. 1848–74), were unpopular with customers, but managements saw that darkness during performance notably pacified audiences. It is unclear when or quite why audiences became as mute and restrained as they are today, but by the early twentieth century darkened auditoria were conventional. Panto and music-hall were exceptions but late-nineteenth-century campaigns to close music-halls as 'vulgar' were ultimately all too effective: panto still operates routines of audience-participation and musicals can provoke great excitement, but intense reactions by playgoers are now rare and under current protocols of spectating would not be tolerated by other audience-members.

The conservatism of modern audiences was noted by Brecht, who spent a life-time evolving a theory and practice to change it. Brecht

---

[17] Charles Lamb, *The Dramatic Essays* (ed. Brander Matthews, London: Chatto and Windus, 1891), pp. 121, 125.

held naturalistic acting and post-Ibsenite plays responsible for encouraging political and social stasis; they spelled "the imminent decline of the west" because they demanded no hard engagement from audiences, and he was fascinated by the cross-class composition and behaviour of spectators at sports events, whom he regarded as the most critically honed audiences in the world:

> When people in sporting establishments buy their tickets they know exactly what is going to take place; [. . .] highly trained persons developing their peculiar powers in the way most suited to them, with the greatest sense of responsibility yet in such a way as to make one feel that they are doing it primarily for their own fun. *Against that the traditional theatre is now quite lacking in character.*[18]

For Brecht the sports match provided a model of an audience using their critical faculties while having fun, and contrary to commentators' claims about his supposed (German, Marxist) dourness it had to be both, not one at the expense of the other. It was an ideal for which he constantly strove in his plays and productions, and through the proactive educational ethos of the Berliner Ensemble which constantly published programmes, pamphlets, and books, and sent out ambassadors. He did not achieve his ideal, but his practice was a radical intervention in modern theatre.

Antonin Artaud (1896–1948), best known for the essays collected in *The Theatre and Its Double* (1938), affected attitudes to audiences. Concerned with primal emotion not intellect, and much influenced by Surrealism and Balinese theatre, Artaud envisioned a *Theatre of Cruelty* confronting audiences with acts of extreme violence, social taboos, and disturbing sexual scenarios. He believed the West had lost touch with its primitive origins and reduced theatre to a banal routine devoid of profound meaning; spectators, he argued, should be overcome by a savage individual and social crisis to connect them with their buried spirituality and base humanity. Perhaps unsurprisingly, he left little to indicate how this might be achieved theatrically, but his importance in the 1960s to Grotowski and Brook (who instituted a series of Theatre of Cruelty experiments), and in the 1990s to Kane, is very clear.

---

[18] Bertolt Brecht, *Brecht on Theatre* (trans. John Willett, London: Methuen, 1974), pp. 6, 8.

Brecht and Artaud are particular examples, but many twentieth-century playwrights have sought to challenge audiences and tried with varying success to force reactions from them. Beckett frequently represented auditors in his short plays, and in *Catastrophe* (1982) inscribed and satirized audience-response through the sound of tape-recorded applause: the final stage-direction reads "[*Pause. Distant storm of applause. P raises his head, fixes the audience. The applause falters, dies. / Long pause. / Fade-out of light on face.*]".[19] The plays of Jean Genet (1910–86) broke sexual taboos of the time and explored theatrical and social illusion; in scene 9 of *The Balcony* (1956), for example, the rear wall is a mirror, and in productions the audience is often reflected and implicated in political meanings.[20] In *Offending the Audience* (1966) by Peter Handke (b.1942) four actors rhythmically harangue spectators from a bare stage and repeatedly attack the complacency of right-wing, bourgeois Austrian theatre-audiences. The most radical working writer-practitioner is again the Brazilian Augusto Boal, whose 'invisible theatre' experiments surpass Brecht by staging provocative scripted scenes in public places in front of unknowing audiences,[21] a radical way of confronting and forcing action from spectators but one which is pressurizing, has critics, and has not in general worked elsewhere.

The censored obedience and silence of modern Western audiences, clear in the common complaint of older theatre-goers about the less-than-silent behaviour of school-parties and young adults, are perhaps beginning to be disturbed by other forces. Theatres everywhere are fighting (and not always winning) a battle to exclude from auditoria mobile phones, pagers, and anything else that can bleep, but at the same time are desperate to attract young playgoers less concerned about audience decorum than their parents. Marketing research is vital to many theatres, and their current audience conventions, however civilized and useful, may not be able to survive the financial need to broaden their appeal.

19 Beckett, *Complete Dramatic Works*, p. 461.
20 Genet, *The Balcony*, p. 83.
21 See Boal, *Games for Actors and Non-Actors*.

24

Critics

Theatre-critics review performances and write on contemporary theatre. They may be journalists writing for the daily or weekly press, or academics usually writing for quarterlies and annuals, but though there are differences in the length of pieces (and in the UK of 'social status') the distinction is not in itself significant. Theatre-criticism *is* distinct from theatre-theory and theatre-history, but a good critic needs to know about both.

The term 'critic' was first used in England in 1544 to describe one who passed judgement, a censurer or caviller; and the first critical work on drama and poetry in England was Sidney's *Defence of Poesie*. By 1605 a 'critic' was specifically one skilled in literary or artistic criticism, and by 1651 the author of a pamphlet criticizing another work or a person who criticized new publications and wrote reviews. Dryden was primarily a poet-playwright, but the elegance and craft of his prefaces to plays and such pieces as *An Essay of Dramatic Poesie* (1668) set new standards of style; like all Restoration playwrights, he feared the censure of the public at large far more than that of individuals, because audiences decided instantaneously (and mercilessly) on a play's success or failure: "We are fallen into an age of illiterate, censorious, and detracting people who, thus qualified, set up for critics".[1]

The professionalization of the theatre-critic came in the eighteenth century when journalistic coverage of theatre began. Steele founded and edited *The Tatler* (1709–10), and with Joseph Addison (1672–1719) wrote extensively for it. When *The Tatler* closed Steele and Addison co-edited *The Spectator* (1711–12), a quality daily with essays

---

[1] John Dryden, *Selected Criticism* (ed. James Kinsley and George Parfitt, Oxford: Clarendon Press, 1970), p. 133.

and articles on manners, morals, and literature; very popular with a growing middle-class readership, and boasting contributors like Alexander Pope (1688–1774) and Mary Wortley Montagu (1689–1762), it was thought exemplary for its wit.[2] Steele later edited the *Guardian* (1713), *Englishman* (1713–14), *Town Talk* (1715), and *Theatre* (1720); and between them Steele and Addison (both playwrights who enjoyed little success) popularized contemporary debate about theatre while keeping up literary standards. They rejected much Restoration drama, promoted sentimental comedy, advocated new plays and genres, satirized styles of staging and acting, and played a significant rôle in shaping eighteenth-century tastes.

The subsequent growth of periodicals and newspapers, many featuring *theatre-listings* and gossip as well as serious theatre-criticism, was extraordinary; the best known include *The Grub Street Journal* (founded 1730), *Morning Chronicle* (1769), *Morning Post* (1772), and *Daily Universal Register* (1785), which in 1788 became *The Times*.[3] Competition for audiences was intense and by the later eighteenth century the overlap of reviewing and publicity was blatant, *puffing* (extravagant reviewing) being much in evidence. Critics often had vested interests in productions, not troubling with subtlety of argument or observation, and it was rumoured that even Garrick indulged in secret self-puffery: the phenomenon was satirized by Sheridan in *The Critic* (1779), where Puff gives a fulsome account of his art to his friends:

> PUFF O lud, Sir! you are very ignorant, I am afraid.—Yes Sir,—PUFFING is of various sorts—the principal are, The PUFF DIRECT—the PUFF PRELIMINARY—the PUFF COLLATERAL—the PUFF COLLUSIVE, and the PUFF OBLIQUE, or PUFF BY IMPLICATION.—These all assume, as circumstances require, the various forms of LETTER TO THE EDITOR—OCCASIONAL ANECDOTE—IMPARTIAL CRITIQUE—OBSERVATION from CORRESPONDENT,—or ADVERTISEMENT FROM THE PARTY.
>
> SNEER The puff direct, I can conceive—
>
> PUFF O yes, that's simple enough,—for instance—A new Comedy or Farce is to be produced at one of the Theatres (though by the bye they don't bring out half what they ought to do). The author, suppose Mr. Smatter,

---

[2] See Angus Ross, ed., *Selections from* The Tatler *and* The Spectator *of Steele and Addison* (Harmondsworth: Penguin, 1982 [Penguin English Library]).

[3] See C. H. Gray, *Theatre Criticism in London to 1795* (New York: Columbia University Press, 1931).

or Mr. Dapper—or any particular friend of mine—very well; the day before it is to be performed, I write an account of the manner in which it was received—I have the plot from the author,—and only add—Characters strongly drawn—highly coloured—hand of a master—fund of genuine humour—mine of invention—neat dialogue—attic salt! Then for the performance—Mr. DODD was astonishingly great in the character of SIR HARRY! That universal and judicious actor Mr. PALMER, perhaps never appeared to more advantage than in the COLONEL;—but it is not in the power of language to do justice to Mr. KING!—Indeed he more than merited those repeated bursts of applause which he drew from a most brilliant and judicious audience! As to the scenery—The miraculous power of Mr DE LOUTHERBOURG's pencil are universally acknowledged!—In short, we are at a loss which to admire most,—the unrivalled genius of the author, the great attention and liberality of the managers,—the wonderful abilities of the painter, or the incredible exertions of all the performers!—[4]   (1.2.151–78)

Thomas King (1730–1805) created the rôle of Puff, and as Sheridan's reviewers realized, Puff's catalogue is modelled on Touchstone's seven "degrees of the lye" (*As You Like It* 5.4.66–103): but no satire could abolish a practice so advantageous to its subjects and practitioners, and puffery remains common today in *blurbs* and endorsements.

After 1800 three theatre-critics emerged whose styles differed but whose passion and critical discrimination were beyond dispute: Leigh Hunt (1784–1859), Charles Lamb, and William Hazlitt (1778–1830). Hunt wrote for the *News* (1805–7), collecting his work as *Critical Essays on the Performers of the London Theatres* (1808), which influenced many later critics. Though he satirized the profession in his 'Rules for the Theatrical Critic of a Newspaper',[5] his iconoclasm was instrumental in raising standards, his style mixed the formal with the colloquial, and his great talent was the detailed analysis of actors' techniques, as an article on Charles Mathews (1776–1835) demonstrates:

We are generally satisfied when an actor can express a single feeling with strength of countenance; but to express two at once, and to give them at the same time a powerful distinctness, belongs to the perfection of his art. Nothing can be more admirable than the look of Mr Mathews [as Sir Fretful Plagiary] when the severe criticism is detailed by his malicious acquaintance. While he affects a pleasantry of countenance, he cannot

---

[4] Richard Brinsley Sheridan, *The Critic or A Tragedy Rehearsed* (London: for T. Becket, 1781); *The School for Scandal and Other Plays*, pp. 308–9.

[5] Rowell, ed., *Victorian Dramatic Criticism*, pp. 349–50.

help betraying his rage in his eyes [. . .]; if he draws the air to and fro through his teeth, as if he was perfectly assured of his own pleasant feelings, he convinces everybody by his tremulous and restless limbs that he is in absolute torture; if the lower part of his face expands into a painful smile, the upper part contracts into a glaring frown [. . .]; everything in his face becomes rigid, confused, and uneasy [. . .] a mixture of oil and vinegar, in which the acid predominates; it is anger putting on a mask that is only the more hideous in proportion as it is more fantastic.[6]

Hunt went on to co-edit the *Examiner* (1808–21). His obvious impartiality was unusual: though a vigorous defender of actors he did not hesitate to chastise when he thought it justified, and his ability to deliver hard judgements with integrity manifested a desire to see theatre taken seriously as an art form.

Lamb, who as playwright fled the brutality of audience censure (< 218–19), rejected the constraints of regular reviewing but freelanced for the *Reflector* (1811–12), *Examiner* (1819), and *London Magazine* (1820–3), collecting work as *Essays of Elia* (1823) and *Last Essays of Elia* (1833). Lamb's understanding was literary, not performative, but he wrote elegies for favourite actors, particularly Robert Elliston (1774–1831), actor-singer Fanny Kelly (1790–1882), and Joseph Munden (1758–1832):

regular playgoers ought to put on mourning, for the king of broad comedy is dead to the drama. Alas! Munden is no more!—give sorrow vent. [. . .] Munden, *the* Munden, Munden with the bunch of countenances, the bouquet of faces, is gone forever from the lamps, and as far as comedy is concerned, is as dead as Garrick! [. . .] With Munden Sir Peter Teazle must experience a shock; Sir Robert Bramble gives up the ghost; Crack ceases to breathe. Without Munden what becomes of Dozey? Where shall we seek Jemmy Jumps? Nipperkin and a thousand of such admirable fooleries fall to nothing, and the departure, therefore, of such an actor as Munden is a dramatic calamity.[7]

Tales From Shakespeare (1807), a children's classic written with his sister Mary, turned plots into short stories, but *Specimens of English Dramatic Poets who Lived about the Time of Shakespeare* (1808) drew attention to playwrights overshadowed by *Bardolatry*.

Hazlitt contributed reviews to the *Examiner, Morning Chronicle, Champion,* and *The Times* from 1813 to 1818, publishing a selection as

6 Ibid., p. 37.
7 Ibid., pp. 40–1.

A View of the English Stage (1818). His main interest was actors' interpretations of rôles, and like Hunt he would express disgruntlement on any subject: "Mr Macready is by far the best tragic actor that has come out in our remembrance, with the exception of Mr Kean. We however heartily wish him well out of the character of Orestes".[8] He thought Mrs Siddons's comeback a threat to her reputation and a loss to the world, lamenting that she tarnished memories of herself as a mythic figure and warning her to cancel further appearances: "if Mrs Siddons has to leave the stage again, Mr Horace Twiss will write another farewell address for her: if she continues on it, we shall have to criticize her performances".[9] Hazlitt's turns of phrase were memorably precise, but his later criticism was mostly in the form of essays concentrating on textual analysis, many of them very fine (including those in *The Characters of Shakespeare's Plays*, 1817).

Hunt, Lamb, and Hazlitt were the outstanding commentators of the time, but many critics were active. American theatre-criticism was established by Washington Irving (1783–1859), whose 'Letters of Jonathan Old Style, Gent' (some about the New York stage) appeared in the *Morning Chronicle* in 1802–3; American newspapers declined for social and moral reasons to publish regular reviews until the 1850s and most reviewing was confined to short-lived magazines in which many pieces were anonymous. In the UK some puffery continued, but John Forster (1812–76), G. H. Lewes (1817–78), and playwright J. W. Marston (1819–90) all wrote with notable force: Lewes's essays for the *Pall Mall Gazette* contained particularly penetrating studies of individual actors and appeared as *On Actors and the Art of Acting* (1875). But in the 1880s and 1890s the sensations caused by Ibsen's *A Doll's House* (1879) and *Ghosts* (1881) developed into prolonged debate about their challenges to playwriting conventions, acting-styles, and staging, and a new generation of critics emerged in both Europe and America.

H. G. Fiske (1861–1942) and J. G. Huneker (1857–1921) fought to establish Ibsen on the American stage: the battle was hard but they won, and the quality of their writing gave dramatic criticism new status in the US. Huneker extended the campaign by advocating the

8 *Victorian Dramatic Criticism*, pp. 62–3.
9 Ibid., p. 19.

works of Strindberg, Shaw, Maeterlinck, and Schnitzler, and in 1905 published *Iconoclasts: A Book of Dramatists*, perhaps the best of his 22 books. In England the argument was graphically encapsulated by the reviews and articles of William Archer (1856–1924), an ardent fan, and Clement Scott (1841–1904), a vituperative decrier. Archer lobbied intensely for Ibsen by translating his plays and bombarded the press with criticism: in the years 1879–1910 he wrote variously for the *London Figaro, World, Tribune,* and *Nation,* and contributed articles to many other publications, determined to educate readers about Ibsen. He exercised restraint and patience, answering charges of immorality and didacticism against Ibsen with careful argument. Scott reviewed for the *Sunday Times* (1863–5) and *Daily Telegraph* (1871–98), a long stint at a prestigious paper where his voice came to represent the views of a 'moral majority'. He never lacked adjectives to castigate Ibsen and his plays, and to modern readers his writing is boorish and unpleasantly personal: reviewing *Ghosts* he calls Ibsen "an egotist and bungler" and the play itself "nasty . . . verbose . . . tedious . . . vulgar . . . deplorably dull . . . debased . . . undramatic . . . utterly uninteresting . . . formless . . . objectless . . . pointless".[10] Neither an intellectual nor a stylist, Scott understood the publicity value of expressing disgust and indignation far better than he understood Ibsen, but reading him conveys the sense of outrage that Ibsen provoked. Archer, however, had a definite sense of changing theatrical landscape, demonstrated in his most notable book of criticism, *The Old Drama and the New* (1923).

Shaw was an oustanding critic as well as playwright: he had learnt from Hunt and Hazlitt, but also from Archer, and the pieces he wrote in the years 1895–8 for the *Saturday Review,* first collected as *Dramatic Opinions and Essays* (1906) and then as *Our Theatres in the Nineties* (1931), are a major resource. He dispensed with any notion of detachment, took enormous pleasure in anarchic or outrageous statements, wrote to provoke and needle, and was a flagrant self-publicist—a combination that makes his writing irresistible. About Irving, the idol of the age, he observed, "The truth is that he has never in his life conceived or interpreted the characters of any author except himself"; and of Shakespeare he claimed that:

[10] Michael Egan, ed., *Ibsen: The Critical Heritage* (London and Boston: Routledge, 1972), pp. 115–25, 187–8.

With the single exception of Homer, there is no eminent writer, not even Sir Walter Scott, whom I can despise so entirely as I despise Shakespear when I measure my mind against his. The intensity of my impatience with him occasionally reaches to such a pitch, that it would positively be a relief to me to dig him up and throw stones at him, knowing as I do how incapable he and his worshippers are of understanding any less obvious form of indignity.

Even his praise was caustic: finding annoyingly little to condemn in Wilde's *An Ideal Husband* (1895) he wrote, "The performance is very amusing. The audience laughs conscientiously".[11] His criticism is not valued only for literary brilliance and amusement: it chronicles individual styles of acting, assesses the worth of many new plays and playwrights, and has much to say about the social aspects of theatre-going.

As the twentieth century progressed theatre ceased to be a subject of intense debate, and English newspapers accorded theatre-criticism progressively less space. Max Beerbohm (1872–1956), half-brother of Beerbohm Tree, succeeded Shaw on the *Saturday Review* (1895–1910) and made a name for himself; James Agate (1877–1947) delighted in flamboyant actors but looked to the past. In America, however, the examples of Fiske and Huneker led G. J. Nathan (1882–1958) to champion O'Neill's early work by publishing it in *Smart Set*, which he co-edited (1914–24) and made into a cult publication. Nathan also wrote for the *American Mercury* (1923–32), founded, edited, and reviewed for the *American Spectator* (1932–5), and was an influence on later American critics. Walter Kerr (1913–96) wrote for the *New York Herald Tribune* (1951–96) and *New York Times* (1966–90), in 1978 becoming the first theatre-critic to win a Pulitzer Prize for reviewing.

In mid-twentieth-century England there were flash-points around Beckett's *Waiting for Godot* (1955), Osborne's *Look Back in Anger* (1956), and *Saved* (1965) by Edward Bond (b.1934),[12] but much reviewing remained run-of-the-mill. One notable critic was Harold Hobson (1904–92), who lobbied for avant-garde playwrights from the 1930s

---

[11] G. B. Shaw, *Our Theatre in the Nineties* (3 vols; London: Constable and Co. Ltd, 1932), II.198, II.195, I.11.

[12] See John Elsom, ed., *Post-War British Theatre Criticism* (London: Routledge, 1981), and Gareth and Barbara Lloyd Evans, eds., *Plays in Review 1956–80: British Drama and the Critics* (London: Batsford Academic and Educational, 1985).

onwards. He wrote for the *Sunday Times* (1944–76), and has been overlooked as a critic deeply informed about continental drama (his books on French theatre reward attention)[13] who was far less parochial or London centred than most. The outstanding figure, however, was Kenneth Tynan, who displayed the same brilliance as Shaw, and wrote for the *Evening Standard* (1952–3), *Daily Sketch* (1953–4), *Observer* (1946–63), and *New Yorker* (1958–60); his reviews and articles were published as *He That Plays The King* (1950), *Curtains* (1961), and *The Sound of Two Hands Clapping* (1975). Tynan was important to the rise of realist political theatre in the 1950s–60s, famously concluding his review of *Look Back in Anger* with the lines: "I doubt if I could love anyone who did not wish to see *Look Back in Anger*. It is the best young play of its decade."[14] His *notices* conveyed the immediacy of his experience in the theatre, adoration of skilled actors, and sparkling wit. Writing on *Waiting for Godot* he declared himself a fervent "*godotista*", and again showed esteem for Beckett in a review of *Krapp's Last Tape* (1958) playfully presented as a scenario entitled *Slamm's Last Knock*, in which the critic, Slamm, is unable to formulate his opinions on the play.[15]

Since Tynan's death theatre-criticism in Britain has been respectable but free of outstanding talent. Hilary Spurling (b.1940) was a provocative reviewer for the *Spectator* in the late 1960s–70s, but is better known for biographies. Irving Wardle (b.1929), Michael Billington (b.1939), Benedict Nightingale (b.1939), Nicholas de Jongh (b.1947), and Michael Coveney (b.1948) are well known to their newspaper-readers but not to the general public, though all have written books on drama as well as reviews. Journalism in Britain is a relatively sexist and closed world, editors tending to appoint those who can write uncontroversially in house-style, not those with exceptional writing skills or opinions. In the US theatre-criticism is of higher quality, and attracts more attention: Frank Rich (b.1949) wrote for *Time* (1977–80), and as chief theatre-critic for the *New York Times* (1980–94) became legendary for hard-edged intellectual reviewing with the power to make or break a show, which did not endear him to New York's theatre-community. John Lahr (b.1941) has written for

13 *The French Theatre Today* (1953) and *French Theatre Since 1830* (1978).
14 Tynan, *A View of the English Stage*, p. 178.
15 Ibid., pp. 161, 232–5.

the *New Yorker* since 1992, demonstrates an impressive knowledge of theatre-history,[16] is very percipient about plays and actors, and is not afraid to go against the grain: his combination of intelligence and stylishness make him the best there now is.

[16] As the son of Bert Lahr, a vaudevillian famous as the Cowardly Lion in *The Wizard of Oz*, Lahr grew up steeped in theatre-lore, and has worked professionally as a dramaturg as well as a reviewer and essayist. His books include a marvellous biography of his father, *Notes on a Cowardly Lion* (1969), the principal biography of Joe Orton, *Prick Up Your Ears* (1978), and an edition of Kenneth Tynan's diaries (2001).

25

Editors

Since the eighteenth century some critics have also been editors, initially of Shakespeare but then of any playwright of scholarly or pedagogic interest. Before the professionalization of literary criticism in the late nineteenth century and the development of the enormous student-market there were no necessary qualifications, and what editors actually did varied widely. The modern consensus is that early texts need modernization and glossing both for students and for a general market, but it is increasingly clear that both didactic and popularizing interventions characteristically overstep their marks.

For early editors of Shakespeare the major issue was to produce a fully coherent text of F1 by collating it with quartos (which might supply uncorrupted readings), correcting throughout, and supplying 'appropriate' stage-directions and supplementary material such as *dramatis personae* (see Display box 2). Some 500 eighteenth-century *emendations*, notably by Theobald, remain accepted, the most famous being *Henry V* 2.3.16–17, Mistress Quickly describing Falstaff's death: F1 reads "for his Nose was as sharpe as a Pen, and a Table of greene fields"; Theobald (arguing that "a" was short for 'ha', a variant of 'he', and 'table' could in Jacobethan handwriting look like 'babld') emended to "for his nose was as sharp as a pen, and 'a [= he] babbled of green fields". For scholarship this helpful one must give thanks, but if supplying supplementary material and eliminating errors continue as core features of scholarly editions, later editorial procedures are highly controversial.

The problem is how to deal with plays that have substantially variant Q- and F-texts, requiring not odd emendations but decisions to include or exclude long passages and whole scenes. For two centuries the quartos were thought generally unreliable, and F1 preferable except where obviously mistaken; in 1909 W. W. Greg (1875–1959)

DISPLAY BOX 2

Major editors and editions of Shakespeare before 1900

1594–1622 Quartos of *2H6, Tit., 3H6, Rom., R2, R3, LLL, 1H4, H5, 2H4, MV, Ado, MND, MWW, Ham., Lear, Tro., Per., Oth.*

1623 First Folio, ed. Heminge & Condell, contains 36 plays—all those in quarto except *Per.*, + *1H6, Err., TGV, Shrew, John, Caesar, AYLI, TN, MM, AWW, Mac., Tim., Ant., Cor., Cymb., WT, Temp., H8.*

1632 Second Folio reprints F1 with some modernization and correction.

1663 Third Folio reprints F2 with some correction; 2nd impression, 1664, adds *Per.* + *London Prodigall, Cromwell, Oldcastle, Puritan Widow, Yorkshire Tragedy, Locrine.* (< 149 n.2)

1685 Fourth Folio reprints F3 with *Per.* and the apocryphal plays.

1709 ed. Nicholas Rowe (1674–1718), 6 vols. Based on F4 but with 'doubtful' plays at the end; modernization and substantial but unsystematic emendation, including added stage-directions; complete act- and scene-division; complete lists of *dramatis personae*; one engraving per play; and a brief 'Life of Shakespeare'. 2nd ed. (9 vols, 1714) included the poems.

1725 ed. Alexander Pope (1688–1744), 6 vols. Based on Rowe with idiosyncratic emendation and passages he didn't like 'degraded to the bottom of the page'.

1733 ed. Lewis Theobald (1688–1744), 7 vols. Based on F1 with some collation of quartos and 300 + emendations still generally accepted; the first to investigate sources; unfairly pilloried by Pope in *The Dunciad* but now recognized as the first attempt at serious scholarship.

1744 ed. Thomas Hanmer (1677–1746), 6 vols. Wildly idiosyncratic, emending and cutting to taste; illustrations by Francis Hayman (1708–76).

1747 ed. William Warburton (1698–1779), 8 vols. Based on F1 with unacknowledged use of Theobald; notable for the abuse of previous editors.

showed many quartos (however variant) to be reliable texts which must be taken into account. The solution he adopted was the *Lachmann method*, developed by philologist Karl Lachmann (1793–1851) to deal with biblical and Homeric texts in multiplevariant versions: Lachmann assumed there was once a 'perfect' copy of each text, exactly as written by God or Homer, which an editor must reconstruct; his method, applied by Greg to Shakespeare, generated a similar assumption. The result was the *eclectic text* in which all

---

1765 ed. Samuel Johnson (1709–84), 8 vols. Based on Warburton, with collation of F1 and Qq and further emendation; noted for the 'Preface' and annotations. Issued in the US in 1795.

1768 ed. Edward Capell (1713–81), 10 vols. Based on F1 fully collated with Qq and earlier eighteenth-century editions; the first to use the Stationers' Register and other Jacobethan documents; a landmark in scholarship.

1773 ed. George Steevens (1736–1800), 10 vols. Based on Johnson; the 2nd ed. of 1778 included 346 pages of introductory matter including the prefaces of Pope, Theobald, Hanmer, and Warburton, Rowe's 'Life' etc.

1790 ed. Edmund Malone (1741–1812), 10 vols. Based on F1 fully collated with Qq; notable for wide use of documentary evidence, a full-length 'Life', and an *Attempt to ascertain the Order in which the Plays* [. . .] *were written*.

1803 First Variorum, ed. Isaac Reed (1742–1807), 21 vols. Based on Steevens–Johnson *cum notis variorum* ('with the notes of various people'); the cumulation of scholarship to date, but the poems are excluded.

1805 ed. George Chalmers (1742–1825). Notable for illustrations by Henry Fuseli (1741–1825).

1818 Family Edition, ed. Thomas Bowdler (1754–1825), 10 vols. Passages thought indecent or improper were cut or otherwise *bowdlerized*.

1821 Third Variorum, ed. James Boswell (1778–1822), 21 vols. Based on Malone; the introductory material in vols 1–3 totals *c*.1,800 pages; the poems are in vol. 20; for years the most important scholarly edition.

1842–4 ed. John Payne Collier (1789–1883), 8 vols. Notable for using material later exposed as forgeries, particularly about Jacobethan casting.

1863–6 Cambridge Shakespeare, ed. W. G. Clark (1821–78), and **W. A. Wright** (1836–1914), 9 vols. Based on F1 fully collated with Qq, using Capell's library (bequeathed to Trinity College, Cambridge); the major Victorian ed.

1864 Globe Shakespeare: a very popular 1-vol. version of the Cambridge ed.

---

passages present in either a Q-text or F1 were merged, but with drama, written for and intrinsically unstable in collaborative performance, there is no reason to think a 'perfect', 'definitive' text ever did or could exist. The eclectic text is an idealized reading version, its untheatricality reflected in the major academic editions to use it, especially Arden 2 and the *New Shakespeare* (see Display box 3); but Greg's became the dominant model for resolving substantive textual difficulty, and was variously applied to other playwrights.

DISPLAY BOX 3

Major editors and editions of Shakespeare since 1900

1871–1953 New Variorum Shakespeare, ed. H. H. Furness (1833–1912), **H. H. Furness Jr.** (1865–1930), **J. Q. Adams** (1881–1946), and **H. E. Rollins**. The most comprehensive ed., published since 1936 by the MLA; earlier vols are badly outdated, but supplements continue to be issued.

1899–1944 Arden Shakespeare, gen. eds W. J. Craig (ed. 1899–1906) and **R. H. Case** (ed. 1909–44), 37 vols (= 'Arden 1'). The first ed. to assign an editor to each play and seek uniform quality of attention; later vols offer an *eclectic text*; now dated but a basic model for many current eds.

1921–66 The New Shakespeare, ed. A. T. Quiller-Couch (1863–1944) and **John Dover Wilson** (1881–1969), 37 vols. A replacement for the Cambridge Shakespeare; used in the Marlowe Society recordings (1957–63); first ed. to use Greg's textual principles throughout, but marred by bizarre typography and Wilson's sometimes obsessively Christian interpretations.

1946–82 New Arden Shakespeare, gen. eds Una Ellis-Fermor (ed. 1946–58), **Harold F. Brooks** (ed. 1952–82), **Harold Jenkins** (ed. 1958–82), **Brian Morris** (ed. 1975–82), 38 vols (= 'Arden 2'). A very scholarly series with exceptional treatment of sources etc. but little interest in stage-history or performance.

1951 ed. Peter Alexander (1893–1969), 1-vol. Single editors are unusual after 1900; based on F1, and using F1-order, but with important Q-only passages added; used for the BBC Shakespeare; rev. with new introductions 1994.

1967–86 New Penguin Shakespeare, gen. eds G. B. Harrison (ed. 1967), **T. J. B. Spenser** (ed. 1967–78); associate gen. ed. Stanley Wells (ed. 1967–86), 38 vols. Based on F1; notable for its introductions and lack of textual notes, maximizing text-per-page; used and endorsed by the RSC.

1974 Riverside Shakespeare, gen. ed. G. B. Evans, 1-vol.; the premier 1-vol. ed. 1974–97, widely used in schools/colleges in the UK/US; notable for excellent introductions and generous illustration; provides current standard act.scene.line references; used for the *Harvard Concordance*.

1982– Oxford Shakespeare, gen. ed. Stanley Wells, 29 vols, in progress. Nearing completion; in general a valuable series with some very good introductions, but earlier vols (pre-1990), often ed. by scholars of an older generation, are conservative and less thoughtful about staging.

1984– New Cambridge Shakespeare, gen. eds Philip Brockbank (ed. 1984–90), **Brian Gibbons** (ed. 1990–), 34 vols, in progress. Nearly complete; notably clear and well illustrated; some (esp. *Pericles*) have been critically controversial; notable for including *Edward III* and some edited Q1 texts.

1986 Oxford Complete Shakespeare, ed. Stanley Wells and Gary Taylor, 1-vol. The most important recent edition, hugely controversial in using early titles and including brief entries on the lost plays, revolutionary in rejecting the eclectic text by publishing both the Q- and F-texts of *Lear*, and wildly idiosyncratic in its textual choices. An old-spelling version and textual companion were published simultaneously; a compact paperback followed in 1987, popular as a cheap alternative to the Riverside.

1995– Arden Shakespeare, Third Series, gen. eds Richard Proudfoot, Ann Thompson, David Scott Kastan, 15 vols, in progress (= 'Arden 3'). An attempt to address the theatrical shortcomings of Arden 2, sharply modern in some vols but patchy; notable for clear typographical design and generous photographic illustration of stage productions.

1997 Riverside Shakespeare, 2nd ed., 1-vol.: a substantial update adding *Edward III*, new textual notes, and critical material; still the market-leader.

1997 Norton Shakespeare, gen. ed. Stephen Greenblatt, 1-vol.; based on the Oxford Complete, but re-annotated for US students; prints Q and F *Lear* in parallel text but includes an eclectic text; contains an overview of the Shakespearean Stage by Andrew Gurr.

In 1980 the Shakespeare Association of America devoted its textual seminar to the possibility that the F-text of *King Lear* represents a revision by Shakespeare (or another) of Q; in 1983 Jerome McGann published *A Critique of Modern Textual Criticism*, attacking the misapplication of Lachmann by Greg and others; in 1986 the *Oxford Complete Shakespeare* abandoned the eclectic *King Lear* by printing both Q- and F-texts. This two-text position is now widely accepted for *Lear*, and more general understandings of Shakespeare as skilled self-reviser are gaining influence but only beginning to be systematically applied to other plays:[1] the arguments are inevitably learned and off-putting to many readers, but the chance to encounter a dynamic Shakespeare

[1] Some Arden 3s include Q-texts as photo-appendices; the *New Cambridge Shakespeare* includes editions of Q-texts, many of which were also transcribed without emendation in the 1990s for the Prentice Hall/Harvester Wheatsheaf series 'Shakespearean Originals'.

rather than a frozen 'classic' is exciting, and readers should welcome the chance to read variant Q- and F-texts for themselves.

For post-Renaissance playwrights textual problems are of decreasing importance because versions seen through the press by playwrights usually survive and have authority. There may be more than one authoritative text—Shaw at various points produced heavily illustrated 'reading editions' with quasi-novelistic stage-directions; de Angelis revised *Playhouse Creatures* (Samuel French, 1993) for a 1997 revival, the revised text appearing in her *Plays 1* (Faber, 1999)—but editors can simply select the copy-text that suits their purposes, and readers (with a little care) can choose the version that suits them or read both/all. For plays edited or anthologized in translation there is also the need to select or commission the translation, a decision subject to ideological and commercial pressures; readers of plays in translation must always be aware of how (un)actable a translation is, and how difficult dramatic registers may be to translate (Racine and Ibsen have suffered badly). The major issues, however, are contextual: play-selection, annotations and supplementary material, and introductions.

Anthologies like Rowell's *Nineteenth-Century Plays* (2nd ed. 1972) are invaluable in making material available but inevitably privilege the few plays they select over the many they omit, promoting some connections over others; the inevitability can make readers and teachers complacent, forgetful that anthologies should always be regarded as cues for further reading. More worrying is the case of C. P. Taylor (1928–81), a prolific playwright who enjoyed national success with *Good* (1981) but wrote most of his more than 50 plays for regional theatres, childrens' theatre, TV, and radio: twenty years after his early death *Good* and one other play that reached a national audience are included in a posthumous Methuen volume for which no editor/s are named, but most of his work is unavailable. *Good* continues to receive attention (including a London revival in 1999) but it and Taylor can only be fully considered by those with access to deposit or specialist libraries.

A clear case of directive annotation is offered by Wertenbaker's *Our Country's Good* (1989), rapidly included in the UK National Curriculum and issued as a Methuen Student Edition in 1995 "with Commentary and Notes by Bill Naismith". The Commentary uses interviews with Wertenbaker and actors in the first production, directed by Stafford-Clark at the Royal Court, and all photographs (inserted between the *dramatis personae* and the beginning of 1.1) are from that production, though several letters to Wertenbaker from inmates involved in a prison-production she assisted are reproduced. Historical contexts are provided for the play, its sources, and much more limitedly for the Royal Court production; the Notes are "intended for use by overseas students as well as by English-born readers" but there is no account of what the Royal Court is and represents,[2] nor any assessment of the political contexts in late *Thatcherite* Britain which informed Wertenbaker's text and both productions. Many readers will sympathize with the implicit political stances of Wertenbaker, the actors, Stafford-Clark, and Naismith, but that should not disguise the facts that a particular (and in many ways narrow) line has been taken but is presented as straightforward help for students. However important the première, the play had by 1996 developed a rich stage-history in many countries: the reactions of other actors, directors, and audiences deserved some consideration, and could have offered sharp insights into both the play and its Royal Court production.

In general it might be said that editing is at once a great blessing and a necessary evil, from which readers benefit but of which they must beware: all editions and anthologies are ideologically and commercially determined, and it is as essential to ask yourself what is missing as to scrutinise what is present.

---

[2] It is the premier English venue for new writing and has radical associations; see the glossary entry.

26

Teachers and readers

Children usually first <u>experience</u> drama as performance, and for some the fun leads happily into play-reading with a lively sense of performative possibilities; but most people first <u>read</u> drama seriously at school, and though many teachers recognize in casting and reading aloud that plays require a different way of reading than novels and poetry, the reductive approach too often embodied in criticism and examining stunts the development of play-reading. There is also a regrettable tendency to treat (expensive) theatre-visits or video-resources as either authoritative or culpably 'unfaithful' to the sanctioned edition of the text, rather than variant possibilities. Religiously governed, socially conservative, and culturally isolated schools may have specific problems with teaching drama as performative, but within any such limits there is a great deal teachers and students can (but often don't) do to enrich and develop their play-reading.

The golden rule is that it is very hard to teach or read drama well while always sitting down and sitting still. Seated voices have flattened delivery, seated bodies inhibited gesture, and seated minds no provocation to calculate dramatic variables; a little unseating can go a long way. One fruitful, under-used resource is to graph or model different features of a play. A scene-by-scene (x-axis) block graph of the number of actors on stage (y-axis), for example, takes only minutes to produce but reveals dramaturgical rhythms, charts act-structures, and pinpoints soliloquies and crowd scenes (try *Measure* and *Coriolanus*). With Renaissance plays charting the distribution of verse, prose, and song is helpful: some directors begin by sellotaping photocopied pages together to produce a broadsheet text (one column per act) on which the three modes can be displayed by colouring and the changes from one to another can be seen in dramatic context. A plan of a Jacobethan amphitheatre large enough to accommodate up to 18 'actors' (paper symbols, plastic figurines) takes longer, but is usable for many plays and is of constant value in reading more complex scenes (multiple eavesdropping, inset-plays) where very different blockings are possible.[1] An amphitheatrical plan can be used in conjunction with a proscenium-arch plan to show how different the physical arrangement of actors must be in differing theatres. There is in *Shakespeare for Dummies* a set of 'play-scorecards' and a marvellous set of symbols for typical Shakespearean plot-devices and actions (including ♥ = Falls in love, ! = Consummates a marriage, M = Goes mad, ⚡ = Visited by supernatural beings, and ⚓ = Shipwrecked),[2] of real use in revealing patterns and comparing productions/texts.

It is also well worth looking at different texts. The advantages of the Folio have often been mentioned, but it is worth stressing that looking at even a sample page or two can be of real help. The automatic use of modernized texts promotes an assumption that school and university students will be hostile to (or unable to cope with) a photocopied page of an F1-facsimile, but our experience is that students of all ages are commonly fascinated to look at unfamiliar typography, and for reading aloud F1 is as performatively superior to a modernized text as the King James Bible is to the New International Version. A valuable exercise with any big speech is to read aloud only the capitalized medial words, which in F1 are often a stress-guide for actors and hence critically a perfect set of stepping-stones through the speech; it is also worth attending to the punctuation, reading not line-by-line but from major punctuation-mark to punctuation-mark (often colon to colon). Try reading aloud fast (as well as more slowly): faced with archaic diction and grammar there is a natural tendency to slow down, but Shakespearean grammar is often clearer if heard fast enough to grasp the overall shape, problematic words or phrases being returned to at leisure and then reintegrated into a rapid delivery. The man himself famously mentioned "*the two howres traffique of our Stage*"[3] (*Romeo*, Pro. 12), but three hours plus is now normal, and even allowing for the prevalence of *discontinuous* over *continuous staging*, an

---

[1] To whom, for example, in *Hamlet* 3.2 does Claudius have his back? Paying audience? or visiting players?

[2] John Doyle and Ray Lischner, *Shakespeare for Dummies* (Foster City, CA, Chicago, Indianapolis, and New York: IDG Books Worldwide, 1999), pp. 127–9.

[3] F1 omits the Prologue; we quote from Q1 (1597).

interval, and laboured stage-business, it is clear we now speak Shakespeare a good deal more slowly than he normally had in mind, mouth, and ear. Similar techniques can be applied to any modern playwright who has exercised control over printed texts: Beckett and Pinter both insist that actors be exact about their various pauses, and readers-aloud can also try to be so; the long and extraordinary speeches that erupt from apparently casual chat in Ibsen, Williams, and Philip Ridley (b.1964) are acutely sensitive to the timing and pitch of their component (non-)sentences; and many plays by Miller, Peter Shaffer, Soyinka, Albee, Stoppard, and others are rapidly revealed, when read aloud, often to demand (and to respond to) highly stylized, even half-chanted delivery. If even a few students in a group are willing to make an effort moments of dynamic antiphony (such as Richard III wooing Lady Anne, the final scene of *Lady Audley's Secret*, the 'chinkle-chankle' bits of Shaffer's *Equus*, or the 'As was' sequences in Soyinka's *Madmen and Specialists*) can acquire compelling dramatic tension with surprising ease, and will spark useful questions about stage positions, sensitivity to tempo, and volume.

Both for Shakespeare and for many modern playwrights film is also a potent resource, but of most help to students if scenes can be compared in two or more film-adaptations. The wooing-scene in *Richard III* is handled very differently in the films starring Olivier (1955) and McKellen (1996), and offers a very informative comparison of period-settings; the performances by Alec Guinness (1914–2000), Richard Briers (b.1934), and Nigel Hawthorne (b.1927) of Malvolio's authority-entrance in *Twelfth Night* (2.3.85–125) realize very different understandings of the man. There are fewer choices with more recent plays, but Beckett's *Not I*, *The Browning Version* and *The Winslow Boy* by Terence Rattigan (1911–77), and Williams's *Cat on a Hot Tin Roof* have been filmed twice. The great advantage of such paired films is that each achieves something the other lacks, and exposure to both usefully inhibits the tendency to treat the version one happens to have seen as somehow definitive. If you have access to a camcorder a little filming oneself also helps: in approaching a given exchange do you find at a particular point that you wish to film the listener rather than the speaker? Is a soliloquy more effective spoken straight to camera or as if no camera were present? A film of any length rapidly becomes a logistical maze, and too great an ambition is counterproductive; if things are kept simple significant lessons can be learnt while a good time is had by all.

For those who have never acted at all the simplest workshops, straightforward trust and warm-up exercises forcing a physical consciousness of self in relation to others, can be a revelation; simple *text-up* walk-throughs of a scene (whether in class or with friends at home) productively force readers to begin to imagine the physical opportunities and limitations of particular stagings, and if at all possible a production should be considered, especially with set-texts. If the resources to mount a whole play are unavailable can a scene or act be done? If some students are unwilling to act or for religious reasons prohibited from doing so can acceptable backstage functions be found for them? If Shakespeare is too daunting begin elsewhere (Beckett's *dramaticules* are handy: 261–2 >). Assisting with a production in any capacity stores the reading mind with theatrical knowledge, not least of the text that is heard over and over again: there is no better way for any group to learn about a play than to perform it. In marking university finals we have both noticed in *practical criticism* and *traditional essay-questions* alike that much of the best writing on dramatic texts turns out to be by students who have been observantly involved (in whatever capacities) in productions: quotations are fuller, more accurate, and better contextualized; text is not unthinkingly privileged over performance, nor any one performance over textual ambiguity; and the relative stylization or naturalistic qualities of dialogue are more often thoughtfully considered. It is not an automatic link—some actors and directors either think or write poorly, and some armchair-readers cultivate first-rate play-reading skills: but the keyword is cultivate. Such skills are neither natural nor automatically acquired, and if not acquired in practice may never be: as they grow the effort needed to read any given play decreases, but the simplest exercises remain of regular value to professionals and it is never too late to start using them oneself.

V

THEATRE TODAY

Another thing I found whilst performing the piece was the number of
people who asked me whether it was autobiographical [. . .]. To that I say
'what difference does it make?'

Claire Dowie, of *Adult Child/Dead Child* (1987)

27

The play-text since the 1950s

All canons are ideologically constructed; in contemporary canons it shows. With limited hindsight and partial experience of unresolved political debates, all critics inevitably project illusion as well as revealing actuality. That contemporary Anglophone playwriting has roots in the 1950s, when certain playwrights (Brecht, Beckett, Genet, Ionesco, Osborne, Pinter) began to make an impact on stages in Europe and the US, is easily agreed, but the degree of discontinuity created by that impact is moot. Given our concern with reading drama we choose to distinguish the continuing play-text from 'challenges' and 'alternatives' to it; broadly speaking, we believe that the political and aesthetic agendas, plays, and beliefs about theatre of the playwrights who came to prominence in the 1950s have been influential because they propagated three new possibilities of exploration: Brechtian epic theatre, social-realist theatre, and *Theatre of the Absurd*. These divisions are in some ways arbitrary—epic and social-realist theatre are closely linked; Churchill has experimented with all three at different points—and any identification or mapping of strands is complex and controversial. Our account, moreover, treats only Europe and North America. Despite the difficulties, it is vital to try to position all contemporary play(wright)s in relationship to recent theatre-history, and to read plays in cultural and socio-political context.

Brecht's epic-theatre project was developed in opposition to Fascism, at a time when Communism seemed a safe, plausible alternative system. No playwright or theatre-maker since has evolved such a coherently systematized body of theory and practice, and Brechtian epic structure, distancing devices, collaborative theatre-making techniques, and treatment of contemporary politics continue to influence playwrights and theatre-companies worldwide. His influence in the

West has largely been in particular acting-techniques and the breaking of illusion: a committed Marxist, he had utopian ideals, but contemporary playwrights using Brechtian techniques, if often left-wing and politically motivated, generally express opposition to beliefs or policies and tend not to offer any preferred ideology in their place.

In Britain Brecht's direct influence was visible in the 1950s–70s in mainstream plays by John Arden (b.1930, *Serjeant Musgrave's Dance*, 1959), Bond (*Lear*, 1971), Hare (*Fanshen*, 1975), Churchill (*Light Shining in Buckinghamshire*, 1976), Edgar (*The Jail Diary of Albie Sachs*, 1978), and in the popular plays written and directed by John McGrath (b.1935) for 7:84 Theatre Company, which toured to working-class audiences.[1] All these plays are concerned to expose injustice to an individual or community and seek to rewrite politics from the point of view of the oppressed; most represent a large sweep of time in retelling an historical event. Bond's *Lear* engages (as Brecht did) with Shakespeare as model and enshrined oppressor, exploring justice, tyranny, and violence even more bleakly than *King Lear*; beginning in mythic prehistory, it moves by act 3 to "the world we prove real by dying in it".[2] Churchill's *Light Shining* explores the fate of the Diggers, a radical group who established communal farms in 1648–9, just after the English Civil War:

> 1ST ACTOR [*announces*]: A Bill of Account of the most remarkable sufferings that the Diggers have met with since they began to dig the commons for the poor on George Hill in Surrey.
>
> 2ND ACTOR: We were fetched by above a hundred people who took away our spades, and some of them we never had again, and taken to prison at Walton.
>
> 3RD ACTOR: The dragonly enemy pulled down a house we had built and cut our spades to pieces.
>
> 4TH ACTOR: One of us had his head sore wounded, and a boy beaten. Some of us were beaten by the gentlemen, the sheriff looking on, and afterwards five were taken to White Lion prison and kept there about five weeks.[3]

---

[1] See Janelle Reinelt, *After Brecht: British Epic Theater* (Ann Arbor: University of Michigan Press, 1994); John McGrath, *A Good Night Out, Popular Theatre: Audience, Class and Form* (London: Methuen, 1981); Maria DiCenzo, *The politics of alternative theatre in Britain: the case of 7:84 (Scotland)* (Cambridge: Cambridge University Press, 1996).

[2] The last line of Bond's 'Author's Preface', first published in 1972.

[3] Churchill, *Plays 1*, pp. 219–20.

The functional speech-prefixes indicate that individual psychology is not a focus, and the actors emphasize their rôle as representatives of a social group. Events are narrated in the past tense, not enacted (a typical epic device), related factually as eye-witness accounts, and stylized in the registers of seventeenth-century commoners; the focus of the scene is the announcements themselves and no stage-action or scenic distraction is permitted. In the 1976 première such Brechtian minimalism was generally observed: a table and six chairs made up the 'set' and were placed at the side of the playing-area when not required; actors played multiple rôles and sat at the edge of the stage watching the action when not playing; scenes were composed as narrative units in their own right; and props were used sparsely.[4]

Playwrights deploy Brechtian techniques variously, adapting them to their own purposes. In *Theresa* Pascal melds techniques of narration and scenic structure with forms of documentary, physical, and dance-theatre, and in *Albert Speer* Edgar deploys many epic devices with great sophistication. Here Speer enacts <u>and</u> narrates past and present as he tries to respond to Casalis's questions about his friendship with Hitler:

SPEER. As ever, he kissed my wife's hand.
    HITLER *kisses* MARGRET's *hand.*
HITLER. Now you see, what I have always told your husband, dear Frau Speer. It is this love of sliding down the sides of mountains in the snow. These long boards on your feet—it's madness! In the fire with them! Please assure me, Speer, you will throw them all away!
    HITLER *holds out his hand.* SPEER *does not take it but speaks again to* CASALIS.
SPEER. And it was his face.
HITLER. And I believe . . . it is your birthday?
SPEER. And I looked at him—his sallow skin, his ugly nose, and thought— how could I not have seen?
    HITLER *smiles, pats* SPEER's *arm.*
HITLER. Well, then. Well, there is it. Well done.
    HITLER *and* MARGRET *go out.* SPEER *stands, takes off his dressing gown, puts on his overcoat.*
SPEER. And for the first time, the magic hadn't worked. And I thought: who is this man, who had meant so much to me?[5]

[4] Ibid., pp. 184–5.
[5] Edgar, *Albert Speer*, pp. 68–9.

The actor playing Speer narrates his past from a present as times co-exist, presenting himself as an old and a young man, involved with and detached from events. He is the grand narrator-manipulator apparently able to stand outside himself, deploying multiple stances and rôles which refract tantalizing questions about Speer's complex personality, numerous masks, and rôle in the mass killings at death-camps. The fictional impossibility of his narration, specifically under-lined at the play's end when 'Speer' represents his own dying and a meeting with an undead Hitler, mixes the real and imagined as frames of time and space collapse. The narrative complexities exceed Brecht's practice and are interesting territory for further experiments.

Modern British social-realist theatre is usually reckoned to begin at the Royal Court in 1956 with Osborne's *Look Back in Anger*: the prot-agonist, Jimmy Porter, rails against a dominant belief in Britain's glory, greatness, and moral superiority; derides class distinctions, the Empire, and capitalist values; and feels betrayed by a system which favours a privileged minority at the expense of a disempowered majority. Porter's bitter, brilliant rant, his destructiveness and self-loathing, touched a nerve with critics who found him an 'angry young man', a voice representative of a postwar generation alienated by grand rhetoric and grimly conscious of economic hardship and social injustice. Porter's verbal assaults were compellingly savage but also exposed as hypocritically self-serving a social silence long sup-posed a form of decency; the play is unwieldy, profoundly misogyn-istic, and now dated, but it is important to appreciate both that it once shocked and that Osborne (and others) passionately believed in the need for such shock. However, *A Taste of Honey* (1958) by Shelagh Delaney (b.1939) is far more radical in its politics and representations, focusing on a working-class mother and daughter, dealing subtly with issues of sexual licence, poverty, interracial relationships, single parenthood, racism, homosexuality, and maternal inadequacy, and giving its characters everyday verbal registers. It was performed not at the Royal Court but by Littlewood's Theatre Workshop, and the fact that Osborne still tends to be thought the more radical playwright suggests much about male-dominated theatre-criticism and continu-ing critical prejudices that promote particular venues and marginalize plays by women.

Social realism was also the preferred style of Arnold Wesker (b.1932), once popular but now rather forgotten; his first plays, *Chicken Soup with Barley* (1958), *Roots* (1959), and *I'm Talking About Jerusalem* (1960) represented working-class life, seeing mass education as the key to social progress. In *Roots* the heroine, Beattie, from a poor rural family, is depicted on a journey to articulacy and political enlightenment, and Wesker had more hope for change than other *kitchen-sink* dramatists. Playwrights such as Churchill, Edgar, Hare, Brenton, and Trevor Griffiths (b.1935) have actively promoted utopian socialism, and argued for it in critiquing capitalism; but Bond's darker views have been more influential.

Bond has for twenty years been critically neglected in his native Britain but is regarded in continental Europe as a major author. *Saved* (1965) became notorious for its brutality, particularly scene 6, in which a baby girl is stoned to death. For Bond the scene represented an inevitable dehumanization bred by the spiralling power-structures of capitalism, reproducing patterns of exploitation and abuse and creating victims who in turn become victimizers. The assault on the baby escalates over eight pages, building up to a frenzied physical and emotional brutishness:

BARRY. Gob its crutch.
He spits.
MIKE. Yeh!
COLIN. Ha!
He spits.
MIKE. Got it!
PETE. Give it a punch.
MIKE. Yeh less!
COLIN. There's no one about!
PETE *punches it.*
[. . .]
COLIN. (*throws a stone*). Right in the lug 'ole.
FRED *looks for a stone.*
PETE. Get its 'ooter.
BARRY. An' its slasher!
FRED (*picks up the stone, spits on it*). For luck, the sod.
He throws.
BARRY. Yyooowwww!
MIKE. 'ear it plonk!
A bell rings.
MIKE. 'Oo's got the matches?
He finds some in his pocket.

BARRY. What yer doin'?
COLIN. Wan'a buck up!
MIKE. Keep a look out.
He starts to throw burning matches in the pram. BARRY *throws a stone.*[6]

These men are aged 18–25: their pleasure in violence is matched only by their inarticulacy and ignorance as they express themselves in brief phrases or indistinct grunts. The baby is to them an inhuman object to be destroyed, the killing undertaken with ritualistic glee in a symbolic act of revenge for their own degraded powerlessness; all moral consciousness is lost in contagious deliquency of action. As hopeful social realism has faded many playwrights have exploited realist dialogue and setting while increasingly excluding party politics and overt ideology from their work, and the dramatic register Bond found in *Saved* has continued to attract imitation.

New realist plays of the 1990s were influenced as much by the salacious violence of film as by Bond. Kane was obsessed with pushing representations of stage violence to an extreme, especially in *Blasted* (< 164), and Ravenhill, Mark O'Rowe (b.1970), Anthony Neilson (b.1967), and Judy Upton (b.1967) have also repeatedly written scenes intended to shock. Some are coherent and powerful, and all repay thought; but media pundits who identified a new 'in-yer-face theatre' celebrated a violence that was often not particularly shocking, certainly not new, and seemed as much a belated attempt by theatre to compete with fashions for sensationalism in film and fine art as anything else.[7] The hype promoted certain playwrights at the Royal Court; other fringe theatres in London (including the Bush, Gate, and Soho Poly) emulated the hyped productions; less sensationalist work (at the Royal Court and elsewhere) was sidelined.

In the US realism was given a strong early platform by Williams and Miller. Blanche Dubois, the tragic protagonist of Williams's *A Streetcar Named Desire* (1947), and Miller's tragedies of the ordinary man in *All My Sons* (1947), *Death of a Salesman* (1949), and *A View from the Bridge* (1955) remain powerfully resonant, but (somewhat as with Bond) a particularly acidic realism in the work of Mamet has generated distinct interest and controversy since his first successes in the 1970s. Mamet's ear for naturalistic dialogue is extraordinary, and his use of

[6] Bond, *Plays 1*, pp. 76–7, 80–1.
[7] See Sierz, *In-Yer-Face Theatre* (< 209 n. 5).

profane and sexual language initially caused considerable offence to audiences. He first came to national attention with his one-act *Sexual Perversity in Chicago* (1974), which begins:

A singles bar. **Dan Shapiro** *and* **Bernard Litko** *are seated at the bar.*

Danny So how'd you do last night?
Bernie Are you kidding me?
Danny Yeah?
Bernie Are you fucking kidding me?
Danny Yeah?
Bernie Are you pulling my leg?
Danny So?
Bernie So tits out to here so.
Danny Yeah?
Bernie Twenty, a couple years old.
Danny You gotta be fooling.
Bernie Nope.
Danny You devil.
Bernie You think she hadn't been around?
Danny Yeah?
Bernie She hadn't gone the route?
Danny She knew the route, huh?
Bernie Are you fucking kidding me?
Danny Yeah?
Bernie She *wrote* the route.
Danny No shit, around twenty, huh?
Bernie Nineteen, twenty.
Danny You're talking about a girl.
Bernie Damn right.[8]

Mamet's dialogue imitates real-life speech patterns with great dexterity, resembling transcription, but the comedy follows a familiar double-act routine with Danny as the *straight man* whose questions and sluggish responses defer the juicy details of what promises to be a highly salacious narrative. The repetitions generate a comic rhythm and emphasize the pleasure the two men take in thinking about the transgressiveness of sex with "a girl": this opening implies that verbally rehashing the sex will be a form of easy gratification at the girl's expense, but the narrative in fact turns at the expense of Bernie who reveals that her demands became so ludicrously excessive he had to run for his life ("**Danny** Nobody does it normally anymore./**Bernie**

---

[8] Mamet, *Plays 1*, p. 47.

It's these young broads. They don't know what the fuck they want.").
In his first Broadway hit *American Buffalo* (1975) Mamet's comic timing was equally assured: he has subsequently become a screenwriter-
director of high repute, and his dialogue has the honed simplicity of
comic film-duos like Laurel and Hardy, turns reminiscent of music-
hall or vaudeville which conjure up Beckett's *Waiting for Godot*—but
what distinguishes him is a style that brilliantly parlays contemporary
idiom into a realist poetics, a feat many attempt but few achieve.

As the left/right politics of the Cold War have been replaced by a
more complex political landscape, many once silenced or ignored
voices (women, ethnic minorities, children, the disabled, unemployed, homeless, and mentally ill, war veterans, the elderly, and
HIV + /AIDs sufferers) have found in theatre a powerful means of political articulation. Albeit slowly, mainstream theatres and publishers
have begun to acknowledge a new diversity, and while white
middle-class males continue to dominate, as does a rather unthinking
realism, things <u>are</u> changing. More women playwrights have been
performed since the 1980s: Liz Lochhead (b. 1947), de Angelis, Prichard, Marina Carr (b.1965), and Zinnie Harris (b.1973) are all currently producing first-class work. Far more non-white writers also
have their work staged, in the UK notably Hanif Kureishi (b.1954),
Khan-Din, 'Biyi Bandele-Thomas (b.1967), and Pinnock, and in the
US, notably Amiri Baraka (Leroi Jones, b.1934), August Wilson
(b.1945), and Ntozake Shange (b.1948). Their work is extremely varied on the page and even more so on stage, but a common concern to
articulate suppressed histories/perspectives and insist on their truth
and importance leads to a prevalent realism, however mediated, and
renewed insistence on holding mirrors up to society, if not nature.

The third strand of 1950s influence is the 'Theatre of the Absurd', a
term invented by Martin Esslin in 1961 to group plays by Arthur
Adamov (1908–70; *Professor Taranne*, 1953), Ionesco (*The Lesson*,
1951, *The Chairs*, 1952, *Rhinoceros*, 1960), Beckett (*Waiting for Godot*,
1953/5, *Endgame*, 1957), and Genet (*The Balcony*, 1956, *The Blacks*,
1959).[9] They have as many differences as similarities, but broadly
speaking Absurdist plays distrusted the supposed logic of language,

---

[9] Martin Esslin, *The Theatre of the Absurd* (1962; 3rd ed., Harmondsworth: Penguin, 1982).

exposed what they saw as the meaningless metaphysical farce of human existence and the ritual emptiness of words, and represented humans as compulsively searching for reason in a universe known to be reasonless. Ionesco's *Rhinoceros* represents a world in which humans become bellowing rhinos and rampage through the streets; *The Chairs* depicts an elderly couple arranging chairs and playing host to dozens of invisible guests before they commit suicide, and ends with the indistinguishable mumblings of a deaf-and-dumb orator who cannot make himself understood; *The Lesson* shows a pupil slowly losing her command of language and submitting to her own murder. Ionesco, Adamov, Beckett, and Genet need, like Brecht, to be contextualized as writers who lived through the Second World War, and if their individual politics are less direct than Brecht's, their work is far more than aesthetic experimentation. Ionesco's rhinos, for example, symbolize the horrible transformations he saw friends and family undergo in accommodating Fascism, and his preoccupation with abuses of language, its power to kill, and people's gullible acceptance of viciously nonsensical rhetoric came directly from his perception of the hold of extreme ideologies in twentieth-century Europe.

Absurdist drama is in its nature blackly comic, demanding inventive design and considerable physical acting-skills. *Waiting for Godot* contains many comic turns, but the miserably failed attempt at suicide with a piece of cord holding up Estragon's trousers leads straight into stage-business about Estragon pulling up his trousers and the final exchange (< 46) is richly Absurd. In *Endgame* (1957) Beckett similarly exposes the empty ritual of living from day to day, the businesses of speaking and doing becoming nothing more than murderously repetitive ways of passing the time:

CLOV: There are so many terrible things.
HAMM: No, no, there are not so many now. [*Pause.*] Clov!
CLOV: Yes.
HAMM: Do you not think this has gone on long enough?
CLOV: Yes! [*Pause.*] What?
HAMM: This . . . this . . . thing.
CLOV: I've always thought so. [*Pause.*] You not?
HAMM: [*Gloomily.*] Then it's a day like any other day.
CLOV: As long as it lasts. [*Pause.*] All life long the same inanities.
   [*Pause.*]

HAMM: I can't leave you.
CLOV: I know. And you can't follow me.
   [*Pause.*]
HAMM: If you leave me how shall I know?
CLOV: [*Briskly.*] Well you simply whistle me and if I don't come running it means I've left you.[10]

Other notable Absurdists include N. F. Simpson (b.1919) whose *The Resounding Tinkle* (1957) and *One Way Pendulum* (1959) enjoyed considerable popularity, and the American Edward Albee (b.1928), whose *The Zoo Story* (1958), *The Death of Bessie Smith* (1959), *The Sandbox* (1959), and *The American Dream* (1960) created a sensation in the US.

Pinter's early plays, such as *The Birthday Party* (1958) and *The Room* (1960) also have some Absurdist qualities, but the early work of Stoppard owes a particular debt to the visual and linguistic experimentalism of Absurdist theatre, particularly *Rosencrantz and Guildenstern are Dead* (1966), *After Magritte* (1970), and *Dogg's Hamlet* (1979), which replaces ordinary English with a nonsense language:

ABEL: (*Respectfully to* DOGG.) Cretinous, git? [*What time is it, sir?]
DOGG: (*Turning round.*) Eh?
ABEL: Cretinous pig-faced, git? [*Have you got the time please, sir?]
   (DOGG *takes a watch out of his waistcoat pocket and examines it.*)
DOGG: Trog poxy. [*Half-past three.][11]

The square brackets and asterisks mark Stoppard's translations into unspoken English; the nonsense language is made comprehensible to audiences through actions, tones of voice, and context. In one reading the whole ludicrous business is an ironic frame for the 15-minute and 90-second versions of *Hamlet* performed at the end of the play: is *Hamlet* too simply a collection of words with which we are familiar? Has its overladen meaning rendered performances ridiculous? As an extended joke the play is in well-timed performance exceptionally funny, but has a pair-play, *Cahoot's Macbeth*, which celebrates the Living-Room Theatre (< 210) practised as protest in Communist Czechosolvakia, where Stoppard was born: the pairing suggests a quite different reading in which people have not persuaded themselves to speak insulting nonsense but been forced to do so by unseen, all-pervasive forces. Comparison with Stoppard's earlier, bleaker, and

[10] Beckett, *Complete Dramatic Works*, p. 114.
[11] Stoppard, *Plays 1*, p. 148.

better-known re-engagement with *Hamlet* (*Rosencrantz . . .*), in which the two minor courtiers whom Hamlet caused to be executed in his place pass the time and ponder their unavoidable irresponsibility for their own fate, also points to a darker, more political Absurdism in Stoppard's *intertextuality* than the comedy of *Dogg's Hamlet* initially suggests.

Two recent plays by Churchill, *Heart's Desire* and *Blue Kettle* (1997), again paired both in print and on stage, also make Absurdist structural experiments with language and form. *Heart's Desire* rehearses different sets of family anxieties around the much-anticipated return of a daughter, Susy, and the play continually resets time to the beginning before Susy has arrived, the actors starting over each time as if her comeback is too traumatic to contemplate. The effect is profoundly comic but the anxious repetitions gradually reveal troubling family-skeletons, including the father's sexual desire for his daughter, while in *Blue Kettle* Churchill replaces various words with 'blue' and 'kettle', at first intermittently but with increasing frequency, to great comic effect but again with growing bleakness as apparent absent-mindedness gives way to questions of euphemism, obsession, and dementia. As with *Dogg's Hamlet* meaning is clarified in production through emotional tenor, the actions and reactions of the actors on-stage, and in reading a very active imagination is required to comprehend the dramatic potentials.

Brechtian epic theatre, social realism, and the Theatre of the Absurd have influenced many contemporary playwrights in many ways, but provide only a starting point for analysis and contextualization. Each play must be considered in its own right: innovative writing and performance often resist traditional analytic approaches; the 'new' in its nature does not conform to expected conventions; and the most significant contemporary writers depart from traditions, melding old and new. Pinter's early plays, for example, weld Absurdist and realistic elements to create a pervading sense of inexplicable menace, a unique quality expressed in the adjective *Pinteresque*. He creates suspense and unease by placing characters in tense, mysterious circumstances they do not fully comprehend themselves, not through well-made plotting; his characters appear to have no motives and uncertain origins, can erupt into extreme violence with no warning, are often themselves filled with anxiety, and seem not to know why they speak or act as they do—but are depicted in naturalistic settings, usually a room in a house, and outwardly appear to live 'normal' lives. In *The Birthday Party* (1958) McCann and Goldberg, under the cover of a celebration, brutally interrogate Stanley, driving him to a breakdown before removing him to an unknown destination. Stanley appears once to have done something for which he is now punished, but it is not clear what, nor who the interrogators are, where they come from, or why they torment their victim in such a bizarre, ritualistic manner. The first meeting between Stanley and his interrogators, whom he has seen and avoided once in act 1, is at the beginning of act 2:

> MCCANN *is sitting at the table tearing a sheet of newspaper into five equal strips. It is evening. After a few moments* STANLEY *enters from the left. He stops upon seeing* MCCANN, *and watches him. He then walks towards the kitchen, stops, and speaks.*
>
> STANLEY. Evening.
> MCCANN. Evening.
>
> *Chuckles are heard from outside the back door, which is open.*
>
> STANLEY. Very warm tonight. (*He turns towards the back door, and back.*) Someone out there?
>
> MCCANN *tears another length of paper.* STANLEY *goes into the kitchen and pours a glass of water. He drinks it looking through the hatch. He puts the glass down, comes out of the kitchen and walks quickly towards the door, left.* MCCANN *rises and intercepts him.*
>
> MCCANN. I don't think we've met.[12]

Only five short, banal sentences are spoken but the body-language indicates an explosive subtext. McCann's tearing of the newspaper, a displacement activity, suggests he is waiting for Stanley but his precision ("*into five equal strips*") gives him a deliberation which bodes ill, suggesting he is nothing if not thorough in any task he sets himself. Stanley's behaviour, stopping and watching McCann, is not a conventional way of greeting a stranger in the house, and Stanley goes through the motions of conversation looking for an escape-route: his thoughts seem to be on an exit via the kitchen but the laughter from outside, and perhaps the thought that Goldberg may be there, stops him. His question "Someone out there?" goes unanswered while McCann resumes tearing; he buys time by drinking a glass of water;

---

[12] Pinter, *Plays 1*, p. 31.

the moment he tries a second escape McCann intercepts him and the victim is netted. Stanley knows he is in great danger, McCann that he will spring, yet their dialogue tries to normalize the moment as a casual encounter.

This clash between the spoken and unspoken is typical of Pinter, whose pauses, silences, and stage-actions can oppose and count for more than his words. In his *two-hander The Dumb Waiter* (1960) Ben and Gus are hitmen who have evidently partnered each other on jobs many times before, and are waiting for their target to arrive; both grow increasingly uneasy and Gus has a sense that Ben is concealing something from him:

> GUS (*tentatively*). I thought perhaps you might know something.
>
> BEN *looks at him.*
>
> I thought perhaps—I mean—have you got any idea—who it's going to be tonight?
> BEN. Who what's going to be?
>
> *They look at each other.*
>
> GUS (*at length*). Who it's going to be.
>
> *Silence.*
>
> BEN. Are you feeling all right?
> GUS. Sure.
> BEN. Go and make the tea.
> GUS. Yes, sure.
>
> GUS *exits, left,* BEN *looks after him. He then takes his revolver from under the pillow and checks it for ammunition.* GUS *re-enters.*
>
> The gas has gone out.[13]

Again the seeming normality/banality of the dialogue is undercut by stage-actions and gazes. Twice Ben evades Gus's probing but something momentous is communicated as they gaze at each other, as though Gus has read a horrible truth in Ben's eyes. The stage-direction "*Silence.*" is Ben's third refusal to name the victim; in the silence Gus presumably shows signs of distress and his subsequent assurances that he is all right ring hollow. When Ben sends Gus to make the tea he immediately checks his gun is primed, and Gus's ill-timed re-entry with a trivial complaint is a moment of grotesque

13 Pinter, *Plays 1*, p. 128.

comedy. Read against the play's ending this scene becomes weightier: Gus stumbles into the room stripped of his jacket, waistcoat, tie, holster, and gun; Ben levels his revolver at him; the final stage-direction reads "*A long silence. They stare at each other.*" Again hidden truths reside in their mutual gaze: did Gus earlier read his own death in Ben's gaze? At what point does Ben know he will have to kill Gus? Why do they feel compelled to act as they do? And who gives the orders to kill? The influence of *Waiting for Godot* is apparent, but the long-anticipated visitor <u>does</u> arrive, and a master/slave hierarchy is ironically played out in the double-act itself. Much of the power of Pinter's early plays comes from a complex, often oppositional dynamic between word and action which disrupts a surface narrative conveyed by the dialogue to expose the darkness, violence, and irrationality in the human psyche.

In contrast, consider Sam Shepard (b.1943), one of America's most critically acclaimed playwrights and like Pinter also an actor/screenwriter, whose influences seem not to be other playwrights, but musical counter-cultures, film, graphic arts, dance, and American myths/dreams, especially the 'Wild West' and Hollywood. Critics argue that he is astonishingly inventive yet lacks discipline,[14] and early plays such as *The Mad Dog Blues* (1971) showed the influence of free jazz-composition, while *The Tooth of Crime* (1972) borrowed from rock-and-roll. Initially, Shepard mixed the fictional, mythic, and archetypal with the prosaic and popular, as in *The Mad Dog Blues*:

GHOST GIRL: That's far enough.

CAPT. KIDD: It's the Indian ghost girl I told you about. (*He speaks to her in an ancient tongue.*) Santo lal gronto. Muchamo no le santiamo.

GHOST GIRL: Buzz off, buster. This is Captain Kidd's treasure. He told me to watch it for him while he was gone.

CAPT. KIDD: But I am Captain Kidd. Don't you recognize me?

GHOST GIRL: He warned me of imposters. And you're about as phony as they come.

CAPT. KIDD: Wait a minute. I'm real. I'm the real Captain Kidd.

YAHOODI: He is. He's the real one.

GHOST GIRL: Oh yeah? And I suppose she's supposed to be Marlene Dietrich or something?

MARLENE: I don't have to stand here and be insulted.

---

[14] See, for example, John Lahr, *Automatic Vaudeville: Essays on Star Turns* (London: Methuen, 1985).

GHOST GIRL: That's right, sister. If you don't like it you know what you can do about it.

MARLENE: Are you challenging me, darling?

GHOST GIRL: Choose your weapons.

MARLENE: Fingernails and teeth.

GHOST GIRL: Okay by me.

(*The* GHOST GIRL *and* MARLENE *square off for a fight.* MARLENE *takes off her boa and her furs.*)

MARLENE: Here, darling, hold these for me.

(*She hands them to* YAHOODI. MARLENE *and the* GHOST GIRL *tear into each other and fight all over the stage.*)[15]

A wild fantasy-scene between Hollywood icon Marlene Dietrich (Maria von Losch, 1901–92), a mythical Amerindian Ghost Girl who talks like a gangster's moll, and the Scots pirate William Kidd (*c.*1645–1701), also celebrated in films, culminates in a kind of imaginative mayhem which Shepard relishes, a spectacular fight parodying Western-style brawls. In one sense Shepard seems to take all Hollywood as a collective American inheritance he can mine and undermine, much as Stoppard has mined Shakespeare; in another the frantic energy celebrates only itself, and however entertaining is in the end as empty as the action is unreal. Shepard's subsequent career similarly defies easy labels: he has been resident-dramatist at the Bush in London and the Magic Theatre in San Francisco; engaged with Miller's tragedies of the American Dream (particularly in *Fool for Love*, 1979, and *True West*, 1980); moved strongly into film as actor (most recently as the Ghost in Almereyda's *Hamlet*, 2000) and screenwriter (*Paris, Texas* won the Golden Palm at Cannes in 1985); and produced one of the most high-profile American political plays of recent years, *The States of Shock* (1991), a post-Vietnam piece set in a roadside diner which premièred on Broadway with John Malkovich (b.1953) during the Gulf War. His preoccupation with the American West continues but has become more with the poverty and landscape of the modern South-West than with the mythic West of Hollywood, and shows signs of social realism as well as a continuing engagement with Miller. His greatest influence has been through his meldings of fact, fiction, and wild imagination, which have inspired the work of playwright-

[15] Shepard, *Plays 1*, pp. 318–19.

screenwriters such as Terry Johnson, whose play *Insignificance* (perf. 1982, filmed 1985) brings together Albert Einstein (1879–1955), Marilyn Monroe, Joe DiMaggio (1914–99), and McCarthy in a hotel-room, and Philip Ridley (also an artist), whose plays *The Pitchfork Disney* (1991) and *The Fastest Clock in the Universe* (1992) represent the seamier side of life in the East End of London as if in a distorting mirror, and most of whose characters are decidedly ghoulish.

In both Pinter and Shepard, dissimilar as they are, both social realism and Absurdism offer some illumination and orientation, and with Brechtian techniques continue to structure much of the contemporary theatrical landscape. Other trends can of course be identified and analysed: there was, for example, in the late 1990s a marked interest in science;[16] another great wave of attention to Irish dramatists, including Anne Devlin (b.1951), Frank McGuinness (b.1953), Carr, Martin McDonagh (b.1970), Enda Walsh (b.1968), and Conor McPherson (b.1971); and a notable Scottish revival, especially of women writers, including (Sue Glover (b.1943), Liz Lochhead, Rona Munro (b.1959), and Jackie Kay (b.1961). All these, however, are still very much movements in progress, and how they can most helpfully be understood remains uncertain.

---

[16] See for example a trio of plays from 1998: *An Experiment with an Air-Pump* by Shelagh Stephenson (b.1955), Wertenbaker's *After Darwin*, and Frayn's *Copenhagen*.

28

Challenges to the play-text

Play-texts have traditionally conformed with certain conventions privileging the presentation of a narrative, more-or-less coherent, and assuming its representation on stage by actors playing specific roles. Their appearance in print conforms with other conventions of dramatic layout, which vary in detail but have fundamentally changed little since the sixteenth century; their look and sound in performance fulfils common expectations about the way plays are staged. The possibility of challenging those conventions of page or stage has always existed,[1] but avant-garde theatre-writers now challenge them more often and radically, asking: What is theatre? What is a play? What is narrative? And what is an actor?

In Europe and America Beckett's corpus of theatre-work, from the first performance of *Waiting for Godot* to the première of *What Where* (1983), offers repeated interrogations of theatre and the nature of plays so brilliantly that it is difficult for playwrights seeking ways of challenging theatre-traditions not to engage at some level with Beckett's work. Initially he observed structural conventions: *Waiting for Godot* and *Happy Days* (1961) have two acts, *Endgame* one. Words are a major feature of all three plays though not deployed to serve traditional plotting or coherent narrative, but after this initial phase his experiments and *dramaticules* centred on reducing theatrical experience to its purest elements: the presence or absence of the actor's voice and body, sound/silence, light/dark, space/confinement, and the presence of an audience. In *Act Without Words 1* and *II* (wr. 1956, perf. 1957, 1960) the play-texts are stage-directions of four and three pages respectively, which map a detailed mime for a solo male actor and for two male actors; the television-play *Quad* (1982)

---

[1] See, e.g., Gertrude Stein, *Last Operas and Plays*.

similarly comprises three pages of stage-directions and notes for four mutes.[2] In *Not I* (1972) the actor is reduced to a "MOUTH, *upstage audience right, about 8 feet above stage level, faintly lit from close-up and below*"; everything else is reduced to an "AUDITOR, *downstage audience left, tall standing figure, sex undeterminable, enveloped from head to foot in loose black djellaba, with hood, fully faintly lit, standing on invisible podium about 4 feet high shown by attitude alone to be facing diagonally across stage intent on MOUTH, dead still throughout but for four brief movements where indicated.*"[3] In *Breath* (perf. 1969) the accumulated conventions of a Western theatre-play are reduced to a minimal schema that lasts about 35 seconds: a curtain rises to reveal a stage "littered with miscellaneous rubbish" with "No verticals"; there is a recorded cry followed by an inhalation of breath and increase in the intensity of light, a hold, an exhalation and decrease in the intensity of light, the same recorded cry, and a brief silence before the curtain falls. The 'play' is described in three numbered points (mocking a three-act structure?) amounting to eight lines; the notes take up seven lines.[4] Character and stage-action are non-existent, the usual aesthetics of set have been subverted, the actor has been removed altogether (the cry and breath are recordings), and any 'narrative' resides in the detritus on stage and the non-verbal sounds. Does the recorded sound constitute a spoken text? The cry itself is described as an "Instant of recorded vagitus" (a baby's birth-cry), and in performance the whole can seem a miniature life, a breath bracketed by the sounds of birth and death that embodies Pozzo's remark in *Godot*, "They give birth astride a grave, the light gleams an instant, then it's night once more."[5] Little of this conforms to our ideas of a traditional scene or sketch but despite its mocking miniaturization has often been presented (one can hardly say 'performed') in a theatre, where the experience of contributing to an audience's self-conscious silence for its duration is exhilarating and moving; it appears in *The Complete Dramatic Works*.

Pinter's earliest work, like that of Beckett, observed most conventions, but he was prompted by Beckett to experiments of his own,

[2] Beckett, *Complete Dramatic Works*, pp. 203–6, 209–11, 451–4.

[3] Ibid., p. 376.

[4] Ibid., p. 371.

[5] Ibid., p. 83.

particularly challenging narrative. In *Landscape* (radio-broadcast 1968, perf. 1969) there are a man and a woman who do not interact: "DUFF *refers normally to* BETH *but does not appear to hear her voice./* BETH *never looks at* DUFF, *and does not appear to hear his voice./Both characters are relaxed, in no sense rigid.*"[6] The narratives they tell may or may not be linked; they could be referring to one another, but when? And what is the situation now?

Beth
He felt my shadow. He looked up at me standing above him.

Duff
I should have had some bread with me. I could have fed the birds.

Beth
Sand on his arms.

Duff
They were hopping about. Making a racket.

Beth
I lay down by him, not touching.

Duff
There wasn't anyone else in the shelter. There was a man and woman, under the trees, on the other side of the pond. I didn't feel like getting wet. I stayed where I was.

Pause

Yes, I've forgotten something. The dog was with me.[7]

Beth's is a lyrical, ethereal, and gentle narrative about being with a man at different moments which haunt her (on a beach, putting flowers in water, ordinary domestic activities), and she frequently returns to the desirability of her own body. Is her narrative from the past? Is she describing Duff or someone else? Or relating a fantasy? Duff may be talking to Beth, but doesn't hear her. His more down-to-earth narrative is about walking the dog and a conversation in a pub, but includes a related confession to a lover of infidelity and culminates aggressively in an imagination of forcing a nameless lover to have sex in which the desire to "bang you" becomes a desire to "bang your lovely head".[8] Readers and spectators alike are left puzzling about the relationship between two figures who share a stage (page) but seem to

---

[6] Pinter, *Plays 3*, p. 166.
[7] Ibid., pp. 168–9.
[8] Ibid., p. 187.

inhabit disconnected worlds; many of Pinter's later works prompt similar puzzlements, including *Silence* (1969) and *Old Times* (1971), which ends with extended silence and two pages of stage-directions,[9] but he has continued to work extensively within established conventions, especially as a screenwriter.

The challenges to narrative and identity in lyricism (poetry/voice) and extended stage-directions (movement/dance) have cued many writers. Duras's *India Song* requires nine principal actors and 20 extras whose movements are specified in long stage-directions, but the dialogue is spoken by four recorded voices and what one hears as an auditor and sees as a spectator cannot unthinkingly be linked (< 107). In *The Hour When We Knew Nothing of Each Other* (1992) Handke recorded the passage of people by his café-table in a series of stage-directions without dialogue, requiring a cast of dozens of actors to move in silence throughout a full-length play. Churchill's *The Skriker* (1994), which releases creatures from Celtic folklore into a modern world, has "just three speaking parts, and the rest of the characters played by dancers, so that a number of stories are told but only one in words".[10]

A more radical approach is evident in the work of Shange, whose *for colored girls who have considered suicide/when the rainbow is enuf* (1975) has often been performed in theatres but began as a mixture of dance, poetry, and music performed in bars. Seven black women, specified by colour of costume, tell of significant moments in their lives, of trauma, joy, failure, success, dreams, desires, struggles, men, children, love, and families.

> *sharp music is heard, each lady*
> *dances as if catching a disease from*
> *the lady next to her, suddenly*
> *they all freeze*

lady in orange
ever since i realized there waz someone callt
a colored girl an evil woman a bitch or a nag
i been tryin not to be that & leave bitterness
in somebody else's cup/ come to somebody to love me
without deep and nasty smellin scald from lye or bein

[9] Pinter, *Plays 3*, pp. 311–13.
[10] Churchill, *Plays 3*, p. viii.

left screamin in a street fulla lunatics/ whisperin
slut bitch bitch niggah/ get outta here wit alla that/[11]

Shange calls *for colored girls* ... a *choreopoem*, one requiring dance-performance, a "theater piece" for which "Those institutions I had shunned as a poet—producers, theaters, actresses, & sets—now were essential".[12] Later choreopoems include *Spell # 7* (1979), set in a Manhattan bar for unemployed actors and musicians where nine friends use poetry, music, and movement to tell each other about the highs and lows of on- and off-stage rôles for blacks in America; *The Love Space Demands* (1992), performed solo by Shange; and *I Heard Eric Dolphy in His Eyes* (1992), in which three musicians and three "dancer/actresses" explore "the violence and lyricism, the incongruities and the constants, as well as the magic and limitations of Afro-American urban life and our music that documents our realities and sometimes impossible yearnings for peaceful, nurturing actualities".[13]

Shange has greatly influenced black writers and women, her works rapidly acquiring classic status for the way in which they rupture theatre-conventions to allow previously excluded voices to sound and be heard, and her different way in theatre has been heeded by many outside her own ethnic and gender-communities. Shepard, for example, worked with the avant-garde director Joseph Chaikin (b.1935) and musicians on *Savage/Love* (1981), a sequence of 20 poems about experiences and perceptions of love. There are no speech-prefixes nor any indication of how many speakers there might be, let alone a coherent dramatic narrative, but two poems have what might be stage-directions (*"face listens"*) or poetically stressed words (*"face"*), the whole was intended for performance, and it ends with a stage-direction, *"(Light fades to black)"*.[14] Shange's radicalism can also be sensed behind the polylingual multicultural work of Guillermo Gómez-Peña (b.1955), particularly the one-man performance-show *1992: a performance chronicle of the rediscovery of America/by/'The Warrior for Gringostroica' aka Guillermo Gómez-Peña* in which specified voices make statements of various kinds:

[11] Shange, *Plays 1*, p. 42.
[12] Ibid., p. xvi.
[13] Ibid., p. 160.
[14] Shepard, *Plays 2*, pp. 322–36.

Nasal voice with megaphone:

[. . .]

Columbus arrived in America without any papers
don't we secretly wish he had been deported right away?

[. . .]

Normal:

I remember drinking out of political sadness
lost between Mexico, Spain and Gringolandia

I drink from shampoo bottle.

[. . .]

Interviewer with French accent:

how exactly has your identity been affected
by your experience of Amerique?

Thick Latino accent:

to 'be' in America, I mean in this America
is a complicated matter
you 'are' in relation to the multiplicity of looks
you are able to display
I am brown therefore I'm underdeveloped
I wear a moustache therefore I am Mexican
I gesticulate therefore I'm Latino
I am horny therefore I am a sexist
I speak about politics therefore I'm unAmerican
my art is undescribable therefore I'm a performance artist
I talk therefore I am, period.

Interviewer:

c'est fascinant

Thick Latino accent:

in order to multiply the perceptual readings of my identity
I always try to create interference during the broadcast
verbi gratia[15]

In performance Gómez-Peña omits or adds sections at will; he states flatly that "The text is never 'finished'".[16] Though in some ways more like a stand-up show and often funny, *1992* is deeply coherent on political and performative levels and the publication of a text, however unfinished, is an invitation to other performers as well as readers.

[15] Levy, ed., *Walks on Water*, pp. 89, 92, 127.
[16] Ibid., p. 87.

The same is true of *Passione* (1993) by Laura Curino (b.1956), an auto-biographical one-woman performance-piece for multiple voices indicated in print by variant founts and display-boxes,[17] and the powerful *Adult Child/Dead Child* (1987) by Claire Dowie (b.1956), a "stand-up theatre play" about damage in childhood which "was written without gender in mind and can therefore be performed by either sex".[18]

A much darker impulse is evident in the later work of Heiner Müller, whose *The Hamletmachine* (1989) premièred the same year as the dismantling of the Berlin Wall. Müller's prefatory note is stark:

> *My main interest when I write plays is to destroy things. For thirty years Hamlet was for me an obsession, so I wrote a short text,* Hamletmachine, *with which I tried to destroy Hamlet. German history was another obsession, and I tried to destroy this obsession, too, that whole complex. I think my strongest impulse is to reduce things down to their skeleton, to tear off their skin and their flesh. Then I'm finished with them.*[19]

The text that follows has five sections; its words mostly seem intended to be spoken, but are often in capital letters; some speech-prefixes are provided but do not always make identities any clearer ("OPHELIA [CHORUS/HAMLET]", for example), and "HAMLET" is distinguished from "HAMLETPERFORMER". The multiple jumbled-jumbling statements from 'Hamlet' culminate in a bizarre stage-direction (*"He steps into the armour, splits the skulls of* MARX LENIN MAO *with the axe. Snow. Ice age."*) not helped by the earlier specification of "MARX LENIN MAO" as *"Three naked women"*[20] or the brief revolutionary coda spoken by 'Ophelia' as 'Electra' which follows. In one reading Müller is simply trashing with vandalistic glee a text that has obsessed many German writers since Goethe, and in having Hamlet kill a naked woman/Marx with an axe manages to offend traditionalists, moralists, feminists, and communists in one fell swoop; in another he may do all that but anticipates and forestalls objections with a deeper interrogation of the palliative, authoritarian rôles that high culture, sexuality, and socialist utopianism have played in German history and culture. When alive Müller gave few helpful answers and it is

[17] The English translation is in Lizbeth Goodman, ed., *Mythic Women/Real Women* (London and Boston: Faber and Faber, 2000), pp. 91–112.

[18] Dowie, *Why is John Lennon Wearing a Skirt . . .* , p. 2.

[19] Müller, *Theatremachine*, p. 86.

[20] Ibid., p. 93.

unlikely a text like *The Hamletmachine* can ever be 'unravelled' or 'solved'; its real test will be whether it continues to be produced or proves only a curio, an epiphenomenon of the general destruction/renewal that attended the collapse of Soviet communist hegemony in Eastern Europe.

The extent to which such challenges to the play-text have become a normal part of the mainstream is clear in the continuing career of Martin Crimp (b.1956). He began with such conventional plays as *Dealing with Clair* (1988), undertook greater structural experiment in *Play with Repeats* (1989), in which orientation in time is deeply uncertain, and reverted to more traditional structures in *The Treatment* (1993) but required conversations supposed to be spoken simultaneously to be printed in parallel-column.[21] He adopted a more radical approach in *Attempts on her Life* (1997), "17 SCENARIOS FOR THE THEATRE" for "a company of actors whose composition should reflect the composition of the world beyond the theatre",[22] which has no speech-prefixes, few stage-directions, and some passages in parallel-column or right-justified. Crimp again reverted to more conventional playwriting with *The Country* (2000), which also lacks speech-prefixes but is a *three-hander* in which most speeches can be assigned to particular speakers without difficulty. He has translated Molière, Genet, Ionesco, and Bernard-Marie Koltès (1948–89), and his confident movement between classical comedy, Absurdism, and his own varied work reflects, like Churchill's career, an assurance that the time-honoured and radical challenges to it can and should co-exist.

---

[21] Crimp, *Plays 1*, pp. 317–18.
[22] Crimp, *Attempts on her Life*, pp. [vi], [vii].

29

Alternatives to the play-text

Current *post-Modernist* trends in theatre broadly reflect interests in *interdisciplinarity* (the creation of dialogues between disciplines such as dance, music, fine art, architecture, writing, performance, sculpture, and film) and in radical explorations of space, time, and the meanings of spectating and auditing.[1] Outcomes may be expressed within a single medium or in *multi-media* work, combining, for example, live performance with film and recorded sound. Robert Lepage (b.1957) in Canada, Robert Wilson, Richard Foreman (b.1937), and the Wooster Group in America, Forced Entertainment in England, and Brith Gof in Wales are all notable practitioners whose interests extend and re-work the aesthetic agendas of Modernist experiments.[2] Their work may involve a script, though not one that is conventional, but more often than not only text appropriately describes the words within their work, which may be spoken live, recorded, or presented visually in different media. Text is merely one element of the work, not privileged above other elements or disciplines, and *interrogates* the interpretative conventions and formulae of traditional forms of theatre; it may be substantial or insubstantial, original writing or *found text*, but is not the main propellant of meaning. Audiences are required to work hard at reading meanings into the work, and as with a painting, sculpture, or piece of music individuals draw different meanings from their experiences of a performance. This difficulty in ascribing meaning to performance is a key feature of the post-

---

[1] For a good introduction see Kaye, *Postmodernism amd Performance*.

[2] See Robert Lepage, *Connecting Flights* (trans. W. R. Taylor, London: Methuen, 1997); Laurence Shyer, *Robert Wilson and His Collaborators* (New York: Theatre Communications Group, 1989); Giannachi and Luckhurst, *On Directing*, pp. 24–9, 78–89.

Modernist, which has been called "the unravelling of the *meaningful*".[3]

Foreman trained as a playwright at Brown University and set up the Ontological-Hysteric Theatre Company in New York in 1968. His post-Modernist concerns were typified in *Total Recall* (1970): fragmentary dialogue, mainly recorded, was spoken without inflection; performers were untrained and directed not to present emotion; furniture and props were suspended from the ceiling; and Foreman positioned himself above the stage, pressing a buzzer to mark phrases of action. He has continued to experiment with attenuated and accelerated stop-start action, striking images, and his own interventions and commentaries in a quest to break spectators' customary processes of interpretation, and he regards writing and directing a play as ways of interrogating spectators' *modus operandi*. His initial use of untrained actors represented a rejection of dominant assumptions about what an actor is and does (play a rôle in certain traditional styles). Training for creators of post-Modernist theatre is a vexed question for academic institutions, but artists such as Allan Kaprow (b.1927) and Claes Oldenburg (b.1929) emphasize that they are driven by desires to challenge modes of seeing rather than any particular discipline. Courses at arts colleges and new universities in Britain and at many higher-education institutes in the US offer programmes which give students foundations in a wide range of skills to create arenas for interdisciplinary performance-work.

Post-Modernist practices are still developing, as is technical vocabulary, and even apparently straightforward words become traps: 'performer' is preferred to 'actor', for example, because 'acting' presupposes certain kinds of actor-training but 'performers' train in other disciplines, some conventional, some not. In Britain there was initially a parochial tendency to polarize 'theatre' and 'performance': some post–1960s British practitioners used a universalizing definition of 'theatre' to define their opposition to what they saw as 'a narrow, bourgeois phenomenon of no interest to audiences'. But theatre cannot be so reduced to a single definition: there are a multitude of cultural forms and different audiences, and though the 'death of theatre' has often been proclaimed in Britain, interest in new plays

[3] Kaye, *Postmodernism and Performance*, p. 22.

and different kinds of theatre is sharp, though of course some types of theatre wane as others evolve. Such polarized usage never flourished in continental Europe or the US, and in general the word 'performance' now indicates that what is under discussion is not the received idea of a play at a theatre but involves other disciplines (though it may include aspects of theatricality and performativity), has a set of different aesthetic agendas, and is not restricted to theatre-buildings or particular modes of staging or representation.

Most Modernist dramatic protests in the 1910s–20s were performed in theatres to theatre-audiences, but in the late 1960s and 1970s the type of *actions* and *events* favoured by *Futurists* and *Dadaists* were rediscovered,[4] and much early post-Modernist performance drew as much on the visual arts as on theatre. *Happenings* and *performance art* were the two main manifestations: 'Happening' was coined by Kaprow in the US for a piece he created in 1959 called *18 Happenings in 6 Parts*, while in Britain the first Happenings took place during the Merseyside Arts festival in 1962 and were directly inspired by the work of Kaprow and composer John Cage (1912–92). Kaprow's assertions about Happenings have been influential, and while different practitioners espoused different definitions Kaprow argued that Happenings should be performed only once, take place in different locations, and treat time as discontinuous and flowing.[5] Kaprow's *Self-Service* (1967) took place over four months in Boston, New York, and Los Angeles; participants chosen from each city took part in as many events as they chose from those offered for their city, selecting the time and place for their activities and incorporating them into their daily lives; there were no invited spectators. Activities included:

> People stand on bridges, on street corners, watch cars pass. After 200 red ones, they leave.
> Couples make love in hotel rooms. Before they check out, they cover everything with large sheets of black plastic film.[6]

Some events overlapped, others recurred, and different unknowing

---

[4] See Goldberg, *Performance Art*, pp. 11–30, 50–75; Hans Richter, *Dada: Art and Anti-Art* (London: Thames and Hudson, 1965).

[5] See Allan Kaprow, *Assemblages, Environments & Happenings* (New York: Harry N. Abrams, 1966); for documentation see Mariellen R. Sandford, ed., *Happenings and Other Acts* (London and New York: Routledge, 1995).

[6] Sandford, ed., *Happenings*, p. 231.

spectators witnessed different acts. *Self-Service* could not with any ease be quantified, described or documented: it challenged notions of performance and spectatorship and did not require 'acting'; actions were real, could be carried out by any adult, and happened in real time, not illusionistic time-frames; diverse locations challenged ideas about space/performance, emphasizing environment rather than enclosed stages. *Self-Service* is itself but the challenges it presented to the assumptions it would overthrow are typical of post-Modernist practices foregrounding determination to collapse conventional boundaries and hierarchies of 'art' and 'performance', and of 'artistic materials' (e.g. oils, bronze, stone, actors) and 'ordinary objects' or 'real, everyday activities'.

Live (or *performance*) *art* also dates to early-twentieth-century Modernist experiments but developed in earnest in the 1960s, focusing particularly on the performer's body with much work concentrating on dance, and many disturbingly masochistic performances of self-mutilation. These were at first 'alternative' and often marginal, but in 1982 Laurie Anderson (b.1947) presented *United States* at the Brooklyn Academy of Music; its impact on the acceptance and spread of live art in the US was enormous. In a one-woman, eight-hour opus of visual, sung, and spoken narrative Anderson stood before a vast screen on which was projected a medley of images, from the hand-drawn to sophisticated technological visuals to operatic backdrops, interrogating the blurring of media-images and art.[7] Other developments include *site-specific* work, increasingly common in the last 15 years; it may involve a performance but is more likely to be a visual art-work made from *found material*.[8] *Installations*, often informed by technology and commonly *interactive*, also belong in the realm of visual art and have developed into establishment art-forms since the 1980s. Post-Modernist art and performance have been embraced in continental Europe and North America but the UK has been slower to absorb it; though the situation is changing, many arts-funders and mainstream practitioners are conservative about the need for traditional narrative in the arts and tend to regard post-Modernist practices as élitist.

One principal problem is how post-Modernist art and performance

---

[7] For a textual excerpt see Bonney, ed., *Extreme Exposure*.

[8] For the best introduction see Nick Kaye, *Site-Specific Art: Performance, Place and Documentation* (London: Routledge, 2000).

can be documented, for any reliance on the printed word or books presents considerable difficulties. How, for example, might one notate the experience of attending Cage's infamous 4′33″ (1952), a silent piece in three movements of equal length, at the première of which a well-known pianist and composer, David Tudor (b.1926), sat at a piano for four minutes, thirty-three seconds, shut the piano-lid during and opened it at the end of each movement? How do creators confront the problem of notating their own work? Cage's 'score' for his later piece 0′00″ (1962), a "solo to be performed in any way by anyone", is a single sheet with one short paragraph of instructions, and asserts that "the first performance was the writing of this manuscript".[9] At the other extreme is the extraordinarily inventive documentation by Clifford McLucas (b.1951) of Brith Gof's "site-specific Theatre Work" *Tri Bywyd* (*Three Lives*, 1995): called "Ten Feet and Three Quarters of an Inch of Theatre", it comprises 12 pages which the reader is invited to photocopy (enlarging by 200 per cent), stick together, and colour. Those who do finish with a sheet 1′3″ × 10′¾″ which has a time-scale on the upper edge, a ruler on the lower edge, and is horizontally divided: in the upper half are four parallel 'tracks' each devoted to one 'performance-unit' (three solo actors and a couple), much as each section of an orchestra has a different stave in a full score; in the lower half are assorted annotations providing clarification, context, etc.[10] The whole can be read as main text with running footnote or two texts locked in mutual interrogation, and with it we reach a point where the meanings of 'reading' and 'drama' exceed definition.

[9] Reproduced in Nick Kaye, *Art into Theatre: Performance Interviews and Documents* (Australia, Canada, China, France, Germany, India, Japan, Luxembourg, Malaysia, The Netherlands, Russia, Singapore, Switzerland, and Thailand: Harwood Academic Publishers, 1996), p. 17.

[10] Reproduced in Kaye, *Site-Specific Art*, pp. 125–37.

VI

EXAM CONDITIONS

TEST PAPER III

2. How did any *one* of the following differ from any one of the other?
   (1) Henry IV, Part I.
   (2) Henry IV, Part II.

5. 'Uneasy lies the head that wears a Throne.'
   (a) Suggest remedies, or
   (b) Imitate the action of a Tiger.

9. Why do you picture John of Gaunt as a rather emaciated grandee?

10. Describe in excessive detail
   (a) The advantages of the Black Death.
   (b) The fate of the Duke of Clarence.
   (c) A Surfeit.

N.B. Candidates should write on at least one side of the paper.

W. C. Sellar & R. J. Yeatman, *1066 and All That* (1930)

30

Practical criticism

Drama is set in practical-criticism papers but response to *seen* or *unseen* extracts may also be required in period or genre papers, and is likely in all cases to be a timed exercise (one hour is common). Briefer needs for practical criticism arise in weekly, assessed, and *open-examination* essays on dramatic topics, where time-pressure may be relaxed or replaced by a word-limit. Few students seem aware that a different writing-style is advisable in timed exams and word-limited essays, but when the need for verbal economy is paramount it helps to use active rather than passive constructions ('When Laertes assails Hamlet' not 'When Hamlet is assailed by Laertes'), to cut introductory clauses ('on the one/other hand', 'it may be argued that', 'it can be said that'), to restrict adjectives and adverbs, and to merge successive sentences with the same grammatical subject ('Estragon says X and does Y.' not 'Estragon says X. Estragon does Y.'). It is where technical terms permitting compact exactitude come into their own: you can paraphrase 'Ibsenite Naturalism, box-sets, and the fourth wall antici-pate the realist demands of film.' or 'He probably exits through a proscenium door.' to avoid the jargon, but it will take longer and inflate the word-count. But technical description is not an end in itself: you are being asked to write an analytical essay and the proper function of jargon is to underpin and focus argument, not substitute for it.

In this as in other things the practical criticism of drama is no dif-ferent from that of poetry and prose, and the general 'rules' taught in schools apply: where possible support points with brief quotations; attend to a range of issues or facets even if concentrating on one; make sure your essay has a beginning, middle, and end that form a coherent whole; if you do not know the work from which an extract comes don't make assumptions you can't support from the extract; be wary of giving 'accounts' by working through an extract from first line to last (rather than analysing thematically), for accounts borrow a structure from the extract and are acutely vulnerable to truncation if time is miscalculated; and so on. There are however two matters which in our experience are over-stressed in schools. One is the use of 'I', which is not forbidden, only restricted to where it is needed—including references to specific performances that you (but not your examiner) have seen. The other is the use of humour, where the rule-of-thumb is not 'No humour' but 'No flippancy': dramatic texts are more likely than poetry or prose to include passages of wit, irony, bawdy, and punning, none of which may safely be ignored, and all are ill-served by po-faced earnestness. There are also points specific to the practical criticism of drama which many students miss:

- Whereas poetry questions commonly involve two passages for candidates to 'contrast and compare' (or equivalent), drama passages tend to be longer and single-passage questions therefore commoner. Consequently *rubrics* (the wording of questions) may be more complex or impose specific requirements, and must always be carefully assessed.

- Drama passages are almost always extracts from full-length plays and suffer from topping and tailing. Examiners may or may not provide contextualization: candidates must remember that unless there is an opening stage-direction the number of different speech-prefixes in an extract does not necessarily correspond to the number of actors on stage—i.e. remember that other speaking rôles may be present but they do not happen to speak in the set passage; and that the presence of mutes (servants, soldiers, etc.) may be vital on stage but unrepresented in an extract.

- Remember to think about what actors may be doing as well as what rôles are saying. Stage-directions included in the extract may give specific instructions, but actors have to be doing all the time and do not usually stand still when speaking: even slight movements (a step towards or away from someone, a smile, a shrug) can significantly affect the sense of spoken words.

- In general, and particularly using performance-evidence, take great care not to *totalise* texts, theatres, productions, performances, or audiences. Formulations such as 'Hamlet says loudly . . . ' or 'The audience sees ... ' provoke the retorts: Which Hamlet? Which audience? At what theatre? Learn as a matter of habit to avoid them, either by specificity ('The 2001 RNT audiences saw ... ', 'Burton's Hamlet shouted the line ... ') or by acknowledging generality ('Many audiences have seen ... ', 'Hamlets often say this loudly').

- Beware anachronism: Shakespeare did not have a fourth wall nor Ibsen a discovery-space, and no original element of their texts can or does encode them; just as post-cinematic playwrights can be influenced by film, but pre-cinematic ones can't. This seems so obvious that one would think no such errors could be made, but we have seen both from otherwise very capable students, especially under time-pressure.

- <u>Never</u> forget dramatic ontology and register: don't attribute to an author words written to be spoken by an actor playing a rôle, and remember that speakers cannot be believed merely because they speak, nor taken to be speaking for anyone but themselves. The meaning of words written for performance is intrinsically unstable and English is very tone-sensitive: 'That's interesting' can when spoken easily mean 'That's very boring.', and though you can never be certain in reading how a line would be spoken in a given performance, you can take care to keep in mind the possibility of more or other than literal meanings. It is of no use academically to learn to read drama well if in writing about it you revert to treating it as if it were a novel.

Know also that in university exams it is becoming commoner to use early texts, especially of Shakespeare—another reason for making yourself familiar with the difference between early and edited texts, particularly with regard to stage-directions and punctuation for actors rather than for readers (capitalization, periods vs. sentences, colons vs. full-stops, etc.).

More specific advice is dangerous, for practical criticism is in its nature an individual exercise, usually without formal *marking protocols*, and a place for students to develop their own style. But this can mask unstructured teaching and it is clear to us both that many students have simply never grasped what they are being asked to do: so a checklist may be helpful.

- In preparation be thorough in acquiring jargon and background historical and generic knowledge, and practise timed work until you are wholly familiar with the contours of the hour (or whatever).

- In exams themselves be calm and thorough. If you have to choose questions glance at each rubric and extract to see if there is anything to put you off a particular question. Read a chosen extract carefully (subvocalizing or 'silently speaking' an extract once helps more than three faster eye-only readings), marking words, stage-directions, and speeches that strike you as critical, ambiguous, or otherwise of particular interest.

- Read the rubric carefully, weighing it against the extract: what are you being asked to do, exactly? Are there obvious or implicit reasons for (or pitfalls in) the wording? Trying to second-guess examiners is unwise but rubrics are usually devised for passages, rather than passages chosen to fit rubrics, and so may reflect a setter's knowledge of particular danger or opportunity.

- If the extract is ascribed and/or dated, or you recognize it and can date it yourself, marshall what you know about the author and the play, including any performances you have seen, but also about the theatre for which that author wrote, its stage-architecture and the conventions then prevailing, and how they differ from those of a modern production. If it isn't ascribed or dated but you can guess with reasonable confidence, go ahead: just remember that it is a guess, and don't use uncertain claims as a foundation for arguments or otherwise offer hostages to fortune. If it isn't ascribed and you haven't a clue, why so? Is it modernized? Or is it in translation, perhaps from a culture with quite different performance-conventions? Or is it not a performative text at all, but a closet-drama or dramatic poem? Look again at the rubric. If all remains blank you should perhaps look at other questions, but if you must answer consider treating your difficulty as itself a principal theme: to be so anonymous the extract must have some unusual qualities deserving comment, which may be deliberate and will certainly pose problems for anyone trying to perform or direct the mother-play.

- Read rubric and extract again, marking (in another colour?) points which now strike you in relation to the knowledge you marshalled, and calibrating what you read against the genres that seem to be present, the kinds of acting and/or delivery they might in one or another theatre suggest or require, and the demands of the rubric.

- If you find it helpful, draft an essay-plan, but <u>keep it brief</u>, using bullet-points or abbreviated reminders of particular issues: plans do not themselves earn marks, and though they aid well-structured argument anyone who has invigilated or marked knows how much time (and potential marks) some students squander on needlessly elaborate plans.

- Now write, <u>and keep writing</u> even if you are unsure of things: do not be afraid to state the obvious <u>once</u> but never be content with doing so; <u>never be afraid to change your mind</u> or admit to error or ignorance—almost all examiners will be more impressed by evidence that a candidate is thinking than by rigid adherence to a (misconceived) plan. If you get tangled up in a sentence or on a larger scale, <u>STOP</u>, work out where you've gone astray and the easiest method of recovering, cross out what you must (but keep it to a minimum: deletions are dead time), and start again. And if you think of a really strong point or well-turned phrase, consider holding it back for the conclusion (where it may be needed) rather than using it at once.

- Do not be afraid to mention another author or work, or quote a critical observation, but <u>keep it sharply to the point</u>: the 'rule' is not 'this text only' in a rigid way, but 'reading this text, now', and that may commonly involve mental comparisons, the only question being whether they are sufficiently helpful or interesting to warrant their use in a timed exam. Literary epigrams or aphorisms are common property, and too rarely used by candidates; but an apposite tag, used lightly or provocatively, is a valuable tool, often given explicit licence by setters who use it themselves.

- <u>Watch the clock!</u> The commonest reason for low marks in practical-criticism papers is short work, usually on the last essay. It's no good realizing with five minutes to go that you're only half-way through your plan: you need to realize with twenty minutes to go that you're only a third of the way through and adjust accordingly, shortening or omitting some points (tough in accounts), and with five minutes to go start to conclude, perhaps with a cracking formulation ready and waiting to take its place.

No one but you can get yourself straight-As or first-class honours, but if you digest and apply the assorted information we have given, follow our advice, and practise diligently, no practical criticism of drama, seen or unseen, should lower your overall grade or class. Much of it will become instead an opportunity to do yourself a favour, not least because the amount of poor writing on drama is staggering, competent scripts are more welcome to examiners than they should be, and good scripts readily command generosity.

Finally, some more abstract and personal advice, for readers to make of what they will. The most engaging photographs are not multidirectionally lit, but raked by monodirectional light that leaves intimate shadows and springs some features into unexpected association and relief; the perfect cutting of a gemstone is not an anatomical dissection. In practical criticism there is surprisingly often a particular issue—a word or stage-direction, a question one might ask at or about a particular moment, a fact about the author or the theatre s/he wrote for—about which many other facts and observations of all kinds will readily group themselves; an angle to employ, or the grounds of an argument, enabling individual points to relate without laborious signposting to an emergent, coherent view taken of the question asked. To find that issue (word, question, moment) fast takes a good eye and/or ear, but eyes and ears can be trained; what it also takes is the habit of looking and listening for it. Thoroughness is vital in preparation, but as the basis for a timed-essay plan has potentially serious limitations: once you have done thorough training of eye, ear, and hand, and are under a time-gun, don't be afraid when idea and opportunity present to trust yourself. Practical criticism tests a practical ability as much as a body of knowledge, and at its best is itself a form and style of professional performance.

31

Period and special papers

Drama, like poetry and prose, is often examined by traditional essay-questions (TEQs). TEQs may be timed, as part of *closed exams*, and typically contain a brief critical quotation or postulation which candidates must discuss with reference to two or three plays by a particular author or of a given genre or period; they are also used in open exams, often with more permissive rubrics, or set as course-essays (with or without a word-limit) which may be required for credit or more formally assessed. In the US Graduate Record Exam, for example, *multiple-choice questions* are also used to test knowledge of drama—but for those no advice is possible.[1]

For timed essays (usually one hour) in closed exams many of the points made in the last chapter apply: the economy of technical jargon, the need to scrutinize rubrics with care, time-watching, and so on. The formulation of TEQ rubrics varies from place to place and paper to paper: in Shakespeare papers genre-based questions are common ('Discuss X in any three comedies'), but in period papers author-based questions are often preferred ('"Z was no playwright, but a frustrated novelist." Assess with reference to at least three of Z's plays'). Past-papers are almost always available in university or faculty libraries, but an amazing number of candidates enter exams without having checked for themselves what sort of questions are likely to be set. It is essential that candidates answer the question asked, not one they would like to have been asked; revision should <u>not</u> involve learning course-essays to reproduce, but rather refreshing one's knowledge of the material used in those essays to deploy as needed in the exam.

---

[1] Every candidate should, however, know before entering whether to guess if they don't know: sometimes it's good strategy, but many multiple-choice papers have deductions for wrong answers specifically to make it a liability.

Examiners have many derogatory terms for essays that have clearly been pre-learned and do not answer the question; only egregiously irrelevant answers are formally penalized but no pre-learned essay is likely to receive high marks.

Given the variety of TEQ rubrics in closed exams more specific advice is difficult and dangerous, but a few points can be stressed. Rubrics <u>must</u> be addressed but do not have to be <u>agreed</u> with; disagreement should always be argued, not simply posited; if you think a rubric self-evidently wrong or stupid be very sure that it is not you who is missing the point. With both genre- and author-based questions remember it is perfectly allowable to make <u>brief</u> reference to other genres/authors to illuminate or clarify a point: many candidates seem very unwilling to do so, preferring to 'play safe', but the result may be narrowness rather than focus. Major points should if possible be supported by an *indented quotation* of several lines (two or three per timed essay is usual); there is little advantage in using longer quotations but much in a larger number of brief *embedded quotations* (a few words) and specific *citations* of particular speeches, actions, or exchanges; stage-directions may be quoted/cited as well as dialogue. Discussion should be crisp: candidates who begin with potted histories or sweeping generalizations ('The Renaissance was a very troubled time . . . ', 'Shakespeare is the greatest playwright . . . ') are playing for time and unlikely to impress examiners; but one who is exact, even in passing, probably will impress ('The first great English burlesque was Buckingham's *The Rehearsal* (1665/71) . . . ', 'Ibsen's London premières were, strictly speaking, private shows, but their influence . . . ').

In open papers and assessed essays candidates will be presumed to have access to texts, criticism, and reference books, so accuracy is essential. In timed papers some latitude is allowed for spelling mistakes, imbrangled syntax, and grammatical solecisms, but in open papers and essays all three may be penalized and even if there is no formal penalty a script showing such carelessness is unlikely to receive high marks. Totalising formulations are also liable to more severe judgement, and a much greater level of specificity about performance evidence would usually be expected, as a minimum the date, venue, and company or leading performer(s) with some quotation from contemporary reviews.[2] Work focusing closely on individual productions should be alert to any textual cuts/additions, as well as to set, design, etc.; programmes and advertising might also be considered. Filmed adaptations should similarly be scrutinized, and any documentation (interviews, web-sites, the 'Making of . . . ' sequences often included in DVD releases) exploited wherever appropriate.

Candidates may have to devise their own essay-titles, and many we have seen reveal a failure to appreciate that for examiners titles create expectations about the essay to follow, and are themselves marked. The commonest mistakes are to make titles either too general ('Renaissance Tragedy'), in which case essays cannot live up to them, or too elaborate and/or specific (the use of a long quotation, for example), in which case essays exceed or ignore them; some students also choose ambiguous or over-clever titles which may mean something to them but without extensive explanation mean little to an examiner. There is no 'right' way of composing a title, but the commonest form is a short, sexy phrase or quotation followed after a colon by a longer, precise statement of the subject ('The Shield of Order: Sir Walter Greg's editorial treatment of Shakespeare'; ' "O, o, o, o, *Dyes*": the textual notation of stage-death in English revenge tragedies, 1580–1614'). You should know more-or-less exactly what the longer phrase is before you start writing, but the sexy phrase can be written or chosen last. Remember that an apposite quotation which does not happen to offer a suitable title can be used as an *epigraph*, like the rubrics from *1066 and All That* prefixed to this section.

Some universities require the provision with longer essays of an *abstract*, a brief summary of the argument, in which case no introductory paragraphs are needed. If no abstract is required the opening paragraphs of an essay should state the subject, specify the major texts to be discussed, and establish both some parameters and the reasons

---

[2] The *Critical Heritage* (Routledge) and *Casebook* (Macmillan) series often include reviews when dealing with play(wright)s, and several series devote individual volumes to the stage-histories of particular plays, including *Shakespeare in Performance* (Manchester University Press) and *Plays in Production* (Cambridge University Press). For more recent UK productions the invaluable resource is *Theatre Record*, published fortnightly since 1981, which collects all major (and many minor) reviews of current shows; Shakespearean productions in or visiting the UK are also considered in regular articles in *Shakespeare Survey* and *Shakespeare Quarterly*.

for them ('Films are specifically excluded from the discussion of casting, as the audition-process and criteria for success are distinct from
those of theatre-practice'). This doesn't mean a first sentence must
begin 'This essay is about . . . ', nor the next 'I will consider playwrights E, F, and G': but this information should be clear to an examiner within a few paragraphs. It is a bad idea to begin with anything
too general, but good to begin with something specific and spiral out
from it, and the needs to provide an introduction <u>and</u> to begin with a
specific are easily reconciled: there are two levels of paragraph-break
('return + indent' and 'return + return'), and if both are used

groups of paragraphs (each indicated by indentation of the first
line) can be clearly separated from other groups of paragraphs by a
blank line (the first paragraph of each group is not initially
indented).

You can therefore begin with a specific example of whatever you
are discussing ('In Beckett's *Endgame* there is a curious moment
when . . . '); use the second and third paragraphs to establish why it
matters ('For actors and directors this poses a serious problem . . . '),
what you will discuss (productions A and B, film-adaptation C) and
your parameters ('Productions D and E are excluded, because . . . ');
then, after a space, begin again on the meat of the essay ('Beckett
came to playwriting late . . . '). Set out like this it sounds mechanical, and in some ways is—whatever exams may be, all require
candidates to jump through certain hoops—but it is important to get
beginnings right, and if you are stuck for a better idea this way of
opening will usually serve you well.

Without time-pressure dramatic quotations are expected to be
longer, more frequent, always accompanied by proper act.scene.line
references, and supported as necessary by foot- or endnotes with full
bibliographical details of the edition used; critical quotations are
usual (but not obligatory), and must also be fully referenced. Some
exam-boards specify particular reference-styles (usually MLA, MHRA,
or Chicago) and it is a candidate's responsibility to be aware of any
such regulation and obey it, but clear and consistent work is unlikely
to be penalized for minor deviations from a prescribed style. Many
candidates let themselves down with inconsistent or inadequate referencing and generally poor presentation, so a short guide is given in

Display box 4. Don't be afraid to make quotations as short or as long as is helpful, but don't use long quotations as padding (examiners will notice), and make sure you analyse (not summarize) what you quote and discuss fully what you quote at length. Do not, however, organize an essay around quotations, patching them together as a substitute for argument: it doesn't work and attracts harsh treatment from examiners. If quoting from a canonical work you may assume that examiners will know it and you should not summarize the plot (though a brief statement of context may be appropriate), but if quoting an obscure or recent work which examiners are unlikely to know well you probably need to give, briefly and cogently, whatever summary detail is necessary to follow your argument.

It is essential that all quotations be indicated as quotations and their sources given in the text or a note. Any failure to do so will leave you open to a charge of *plagiarism*, the deliberate attempt to pass off another's work as your own, and protestations of innocent error will not necessarily be believed or accepted. Some students associate plagiarism only with its grossest forms, the purchase of essays or whole-sale unacknowledged copying of published criticism, offences which in many universities are dealt with by plagiarism courts and can lead to expulsion; but any unacknowledged use of key phrases, specific critical points, or individual interpretations can be regarded by examiners as plagiarism, and in this matter you should always be safe rather than sorry. Some phrases originating in specific works become common property, but care is the watchword: 'mind's eye', for example, need not be attributed to Shakespeare nor 'epic theatre' to Piscator, but "willing suspension of disbelief" should be attributed to Coleridge (*Biographia Literaria*, ch. XIV), and "empty space" to Peter Brook's 1968 book of the same name. Even if such usage is not taken as plagiarism failure to attribute may be taken for ignorance and may earn a demerit.

Conclusions are not summaries of what you have already said, nor necessarily single sentences or paragraphs, but places where the wider implications of your argument are made explicit and general lessons drawn. A group of concluding paragraphs, each dealing with one implication or generalization, can usefully be separated from the end of the main body of argument by a blank line; and if you find yourself stuck for a conclusion consider the possibility that you have

DISPLAY BOX 4

The presentation of written work

Main text should be double-spaced on A4 (UK) or quarto (US) paper, with margins of 1"/2.5 cm. Pages should be properly numbered with arabic numerals in the centre of the footer. Titles of plays and books should be in italics (or with single underline),[3] and titles of texts that are items within a book within single inverted commas—thus *Macbeth* or <u>Macbeth</u>, but 'Tradition and the Individual Talent'. *Hamlet* (<u>Hamlet</u>) = the play, Hamlet = the rôle, and 'Hamlet' = confusion.

Short quotations (less than 2 lines of verse or 20 words of prose) should be "embedded in your text within double inverted commas"; longer quotations, preceded by a colon:

> should be indented from both margins, single-spaced with an additional single space above and below, and should <u>not</u> have inverted commas around them.

<u>Embedded</u> quotations of verse should indicate lineation by a forward slash (/) with a space on either side; <u>indented</u> quotations of verse should reproduce lineation; the lineation of prose need not be noted if there is no reason to do so.

All direct quotations <u>must</u> be absolutely accurate in words and punctuation. An obvious *typo* in the original can be corrected [within crotchets], or add [*sic*], meaning "thus", to make clear it is not your typo. Any other changes you make—e.g. replacing a pronoun with a proper name—<u>must</u> be crotcheted. The <u>only</u> possible exception to this rule is suspension-marks, which you <u>must</u> use if you omit word/s from a quotation: "Approach, thou beacon, to this under globe", or "Approach . . . to this under globe"; <u>but never</u> "Approach to this under globe". Many scholars now write "Approach [. . .] to this under globe", so that authorial/editorial ellipses are distinguished.

The first time you quote from a source you <u>must</u> give a full reference in a foot- or endnote, using a superscript or parenthesized index—[1] or (1); notes are usually single-spaced. The most complete form is:

Author, *Title* (Place of publication: Publisher, date), page reference.

Some style-manuals prescribe more limited forms (publishers are typically omitted); if in doubt the full form is safest. If there is an editor and no author as such, the editor's name replaces the author's and is followed by 'ed.'. If there is both an author and an editor put the author before and the editor after the title:

William Wordsworth, *Poetical Works*, ed. E. de Selincourt and H. Darbishire (5 vols, Oxford: Oxford University Press, 1940–9), IV.279.

---

[3] An old printers' convention: <u>single underline</u> = *italics*; <u>double underline</u> = SMALL CAPITALS; <u>triple underline</u> = LARGE CAPITALS; <u>wavy underline</u> = **bold**.

In the page reference—IV.279—the roman numeral indicates a volume, and the arabic page-number follows a full-stop; after a volume-number the abbreviation 'p(p).' is not required. If you are using a modern edition of an old work it is helpful to include the date of first publication before that of the edition you are using:

Charles Dickens, *Hard Times* (1854; Harmondsworth: Penguin, 1969), p. 236. All necessary information is usually on the title- or copyright-pages. For an article in a periodical, the form is:

Author, 'Title', *Name of Periodical*, volume-number (date): page-reference.

If the periodical uses roman numerals for volumes so should you; again, 'pp.' is omitted. For an essay in a collection the form is fractionally different:

Author, 'Title', in Editor, *Title* (Place: Publisher, date), page reference.

The plural 'eds' and 'vols' are contractions, not suspensions, and therefore take no following suspension-mark. An italicized title embedded in another italicized title reverts to roman type. Subsequent references to a source may be shortened to author and/or (short) title + page-reference and given in parenthesis immediately after a quotation—e.g. (Empson, p. 56) or (*Hard Times*, p. 56). Never use a short title unless you have previously given the reference in full.

When quoting repeatedly from the same source indicate in an initial note which edition you're using and follow each subsequent quotation with a parenthesized act.scene.line reference, e.g. (*Hamlet*, 1.4.23). Just (1.4.23) would be sufficient if no other play has been mentioned since the last quotation. Act. scene.line references used for drama are now usually arabic, as 1.4.23, but in older works you will see the increasingly archaic form I.iv.23.

If you have access to a scanner consider photo-quotations. For most texts they will not be needed, but if you are using a facsimile, for example, you should probably let your examiner see exactly what you see; illustrations of stages, scenes, actors, etc. may also be useful. (Be aware, however, if you have a word-limit, that in computer word-counts an entire photo-quotation will register as one word, and photo-quoted text must be hand-counted.) The sources of photo-quotations should be given as for any other quotation, and any reduction/enlargement specified.

Your *bibliography* should list in alphabetical order all works you quote or cite, and whatever other works you have substantially used. The form is the same as in foot- or endnotes, but place authors' initials or first names after their surnames to obtain a neat alphabetical listing and use capitals for surnames. Bibliographical entries should be internally single-spaced, but have a space between each entry. It can help the appearance and clarity of bibliographies to use a hanging indent (where every line after the first is indented), as we do (374 >). If your bibliography is long (more than, say, 20 items) you may divide it into sections, usually 'Primary'/'Secondary' works.

anticipated it, and see if any points you've tagged on to a particular paragraph or analysis within the essay could be moved to the end and treated in more depth or a fuller context. Remember that 'resolution' can mean either 'narrative closure' or 'optical focus', and that it may be a mistake to try and close things down or tie everything up, when all that is necessary is to see things clearly and say with well-earned exactitude what they are and how they relate.

A bibliography is usually required. Its omission may incur formal penalty, and any sloppiness of presentation, error, or omission is likely to be noted (we both know examiners who read the bibliography first). You should keep legible notes of the publication details of everything read in preparing work and full references for every quotation you copy down: there's nothing worse than last-minute panics where you go back for the book and find it's out of the library or have to go through the whole of *Hamlet* looking for one quotation. Details of organization and layout, etc. are given in Display box 4.

In many ways the real trick is to balance the various elements of your argument (historical background, textual and critical quotation/citation, biographical data, performance observation, reviews, personal contention) without becoming over-committed to any of them. Otherwise competent work is often marred by overstatement or poor formulation, so that, for example, a speech is quoted as if it were the key, a straightforward revelation of absolute truth to which all else must be subordinate: that may be possible in novels or poems but is rarely so in drama. Similarly, critical observations which appeal to a candidate are often quoted as incontrovertible fact: one may contain such facts but all (however acute) are interpretative opinions, not facts. With drama-criticism by scholars who are not theatrically minded and prone to reducing drama to text this danger is acute, but all critical quotations should be handled as contributory evidence, not achieved truth. In open exams there is little time for revision, so it is important to try to formulate well first time, but all essays should receive at least one careful read-through to correct any slips, and untimed longer work (term-papers, dissertations, etc.) should go through several drafts in which serious attention is paid to style as well as factual accuracy and argument. One useful test is to read your own prose aloud: as a rule-of-thumb, if you cannot make the syntax and meaning clear to an auditor with your mouth it will not be immediately clear to a reader, and should be improved (typically a sub-clause will need moving or cutting).

Especially if you are unused to word-processing leave time for proper proof-reading, making corrections, and reprinting. There will be errors, both simple typos and inconsistencies of printed style: there always are. Computer spell-checkers take a lot of the strain but have limited, idiosyncratic vocabularies, miss errors that produce valid words (pots/post, bard/bare, there/their), and happily substitute gibberish for sense. No existing grammar-checker is worth diddly; and punctuation-checkers don't exist. Use technology by all means; to rely on it is foolish. Be aware, also, that proof-reading is a different mode of reading, demanding sustained dis-engagement from the sense of the text; the more caught up by narrative, syntax, or rhythm you allow yourself to become, the less likely you are actually to register errors errors on the page. You may have experienced this in suddenly noticing a typo on a page you have read before: your eyes have passed over it but so has your mind. The hardest error to spot is notoriously a duplicated word at the end of one line and the beginning of the next: beware. (Did you spot it?) If you know yourself to be bad at such disengagement and tend to let errors through, there are two sure (but very time-consuming) strategies: use two proof-copies and have someone read each word and mark aloud while you check them; or read backwards, word-by-word, looking individually at each (you need to proof forwards as well).

Such reading, and the general business of knowing when your script is fit for your examiners, demands a sharper way of looking at the page than is common, but pays dividends. Remember that English offers you a system of punctuation both flexible and exact, which exploited properly will enormously help your prose: very many students are unable or unwilling to use colons and semi-colons, confuse dashes with hyphens, and stick clauses together using commas as all-purpose glue. You wouldn't ignore certain letters, to write without R, T, and D for example; but many people do that to non-alphabetical marks, which are just as important.[4] Word-processing and digital scanning have made careful, exact academic documents easier to produce; written work can easily be made impressive with title- and

---

[4] There is a summary guide to punctuation in Lennard, *Poetry Handbook* (< 1).

contents-pages, epigraphs, page-numbering, running-heads, photo-quotations, illustrations, and a palpable absence of minor errors—but too rarely is.

Finally, if you want further advice or help, <u>ask in good time</u>. Last-minute panics are no use to anyone. Don't waste good work with slipshod syntax, poor presentation, or careless error: they will always imperil a high grade. It may seem daunting, but with practice you will find you automatically formulate well and format correctly as you go, and examiners will read with generous pleasure the documents you produce.

32

Sample answers

These five timed TEQs and practical criticisms were written either during their authors' preparation for the Cambridge English Tripos 2001 or in the exams themselves. The questions all come from Tripos papers of recent years, in Shakespeare, Literary Criticism, and Tragedy; the answers were all written in one hour except number 5, which takes the Tragedy paper option of a single three-hour answer. Spelling mistakes and solecisms attributable to haste have been silently corrected, and the style of quotations and emphases standardized, but answers have otherwise been transcribed without alteration. Passages set for comment were <u>not</u> identified in the question-papers, but for the benefit of readers we have supplied authors, titles, and dates in crotchets. The explanatory note to passage (a) in question 4 <u>was</u> provided in the paper. It is coincidental that both practical criticism questions require the comparison of drama with another genre; such comparisons are common in close-reading papers, and it did not seem helpful to exclude these examples because their focus is not purely dramatic[1].

We do <u>not</u> offer these essays to you as models to imitate (though all are good, and served their authors well) but as illustrations of what is really done, and how. To choose what to write is also to choose omissions; you, assessing both question and answer, can step into an examiner's shoes to judge for yourself how good you think an answer is, what it achieves and lacks; to ponder what the question asks or calls for; and to consider how <u>you</u> would tackle the question, given one hour to do so. Whether you are preparing for similar exam-questions yourself or know someone who is, and whether you read plays professionally or simply for fun, it is interesting and helpful to

---

[1] For examples of essays specifically on poetry see Lennard, *Poetry Handbook*. (< 1)

discover what sorts of formal questions examiners ask and what sorts of answers students give. And it is to the abilities intelligently to enjoy reading and writing about drama that we (and this book) are devoted.

ONE

Q. *What considerations have governed the translation of passage (a) into passage (b), from novel to film-script?*

(Isabel's step-daughter Pansy Osmond has attracted the attentions of Lord Warburton. but he has returned to England without proposing marriage.)

(*a*) Madame Merle was very rarely insolent, and only when it was exactly right. It was not right now, or at least it was not right yet. What touched Isabel like a drop of corrosive acid upon an open wound was the knowledge that Osmond dishonoured her in his words as well as in his thoughts. 'Should you like to know how I judge *him*?' she asked at last.

'No, because you'd never tell me. And it would be painful for me to know.'

There was a pause, and for the first time since she had known her Isabel thought Madame Merle disagreeable. She wished she would leave her. 'Remember how attractive Pansy is, and don't despair,' she said abruptly, with a desire that this should close their interview.

But Madame Merle's expansive presence underwent no contraction. She only gathered her mantle about her and, with the movement, scattered upon the air a faint, agreeable fragrance. 'I don't despair; I feel encouraged. And I didn't come to scold you; I came if possible to learn the truth. I know you'll tell it if I ask you. It's an immense blessing with you that one can count upon that. No, you won't believe what a comfort I take in it.'

'What truth do you speak of?' Isabel asked, wondering.

'Just this: whether Lord Warburton changed his mind quite of his own movement or because you recommended it. To please himself I mean, or to please you. Think of the confidence I must still have in you, in spite of having lost a little of it,' Madame Merle continued with a smile, 'to ask such a question as that!' She sat looking at her friend, to judge the effect of her words, and then went on: 'Now don't be heroic, don't be unreasonable, don't take offence. It seems to me I do you an honour in speaking so. I don't know another woman to whom I would do it. I haven't the least idea that any other woman would tell me the truth. And don't you see how well it is that your husband should know it? It's true that he doesn't appear to have had any tact whatever in trying to extract it; he has indulged in gratuitous suppositions. But that doesn't alter the fact that it would make a difference in his view of his daughter's prospects to know distinctly what really occurred. If Lord Warburton simply got tired of the poor child, that's one thing, and it's a pity. If he gave her up to please you it's another. That's a pity too, but in a different way. Then, in the latter case, you'd perhaps resign yourself to not being pleased—to simply seeing your step-daughter married. Let him off—let us have him!'

Madame Merle had proceeded very deliberately, watching her companion and apparently thinking she could proceed safely. As she went on Isabel grew pale; she clasped her hands more tightly in her lap. It was not that her visitor had at last thought it the right time to be insolent; for this was not what was most apparent. It was a worse horror than that. 'Who are you—what are you?' Isabel murmured. 'What have you to do with my husband?' It was strange that for the moment she drew as near to him as if she had loved him.

'Ah then, you take it heroically! I'm very sorry. Don't think, however, that I shall do so.'

'What have you to do with me?' Isabel went on.

Madame Merle slowly got up, stroking her muff, but not removing her eyes from Isabel's face. 'Everything!' she answered.

Isabel sat there looking at her, without rising; her face was almost a prayer to be enlightened. But the light of this woman's eyes seemed only a darkness. 'Oh misery!' she murmured at last; and she fell back, covering her face with her hands. It had come over her like a high-surging wave that Mrs Touchett was right. Madame Merle had married her. Before she uncovered her face again that lady had left the room.

Isabel took a drive alone that afternoon; she wished to be far away, under the sky, where she could descend from her carriage and tread upon the daisies. She had long before this taken old Rome into her confidence, for in a world of ruins the ruin of her happiness seemed a less unnatural catastrophe. She rested her weariness upon things that had crumbled for centuries and yet still were upright; she dropped her secret sadness into the silence of lonely places, where its very modern quality detached itself and grew objective, so that as she sat in a sun-warmed angle on a winter's day, or stood in a mouldy church to which no one came, she could almost smile at it and think of its smallness.

[Henry James, *Portrait of a Lady*, 1881]

(b) *Isabel, choked with bitterness, turns to leave:*

ISABEL: Should you like to know how I judge him?
MADAME MERLE: No, because you'd never tell me. Stay, please.

Madame Merle sits on one of the little chairs. Isabel hesitates, then sits. Leaves thick on the ground around them.

MADAME MERLE: I want if possible to learn the truth.
ISABEL: What truth do you speak of?
MADAME MERLE: Just this: whether Lord Warburton changed his mind quite of his own accord or because you recommended it. To please himself, I mean, or to please you? Now don't be unreasonable, don't take offense. If Lord Warburton simply got tired of the poor child, that's one thing, and it's a pity. If he gave her up to please you, it's another. If that's the case, let him off, let us have him!

Isabel horrified: the strange truth, that Madame Merle's interest is identical to Osmond's.

ISABEL: Who are you—what are you?
MADAME MERLE: Ah, you take it like that.

Madame Merle stands.

ISABEL: What have you to do with me?

Isabel looks up at Madame Merle. Isabel's "face was almost a prayer to be enlightened. But the light of this woman's eyes seemed to be only a darkness."

MADAME MERLE: Everything.

     Later that afternoon in the country outside Rome.

Isabel's carriage and driver wait by the roadside.

Isabel's tiny figure in the distance, in the growing blues and purples and browns of the campagna.

Isabel walks in grove of tall, dark cypresses. A small wind makes a soughing noise in trees as Isabel walks in their cold shade, contemplating the ruins of her happiness. "It had come over her like a high-surging wave that . . .

Osmond had married her for her money and Madame Merle had brought about their union."

[Laura Jones, *Portrait of a Lady: The Screenplay*, 1997]

A. The first thing to point out is that passage (b) is not, in fact, a film-script. Film-scripts are full of technical information concerning camera angles and shot changes, as well as other material which makes them a blueprint for the film the audience sees. Passage (b) therefore seems more inadequate than, I suspect, is the case in the actual film. The most noticeable elision necessitated by the form of script with which we are presented is its use of quotation from the novel as a code for concepts which could not be translated into cinema. I will, however, return to this.

Taken as it stands, passage (b) is very obviously much shorter than passage (a). Not only has the third-person narrative voice disappeared, as well as the interior monologue, but the direct speech has been slashed in length, cutting out a lot of material, most notably any direct reference to Isabel's husband Osmond. Why is this? Films, especially adaptations of novels, often feature, if sporadically, narrative voice-over taken from the source-text. Less frequently, films feature internal monologue. The film-adaptation of George Perec's *A Man Asleep* preserves substantial chunks of the unusual second-person narrative, while the voice-over and internal monologue are both staples of the 1930s detective-movie.

Why, then, have narrative and monologue disappeared from passage (b)? The majority of film is set in a naturalistic environment. With a few notable exceptions (e.g. Jarman's *Edward II*), film sets and props undergo a far smaller degree of abstraction than, for instance, on stage. Film tends not to suggest, but to create, a broadly 'realistic' setting achieved by enormous attention to detail. And the desire for realism also, I suggest, accounts for the loss of narrator and internal monologue in passage (b), both of which devices accentuate the artificiality of a film.

The same consideration in part accounts for the drastic shortening in the length of the dialogue. Despite the naturalistic tone of the novel, certain speeches are non-naturalistic in a certain way. For instance, take Madame Merle's long speech beginning "Just this". At the start of the speech she says:

> Think of the confidence I must still have in you, in spite of having lost a
> little of it [. . .] to ask such a question as that!

Despite being in direct speech, Mme Merle is in fact narrating upon
her own speech, supplying an internal monologue for Isabel as to
what she should 'think' of the conversation. The effect is complex,
but relies on Mme Merle's voice momentarily supplanting that of the
narrator, and thus could not be done in film—unless Mme Merle were
suddenly to take control of one of the cameras.

More straightforwardly, the grammar of film, though complex,
cannot handle long, complex verbal text. Simplicity in storytelling (if
not in meaning) is the key. There is an apocryphal story of the interview process at the film school attended by Kieslowski, in which
interviewees were asked to outline how they would film the flushing
of a toilet. The very few who could convincingly describe such a simple thing were admitted. So, here, long speeches are eschewed in
favour of short lines conveying the pith of the original speeches. It is
also possible that the film-version reflects contemporary taste for
short lines riddled with subtext. One exchange in particular exemplifies Harold Pinter's doctrine that 'what is not said' is more important
than what is:

> ISABEL: What have you to do with me?
>
> *Isabel looks up at Madame Merle. Isabel's "face was almost a prayer to be
> enlightened. But the light of this woman's eyes seemed to be only a darkness."*
>
> MADAME MERLE: Everything.

This need for apparent simplicity in dialogue is counterpointed by the
alternative ambiguity allowed by images. Thus a certain obliqueness
of statement in passage (a) becomes textually clear but visually
ambiguous in (b). This is what I referred to when I wrote that this
'film-script' encodes filmic grammar through quotation. In (a), we
read of Isabel's reaction thus:

> It had come over her like a high-surging wave that Mrs Touchett was right.
> Madame Merle had married her.

In (b), we find the direction:

> *It had come over her like a high-surging wave that . . . Osmond had married her
> for her money and Madame Merle had brought about their union.*

The screenwriter imports text from outside the immediate extract to render the scene far less enigmatic than in the novel. But this is because the quotation functions as an instruction to the actor—imagine the instruction carried out in the film, and the cryptic enigmaticality of the novel returns: all the actual shooting script would describe is an actor walking through a grove of trees ('FX: wind')—with the sentiment, apparently simplified, having to be rendered wordlessly by the actor.

The above analysis can be applied to many other passages of the script—imagining the enactment of the subtext by actors brings back the complexity of the novel, but translated into the grammar of film.

Tom Perrin

TWO

Q. *"Shakespeare's comic heroines show us how to regard ourselves as other." Discuss.*

A. It has been argued that female rôles in Shakespeare necessarily represent the 'other' since Shakespeare, as a man, wrote the self into his male protagonists. It is true that female rôles do provide an 'other' to central male rôles. They may provide off-centre parallels with a twist to the male point of view (as Ophelia's madness, a possible bid for freedom, is said to parallel Hamlet's playing for freedom in his feigned madness) or direct contrasts to characteristics of the male rôle. Shakespearean comic heroines often teach their male counterparts how to view themselves as 'other' by presenting them with an image of themselves. They also teach the audience the possibilities of being 'other' in the fluidity shown in their characters when they use disguise.

Viola, in *Twelfth Night*, is an example of a female foil to a male rôle. She suffers her love for Orsino in silence, revealing it early in the play to the audience only:

> Yet a barful strife!
> Whoe'er I woo, myself would be his wife.

providing an 'other', in fact an opposite, to Orsino's self-indulgent overdramatised love, long-windedly expressed in the first fifteen lines of the play: "If music be the food of love, play on, [. . .]".

In *Love's Labour's Lost* the Princess's sympathetic attitude to the actors in the pageant in 5.2—'Alas, poor Maccabeus, how he hath been baited'—provides a contrast to the mocking behaviour of the King and his lords. But as well as providing this contrast to the audience, the women in this play seek to teach the men how to be other. They tailor their lesson to their pupils and, by playing a trick—disguising themselves as each other—to mirror the men's trick—disguising themselves as Muscovites—they force the men to view trickery from the point of view of the victims—to regard themselves, tricksters, as other. The moral of this lesson is made explicit in the final scene of the play when Rosaline tells Berowne 'A jest's prosperity lies in the ear / Of him that hears it, never in the tongue / Of him that makes it', so that Berowne must learn to position himself as 'the ear', the other to 'the tongue' he has so far played.

It has been well observed how Rosalind uses her disguise as Ganymede to teach Orlando about love. Again, she does this by presenting to him an other, male construction of the feminine as "changeable, longing and liking, proud, fantastical, apish, shallow, inconstant, full of tears, full of smiles". By presenting them in this unusual frame—a male, Ganymede, playing a woman (and to the audience even more complex—Ganymede being played by Rosalind who, in Elizabethan theatre, would have been played by a boy)—she enables Orlando to take another point of view and to see the limitations of these constructions.

Rosalind's disguise also teaches the audience 'how to regard ourselves as other' by being a demonstration of her ability to be other. Within the guise there is the fluidity of character in Ganymede's presentations of Rosalind. Within the rôle of Rosalind is the fluidity of a woman who can dress, and play, the male rôle. In the performance of the Elizabethan boy-actor is the demonstration of a boy's ability to play a rôle of fluid gender and temperament, or to play many rôles and be fluid in moving from one to an-other. This is made obvious in the epilogue in "If I were a woman, I would kiss as many of you as had beards that pleas'd me, complexions that lik'd me, and breaths that I defied not."

Other cross-dressing comic heroines make this demonstration.

They often make other alterations to their character to demonstrate the possibility in disguise for one to be an-other. In *The Merchant of Venice*, Portia is a fake doctor, influenced by the Commedia character *Il Dottore* (of false learning). Viola in *Twelfth Night* has a sword but proves, in male terms, a coward when drawn into a fight with Sir Andrew. As a false man she is also a false soldier echoing the Commedia rôle of *Il Capitano*.

Viola's disguise is deliberately intended to place her in society as an-other to what she would be. She takes it on as a protection from the fact that she is a woman in a strange land and takes on the name Cesario, meaning 'of Caesar' and therefore protected. However this also derives (as 'Caesar' does) from *caesus*, to cut, and signifies Viola's taking on of the rôle of an eunuch and initially placing herself as outside, and other to, the romantic interactions of the plot.

Disguise is probably the most significant way in which Shakespeare's comic heroines 'show us how to regard ourselves as other', as their use of it demonstrates the fluidity of rôles one can have—one's ability to be other. (The transformation of Katherina in *The Taming of the Shrew* is a demonstration of this fluidity without disguise.) Disguise is one way of presenting a twist to the point of view, something female characters sometimes do deliberately in teaching male characters, and something they can also do merely through their presence on stage!

Jacinta Lawrey

THREE

Q. *Write a general essay on Shakespeare giving your view of his sense of tragedy.*

A. Generic essentialism which rigidly divides between genres is perhaps naïve. It is my contention that Shakespeare's sense of tragedy is intimately engaged with his sense of the comic. Ruskin claimed that 'Comedy is Tragedy if looked at closely enough' and many of Shakespeare's tragic protagonists may be seen as exposures of the tragic inhering in the comic. For this reason, analysis will not be limited to the tragedies themselves. I would argue that the tragic can be traced through Shakespeare's insistence on characters being denied the postures and identities they propose for themselves. This can be best explored through a sequential examination of specific texts.

Within the comic wrangling of *Love's Labour's Lost* there is, perhaps, a whisper of the mature comic sense. The news of the death of the King of France interrupts the process of romantic alignment. Berowne laments, 'our wooing doth not end like an old play / Jack hath not Jill'. The King of Navarre may reassure that the delay is but a year, but Berowne regrets 'that's too long for a play'. This sense of a discomforting of comic anticipation and a disorientation of the character's self-proposed identity (in this instance, successful wooer) is arguably central to Shakespeare's tragic sense.

It is, perhaps, most interestingly developed within Shylock in *The Merchant of Venice*. Shylock is, from one perspective, the *senex* of classical comedy. He has an eloping daughter (Jessica) and his attachment to the 'law of Venice' echoes the appeals of other comic fathers (witness Egeus's claims on 'the law of Athens' in *Midsummer Night's Dream*). The pound of flesh, however, is provocatively the tragic *in potentia*. Bassanio notes that Antonio has engaged to 'feed my means', and Shylock would 'feed my revenge' and 'feed fat the ancient grudge I bear him'. This identification with feeding, aside from evoking the predator-creditor caricature of Jewry, gives the pound of flesh the savour of the Eucharist. It acquires a symbolic gravitas. Shylock's deprival of it occurs through the quintessential mechanism of comedy, the quibble, but simultaneously generates a tragic disfunction. Shylock's attachment to 'my bond' and his rejection of mitigating acts of mercy, because they are not 'nominated' in the bond, reflects, from a Saussurean perspective, a rigid attachment to the integrity of *signifier* and *referant*. It is a rigidity which, from the Bergsonian perspective, is the quintessential target of comedy. He exhibits *raideur* or an 'inelasticity of character' and a 'separatist tendency'. Portia's division between 'flesh' and 'blood' is at once a *reductio ad absurdam* of this rigidity and the operation of comic inversion. It is a semantic enactment of the 'turnabout' ot 'topsy-turvy' freedoms of the 'carnivalesque', identified by Bakhtin.

Shylock's comic *raideur* is tragic, however, exactly because we sense his refusal to be assimilated into the fluid interchange of comic possibilities. While the Duke stipulates that he 'presently become a Christian' he is not a comic villain who, like Oliver in *As You Like It*, can say of a past, criminal self '"Twas I, but 'tis not I'. Such a juggling of identities is his daughter's romance prerogative. She can hope to 'Become a Christian, and thy loving wife'. However, Shylock, in a manner comparable to Berowne, is denied his <u>generic</u> identity. His tragic bond is carnivalised and, looking to a different genre, he too might say that his enterprise does not 'end like an old play'.

The notion that Shakespeare's <u>tragic</u> sense paradoxically lies in the pain by which the <u>comic</u> robs characters of the decorum of a comprehensible and anticipated posture is seen equally in *King Lear*. On the heath Lear plucks at his skin, crying '"Twas this flesh begot / Those Pelican daughters'. Poor Tom immediately interjects 'Pillicock sat on Pillicock hill / Alow, alow, loo, loo'. Just as Shylock's bond is comically inverted, Lear's attempt at tragic self-definition is violated by a quibble. The 'Pelican' is a common trope for Christ (witness the blazon of Corpus Christi College). Lear's Pelican offers a potential decorum, a conventional tragic posture which can be inhabited. Shakespeare's tragic sense, however, is seen exactly in the denial of this decorum. The Pelican is degraded to a Pillicock, the body of Christ becomes a phallic pun. Lear's pain truly is that of 'unaccomodated man'—of a comic *senex* displaced into a tragic universe and repeatedly humiliated in his attempts to find a tragic grandeur.

Extending into the Roman plays, this sense of tragedy can equally be seen to be operative. Antony seeks to define himself as a martial hero. He scorns Caesar for his perpetual use of troops rather than personal combat ('he alone | Dealt on lieutenantry'). He longs for the grandeur of personal combat ('sword against sword / Ourselves alone') and yet he is repeatedly denied such martial self-realisation. His speeches imagine the heroic body as autonomously operative. He protests, for example, that he 'quarter'd the globe' with 'my sword'. The reality, however, as one of his officers concedes, is that 'Caesar and Antony have ever won / More in their officer than person'. Reporting that Caesar has rejected the offer of hand-to-hand combat, Enobarbus wonders how Antony can 'dream / Knowing all measures, that the full Caesar / Will answer his emptiness'. Antony's Rome is a geopolity defined by 'ships, coins, legions'. The 'full Caesar''s logistical pre-eminence translates into a density of being—fullness.

Identity is socially contingent. Antony, like Berowne, Shylock, and Lear, finds himself disoriented—seeking a posture which circumstances deny him. The tragedy is his emptiness, his inability to eclipse himself with 'tragic' decorum and his reduction to being hauled about because his embarrassed body is neither dead nor alive, but dawdling somewhere in between. Having seen, in *Julius Caesar*, his heroic counterpoints eclipse themselves in rapid succession, he may well wonder, like Berowne, why he can't end himself 'like an old play'.

This attempt to proffer one vision of Shakespeare's tragic sense is necessarily partial, but it points to a 'sense' in which comic incongruity and tragic disorientation are fruitfully involuted.

Jamie McClelland

FOUR

Q. *'Coarseness is not always stupid.' Examine and discuss these two pieces of writing (the poem is complete).*

(a)   Cordelia. Was ever such an insipid piece of antiquity? Pray, Sir, forbear these impertinences, and assure your self I hate an old fellow for a husband, as much as an old gown, or an old piece of wit, that after forty years oblivion, with a new name, is publist for a new *Lenten* play.

   Fumble. What does she say now? But no matter, I'll go on. Well, said, Bird, well said. *Bona fide*, thou hast wit in abundance; that colour, and such a sort of nose, never fail. But come, we lose time, I know 'tis ordain'd I must marry thee. I am the man that must gather the rosebuds.—Ah Rogue!—I'll warrant thou'rt a swinger and Ifack that black a top there fires me strangely. I am all flame, and *bona fide*, me thinks as youthful and mercurial as any spark of 'em all.

SONG.
And he took her by the middle small,
And laid her on the plain;
With a hey down derry down, come diddle,
With a ho down derry, &c.

What think you, Madam? Am I old?

Cordelia. So old, that your presence is more terrible than a deaths-head at supper. For my part I tremble all over. There's a kind of horrour in all your antick gestures; 'specially those that you think become you, that fright worse than the Devil; (*Aloud*) than the Devil, Sir.

Fumble. The Devil! What of him, Bird? Pish, the Devil's an Ass, I ha' seen't in a play; and ifack we lose time talking about so worthless a matter. Lovers should ne'er be slow in their affairs. For, as my good friend *Randolph* tells me, nothing is like opportunity taken in the nick; in the nick, Sweet-heart!— *Icod*, I was waggish again, I was waggish agen ifack.—Come, Bird, come.

Cordelia. What will you do, Sir? Heav'n, how he tortures me!

Fumble. Come along then.—I have got a priest ready, and paid for the licence and all.—Prethee let me kiss thee; I long to practise something that might please thee. Never was man so alter'd! Never! Come, prethee Bird.— Come; ifack I have not patience.

Enter Governess *and Sir* Roger.

Governess. Here's Sir *Roger Petulant*, my dear mouse, desires to speak a word or two with you.

Cordelia. Oh here's some hope of deliverance! Sir *Roger*, your humble servant. Come hither, *Lettice*, and stand just in my place. I am so tortur'd with this old fellow—Prethee be kind to him, and follow him whither he'd have thee; it may be a husband in thy way, and a good estate.

Governess. A husband! Marry that's fine! I warrant you, sweet mouse, I'll be very punctual.

Cordelia. So, now let us slip aside and observe; 'twould be an excellent revenge if he shou'd marry her.—He's coming to her already, and his eyes are so old and dim that he perceives not his mistake. (*They step aside.*)

Fumble. Delays, Sweet-heart, are dang'rous ifack; I have consider'd it. The time I have liv'd in the world has given me the benefit of knowing more than another of fewer minutes.—Along, along—I say, thou shalt be my queen, my paramour, my *Cleopatra*, and I will live another age in love, and then farewel old *Simon*, ifack. Come, come along.

[ifack: commonplace substitution for *in faith*]

[Thomas D'Urfey, *A Fond Husband*, 1677]

(*b*)   *A Song of a Young Lady to Her Ancient Lover*

Ancient person, for whom I
All the flattering youth defy,

Long be it ere thou grow old,
Aching, shaking, crazy, cold;
    But still continue as thou art,
    Ancient person of my heart.

On thy withered lips and dry,
Which like barren furrows lie,
Brooding kisses I will pour
Shall thy youthful heat restore
(Such kind showers in autumn fall,
And a second spring recall);
    Nor from thee will ever part,
    Ancient person of my heart.

Thy nobler part, which but to name
In our sex would be counted shame,
By age's frozen grasp possessed,
From his ice shall be released,
And soothed by my reviving hand,
In former warmth and vigour stand.
All a lover's wish can reach
For thy joy my love shall teach,
And for thy pleasure shall improve
All that art can add to love.
    Yet still I love thee without art,
    Ancient person of my heart.

[John Wilmot, Earl of Rochester, pub. 1691]

A. Coarseness is certainly not always stupid in these two passages, although one is left wondering about the wisdom of old men. Both passages concern elderly amorous males, one of whom is coarse in his language, the other of whom is the addressee of a somewhat smutty poem.

There is little doubt in each case that coarseness is funny. The central question in each case is 'why?' Do we laugh primarily <u>at</u> Fumble, or <u>with</u> him? When we laugh at him, is this a result of his coarseness? Are we laughing because of his wit? or because of his stupidity? Similarly, with (b), it would be hard not to find the poem amusing. But just what is its tone? Do we take the young lady at her word and imagine the poet to be satirising her love for a withered old man? or do we find the young lady in fact double-bluffing us with a witty hyperbole that turns the conventions of love poetry back in the reader's face, along with his or her preconceptions about love? Either way, it is not at all certain whether the relationship between coarseness and stupidity is funny because it is there, or funny because the poet or dramatist is playing on the fact that one expects it to be there.

Let us look at (a) first. Fumble is without much question a fool and *senex*. His age and accompanying deafness and bad eyesight make him the butt of numerous jokes, including Cordelia's central prank, the swapping of herself for the old Governess. We laugh at Fumble for his appropriate and foolish name (if we've seen the script or programme at a performance). We laugh at the anticlimax when Cordelia declares with vigour that:

I hate an old Fellow for a husband [. . .]

and the unhearing Fumble replies:

What does she say now? But no matter [. . .]

We might chuckle at the old-buffer-ish bluster of his speech, his frequent and unnecessary repetition ('I was waggish again, I was waggish agen ifack.') that reminds one of that modern *senex*, *Coronation Street*'s Fred Eliot.[2] Most of all, we laugh when Fumble fails to notice the substitution of the Governess for Cordelia. We laugh at his foolishness, but what about his coarseness?

Cordelia says in line 3 that she hates 'an old piece of wit', but presumably would approve of a new one. Fumble's wit is in fact often sophisticated and if it is coarse in tone is frequently reminiscent in some respects of Shakespeare's Fools. His song combines his old-duffer bluster ('hey down derry down [etc.]') with a reasonable pun on laying down and sex: 'took her by the middle small' being both waist and vagina (Rosencrantz and Guildenstern make the same joke in *Hamlet*, when they refer to themselves as 'in the very middle of her favours'). Similarly Fumble gets a second good line at line 20. Once again having been the butt of a deafness gag, Fumble gets a metatheatrical quip with 'the Devil's an Ass, I ha' seen't in a play', referring to Jonson's *The Devil is an Ass* and then deflating Cordelia's insult by declaring that plays are 'worthless'. Admittedly this is more the

---

2 *Coronation Street*: a popular British TV soap opera, broadcast since 1960.

playwright's joke than Fumble's, but it does demonstrate that his coarse and bawdy language is frequently expressed with an intelligent wit, even if Fumble is himself a fool.

In (b), as I have suggested, the case is slightly more complex. It is possible that the poet is satirising the stupidity of the young lady's lust for the ancient lover. In emphasizing the 'withered lips and dry', the 'barren furrows', and the seamy details of the final stanza, which is really more than we need to know (in contrast to the false modesty of 'Thy nobler part, which but to name | In our sex would be counted shame'), one might find a mocking portrait of a crude and stupid young lady. As with the depiction of Fumble, the poem has a fully developed wit which may be the poet's, but may be the young lady's. The humorous bathos of 'Nor from thee will ever part', when compared to what seems an inadvertent pun on 'Thy nobler part', seems to belong only to the poet. However, the similar quibble on 'art' and 'love' at the end of the poem, suggesting the lady knows the art of love*making* but that her love is not a sham, seems to be spoken in the persona of the lady herself, once again phrasing coarse sentiment in an intelligently crafted wit.

Indeed, a further reading of the poem might find something deeply sardonic in the young lady's own tone. Though she claims to love without art, might she have ulterior motives for taking an ancient lover? Without seeming to intend to, the lady dwells rather too often for too long on the decrepitude and death of her beloved than is comfortable. At line 4 she does not wish him to be youthful but rather *not* to be:

Aching, shaking, crazy, cold

This has the effect not of evoking the wished-for youth but the more likely decline into illness, madness and death. Similarly in stanza 3 our ancient lover might not wish to be reminded that his shrivelled member is 'By age's frozen grasp possessed', even if only in contrast to the young lady's 'reviving hand'. Frequently the lady writes of restoring the lover's youth, to 'recall' a 'second spring' rather than love him for what he currently is. And indeed, the whole poem reverses convention by coming <u>from</u> the woman <u>to</u> the man, in what could be seen in poetic terms as an emasculating gesture. All of these details suggest that while Fumble may be a fool for all his wit, the young lady's coarseness is a clever disguise for other intentions which perhaps look to a reward beyond the ancient lover's death.

Tom Perrin

Five

Q. *'A singularity of English tragedy, so repulsive to French feelings that Voltaire used to call Shakespeare a drunken savage, is its peculiar mixture of the sublime and the base, the terrible and the ridiculous, the heroic and the burlesque.'*

A. It is, from a certain point of view, true that English tragedy, especially in its golden age in the Renaissance, appears to be a disordered and perhaps 'impure' form. Sidney, in the *Defence of Poesie*, complains of the Shakespearean mingling of kings and clowns on stage together. However, I believe that, if tragedy is seen in a wider context, such distinctions often become part of a small-scale historical view that takes little account of the different things that have been called 'tragedy' over the course of the history of the genre. Thus it is neither singular nor peculiar to 'English tragedy' that such generic mixing should go on.

Much of the blame for the existence of this sort of critical viewpoint must be with Aristotle. Not only did his *Poetics* (along with a Renaissance re-reading of Horace) form the basis for the Neoclassicism that found Shakespeare at best 'indecorous' and at worse a 'drunken savage', but it is Aristotle who initially draws distinctions based on the difference between 'base' and 'sublime', 'comic' and 'tragic' in the Western critical canon. Aristotle frequently draws these sorts of distinctions, writing of early tragedy that:

> its plots were at first slight, its expression comical, and it was a long time before it acquired dignity

And what is comedy but 'a mimesis of people worse than are found in the world'? Hence early on lines were drawn by which comedy and baseness are aligned in opposition to tragedy (and by extension seriousness) and nobility, sublimity, heroism.

When Aristotle's *Poetics* was translated into Latin in 1498 Renaissance scholars rushed to extrapolate from it rules for their own drama. Especially in continental Europe, playwrights were soundly chastised if their work did not conform to Aristotelian unities or was not sufficiently exalted in tone. This attitude was reinforced by the rediscovery of Hermann the German's Latin translation of Averroes's gloss on Aristotle (1256) in which tragedy was characterised as a *laudatio*. Tragedy was felt to be, whether ending happily (like Euripides's *Alcestis* or *Helen*, for instance) <u>or</u> sadly, a moral lesson in praise of virtue. Comedy, characterised as *vituperatio*, was designed to show up moral faults. Hence comedy and tragedy, and their inherent baseness and nobility, were further divided by Renaissance theorists.

In England, by contrast, less theoretically prescriptive models often prevailed. Encouraged by a system in which both genres were performed in the same theatres, tragedy and comedy often blurred, so much so that, despite the Neoclassicism of Dryden and the Augustans, by 1839 Hallam's *History of Literature* could define tragedy as plays which 'are concluded in death'. In England there was no need for a strict theoretical defence of 'tragicomedy', such as Guarini made in Italy in 1601: the Neoclassical model was not so strictly entrenched.

However, what I would like to argue in this essay is that this debate over genre, often extended in critical writing to cover such phenomena as twentieth-century 'tragicomic' Absurdism, is in fact more localized in the Renaissance than is often considered to be the case. I hope to demonstrate that 'baseness', 'burlesque', 'ridiculous' and other such terms are a powerful force in Greek tragedy, Shakespearean tragedy and much of what modern critics are often reluctant to call 'modern tragedy'. Comedy, comedic structures and comic elements play an important rôle, in some cases even in their absence, in many tragedies and are not simply a 'singularity' (and a 'repulsive' one at that) of English tragedy.

In certain Greek tragedies, notably those of Aeschylus and Sophocles, there truly does seem to be no place for the 'base', 'ridiculous' or 'burlesque'. In such tragedies the outcome is frequently the completion of some form of bargain with Fate. This view is a reductive one in the face of the complexities of the plays, but nonetheless can be seen in operation. In Aeschylus's

Agamemnon, Clytemnestra attempts to present herself as the blameless agent of Fate:

> You say this work is mine, call me
> Agamemnon's wife. You are so wrong.
> Fleshed in the wife of this dead man
> The spirit lies within me,
> Our savage ancient spirit of revenge

Clytemnestra is not (she claims) even herself, but is rather the 'spirit of revenge' (elsewhere called 'the curse') manifested in a body. Hence her murder of Agamemnon was simply the acting-out of an inevitable process.

In *Oedipus Tyrannus* (a play much cited by Aristotle) such a conception of fate is even more pronounced. At the start of the play Oedipus's fate is already sealed—he cannot avoid it. But following his blinding the tragedy has been worked out. The plague is lifted from Thebes and Oedipus is free to wander Attica. His bargain has been acquitted. Some critics have gone so far as to make the blinding a grasping of existential freedom. In his 1991 introduction to the play, Diskin Clay writes that 'Oedipus's life belonged to Apollo, but his blindness he claims for himself'. Similar things have also been said about Heracles's suicide in *The Women of Trachis*.

In his reworkings of Greek myth, Jean Anouilh conceives of this type of Greek tragedy as not simply not including the 'base' and 'ridiculous' but positively struggling to keep them out. Tragedy becomes a self-indulgent process, a turning-away from the real business of life. In his *Antigone* (1942), Creon tells Antigone that:

> nothing less than a cosy tea party with death and destiny will quench your thirst. The happiest hour of your father's [Oedipus's] life came when he listened greedily to the story of how, unknown to him, he had killed his own father and dishonoured the bed of his own mother

In contrast to this, 'tragedy', the chorus tells us, 'is clean. It is restful. It is flawless.' It is a system, like an uncoiling spring. We note how Creon's attack on Antigone's tragedy comes in the form of a joke designed to destroy its dignity—her suicide becomes 'a cosy tea party with death and destiny'. The point is emphasized in Anouilh's *Eurydice* (sometimes translated as *Point of Departure*). Again a dichotomy is established between comic life and tragic death. In life, perfection (sublimity) cannot survive. Monsieur Henri tells Orpheus:

> Walk through life with your little Eurydice. You'll meet her at the exit with her dress covered in finger marks. You'll find her strangely soiled

By contrast, death 'is beautiful. She alone can create the perfect setting for love.' Life is characterized as 'ridiculous', and is personified by Orpheus's father, whose affable humour confirms his untragic nature: given a cigar 'rolled on a young girl's thighs' shortly before Orpheus's death he again robs the scene of its dignity, provoking a laugh with the sleepy ejaculation:

> I feel as if I'm smoking the thigh itself!

Viewed through Anouilh's reappraisal, tragic sublimity and heroism becomes not the noble work of a Voltaire or a Racine, but a struggle to shut out life, humour and baseness; the 'drunken savage' becomes a figure whose absence speaks loudly indeed. But if Anouilh is reappraising a French tradition of tragedy through a reworking of Greek myth, he does so at the risk of ignoring the fact that much other tragedy, both Greek and Shakespearean, is predicated upon this same struggle. In some other of the plays of Sophocles, most of Euripides, and almost all of Shakespeare, the tragedy is itself the loss of a battle with Anouilh's 'life'. The acquittal of a bargain with Fate is replaced by the inescapable clutches of what Ted Hughes translates as 'Necessity' (in his *Alcestis*), from which one can never, unlike Orestes, be let off.

For Aristotle tragedy achieved its generic status as separate from the 'satyr-style' when its expression ceased to be 'comic' and it acquired 'dignity'. 'Dignity' is a key word here: it lies behind all of the oppositions put forward in the question. Yet, paradoxically, it is also central to the model of tragedy we will now examine. The infection of the 'clean' tragedy by 'life' results in an indignity that is itself central to tragedy.

In the nineteenth century Schopenhauer (in *The World as Will and Representation*) defined tragedy as the overcoming of man's will by the ceaseless workings of the world: 'the description of the terrible side of life [. . .] the scornful mastery of chance'. I have shown how this 'chance', this unsystematizable element of life, is frequently encoded in the 'base' and the 'ridiculous'. In Sophocles's *Ajax*, Ajax's suicide is caused precisely by his refusal to admit this element into his heroic existence: he fears terribly the loss of his 'dignity' and expresses this as a fear of laughter, a fear of becoming ridiculous:

O! What a mockery I have come to. What indignity!

Similarly, Athena describes his position to Odysseus as laughable:

But to laugh at your enemies—
What sweeter laughter can there be than that?

The case is similar again with *Philoctetes*: his fear of indignity, and the latent indignity with which he is characterized by Odysseus.

But this model becomes fully developed in Euripides. In Euripides the 'mastery of chance' is only 'scornful' since man cannot choose which he ends up with: thus disastrous and happy endings are equally prevalent in Euripides—what is constant is the tragic protagonist's inability to manipulate events in their favour (*Helen*, *Alcestis*, and *Medea* all end with the words 'the things we thought would happen do not happen'). This in turn allows the infusion of comic elements into the partially comedic structures of Euripides's plays. In *Alcestis* Admetos's grief is prevented from attaining tragic grandeur by the comic entrance of the drunken Heracles (complete, in Northern Broadsides's recent production of Ted Hughes's version, with a noisy oompah band). The operation of chance is key: as Hecuba says in *The Trojan Women*:

Those forces which
control our fortunes are as unpredictable
as capering idiots

As with Creon in Anouilh's *Antigone*, the uncontrollable operation of life is represented as a base and ridiculous figure, a capering idiot. Similarly, both Phaedra and Pentheus meet destruction because they will not 'roll with the punches' of life. The Nurse tells Phaedra that 'someone she [Love] finds full of pride and arrogance—Why, what do you think? / She takes and tramples in the dust'.

It is a tragedy stemming just from these elements that is key in Shakespeare rather than some peculiar British lack of decorum on stage. I have shown that Greek tragedy frequently bolts its doors (successfully and unsuccessfully) in fear of the intrusion of the ridiculous.

In Shakespeare these bolts, which often break in Euripides, are smashed time and time again.

The figure of the Fool is important here. The Fool is never a noble character, is theoretically ridiculous, and is often involved in burlesque. In Shakespearean comedies the presence of the Fool often serves to prick the pretensions of the central characters, who believe that they can control the events around them. Their fate is dependant on waiting for the wheel of fortune to turn in their favour, instead of attempting to impose their Will on an unheeding world. Celia in *As You Like It* explains the symbolic significance of Touchstone's arrival:

> Though Nature
> Hath given us to flout at Fortune, hath not
> Fortune sent in this Fool to cut off the argument?

It is interesting that in *Love's Labour's Lost* Berowne articulates this sort of sentiment with direct reference to the Ajax myth, claiming with a logic more characteristic of the Fool that he is a fool since he cannot control his love which, like Ajax, has slain him, a sheep. It is ironic that the disordered operation of chance that Ajax cannot cope with is characterized as Ajax himself.

In Shakespearean tragedy, by contrast, the Fool is frequently marginalized, and is unable to keep the characters in check. *Hamlet*'s gravedigger, *Macbeth*'s Porter, and *Othello*'s clown get only one scene apiece. Even *King Lear*'s Fool vanishes during the third act. But the marginalization of the Fool, paradoxically, allows his 'repulsive' characteristics directly into the heart of Shakespearean tragedy. Tragic protagonists who attempt to impose an order upon their surroundings frequently end up the victim of forces beyond their control, often encoded as characteristics of the Fool. Othello calls himself 'O Fool! Fool! Fool!', and Hamlet puts on his 'antic disposition'.

But *King Lear* must form the centre of such an argument. Lear's Fool draws frequent parallels between himself and Lear ('The sweet and bitter fool / Will presently appear / The one in motley here / The other found out there'), and in the end Lear, in his madness, becomes more base and ridiculous than the Fool ever was, all because he is 'Fortune's Fool'. Lear's tragedy is hence directly tied to the interruption of ridiculous disorder into his ordered world. Tragedy and comedy become fused in the *senex*-figure of King Lear. In *Madness and Civilization*

(1967) Michel Foucault articulates just this point when he writes that 'madness becomes the great *trompe-l'œil* in the tragicomic structures'.

Thus the interruption of the 'low' forms into the 'high' can be traced from even the most apparently 'sublime', 'heroic' and 'terrible' classical tragedy into the English tragedy where Voltaire found their presence 'repulsive'.

But furthermore, this 'interruption' and fear of interruption can be traced further, to the modern 'Absurdist' drama. The *Encyclopædia Brittanica* says that Absurdism 'suggests that laughter is the only response left to man when he is faced with the tragic emptiness and meaninglessness of existence'. The presence of the word 'tragic' here ought to give us pause. What might be the same about tragedy and Absurdism? Is it simply that, like the laughing Titus Andronicus, we have no more tears to shed? Let us look at a passage from the most famous Absurdist play, Beckett's *Waiting for Godot* (1956):

> VLAD: What do we do now?
> EST: Wait.
> VLAD: Yes, but while waiting.
> EST: We could try hanging ourselves.
> VLAD: Hmm. It'd give us an erection.
> EST: (*highly excited*) An erection!

Here the knob-joke defuses the potential for catastrophe implied by the threat of suicide, and also destroys the dignity of Estragon, who is, comically, more excited by the possibility of an erection than he is concerned about dying. Thus the low comedy suffuses the high tragedy to the extent that there is no longer the possibility of catastrophe. It has, in a sense, already happened. Let us construct a continuum: Ajax commits suicide instead of allowing mockery and ridicule to intrude on his identity; Hecuba's tragedy is that Destiny is itself as ridiculous as a capering idiot; Lear's tragedy is that his ignorance makes him, in the end, ridiculous himself; Vladimir and Estragon are already ridiculous—they are, in a way, beyond tragedy, but still embedded in its tradition.

Finally, why is this continuum important? It is important because it shows the increasing proximity, and the eventual intermingling, of the low and high forms in the tragic tradition. Importantly, Greek tragedy is seen to participate in such a tradition, and the direct line from Aeschylus and Euripides through Aristotle to Racine is broken by an English tragedy far from 'peculiar' in its concern with the ridiculous.

Tom Perrin

Glossary

The bracketed numbers following each entry are page-references to significant and illustrative (but not all) uses of the term.

A

above in Jacobethan amphitheatres the first floor of the tiring-house, used for any raised element of theatrical space-within (battlements, etc.). (136, 141)

abstract a brief summary of the argument and/or contents of an essay or other document, which may be required in examinations. (285)

act (1) as verb, to perform a rôle in a play. (2) as noun, one of usually several sections into which a play may be divided; five- and three-act plays are traditional, but two- and one-act plays are also standard modern forms. Acts may be sub-divided into scenes. (5)

act-division dividing a play into acts; the break between acts. In editions of Renaissance plays these are often created by editors. (5)

action a short performance/event designed to disrupt proceedings and intended as a political or aesthetic protest; the Italian Futurist Filippo Tommaso Marinetti (1876–1944) favoured actions which provoked theatre-audiences to such violence as flag-burning or hurling abuse/missiles. (271)

actor one who plays a rôle in a play. The feminine form is 'actress', but this was often used insultingly, and critics now use actor as a unisex term, specifying male or female actors if necessary. (10, 17)

actor-manager a theatre manager who also takes leading rôles in his/her productions; a dominant type of impresario from *c*.1700 to 1914. Cf. 'player-managers' in sport. (85, 159, 177, 197)

Actors' Studio a controversial workshop studio for professional actors admitted by audition but charged no fees, founded by Elia Kazan, Cheryl Crawford, and Robert Lewis in 1947; Lee Strasberg was Artistic Director from 1951 to 1982, and many eminent American actors are members. (184)

act.scene.line reference one of the form III.ii.1 or 3.2.1, meaning 'act 3, scene 2, line 1'. Stage-directions are usually omitted from the numbering, and attached to the preceding line of dialogue, so '4.3.21.s.d.' means the stage-direction immediately following act 4, scene 3, line 21; the opening stage-direction of that scene would be '4.3.o.s.d.'. (4, 5, 289)

adaptation a significantly altered version of a text. Novels may be adapted as stage- or screen-plays, but play-texts may also be adapted for touring, a different performance-space, etc. (28)

ad lib from Latin *ad libitum*, 'at will, without restraint'; an improvised (unrehearsed) line used for topical reference or comic effect, or to cover a memory-lapse or technical hitch. Also a verb (hence ad libbing). (70)

administrative staff within the production staff, those whose jobs are not artistically creative, including accountants, secretaries, etc. (204)

affective memory a Stanislavskian term, a.k.a. emotion memory; an actor's stored memory of sensations, smell, sight, sound, touch, and taste, which through training can be called upon in an instant to help them connect with a line or scene they are playing. The richer their repository, the greater an actor's creativity. (183)

afterlife a term coined by Jonathan Miller to describe the successive performances of a classical play, each of which serves to recreate and reinterpret it. (169)

agit-prop Russian *agitatsiya-propaganda*, 'agitation-propaganda'; unsophisticated consciousness-raising theatre which privileges political message above art and can be performed in any location. (100)

Aldwych farce lit. those put on at the Aldwych Theatre in the 1950s–60s, especially the work of Ben Travers; more generally a type of farce typified by wit and satire, as opposed to bedroom and Whitehall farces. (95)

alienation in (post-)Brechtian dramatic theory the word most often used to describe techniques (including masks, song, projected images, and highly stylized delivery) which disrupt narrative flow, break audience-expectations, and alienate audiences from dramatic illusion. Brecht's word is *Verfremdungseffekt*, 'the effect of making things strange'. (102–3)

alliterative verse composed of lines within which keywords alliterate, which often follow prescribed metrical patterns, and which may or may not have terminal rhyme. Most Mysteries and some Moralities use alliterative verse. (71)

alternative comedy loosely used in the UK from the 1980s to describe successive waves of self-consciously oppositional stand-up, radio-, and TV-comedy, often anti-Thatcherite but ranging from the mildly surreal violence of *The Young Ones* to the witty political pranks of the *Mark Thomas Product*. In the US 'alternative theatre' is a similarly broad and contested label for post–1960s 'non-commercial' theatre. (211)

amphitheatre lit. 'theatre on both sides'; in present usage, circular theatre-spaces lacking a proscenium wall. (130–2, 135–8)

amplification of sound, to increase in volume. (107)

anachronism an element in anything that is out-of-time, such as a telephone in an Elizabethan play or a sword in a twentieth-century one. (121, 279)

angiportum in Roman theatres, a back-alley conventionally supposed to run behind the houses whose front-doors were visible to the audience. (133)

annotation the provision of explanatory notes by author, editor, or critic. (18, 35)

anti-Aristotelian of dramatic practice or theory, opposed to rigid, neo-classical interpretations of Aristotle's *Poetics*. (66)

anti-essentialist of genre, a view that no one element is essential (e.g. there can be tragedy without a death). (51)

anti-masque a pendant form developed by Ben Jonson, in which grotesque and disharmonious characters, dialogue, etc. heighten by contrast the beauty and harmony of the masque proper. (57, 85)

antiphony the structure of music/words with two interlocked parts/voices. (68–9, 240)

anti-theatricality opposition to theatre, usually religious or moral. (68, 90, 133, 214)

apostrophe a mark of punctuation (') used in possessives (the boy's play, the boys' play), or to indicate elision (never → ne'er, in the → i'th'), which affects rhythm, especially in dramatic verse. (31)

apron-stage a stage mostly behind but extending shallowly through a proscenium-arch, then spreading to the sides; see **thrust-stage**. (142)

Arcadia a mountainous district in the Greek Peloponnese which became the standard location of pastoral. In Virgil's *Eclogues* (*c*.40 BCE) Arcadia became an ideal place, assimilable to Eden—hence the shock of the tomb or skull inscribed *Et in Arcadia Ego* (either 'I too lived in Arcadia' or 'Even in Arcadia I am'); pre-Virgilian Arcadias were charming rather than ideal, accommodating both death and winter. Shakespearean Arcadias, like the Forest of Arden, tend to be pre-Virgilian. (80)

Arden 1 the first series of Arden Shakespeares, 1899–1944, and the first to assign an editor to each play; very influential but now dated. (19, 34)

Arden 2 the second series of Arden Shakespeares, 1946–82, exceptionally scholarly in the treatment of sources, etc. but persistently uninterested in stage-histories and performance. (19, 202, 233–4)

Arden 3 the third series of Arden Shakespeares, begun in 1995 and still in progress. Notably modern and clear in design, and very positive about both performance and textual scholarship. (19, 235)

Aristotelian (or neo-classical) **unities** a retrospective oversimplification of a discussion in Aristotle's *Poetics*, the supposed necessity for 'good' plays to have unity of time (occurring in a single revolution of the sun), place (only one location), and action (nothing irrelevant, no sub-plots). Dr Johnson famously mocked the unities in his *Preface to Shakespeare* (1765). (62)

Arlecchino a Mask in *Commedia dell'arte*, one of the *zanni*. The name probably means 'little devil'; the Mask, which may derive partly from a French wild-man figure covered in leaves, combines a limited mind with an exceptionally agile body in a patched and coloured costume. Arlecchino is fruitlessly devoted to Columbina, and is the source of English Harlequins. (79)

artistic director the person in charge of the artistic policy of a theatre or theatre-company, usually including the choice of plays to be produced. (9, 159)

audience-participation the organized involvement of the audience in singing, hissing villains, etc. (91, 219–20)

audition a competitive performance for admission to a drama school, or a competitive acting-test performed before a director in the hope of being selected for a production. (184)

auditorium lit. 'place of hearing'; in proscenium-arch theatres the place of the audience, including the stalls, circles, and boxes. (11, 141–6)

aulaeum in Roman theatres, a large curtain covering the *frons scaenae*. (134)

aulos, aulos-player a Greek instrument resembling a flute; the player accompanied tragic choruses. (58)

authority-entrance one arresting the action, as by a King or Duke. (136)

avant garde lit. 'vanguard of an army'; from the late nineteenth century on, artists and patrons of the arts in the forefront of change, championing styles, etc. that have yet to gain popularity. (99, 261)

B

back-drop a (painted) cloth in front of which actors perform; in perspectival scenery the rear-most illusion. (131, 139)

Bad Quarto(s) a term for six Shakespearean Qq1 (*The First part of the Contention betwixt the two famous Houses of Yorke and Lancaster, with the death of the good Duke Humphrey*, 1594 (= 2H6); *The true Tragedie of Richard Duke of York, and the death of good King Henrie the Sixt, with the whole contention between the two Houses Lancaster and Yorke*, 1595 (= 3H6) *An Excellent conceited Tragedie of Romeo and Iuliet*, 1597; *The Chronicle History of Henry the Fift*, 1600; *A Most pleasaunt and excellent conceited Comedie, of Syr* Iohn Falstaffe, *and the merrie Wives of* Windsor, 1602; and *The Tragicall Historie of Hamlet*, Prince of Denmarke, 1603) which have significantly shorter and otherwise variant texts, and are believed to be memorial reconstructions. Recent scholarship has demonstrated most to be (whether or not memorially reconstructed) adaptations, probably for touring, and all play far better on stage than their academic standing would suggest. (28, 148)

Bardolatry the uncritical worship of Shakespeare, 'the Bard'. (225, 228)

barker a performing salesman, advertiser, or tout who 'barks' a sales-patter. (78)

barn-stormer an itinerant actor who typically performed in barns and needed an exaggerated, crowd-grabbing style; transferred approvingly and censoriously to any highly energetic show which gets an audience going. (113)

bedroom farce farces in which sexual machinations and complications form the basis of the plot; see **Aldwych** and **Whitehall farce.** (95)

Benevolent Agent in pantomime, the fairy godmother, genie, or equivalent who magics things right. (92)

Berliner Ensemble the premier East German theatre company, founded by Brecht in 1949, whose tours in the 1950s–60s were a primary means of disseminating his influence and the practices of epic theatre.
(127, 167, 188, 220)

bibliography an appended list of the books quoted and cited in an essay, or read as preparation. (289–90)

bio-mechanics a method of demanding physical training developed by Meyerhold between 1905 and 1930 in opposition to Stanislavski's System. (184)

black-face pertaining to comic performances by white actors who 'blacked up' their faces to perform song-and-dance routines considered stereotypically black. Popular in the nineteenth and twentieth centuries, it has been all but destroyed by political correctness. (93)

Blackfriars (Theatre) a former monastery within the City of London, and as such a 'liberty', outwith local-government control; the home of two Jacobethan hall-theatres. The first Blackfriars (1576–84) was used by the Children of the Chapel Royal to perform Lyly and others; the second Blackfriars (1600–42) was planned by James Burbage in 1597, but adult performances were objected to by local residents and the space leased to the Children of the Chapel Royal from 1600 to 1608, their glory years. In 1608 Richard Burbage regained control, and from 1610 the Blackfriars was the winter-home of the King's Men; a smaller space than the Globe, it is particularly associated with Shakespeare's late plays. (138–9)

black hole a simple, generally rectangular, modern theatre-space, a room painted black or draped in black cloth. (129, 144)

blackletter a general name for a Renaissance family of founts of type including gothic; this one is Old English Text. (28)

blackout the extinguishing of all lights on stage and in the auditorium— total darkness. (106)

blank verse unrhymed iambic pentameter, widely used by Shakespeare (as in Hamlet's "To be or not to be" speech). (20)

blocking working-out in rehearsal actors' on-stage positioning and movement; the scheme of such movement in a given production. As a rehearsal-technique blocking was especially popular from c.1920 to 1960. (127)

the Blue Book *Scheme and Estimates for a National Theatre* (1907) by William Archer and Harley Granville Barker. (187)

blue pencil the mark of the censor, and as *blue-pencil*, to censor, supposedly because successive Lord Chamberlains used the colour to mark cuts; *OED2*'s earliest citation is from the *New York Herald* in July 1888. (207)

blurb summary advertising-copy printed on the back/dust-jacket of a book. (224)

the Book a master-copy of a text in which the cuts, emendations, technical cues, stage-business, etc. of a production have been entered as annotations. Also known as the prompt-copy, though not necessarily used by the prompter. (18, 147–8)

Book-holder an enigma: the only known permanent functionary in Jacobethan companies, but whose exact functions are not known. When Books were the only complete texts of plays they (and their associated cue-scripts) represented a major company investment, and had to be secured both for ready use and against theft; but it is widely thought Book-holders also acted as prompters and stage-managers, supervised musicians, use of the thunder-run and other special effects, etc. (205)

bowdlerized of a text, having 'offensive' or 'rude' passages removed or altered; from Thomas Bowdler (1754–1825), editor of *The Family Shakespeare* (1818). (233)

box(es), box-seats enclosed private seating in an auditorium, usually expensive. (136, 142)

box-office lit. the room or booth in a theatre-foyer where tickets are sold; hence also receipts from and popularity measured by ticket-sales. (64)

box-set a walled and sometimes partly-roofed set of a room, invented in the later nineteenth century, placed like an open box on its side against a proscenium arch for drawing-room drama, etc. (143, 195)

braggart soldier see *Il Capitano, miles gloriosus*.

breeches part a male rôle played by a female actor, a common feature of early eighteenth-century English comedies. (178)

Brighelia a Mask in *Commedia dell'arte*, a dominant *zanni*. *Brigare* means 'to intrigue'; Brighella is usually clever and bossy. (79)

Broadway a street in central Manhattan running through the heart of the theatre-district; hence from the 1850s a collective term for mainstream New York theatres, particularly those between West 44th and 50th streets. See **off-Broadway, off-off-Broadway, West End**. (94)

broken brackets crotchets missing the lower horizontal bar, ⌐ ⌐, used in some modern editions to indicate a particular aspect of text or editing. (31)

burlesque a word imported from seventeenth-century France, but ultimately from Italian *burla*, 'ridicule, a joke'. (1) as verb, vigorously to parody and/or pastiche a current success or genre. (2) as noun, a work which does so, particularly in Restoration and eighteenth-century theatre, and the genre to which such works belong. (89–90)

byplay action, usually wordless, carried on aside while main action proceeds. (126)

C

canon strictly, a body of works accepted as authentic and thereby distinguished (like the books of the Bible) from apocrypha; more loosely, as in 'taught canon', the body of works distinguished by being set and taught. Many canons, both historical and contemporary, privilege the work of wealthier and more educated white males. Canon formation is now a much contested and debated subject, and many alternative canons have been proposed. See also **high canon**. (145, 245)

capitalization the provision in a text of capital letters, including wholly conventional capitals (proper names, initial words in each line, etc.), but also the Jacobethan and Restoration capitalization of medial words as a stress-guide for actors. (29)

Il Capitano The Captain, a stock-character in *Commedia dell'arte* descended from the *miles gloriosus* ('braggart soldier') of Plautine comedy, the type exemplified by Shakespeare's Falstaff. *Il Capitano* looks fierce, and boasts greatly, but is a complete coward. (61, 79, 81)

carnival from Latin *carne*, meat, + *vale*, farewell; originally the Shrove Tuesday feast when meat and other rich foodstuffs forbidden during Lent were finished, but used loosely for festivals of revelry, sometimes with a particular sense of authority being suspended for the day. Venetian *carnivale* was a source of *Commedia dell'arte* rôles. (71, 78)

Caroline of the reign of Charles I (1625–49); Caroline theatre was truncated in 1642. (77)

cast (1) as verb, to choose actors for the rôles in a play. (2) as noun, the actors in a play, collectively; hence cast-list, etc. (10)

casting director one responsible for casting, with particular knowledge of who is available, fees, etc.; common only in large productions or companies. (204)

catastrophe lit. 'sudden turn'; in theatre, the stroke that brings about the dénouement of a play. As the general meaning of the word suggests, there is a particular association with tragedy; but cf. *Lear* 1.2.134, "Pat: he comes like the Catastrophe of the old Comedie", and Beckett's *Catastrophe*. (172)

catchword the first word or syllable of text on a page or in a column reproduced at the bottom right of the previous page or column, as an aid to readers (especially readers-aloud); catchwords fell out of use during the eighteenth century. (28)

catharsis a much disputed word used in Aristotle's *Poetics* to refer to the effects of watching tragedy; its literal meaning concerns medical purging, and Aristotle associates it with pity and terror, but it is unclear whether these emotions purge or are purged. (62)

Il Cavaliero the Cavalier, a Mask in *Commedia dell'arte*, a genuine soldier mistaken for *Il Capitano* and liable to thrash his challenger. Sebastian in *Twelfe Night* acts as *Il Cavaliero* in beating Sir Toby and Sir Andrew. (78–80)

character a person in a play, used as an equivalent of 'rôle' (who played the character Hamlet?), but often serving to misdefine 'rôle' as "moral and mental constitution" (what is Hamlet's character like?). (13, 103)

Chefdramaturg the chief dramaturg at a mainstream German theatre, who does the work of literary managers in Britain but may also undertake production dramaturgy. (187)

Chief Villain in pantomime, the leading baddy—e.g. Captain Hook in *Peter Pan*. (92)

children's companies in Jacobethan theatre-practice companies of sub-adult boys, evolved from choirs, who presented adult drama from the 1570s to 1615, and were particularly in vogue 1600–8. The best known are the Boys of St Paul's and the Children of the Chapel Royal, who used the Blackfriars 1601–8 and for whom Jonson, Marston, and Beaumont wrote. The last of the major children's companies was Beeston's Boys (after their master Christopher Beeston), performing 1637–42. (62, 176–7)

choregos in Greek drama a rich citizen who funded a production and was responsible for training the chorus. (124)

choreopoem a term coined by Ntozake Shange (b.1948) to describe theatre-pieces that began life as poems for cabaret-style performance and expanded into stage-works that combine lyrical text with dance and music. (265)

chorus a group of performers who speak and move as a unitary rôle, perhaps in unison. A *coryphaeus* may give the beat. Greek tragic choruses were of 12 (later 15) male performers, comic choruses of 24. (53, 58–9, 69, 124, 131)

circle a mid-level gallery in an auditorium; the standard modern term. (144)

citation a mention of a book, line, stage-direction, etc. which is not quoted. (284)

citizen comedy a Jacobethan variant set in London and featuring tradesmen and their wives; examples include Dekker's *Shoemaker's Holiday* (1599) and Middleton's *Chaste Maid in Cheapside* (c.1613). (63)

City Dionysia the major dramatic festival in Athens, five days in spring primarily devoted to tragedy. (57)

clever slave a stock-rôle in Greek New Comedy, greatly developed by

Plautus; often a likeable rogue, and always responsible for solving his (less clever) master's problems with a ruse. Jeeves (in *Jeeves & Wooster*) is an outstanding modern example, and Baldrick in *Blackadder* ("I have a cunning plan") is an inverted version. (61, 74)

closed exam one held in a specific place at a specific time. (283)

closet-drama plays written to be read (by the author to friends, by amateurs to one another, or silently) but not performed. (60, 90)

close-up in film, a shot in which the object is focused on in detail and is therefore relatively large in the frame. Often abbreviated to CU, MCU (medium close-up), and ECU (extreme close-up). (87, 111, 204)

clowns (1) in Jacobethan stage-plays rustics, peasants, and other uneducated (but not therefore unsophisticated) rôles, often played by (2) actors who specialized in such rôles and were commonly star-turns, liable to ad lib and invent extra stage-business for themselves; they also performed jigs. These clowns drew heavily on the *zanni* in *Commedia dell'arte*, but were also influenced by travelling entertainers, and have existed in various forms in every period since, flourishing in Harlequinades, music-hall, and in the plays of Beckett and Fo. (3) in circus, a kind of comic performer, often in white-face and/or with a red nose, specializing in slapstick; principally descended from Pedrolino, but much influenced by Charlie Chaplin. (19, 175–6)

collaboration of writing, when more than one writer engages in working on a play; the adjective is collaborative. (157)

collation the comparison of texts to identify variant readings.

colloquy lit. 'speaking together'; dialogue between two or more actors/rôles; see **soliloquy**. (143)

Columbina a Mask in *Commedia dell'arte*, the principal female counterpart of the *zanni*. Usually maid to the first female lover, Columbina is kind and sensible, but often the target of both Arlecchino (romantically) and Pantalone (sexually). (79)

comedian until the seventeenth century simply an actor, a sense preserved both in Shakespeare and in French, but thereafter, in theatre, specifically a comedic actor or entertainer, often of relatively low status (hence the loosely derogatory modern sense). (173)

comedic concerning comedy as a form and art; a usefully narrower word than 'comic' (terminal marriages are comedic but not necessarily comic). (56)

comedy from Greek *komos*, a revel; one of the two fundamental Greek genres, the pair of tragedy, symbolised by the smiling mask. In Aristotelian and other essentialist genre-theory comedy is supposed to be concerned with society rather than the individual, with street-rather than high-life, and to end in the union of lovers, traditionally in marriage; in non-essentialist theories it relates to any amusing and/or irenic elements of action and dialogue. Shakespearean comedy is broadly associated with prose and song rather than blank

verse. See also **citizen, Old, Middle, musical, New,** and **Restoration comedy, comedy of humours, dark comedies, screwball comedies,** and **sitcom**.
(49, 55–66, 80)

comedy of humours a variant based on the Renaissance 'theory of humours' in which excess or defect of blood, phlegm, yellow bile, and black bile determined how sanguine, phlegmatic, choleric, or melancholic one's character was. Chapman began a fad for characters dominated by one or another humour with *An Humorous Day's Mirth* (1597), and the trope was used by Jonson in *Every Man in his Humour* (1598). (63)

comic business see stage-business.

command-performance a private performance commanded by a noble patron, etc. (85, 124, 138, 211)

command-point that point on a stage from which an actor is visible to all members of an audience and all other on-stage actors; the place from which action and audience can be best dominated. (131, 137)

Commedia dell'arte an extremely influential improvised Venetian play-form and theatre-style of the sixteenth to eighteenth centuries partly derived from Roman comedy, which features Arlecchino (Harlequin), Pantalone (Pantaloon), the Spanish Captain (or braggart soldier), the false Doctor (Pedant or Mountebank), and others. Descendants of *Commedia* include French Pierrots and white-face mimes, and English Harlequinades and Punch-and-Judy shows. (20, 61, 77–81, 91, 121)

Commedia erudita Italian, 'learned comedy', written plays acted, often by amateurs, without masks or improvisation. Many drew directly on Plautine and Terentian comedy. (77–8, 85)

commission a contractual agreement to write and deliver a play to a theatre by a specific date for a specific sum of money. (107)

community-play a play commissioned by and written for a specific community, the cast of which may contain professional actors as well as amateur actors from the locality. (104, 161)

company a practical and financial association of actors (and sometimes administrators and others); the business sense should always be remembered. (77, 148)

company- (theatre-) structure the number and organization of officers and functionaries within a company/theatre. (203)

compositor in cold-metal printing the person who takes individual type-letters, marks, and spaces from type-cases and sets them in correct sequence. Composing is distinguished from 'imposing', or arranging the set type in pages on the press. Most composing is now done by keyboard, but the word is still used. (9, 147)

comps from 'complimentary tickets'; those given free to reviewers, etc. (203)

Constructivist of sets, especially in the early twentieth century, anti-realist, using mechanical structures, often powered. (There are other meanings in architecture.) (198)

continuous staging performance in which there is no clear break between scenes or acts, and actors entering for a new scene do not usually wait for the stage to be clear before doing so. It is associated with minimalist staging as there is no time for changes of set, etc. (239)

copy the text which compositors follow in setting type. (147)

copy-editor in printing the person responsible for checking a typescript for mistakes and inconsistencies, and for marking up the typescript to make all printing instructions clear to the compositors (9)

copyright the legal entitlement of the owner of a dramatic work to claim a fee in exchange for their permission for its performance or publication.
(4, 157, 159)

copy-text the existing text which an editor adopts as the basis of a new edition; it may be corrected or altered by collation with other editions, but is the default text, preferred unless there is a good case for a specific change. (22)

to corpse, corpsing of actors, to laugh personally when in character, so called because it 'kills' the rôle being presented. In metatheatrical and other self-aware acting corpsing can pass off without difficulty, or be an opportunity, but in theatres of illusion it is powerfully destructive. (184)

coryphaeus the leader of a chorus, probably a 'conductor' and focus. (59)

costume-designer one responsible for the overall design and harmony of costume, including accuracy of period-detail. (204)

costume-drama a twentieth-century term for plays, films, or TV-dramas that foreground and rely on the accurate use of period-detail, particularly costume, to bring a historical period to life; prime examples include BBC TV-adaptations of Austen and Dickens, and the films of Ismael Merchant (b.1936) and James Ivory (b.1928). (110)

costumier one who makes costumes. (204)

côterie (audience) a small, élite audience of theatre-goers; plays written for côteries can afford to make learned or in-jokes. (142)

cothurnus a high-soled shoe worn for tragedy by Roman actors. (134)

coup de théâtre a moment of spectacle in a play providing a brilliant and unexpected effect. (92)

court-room drama a play or film all or part of which is set in court and revolves around a trial. (112)

create rôles are created by the first actor to perform them; the term potently suggests the importance of first performances. (173)

creative staff within the production staff, those whose jobs are artistically creative, as distinct from administrative staff. (204)

cross-casting principally the casting of men in female rôles or women in male rôles, but by extension any systematic casting against type. (178)

cross-dressed usually a man dressed as a woman or vice versa, but also potentially an actor dressed as an animal, etc. In productions where all female rôles are played by men those actors are cross-dressed, but the term is commonly reserved for rôles who cross-dress within the play, as Rosalind does in *As You Like It* and Portia in *The Merchant of Venice*. (35)

crotchets square brackets [like these], used to distinguish changes and additions to a text in quotation, and by editors of academic editions to indicate alterations to the specified copy-text. In textual collation single crotchets are commonly used to separate the lemma (the word or words to which the textual note refers) from its variant readings: thus 'gun] guns Q1; pistols F.' means that where this text reads 'gun', the text labelled Q1 reads 'guns', and the text labelled F reads 'pistols'. (19)

Cubist of sets, especially in the early twentieth century, anti-realist, using multiple perspectives, geometric forms, and coloured planes. (There are other meanings in criticism and art history.) (198)

cue any line or action to which an actor is supposed to respond in performance. (15)

cue-script an actor's learning-script which gives only their own lines and cues (usually the last few words of someone else's speech). It is often now cheapest to buy each actor a printed copy of the text in which to highlight their own lines and actions, but when all copying was by hand cue-scripts were an obvious time-saver, and their use affects performance. (15, 147–8)

curia a political meeting-room in the Theatre of Pompey in Rome. (133)

cycle a sequence of plays, usually individually short, which collectively tell a complex story; there is no formal rule about the number of plays, but sequences of fewer than five plays are rarely called cycles, and the Mystery-cycles have dozens. (71)

Cyclorama a large semi-cylindrical surface invented in the 1840s to improve the quality of stage-illusion; if the proscenium-arch is the upright stem of a capital 'D', the Cyclorama is the bowl. (143)

D

Dadaism from French 'Dada', 'a hobby-horse'; a movement dating from 1916 characterized by a repudiation of traditional conventions in art, theatre, and literature, and intended to outrage and scandalize; Tristan Tzara (1896–1963) is considered its founder. (271)

dark comedies loose term for Shakespeare's late Elizabethan comedies (e.g. *The Merchant of Venice, Twelfe Night, Measure, for Measure*) which qualify or deny comedic endings, and include insoluble sadnesses. (52, 82)

dash a mark of punctuation (—) which in dramatic texts usually indicates either an abrupt change of subject or that the speaker is interrupted and cut short by the next speech (cf. **suspension-marks**). (16)

dead air in radio, periods of non-transmission (e.g. overnight); silences are difficult to use in radio-plays because they can be mistaken for dead air. (109)

decorum the seemliness of a particular genre; tragic decorum might be broken by ribaldry, comedic decorum by suffering or philosophy. (62, 81–3)

delivery how lines are spoken; personal stage-directions—*angrily, slowly, loudly*—often specify delivery. (16)

dénouement from French, 'unravelling'; the final working-out of a plot, also known as the *catastrophe*. (78)

deposit library a library in which a work must be deposited to establish copyright; a book published in the UK must by law be sent to the British Library, Bodleian Library in Oxford, Cambridge University Library, National Library of Scotland, and the library of Trinity College, Dublin. (152)

descends, descent in Renaissance stage-directions an indication that an actor (usually playing a supernatural rôle) should be lowered on a wire. (85–6)

designer in theatrical production the person who conceives and designs the set and often the general 'look' of a production, extending to costume, wigs, props, and potentially style or movement. Designers have steadily risen in importance since the advent of the director, and many director-designer partnerships operate as teams. (10)

deus ex machina Latin, 'god out of the machinery'; originally a classical dénouement, the spectacular appearance of a god suspended in the air to set things right. Though a feature of Shakespearean inset-masque, the phrase now tends to mean 'a ridiculously contrived ending'. (86)

deuteragonist lit. 'second player'; the second actor/rôle in Greek tragedy. (60)

development the training of new playwrights. Companies such as Paines Plough workshop and produce the work of new playwrights and seek to improve their knowledge of stage-craft and writing skills. (160)

development dramaturg from the German *Entwicklungsdramaturg*, one who helps new writers develop their writing and stage-craft; often called writing-tutors or mentors, they are generally playwrights or directors. They are still controversial in Britain: some view them as worrying signs of a nannying mentality among arts establishments, others think their experience a valuable teaching tool. Success depends on the relationship of mentor and pupil, which is where things can most easily go wrong. (191)

development dramaturgy the work done by a development dramaturg in helping to develop a new writer's sense of structure and stage-craft. (191)

devised of a performance, generated (usually through improvisation) by a company of actors; of text, generated through such a process, not by a single author. The process is known as devising. The decision to devise is usually specifically intended to overturn the established hierarchy of playmaking, especially the authorities of playwright and director. (162)

dialogue (1) those parts of a printed text intended to be spoken, as distinct from stage-directions, etc.; (2) those parts of a performance that are spoken, as distinct from stage-business, etc.; (3) as distinct from 'monologue', 'soliloquy', etc., an exchange between two actors/rôles. (15)

dimming in theatre, reducing the intensity of stage-light. (106)

director in modern theatrical production the person in overall charge of an individual production, responsible for organizing and managing rehearsals and bringing a coherent overall artistic interpretation and/or performative style to the performances. The director as a named and chief functionary dates only from the later nineteenth century. (1, 17)

discontinuous staging performance with clear breaks between scenes and acts, either with a clear stage or a drawn curtain. It is necessary if significant changes of set are required between scenes. (239)

discovered in stage-directions an indication that an actor, tableau, etc. should be suddenly revealed to the audience, often by drawing aside a curtain. (134)

discovery-space in Jacobethan amphitheatres the double-width, curtained, central entrance/exit, favoured by rulers, processions, and others possessing or desiring authority, but also clowns and Fools who could first peep through the curtains. Tableaux could be discovered, and large props (beds, thrones) concealed to be thrust out as needed. (136–7)

distegia in later Roman theatres a first-floor balcony on the *frons scaenae*; the equivalent of the Jacobethan 'above'. (134)

distribute, distribution the assignment of lines to particular rôles/actors; applied to classical choric speeches, 'distributed' is opposed to 'in unison'. (58)

dithyramb a choric dance to a god, particularly Dionysus, from which Greek tragedy probably developed and which were included in tragedies. (53, 57)

documentary drama (docudrama) plays containing documented (non-fictional) written, spoken, or visual source-material assembled to make a hard-hitting political point. (100–1)

documentation the process of recording performance, and the record made; printed texts, the Book, video- and audio-tapes, lighting- and sound-plans, the programme, interviews with actors, directors, and technical crew, and documentaries are all forms of documentation. (15, 273)

domestic tragedy a variant rejecting the supposed need for an aristocratic or noble protagonist, and often concerned with bourgeois marriage. (63)

doorman the keeper of the stage-door. (205)

Dorian Doria was an area of central Greece; the Dorian mode of music was characteristically simple and solemn, and influenced later Western music. (59)

Il Dottore the Doctor, a principal older Mask in *Commedia dell'arte*; often named Gratiano, *Il Dottore* is usually fat and always pompous, a pedant whose learning is false or misapplied. He is Pantalone's neighbour and rival, and may be the father of one of the lovers. (79)

downstage on a raked stage, closer to the audience. (142)

dramatic irony a term supposedly characterizing either moments of irony between rôles, or more complex performative ironies contrived by the playwright for the appreciation of the audience but not necessarily understood by the rôles involved. The coincidence in both irony and theatre of doubleness and gaps makes it hard to use with precision. (3–4)

dramatic motivation in a particular scene, what a rôle has to do, often confused with Stanislavskian and Freudian ideas about overall psychological coherence. Iago's dramatic motivation in *Othello* 3.3 is to persuade Othello of Desdemona's adultery with Cassio, but the larger coherence of the rôle involves his self-deceptions, partial embodiment of a Vice-rôle, etc. (183)

dramaticule an eighteenth-century term defined by *OED2* as "A miniature or insignificant drama"; used by Beckett as a subtitle for *Come and Go* (1967), and thereby popularized as a general term for his (very) short works.
(241, 261–2)

dramatis personae lit. 'the persons of the play'; a list of the rôles in a play, now usually printed immediately between title-page and opening scene. (231)

dramaturg lit. 'a worker/maker of drama'; often used without qualification (which continues to generate confusion) but usually either a production or development dramaturg. (120, 128, 186)

dramaturgy (1) the structural composition of a play (the dramaturgy of Shakespeare's *Hamlet*); some commentators also use the word broadly in relation to an author's work (Brechtian dramaturgy, Shakespeare's dramaturgy). (2) the work of a dramaturg. (3) a collection of writings on drama, after the *Hamburgische Dramaturgie* (1768–9) by G. E. Lessing. (186)

drawing-room drama plays (especially of 1875–1950) typically set in drawing-rooms, and often assuming a realist box-set. (90, 143)

dress-circle a gallery in the auditorium, adjacent to the pit; in the nineteenth and earlier twentieth centuries evening-dress was expected for those seated there (but not in higher, cheaper circles). (144)

dresser one who helps actors to (change) dress; often skilled valets, as celebrated in *The Dresser* (1980, filmed 1983 with Albert Finney (b.1936) and Tom Courtenay (b. 1937)) by Ronald Harwood (b. 1934). (205)

dressing-room a room where actors can prepare, and to which they can retreat; individual dressing-rooms are a mark of status. (127)

dress-rehearsal a rehearsal, usually immediately before opening, using full costume, etc. (10)

droll a brief excerpt from a play performed in its own right. (63)

to dry, drying of actors to forget lines in performance and be unable to fribble through. (184)

dumb-show sometimes an alternative for *mime*, action without words, but specifically a brief stylized mime summarizing the plot performed before the play (or each act) in some Late Mediaeval and Early Modern drama. (85)

E

early editions sixteenth- and seventeenth-century editions of plays, particularly Shakespearean quartos and folios. (4, 23–30)

Early Modern of the period 1500–1700 CE. (62)

eclectic text a composite text of Shakespearean plays with variant Q and F1 texts, including all passages from both. (232–3)

editor (1) in publishing, the person responsible for accepting or rejecting typescripts and managing the process of publication; the author's main contact. (2) in academia and criticism, a person who prepares for publication a literary work by someone else. Editors will often claim to be neutral, and to be presenting the author's 'final intentions', but ideological and political agendas are usually visible. (9, 22–35)

education officer in larger companies/theatres one with responsibility for liaison with schools and the general promotion of theatre as education. (205)

eisodos, eisodoi in Greek amphitheatres, paired side-exits, not piercing the *skênê*; one led to distant places, one to near places; one might be wider to allow processional entrances. (131, 133)

ekkyklêma lit. 'something rolled-out'; in Greek amphitheatres a wheeled trolley on which objects or tableaux could be thrust out through the door in the *skênê*. (130–1)

elision the omission of one or more letters from a word, usually indicated by an apostrophe (of the clock → o'clock, hunting → huntin'); the missing letters are *elided*. Elision may critically affect rhythm in dramatic verse. (31)

Elizabethan of the reign of Elizabeth I (1558–1603). (52)

elocutionary of punctuation, guiding the voice, not syntactical. (149)

embedded quotation one within inverted commas within the main body of a text. (284, 288)

emblematic costume one expressing function or status, often without regard for period-accuracy, etc. (193)

emendation an editorial alteration to a copy-text. (231)

emotion memory see **affective memory**.

entrance the arrival of one or more actors/rôles on stage; also the door or other means by which to do so. In epic theatre actors may be visible before entering. (22)

epic a classical genre of poetry; epics are usually long accounts of conflicts between peoples and of nation-formation. Major epic poets include Homer, Virgil, and latterly Milton. (66)

epic theatre a term used by Brecht for a coherent dramatic theory and practice characterized by sequential scenes rather than continuous narrative, alienation rather than illusion, and political urgency.
(66, 101–3, 189, 245–8)

epigraph a short motto or quotation prefixed to a text, typically between the title and the first paragraph. (285)

epilogue (1) an exductory speech or scene; (2) as Epilogue, a special rôle, one who speaks an epilogue to a play. (143, 158, 215)

epistemology how we know things, the study of knowledge; see ontology. (11)

essentialist of genre, a view that at least one element is essential (e.g. all tragedies must include a death). (51)

event a term used by the Fluxus movement in the 1960s to describe a short action that was self-contained; subsequently used loosely for various kinds of live art. (271)

exclusivity the idea that genres are mutually exclusive, and no art-work can be of two genres; a primary problem with essentialist theories of genre. (51)

exduction see **induction**.

exeunt see **exit**.

exit lit. 's/he leaves'; the departure of an actor/rôle from the stage (the plural is 'exeunt'); also the door or other means by which to do so. In epic theatre actors may be visible after exiting. (22)

Expressionist of sets, anti-realist, using distorted perspective and colouring, often to represent dark and disturbing states of mind. (There are other meanings in criticism and art history.) (54, 197–8)

extra a small non-speaking rôle, typically a member of a crowd, for which little acting-skill is required. The term is occasionally used in theatre, e.g. if invited members of the public are used to bolster a stage-crowd, but is common in film where the access and experience work as an extra offers has for some been a key to success. (182)

extra-dramatic outwith the dialogue and fiction of a play; prologues and epilogues, for example, are extra-dramatic address. (142)

F

F1 see **First Folio (F1)**.

facsimile an edition which exactly reproduces another edition, often photographically. (4, 28, 150, 289)

fade-out in theatre, a gradual dimming of stage-lights to darkness. (106)

fade-up in theatre, a gradual augmentation of stage-light. (106)

fading in theatre, a gradual alteration of light. (106)

fair-copy a hand-written or typed copy of a text free of corrections and errors, as distinct from foul papers. (149)

farce from Latin *farsa*, stuffed; a comic play in which scenes are intricately manipulated to deliver increasingly exaggerated situations at accelerating pace. (94–5)

farceur a writer of farces. (95, 128)

'Filthy Words' decision a 1978 US Supreme Court decision which effectively established a list of seven words that could not be broadcast; the name comes from the monologue 'Filthy Words' by George Carlin (b.1937). (209)

fire officer a local-government official who inspects theatres and productions to ensure that fire regulations are observed. (204)

First Folio (F1) *Mr. William Shakespeare's Comedies, Histories, & Tragedies. Published according to the True Originall Copies*. (London: Isaac Jaggard & Ed. Blount, 1623). The first collected plays of Shakespeare, and the only authority for 18 plays; the term *folio* means that each sheet of paper had been folded only once, and implies a large, handsome book. Facsimiles are available from Norton (hardback) and Applause/Routledge (paperback). (4)

first gallery in Jacobethan amphitheatres and Restoration theatres the lowest gallery in the auditorium, next to the pit; in later theatres it became the dress-circle. (138, 144)

first night the official opening night of a play, now usually not the first performance but scheduled after things have had a chance to settle down. (10)

first tetralogy Shakespeare's *1, 2, 3 Henry VI* and *Richard III*. (41)

first world in Shakespeare, the world in which a play opens, usually courtly or urban and in some way oppressive or corrupt; see **green world**. (82)

flagship company/theatre one built or founded with a national purpose or enjoying major subsidy. (127)

flats (wings) framed rectangles of canvas bearing painted scenes, usually perspectival, and arranged at angles (usually behind a proscenium arch) to create for the audience an illusory sense of depth and location. (139, 141)

fliers small (usually A5 or equivalent) advertisements, handed out or mailed. (204)

flies the area above a proscenium-arch stage, into which flats, etc. can be lifted out of audience-view. (142)

folio a book printed on sheets of paper which have been folded only once, giving two pages (four sides of text) to each sheet. Folios are usually large, a suitable format for collected works. (23, 148–9)

Fool (1) a popular entertainer, with a bright multi-coloured costume (motley), and a wooden dagger and/or ladle to carry; also (2) a position at court, a royal entertainer licensed (within variable limits) to be disrespectful; subsequently (3) a number of complex scripted rôles in Elizabethan drama, most famously Shakespeare's *King Lear*. Fools often acted as master-of-ceremonies at carnivals and some feasts, and could dispense both wisdom and moral force. 'Natural fools' were genuine simpletons, but all varieties of theatrical fool are anything but. (73–5, 137)

footlight one positioned to shine upwards from the stage-boards. (105)

Fop a supposed stock-character in Restoration comedy, dandified, vain, and usually gullible; a foil for the Rake. (64)

forestage in Restoration theatres that part of the stage in front of the proscenium-wall, where the front rows of the stalls would now usually be; particularly associated with comedic performance; see **scenic stage**. (64, 95, 140–1, 177)

form the shape/structure of an art-work, as distinct from its content; established shapes/structures (sonnet, concerto, portrait, etc.). (49)

forum theatre a form of theatre invented by Boal in which a community seeks radical alternatives to local problems by creating, enacting, and discussing other narratives. (104, 185)

foul papers a copy of a text with deletions, additions, corrections, etc. scribbled in; an author's working drafts, as distinct from fair copy. (23)

found material readily available, everyday material, perhaps gathered on site, and used to create a piece of art, e.g. litter, leaves, pebbles, newspaper. (272)

found text text not created especially for a performance but taken from another source, e.g. a book, flier, graffiti, advertising-copy, or packaging. (269)

fount (US **font**) a particular design of type-letters, numbers, and marks; each fount will include several faces, such as *italic* and **bold**. (28)

fourth wall an imaginary wall of glass filling a proscenium arch, supposed in (post-)Naturalist theatre to be transparent to an audience but not to actors. (99, 143)

foyer the entrance-hall of a theatre, between the street-doors and the auditorium. (11, 144)

fribbling (through) a useful seventeenth-century word for an actor's resort to roughly appropriate ad libbing if exact lines are forgotten. (126)

fringe theatre in the UK, originally experimental and/or unconventional low-budget theatre on the fringe of the Edinburgh Festival during the 1950s and 1960s; subsequently a generic term for such theatre, especially in London.

The growth of fringe theatre was notably boosted by the abolition of stage censorship in 1968. See **off-off-Broadway, West End**.   (144, 185, 212)

frons scaenae in Roman theatres, the rear wall of the stage, pierced by three doors; the equivalent of the Greek *skênê* and Jacobethan tiring-house wall.   (133, 135)

front-of-house in theatres, the area open to the public.   (206)

Futurism an art movement originating in Italy in 1909 with Marinetti's *Futurist Manifesto*, characterized by a violent departure from traditional forms and particularly concerned with the expression of movement.   (271)

G

gallery, galleries raised areas of seating encircling an auditorium.
     (133, 135, 138, 142)

gangster-movie a genre established during the Prohibition and Depression eras in the USA (1919–34), concentrating on gang warfare and criminality; always popular, the genre was greatly boosted in the 1990s by Tarantino. (112)

gaslight a means of providing lighting in theatre through gas flame, in use for most of the nineteenth century.   (106, 142)

gendered of theatre or theatrical spaces, restricted to or representing areas supposedly 'proper' to men or women.   (130, 132)

generic décor a decorative scheme used for a particular genre, such as black drapes for tragedy, cityscapes for comedy, etc.   (134, 137)

genre (1) an imprecise method of grouping art-works according to any specified criterion; a category between medium and form. (2) a process by which art-works, during and after consumption, arouse and fulfil or defeat a consumer's expectations, and are compared to other art-works. (3) the collective noun for named patterns of expectation generated by art-works.
     (49–55)

get in the process of bringing the set, costumes, props, etc. into the theatre before a run begins.   (205)

get out the final dismantling and removal from the theatre of a set when a run ends.   (205)

Globe I the first theatre on that site, 1599–1613; built from the transported timbers of The Theatre in Shoreditch (1576–99), it burnt down when wadding from a small cannon caught in the thatched roof during a performance of Shakespeare's *Henry VIII*.   (1)

Globe II the second theatre on that site, 1613–42; it cost *c*.£1,300 to rebuild, and had a tiled roof. Closed with all theatres in 1642, it was demolished in 1644.   (1, 137)

Globe III also known as 'Shakespeare's Globe', the reconstruction opened (after much effort by Sam Wanamaker, 1919–93) in 1997, on the south bank of the Thames, near the site of Globes I and II. (1, 195)

glosses brief paraphrases of obscure or ambiguous words or phrases, such as editors usually provide in annotation. (18)

gods a slang term for the upper(most)-circle of proscenium-arch theatres. (144)

Good Quarto as opposed to 'Bad Quarto', one that was printed from reliable copy, and not memorially reconstructed; often specifically Q2 *Hamlet*. (28)

gothic of script and type, having no curves, so that B, P, etc. are made wholly of straight lines. All gothic type is blackletter, but not all blackletter founts are gothic. (28)

gothic drama a Romantic genre characterized by mysterious settings, supernatural happenings, and plots which disturbingly treat social taboos. (90–1)

Grand-Guignol a sensationalist mix of horror and farce, typically in plays milking psychological suspense or dramatizing notorious murders; from the Théâtre de Grand-Guignol in Paris, founded by Oscar Méténier (1859–1913), which provided such fare from 1895 to 1962. The influence of Edgar Allen Poe (1809–49) is notable. (44)

grand opera full professional opera without spoken dialogue; the classic repertoire as performed in the great opera-houses; see **light opera**. (87)

green-room a room where off-stage actors can wait; a common-room during rehearsals and performance. (127, 128)

green world in Shakespeare, the alternative to the **first world**, usually reached by act 2 and dominating the rest of the play (e.g. Arden in *As You Like It*, Belmont in *Merchant*, Cyprus in *Othello*). Coined by Northrop Frye, (1912–91) to describe the structure of Shakespearean comedy, but though the green worlds of Shakespearean tragedy are more bleak than green the term still applies. (82)

Grex figures from Latin *grex*, 'a flock'; rôles representing audience-members who spectate and commentate, often unfavourably (though they tend to disagree with one another), but do *not* become involved in the action. The best-known examples are Mitis and Cordatus in Jonson's *Every Man Out* (1599), and Waldo and Stadtler in *The Muppet Show*. (216)

groundlings in Jacobethan theatre, those who stood in the pit; a collective term for various small bottom-feeding fish, seized into theatrical use by Hamlet: "O it offends mee to the Soule, to see a robustious Pery-wig-pated Fellow, teare a Passion to tatters, to verie ragges, to split the eares of the Groundlings: who (for the most part) are capeable of nothing, but inexplicable dumbe shewes, & noise" (3.2.8–12). (214)

ground rows long low flats, often shaped (as rooftops, trees, etc.). (194)

H

hack-work a derogatory term applied to rapidly written and commercially opportunistic plays which the playwright has undertaken wholly for money.   (151)

hack-writer one who dashes out work rapidly for money. The term is derogatory (a hack is a horse kept for hire), implying lack of literary skill; used of nineteenth-century playwrights who bashed out work in days.   (161)

hall-theatre a Jacobethan theatre with stage architecture like that of the amphitheatres but in a roofed hall; the best known, used by the King's Men from 1608 and associated with late Shakespeare, was the Blackfriars.   (138–9)

hamartia a much disputed word from Aristotle's *Poetics*, often wrongly translated (notably by S. H. Butler, 1850–1910) as 'tragic flaw', the weakness (pride, lust, over-confidence, diffidence, etc.) which causes a tragic figure to fall. The exact meaning is unclear, but the consensus is now for something like 'error arising from ignorance'.   (62)

Happening a term invented by Allan Kaprow in 1959; a form of live-art event initially driven by experimental visual artists, which came to represent a form of protest/provocation. In Britain the performance-aesthetic of Happenings developed a close connection with the music-scene which differentiates it from developments in continental Europe and the US.

Harlequinade originally a late seventeenth- and eighteenth-century English form of comic and acrobatic performance featuring Harlequin, a complex figure derived via the French Arlequin from Arlecchino in *Commedia dell'arte*. The Harlequinades of John Rich (?1682–1761) were the beginnings of pantomime, and though Harlequin has been sufficiently displaced by later styles of clowning to become emblematic of a bygone world he can still be seen, especially in mime. The word is sometimes used loosely to represent the many kinds of comic performance derived from *Commedia*.   (20, 91)

Hays (Office) Code a code of 'decency' to which Hollywood movies and comics were subject 1930–66, named for Will Hays (1879–1954), president of the Motion Picture Producers and Distributors of America (1922–45).   (209)

Health and Safety issues a general, and in the UK official, blanket-term for fire regulations and everything controlled by employment law; the manifest dangers of stage-fights, falls, and special effects, and the many perils of the backstage-area, make responsibility for Health and Safety a critical job.   (204)

Heaven(s) in Jacobethan amphitheatres a painted roof covering part of the stage and containing wire-flying machinery, etc.   (136–7)

Hell a term sometimes used for the understage area in Jacobethan amphitheatres, accessed via the stage-trap and from the tiring-house.   (137)

hierarchy the relations of genres to one another; a primary problem with essentialist theories of genre. (There are more general meanings.)   (51)

high canon the national canon of approved literature; the 'classics'. In English the high canon of drama comprises such authors as Marlowe, Shakespeare, Congreve, Sheridan, and Wilde. When applied to contemporary writing the term usually refers to those living (or recent) authors, such as Beckett, Pinter, and Churchill, who have been widely recognized as outstanding talents and become widely taught in schools within their lifetime, particularly by inclusion in compulsory national curricula. See also **canon**.   (108, 151)

history play, histories a genre developed by Shakespeare and established for posterity by F1 (*Mr. William Shakespeares Comedies, Histories, & Tragedies*); besides Shakespeare's 10 chronicle histories covering the reign of King John, the period *c*.1390–1485, and the reign of Henry VIII there are about 30 Jacobethan histories, most notably Marlowe's *Edward II* (*c*.1592) and Greene's *James IV* (c.1590).   (57, 81)

house-lights in modern electrified theatres, the lights in the auditorium, usually dimmed for performance.   (2, 144, 219)

house-manager one reponsible for everything front-of-house.   (206)

house-style the typographical style of a particular publishing house; in one house-style all stage-directions may be in lunulae; in another only stage-directions within speeches; and in a third none. The attractiveness and clarity of house-style is a site of commercial competition.   (21)

hubris presumption against the Gods, such as Prometheus stealing fire and Icarus flying too high; in Aristotle's *Poetics* a major cause of tragic action. (62)

hypertext properly, any text that operates on another, such as an index or appendix; now usually a multi-page, multi-element text on the web or CD with embedded links from words, etc. to supplementary information.   (18)

hyperverse the universe of connected hypertext pages.   (18)

I

iambic pentameter a five-beat verse line (ti-TUM ti-TUM ti-TUM ti-TUM ti-TUM) common in English poetry and dramatic verse; unrhymed iambic pentameter is 'blank verse', Shakespeare's basic verse-form.   (20)

illegitimate theatre in the period 1662–1843 unofficial drama with music and song, invented to evade theatre licensing laws.   (64, 89)

illusion a complex word often used loosely, but centrally concerned with perspectival scenery and special effects (e.g. sudden disappearances, beheadings), and so with the attempt to deceive the senses (but not the minds) of spectators by simulation. It may usefully be contrasted with 'realist' sets, which do not use, e.g., an illusory or painted chair, but the real thing. The phrase 'theatre of illusion' is, however, used to cover the nature of performance both on the scenic stage of Restoration theatres and in proscenium-arch theatres, including Naturalist plays demanding realist sets—in which case it specifically excludes both the metatheatricality common to the Shakespearean stage and Restoration forestage, and such anti-Naturalist techniques as Brechtian epic theatre. (87)

imposition in printing, making up pages on the bed of the press. (147)

impresario lit. 'undertaker'; one who promotes a show, the first-mover. (203)

improvisation (impro), improvised (1) unscripted, ad libbed, invented in performance. (2) a rehearsal or performance technique requiring actors to invent lines and/or actions within a prescribed scenario. (74, 77, 162)

indented quotation one distinguished from the main text by a narrower measure and spacing above/below. (Smaller founts may also be used.) (284, 288)

induction lit. 'leading in'; an opening scene or scenes which establish a frame for a play. The best-known example is the 'Christopher Sly' scenes at the beginning of Shakespeare's *Taming of the Shrew*, which show Sly as a spectator of the play about Katerina and Petruchio. The corresponding final scene(s), returning to the frame, are the exduction. (148)

Innamorati a collective term for the lovers in *Commedia dell'arte*. (79)

inset(-play) a play-within-a-play, requiring some actors to play actors and some to play an on-stage audience. Inset-plays may replicate the form of their host play or be deliberately distinct, as Shakespeare's usually are; and in either case serve to manipulate generic expectations. See **metatheatre**. (74, 82, 85, 215–16)

installation material placed to articulate and take account of its space. (272)

interactive of an art-work or performance, requiring the agency of the viewer; active participation may be as simple as pushing a button or as complex as full participation in performance. (272)

interdisciplinarity the creation within a performance or art-work of dialogues between different disciplines; the adjective is interdisciplinary. (269)

interludes originally short pieces played between the parts of something else (acts of a play, courses of a meal, etc.), but used in scholarship as a catch-all term for short sixteenth-century dramas of uncertain genre. (73)

interrogate of an art-work or performance, to ask challenging philosophical and aesthetic questions about form/content/spectatorship. Interrogating modes of seeing is a major impetus behind much post-Modernist work. (269)

intertextuality generally, the relations between texts; more specifically, the aspects of a given text which derive meaning from relations with another text or texts. (255)

interval a break between the parts of a play, or between successive performances. The practice of dividing almost all plays with an interval is largely of twentieth-century origin, and for many theatres is now a financially critical opportunity to ply audiences with drink and food. (73)

in the round of performance, with audience on all sides. (145)

invisible theatre a form of theatre developed under dictatorship by Boal in which a small group of actors perform politically sensitive scenarios to passing 'spectators', who are unaware that what they are watching is scripted and who may or may not intervene in the proceedings. (104, 211, 221)

issue-play one dealing with a specific issue in relation to a specific audience or community (black, gay or lesbian, prisoners, etc.). (103–4)

italicized set in slanting or italic letters, *such as these*, which are distinct from upright roman letters. (3, 16, 29)

J

Jacobean of the reign of James VI of Scotland and I of England (1603–25). (77)

Jacobethan a portmanteau of Elizabethan and Jacobean, hence, strictly, of the period 1558–1625, but often used primarily because the careers of Shakespeare, Jonson, Marston, Dekker *et al.* straddle the change of monarch in 1603. (77)

jig a short comic afterpiece to a play popular in the Elizabethan theatre, consisting of rhymed verses, often on topical issues, sung and danced by a group of actors with the clown playing a key rôle. Tarlton and Kemp were the jig-masters of their day. (176)

K

Kathakali dance-drama from Kerala, south India, dramatizing great Indian epics through a mixture of dance, music, and acting. (185)

Kennedy Center an arts complex in Washington, D.C., housing five theatre-spaces, built in 1971 to commemorate John F. Kennedy. (129)

kitchen-sink drama a term derived from fine art (the kitchen-sink school) for certain plays and screenplays of the late 1950s and early 1960s which signalled their politicized departure from middle-class drawing-room drama by choosing working-class kitchens instead. The best-known names are Wesker and novelist-screenwriter Alan Sillitoe (b.1928); the term is sometimes extended to Osborne and Delaney but now thought more patronizing than useful. (249)

L

Laban notation a special system of recording physical movement and dance choreography, developed by Hungarian Rudolf von Laban (1879–1958). (15)

Lachmann method a way of collating variant copies of a text to establish an authoritative text, developed by Karl Lachmann (1793–1851) for use with Homeric and biblical texts, and influentially applied to Shakespeare by W. W. Greg (1875–1959); most twentieth-century editions of Shakespeare print eclectic texts based on Lachmann's and Greg's procedures. (232)

Lady Chatterley trial the 1960 UK trial of Penguin Books for an 'obscene libel', publishing the words 'fuck' and 'cunt' in *Lady Chatterley's Lover* (1928) by D. H. Lawrence (1855–1930). The trial was a *cause célèbre*; to everyone's surprise Penguin were acquitted, effectively ending state censorship of printed verbal obscenity. (208)

Late Mediaeval of the period 1300–1500 CE. (62)

Laterna Magika lit. 'magic lantern'; a form of theatre developed by Svoboda in the 1950s, using live performers against multi-screen film projections of themselves. Subsequently also a theatre in Prague. (198)

legitimate theatre in the period 1662–1843 officially licensed drama without songs, dances, or musical interludes. (64, 89)

Lehrstück lit. 'learning play'; a short, participatory play with a direct political message, a form developed by Brecht. The plural is *Lehrstücke*. (102)

Lenaia the minor dramatic festival in Athens, three days in winter devoted primarily to comedy. (58)

light opera burlesque and comic opera including spoken dialogue and performed in ordinary theatres. Musicals are *de facto* light opera, but the terms imply status that matters to some people. (87)

lighting-board in theatre, a control-board attached to a computer which controls all stage- and house-lights. (106)

lighting-box the room, now often high in the auditorium, from where stage- and auditorium-lighting is controlled. (106, 144)

lighting-designer one responsible for the overall lighting-scheme of a show. (204)

lighting-plan a detailed lighting 'map' of a show drawn up by the lighting designer in consultation with the director. (106)

lighting-technician one responsible for working the lighting-board during performance. The term could be, but usually is not, applied to the stage-hands and others who must in Renaissance and Restoration performances have been responsible for lightning-effects, etc., and to those who worked gas- and limelight installations. (103)

limelight intense light provided by heating quicklime in an oxyhydrogen flame, in use in theatres from 1837 until the 1890s. (106)

line a single sequence of characters read from left to right; more generally, as lines, the words an actor must learn and speak. (5, 15)

lineation the division of a text into lines, usually unimportant in prose but potentially critical in dramatic verse. (29)

line of business the kind of parts for which an actor was engaged; the first recorded use is 1775, and it highlights the custom of actors becoming known for certain types of rôles in the stock-companies from the late eighteenth to the late nineteenth century. Such typecasting was then the norm and did not have the negative connotations it has today. (179)

literary agent a person employed by writers to find buyers for their work (for playwrights, theatres, or companies), negotiate fees, and take care of all legal and contractual aspects. Peggy Ramsay (1908–91) was England's most famous agent for playwrights. (160)

literary manager in theatrical administration a functionary responsible for dealing with unsolicited typescripts and commissioning new work; they may also be concerned with developing young writers. The term was popularized by Granville Barker and Tynan, who brought it into mainstream British use by adopting it as his title at the NT in 1963. It is sometimes used as a 'translation' of the German and French term 'dramaturg(e)', but the relations between dramaturgs and literary managers are complex. (9, 187–8)

liturgy the structure and verbal 'script' of a Christian service including the sacrament of Communion. (68)

live art notoriously difficult to define, live art is perhaps best understood as an umbrella term for many post-Modernist practices which include live performance (whether by performer or spectator); since the late 1970s it has absorbed the term 'performance art', can include Happenings, actions, events, interactive installations, and site-specific work, and means different things to different theorists and practitioners. (272)

living newspaper a revue-style theatre which offers alternative interpretations of current events, used as a part of agit-prop as well as a form in its own right; it is still commonly seen in television satire and political comedy. (100)

Living-Room Theatre originally a form of theatre devised in the 1970s by the Czech actor Pavel Kohout (b.1928), the performance of reduced texts of classic plays on demand in people's houses; subsequently any such take-away theatre. (210)

long-s the f-shaped 's' used until the eighteenth century. (27)

long-shot in film, a shot in which the object is placed at a distance and is therefore small. Abbreviated to LS, MLS (medium long shot), or ELS (extreme long shot). (111)

Lord Chamberlain in the UK, a Royal official, responsible from 1737 to 1968 for licensing stage-plays for performance. (90, 207–8)

Lord Chamberlain's/King's Men the most successful company on the Jacobethan stage, both before and after their change of name in 1603. Shakespeare was a sharer from 1594 to 1611; the star-actor 1594–1619 was Richard Burbage. (2)

lower-case of type-letters, small, like these, not UPPER-CASE. In hand-printing the small letters were in the lower-case of type. (15)

lunulae lit. 'little moons'; round brackets (like these). (16, 29)

M

Macro plays *Perseverance, Mankind,* and *Wisdom,* so called after an owner of the manuscripts, the Reverend Cox Macro (1683–1767). (73)

madcap a late-sixteenth-century term for one who behaves impulsively and exuberantly, as if mad, sometimes used to describe such characters as Simon Eyre in Dekker's *The Shoemaker's Holiday*; in the twentieth century it became particularly associated with couples in film comedies of the 1930s–40s, notably those starring Cary Grant (Archibald Leach, 1904–86) and Katherine Hepburn (b.1909). (64)

make-up artist one who makes-up actors for performance; even simple making-up requires art, and non-naturalistic making-up is a skill. (205)

malapropize, -ism to use the wrong word, a word wrongly used; an eponym from Mrs Malaprop in Sheridan's *The Rivals* (1775). (78)

marginalia notes written or printed in the margin of another work; the singular is marginalium. (119)

marketing officer one with responsibility both for advertising the show (company, theatre) and for selling advertising space in the foyer and programmes; often the head of a team. (204)

marking protocol a checklist of specific points, issues, or errors which examiners must in marking reward or penalize. (279)

mask a facial covering used in all classical and some other drama; full- and half-masks are distinguished, as are distorted masks (for comedy), with exaggerated volumes of one or more features, and neutral masks (for tragedy), naturally proportioned. (53, 58)

Mask with a capital M, a particular rôle in *Commedia dell'arte*. (78–9)

mask-work rehearsal and workshop exercises to enable actors to perform in masks; also the (exhausting) work of masked performance. (204)

masque a highly stylized Renaissance form, an aristocratic entertainment enacting harmony and virtue, often politically charged and performed by nobles for the monarch; the Jacobean and Caroline masques of Ben Jonson and Inigo Jones were highly spectacular and technologically innovative.
(57, 85–6, 193)

masquing-house a Jacobethan theatre specifically designed for masques, the stage being deep enough to allow the use of perspectival illusion. The best known was at Whitehall. (139)

Master of the Revels in England, a Royal official, responsible from 1574 to

1737 for licensing stage-plays for performance; the records of Renaissance Masters, especially Henry Herbert (1594–1673, Master 1624–42, 1660–73), are a valuable source for theatre-historians. (90, 207–8)

matinée lit. 'morning performance'; now usually an afternoon performance. In contemporary London theatre matinées are usually on Wednesdays, Thursdays, and Saturdays. (181)

mêchanê in Greek amphitheatres, a crane used to allow flying entrances/exits over the *skênê*. (181)

medium a mode or technology in which art can exist: music, print, film, performance, plastic art (e.g. sculpture), fine art (e.g. paint). (49)

melodrama lit. 'drama with music'; specifically a nineteenth-century form of theatre with conspicuous musical accompaniment to overwrought text, exaggerated emotions, and declamatory acting; hence a semi-pejorative term for hammy or overdone theatre. (64, 87, 92–3)

memorial reconstruction an explanation of some early editions which supposes the text to have been dictated to the printer by an actor, probably for money and inevitably with very many errors. (38)

metatheatre a complex term most often used to mean drama that is aware of its status as drama, and so exceeds both naturalistic acting and illusion; in Shakespeare it applies to inset-performances, such as the inset-plays in *Hamlet* and *Dream*, prologues, epilogues, dialogue that names parts of the performance-space, allusions to the 'true' gender of boys playing female rôles, intertextual invocations of other plays, etc. (82, 84–5)

the Method, Method acting a mainly American development of Stanislavski's theories and System. Its principal exponent was Lee Strasberg at the Actors' Studio; Method actors are trained to seek out and to identify with their character's inner motivations. (184)

Middle Comedy Greek comedy of 404–c.321 BCE, an intervenient period of major change without a major dramatist which saw the decline of the comedic chorus. (61)

middle-gallery the second circle, in Jacobethan amphitheatres open to anyone paying extra pennies, but in Restoration theatre associated specifically with bourgeois citizens. (142)

mike, miked back formations from 'microphone'; 'to mike' is to attach a microphone to someone or something. (107)

miles gloriosus the 'braggart soldier', a stock-character in Plautine comedy (and the title of one of his plays). See *Il Capitano*. (61, 81)

mime though it has complex classical roots, in contemporary use mime means (1) a style of silent acting, commonly with imaginary props and somewhat exaggerated (e.g. 'He mimes lighting a pipe'); and (2) actors trained in that style, especially in the French white-face tradition exemplified by Marcel Marceau (b.1923). (19, 185)

miracle-plays those dealing with miraculous events at saints' shrines, etc. (72)

mise-en-scène lit. 'putting-on-stage'. The French term for stage-production (a producer is a *metteur-en-scène*), used to designate everything materially necessary for a stage-performance, from costume and props to the set and lighting. (11)

mock-death a reported death, believed but not 'true'. Shakespeare used the device repeatedly both in comedy (Hero in *Much Ado*) and tragedy (Juliet in *Romeo*), and it can be extended to events like the supposed loss of Antonio's ships in *Merchant*. (39)

mock-up a practice-version of a set or stage used in a rehearsal-room. (127)

Modellbuch a Brechtian term; in the Berliner Ensemble, a meticulous photographic record of a production designed to show the techniques of epic acting and staging, produced as a book to facilitate dissemination. (189)

Modern of the period after 1700 CE. (62)

modernized of texts, made modern, comprising the choice of a new fount, redesigned and contemporarily conventional layout, changes in orthography, wholesale repunctuation, and usually the extensive addition of stage-directions. (28)

monologue a lengthy speech or scene in which only one person speaks (cf. dialogue); also a play or film-script intended for a single performer. (107)

montage in Brechtian theatre, the cutting and organization of autonomous scenes into a whole play. (There are other meanings in film studies and art history.) (102–3)

Morality (play), Moralities a loose term covering allegorical, satirical, or otherwise didactic plays, primarily of the fourteenth to sixteenth centuries; sometimes primarily those with allegorical rôles (Everyman, Pride, etc.). (71–5, 81)

Moscow Art Theatre (MAT) an ensemble company founded in 1898 by Constantin Stanislavski (1865–1938) and Vladimir Nemirovich-Danchenko (1858–1943) to promote post-Ibsenite Naturalism. Stanislavski's productions of Chekhov's plays rapidly established its international reputation and attracted other great names, notably Meyerhold and Craig. Based at the Hermitage Theatre (renamed the Gorky Theatre in 1932) from 1898 to 1973, using different studio-theatres, and then at a purpose-built MAT on Tverskoi Boulevard. Its Soviet history is complex, including a division between a Chekhov MAT and a Gorky MAT. (84–5, 166, 197)

motley etymology unknown; originally a cloth woven of mixed threads (cf. tweed, homespun), but subsequently a garment made of mixed cloths, implicitly brightly coloured and/or clashing, and hence a costume for Fools (the usual Shakespearean sense). (79)

Motley with a capital M, the business name of an influential team of female stage-designers based in London from the 1930s to the 1960s, and particularly associated with Gielgud and Olivier. (198–9)

movement-director a specialist in theatrical movement, often but not necessarily of a particular kind or style; physical-theatre companies may have permanent movement-directors, others will tend to hire as needed. (204)

multi-media of an art-work or performance, having recourse to more than one medium, e.g. mixing painting with video, or performance with film. (269)

multiple-choice question one in which a number of possible answers to a question are given, candidates having to mark one as correct. (283)

musical a popular form of light opera combining dancing with songs and dramatic plot; a major American twentieth-century form of entertainment, particularly associated with Broadway theatres and film. (87, 93)

musical comedy comic drama which evolved in the 1890s with little emphasis on plot and much emphasis on spectacle and song; barely distinct from light opera, musical comedy evolved into twentieth-century musicals. (93)

musical director a specialist in theatrical music, who may also compose and will superintend the rehearsal (and often performance) of musicians; in musicals sometimes an equal of the director. (204)

music-hall a variety entertainment of songs and comic turns which flourished *c.*1850–1914 and influenced both early film and Beckett.

(45, 93–4, 144, 219)

mute as noun, a non-speaking rôle. (37, 109, 262, 278)

Mystery play/cycle, Mysteries a sequence of short plays, dealing with one of two Christian mysteries, the history of the world from creation to doomsday or the life of Christ from Incarnation to Resurrection. (71–2)

N

National Theatre (NT), Royal National Theatre (RNT) campaigned for since 1848, but founded at the Old Vic, London, in 1963; the current site on the South Bank opened in 1976, with two large theatres, the Olivier and Lyttelton, and a studio-theatre, the Cottesloe; the NT performs classics, new plays, and (increasingly) musicals, and is the most prestigious producing-house in London; the Artistic Directors have been Laurence Olivier (1963–73), Peter Hall (1974–88), Richard Eyre (1988–95), and Trevor Nunn (1995–); Nick Hytner (b.1957) is due to take over in 2002. It was renamed the RNT for its silver jubilee in 1988. (54, 72, 187–8, 190)

nativity-play one dealing with the birth of Christ. (70)

natural fool a person of small wit; see **Fool**. (74)

Naturalism an artistic movement operating in the 1880s–90s, that advocated a combination of realist sets with as naturalistic as possible a style of acting to stress the relationship between humans and the material environment. (98–9, 126, 166, 183, 197–8)

naturalistic a complex word used very loosely and often confused with **Naturalism** and **realist(ic)**, but applying specifically to acting-style. Naturalistic acting seeks to minimize the gap between actor and rôle, and is most usefully contrasted with 'stylized' acting, which tends to foreground that gap; but each element of an actor's performance may be more or less naturalistic, or stylized. Naturalistic movement would be 'normal' walking or running, while stylized movement could be in unison, choreographed, or comically exaggerated; naturalistic delivery implies speaking 'as people do', while stylized delivery could respect verse as verse or be accompanied by formal gestures. Every age tends to think its own preferred acting style 'more naturalistic' (i.e. a better representation of 'reality') than that of other ages, and to perform older plays in new ways: and it follows that non-naturalistic dialogue (e.g. blank verse) may be delivered naturalistically (as if prose). Criticism which assumes texts to be naturalistic often treats rôles as characters and may have problems with metatheatre. (14, 143)

neo-Classical deriving from the Renaissance rediscovery of classical ideas and writings; of dramatic theory and practice, a rigid interpretation of Aristotle may be implied, e.g. a strict maintenance of generic decorum. (62)

neutral of masks, naturally proportioned without distorted/exaggerated volumes. (58)

New Cambridge Shakespeare a major one-volume-per-play edition, in progress since 1984; notable for including editions of Qq and *Edward III*. (235)

New Comedy classical Greek comedy after *c*.321 BCE, with five-act structures, no chorus, and emergent stock-characters; the world of Menander. (61)

New Shakespeare a major one-volume-per-play edition edited by Quiller-Couch and Dover Wilson, published 1921–66; now widely disparaged for bizarre textual decisions and typography and aggressively Christian interpretation, particularly of *Measure* and *King Lear*. (233–4)

Noh theatre a form of Japanese theatre created by Kanami (1333–84) and his son Zeami (1363–1443), reflecting the ritualistic codes of samurai warriors and performed only by men. There is a specific stage-design, and most action revolves around two masked actors, the *shite* and the *waki*. Some European playwrights were influenced by the tradition, notably Yeats. (185)

Notate lit. 'notes'; Brecht's term for written critical observations of rehearsal and performance, required in the training of directors and dramaturgs. (189)

notes (1) in theatre-practice, observations/instructions by a director to actors and stage-crew, typically given orally after a rehearsal or performance. (2) in academic editions of texts, explanatory information or comment provided at the foot of the page or after the text. (18)

notice originally a brief description of a play, the actors appearing in it, and any notable features of the production, critical evaluation being minimal or non-existent; now largely synonymous with review. The word is first recorded in 1835, but the practice began in the eighteenth century. (229)

O

objective a Stanislavskian term denoting the identification of a character's motivation/desire within a single unit of action. (183)

octavo a book printed on sheets of paper which have been folded three times, giving eight pages (16 sides of text) to each sheet. Octavos are usually small, a suitable format for pocket editions. (23)

off-Broadway in New York, from the early 1950s, an alternative to the glossy commercial tradition of Broadway; low-budget productions of plays by Tennessee Williams and Albee were notable off-Broadway successes. (144)

off-off-Broadway in New York, from the early 1960s an alternative theatre-scene in Greenwich Village and the Lower East Side, developed from concerns that off-Broadway had become commercialized by success. (144, 185)

off-stage of actors, not visible to the audience (in epic acting actors who have exited from the action may remain on-stage); the equivalent in theatre-space of theatrical space-without. (60, 130)

oikos in Greek thought, the private, 'feminine' and domestic space of home and hearth, often mapped on to the theatrical space-without immediately behind the *skênê*. (130, 132, 141)

Old Comedy Greek comedy of *c.*490–404 BCE, the world of Aristophanes, with full chorus and costume. (60–1)

omphalos in Greek amphitheatres, a navel-stone marking the centre of the *orchêstra*. (131)

onkos in Roman tragedic practice, a distinctive mask with a high forehead (exaggerated upper volume). (134)

on-stage of actors or action, visible to the audience; the equivalent in theatre-space of theatrical space-within. (60, 130)

ontology how things are, the study of being; see **epistemology**. (11, 279)

open exam one in which papers are issued and candidates may then depart, completed scripts being due in a specified time, typically 8, 24, or 72 hours. (277, 283)

opera a Renaissance form of élite musical drama in which music is primary and all dialogue sung; opera-houses must therefore make acoustic design central and provide a full-size *orchestra-pit*. (36–7)

oratory lit. 'speaking, pleading'; the art of public speaking, studied by lawyers, politicians, etc. as well as by actors. Oratory is often accompanied, even today, by exaggerated and formal gestures, and in discussions of Renaissance acting may be used in (derogatory) contrast to personation.　　(174, 178)

orchêstra lit. 'place of dancing'; in Greek amphitheatres, a circular acting-area used particularly by the chorus, between the rectangular stage in front of the *skênê* and the audience.　　(131, 133)

orchestra-pit in opera-houses and proscenium-arch theatres designed for musical drama, a pit between the stage and stalls for the musicians.　　(141)

orthography 'correct' spelling, and (the study of) systems of spelling which are correct at one time but subsequently change.　　(28, 31)

outreach staff those in a theatre/company education department who are charged with attracting new audiences by proactively contacting schools, businesses, etc. to arrange talks, workshops, theatre-visits, etc.　　(205)

overlap both as verb and noun, the requirement that (part of) two or more speeches be delivered simultaneously. Caryl Churchill (b.1938) has developed new notation for overlaps.　　(21)

oversound also 'sound-over'; in film, sound that is not represented as being directly audible within the world of the film itself, e.g. voice-over.　　(107)

Oxford Complete Shakespeare the major recent one-volume edition, edited by Stanley Wells and Gary Taylor, published in 1986 to enormous controversy. Q-titles were preferred, entries on the two plays known to be lost were included with some dubiously attributed poems, and the eclectic text of *Lear* was abandoned, both Q1 and F1 texts being printed.　　(235)

Oxford Shakespeare a major one-volume-per-play edition, in progress since 1982.

P

pageant-wagon a wheeled stage used for performance either while moving, or at successive venues; civic and guild performances of mystery cycles were staged in this way.　　(71, 134–5)

Pantalone the Pantaloon, a stock-character in *Commedia dell'arte* descended from the *senex* or 'old man' of Plautine comedy; Pantalone is the father of the female love-interest, and jealous of his daughter's chastity and the money for her dowry. The rôle is common in Shakespearean comedy and tragedy, for example Baptista in *Shrew*, Polonius in *Hamlet*, and Desdemona's father (Brabantio) in *Othello*.　　(20, 61, 80, 82)

pantomime (panto) a Christmas entertainment derived from *Commedia dell'arte*, developed in the early eighteenth-century, and incorporating popular song, topical comedy, and audience-participation rituals. Now often based on fairy-tales, pantomimes remain staple Christmas fare, commonly feature leading TV personalities, draw a socially wide family audience, and are financially vital to most regional English theatres.　　(91–2, 144, 219)

Pantomime Dame in pantomime, a flamboyant, exaggerated older woman, always played by a (notably unfeminine) man; the best known is perhaps the Widow Twankey in *Aladdin*. (92)

Pantomime Horse (or other animal) a costume-animal requiring two actors; the source of a common acting joke about playing the 'rear-end' or being 'promoted' to the 'head-end'. (92)

paraskênia in Greek amphitheatres, wings extending beyond the *skênê* and leading to the *eisodoi*; stages with such wings. (131)

passion-play one dealing with Christ's Passion (torture and crucifixion).(70)

pastiche from Italian *pasticcio*, a pie; originally a composition made of fragments from different sources, a "medley; a hotchpotch, farrago, jumble" (*Sh. OED*), and still sometimes used in this sense (cf. satire); but in current use pastiche is to style or genre as parody is to an individual work. Thus one might parody *Hedda Gabler* but would pastiche Ibsen or tragedy. (89–90)

pastoral a classical form of poetry featuring the refined love of shepherds and swains, etc. in rural settings; dramatically important in tragicomic theory and practice as a setting in which tragedy and comedy can blend. Shakespearean green worlds are often pastoral. (80)

pathos lit. 'suffering, feeling'; the quality in artistic representation, often visual and musical, which excites feelings of pity and sadness. (92)

patter rehearsed, frequently used, and often rapidly delivered speech, such as that of barkers, salesmen, army sergeants, etc. (78)

Pedrolino a rôle in *Commedia dell'arte*, 'little Peter', unusually not masked but in white-face, giving him a range of expression the Masks lack. The youngest and ill-treated son, often a servant to Pantalone, and the main source of the French Pierrot. (78–80)

pendant of forms or genres, not occurring independently; a form that hangs from another, as satyr-plays from tragedies. (57)

performance art a pre–1970s term for what is now usually called live art. (271–2)

period (1) a classical, rhetorically defined unit of syntax and argument, composed of *cola* (colon-to-colon) and *commata* (comma-to-comma), and closer to the modern paragraph than the modern sentence; periods were the dominant method of organizing prose until the late seventeenth century. (2) latterly, and in the USA, a full-stop. (29)

period-detail incidental details of life in a historical period, such as styles of clothing, furniture, props, and language, used to further the illusion of a play set in that period. (121, 195)

personation the playing of a recognizable, sustained character-rôle, used by Jacobethans to distinguish a new type of acting from traditional oratory. (173–4)

perspectival scenery painted boards or cloths which give an illusion of depth and may be used as a backcloth or placed at an angle to the audience. (85, 139, 140–1, 178)

photo-quotation an inserted photograph of text used as a quotation; now usually a scanned image. (23, 289)

Phrygian Phrygia was a country in Asia Minor (within modern Turkey); the Phrygian mode of music, though it had some influence on later Western music, was more distinctly 'Eastern', as modern Arabic music is. (59)

phylakes simple Greek wooden or temporary stages. (130)

physical theatre any approach to performance that privileges physical fitness and acrobatic skills above psychological (particularly Stanislavskian) approaches to 'character'. The best-known teachers of physical theatre have been Meyerhold, Grotowski, and Decroux. (164, 184–5)

pictorial of staging or theatre, concerned to present a picture, typically with perspectival scenery and elaborate sets but also costume, tableaux, etc. (93)

Pierrot A complex Franco-Italian figure derived from Pedrolino (Little Peter), the ill-treated youngest son in *Commedia dell'arte*. Popularized by Molière, Pierrot had by *c*.1675 his characteristic loose white costume and white-face, and in a powerfully sentimental form survives to this day, especially in mime. He is probably a principal source for the white-faced (as opposed to red-nosed) circus-clown who often has on one cheek a painted tear. (20, 79)

Pinteresque the adjective from Harold Pinter (b.1930), deriving from his early work and best-glossed in the phrase 'comedy of menace'. (255)

pit in Jacobethan amphitheatres the standing-area for audiences, the floor of the amphitheatre, between the edges of the stage and the first-gallery; in Restoration theatre the same area, now equipped with some seating and used particularly by gallants, prostitutes, etc. (38, 141)

plagiarism passing off another's work as your own by failing to indicate that it is a quotation; a heinous academic sin, and in most legal codes a quasi-criminal offence, the theft of intellectual property. (287)

platea in Roman theatres, the rectangular stage-area immediately in front of the *frons scaenae*; see **via**. (33)

platform-stage the simplest kind of stage, a platform without architecture. (134–5)

Plautine the adjective from Titus Maccius Plautus (*c*.250–184 BCE), a great Roman comedic playwright particularly associated with the development of slave rôles (clever, treacherous, incompetent, etc.). Plautus also used the *senex*, the old and authoritarian father-of-the-heroine jealous of his daughter's chastity and dowry, and the *miles gloriosus* or braggart soldier; his work deeply influenced *Commedia dell'arte* and Shakespeare. (51, 61, 74, 78)

play-bills eighteenth- and nineteenth-century posters advertising performances, which gave far more information than is usual today but were without pictures. (194)

player an actor; the usual term until the early seventeenth century. (173)

play-reader in theatrical administration a functionary responsible for reading new plays and reporting on their quality and suitability for production. Play-readers have always been vital to theatres, and often work closely with the literary manager and artistic director, but are almost wholly ignored in dramatic criticism and theatre-history. (9, 20, 187)

play-within-a-play see inset (-play).

point "A gesture, vocal inflection, or some other piece of theatrical technique used to underline a climactic moment in a speech, rôle, or situation; a moment so underlined usu. used with the implication that the integrity of the performance as a whole is being subordinated to the desire for immediate applause." (*OED2*, IV.10.c). The first recorded use was in 1822; Edmund Kean's points were particularly admired and his style influential. George Taylor defines it more specifically as the moment when an actor suddenly strikes a new note or posture to create the impression of a new passion. (179–80)

point-of-view shot in film, a shot taken from the point of view of a particular character on-screen, the camera substituting for the character's eyes. Abbreviated to POV. (111)

polis in Greek thought, the public, 'masculine', and civic space of city and politics; often mapped on to theatrical space-within. (130, 132, 141)

Porticus Pompeii a large park within the Roman Theatre of Pompey. (133)

post-Modernist a term with many definitions, often used as a buzz-word without regard to any of them. We always use the hyphen and capital 'M', and mean 'coming after, and having absorbed, Modernism' (i.e. an international movement, principally in the arts in the first third of the twentieth century and troublingly coincident with Fascism, characterized by the rejection of long-established artistic paradigms in favour of new paradigms). Other specific definitions, centred on the ways in which IT has restructured information-storage and articulation, have been advanced by the French philosophers Jean Baudrillard (b.1929) and Jean-François Lyotard (b.1924), and the American Marxist critic Fredric Jameson (b.1934), for whom post-Modernism is a distinctive phase of late capitalism. (269–70)

practical criticism the exercise of close reading, examined in many universities by setting passages of drama, poetry, or prose upon which candidates are required to comment in detail, usually within a sharply limited time. The term was popularized by I. A. Richards (1893–1979), and has been hugely influential; it has also been condemned as soulless and unattractive to students, but the practice, under various names, remains a staple and usually enjoyable exercise in teaching literature. (241)

pratfall in comic stage-business a fall in which someone lands on their prat, or arse. (66)

press-night a designated night early in a production, after the previews, to which reviewers are invited; it may also be the first night. The convention of having a press-night seems to date only from the 1970s. (10, 17)

presswork in printing, work on the press itself: inking, paperwork, pulling, etc. (147)

previews the first few performances of a production, preceding the press- and first nights; a settling-in period to get things running smoothly. (10)

Principal Boy in pantomime, the hero, always played by a female actor. (92)

problem play a term coined in the late nineteenth century for plays such as Ibsen's *An Enemy of the People*, in which the plot turns on an insoluble difficulty, applied by the critic F. S. Boas to some Shakespearean plays, and subsequently distorted in critical usage to imply that the problem is generic indeterminacy: *Troylus*, *Measure*, and *All's Well* are the usual suspects, but *Caesar*, *Hamlet*, *Anthony*, and *Cymbeline* have all been indicted. (63)

producer before *c.*1939 an alternative name for directors, but now (as in film) the most senior non-creative officer in a production, with overall responsibility for finance, procurement, hiring, and publicity. (203–4)

producing-house a theatre that produces shows, often with a resident company. (204)

production dramaturg from *Produktionsdramaturg*; a post-Brechtian term for one who works with a director, acting as a researcher, adviser (usually textual), sounding-board for ideas, and critic of process. (189)

production dramaturgy the work of a production dramaturg. (189–90)

production staff a general term for those involved in creating a show who do not have to be present for performance. (205)

profit-sharing the sharing of box-office profits. (159)

programme (US program) (1) the plays put on at a specified venue; the choice of texts to perform over a season. (2) a glossy pamphlet sold to audiences which typically includes a cast-list, company-biographies, a brief critical essay on the play or its author, and much advertising. The educational use of programmes began with Brecht and was imported to the UK in the mid-1960s by Kenneth Tynan at the NT. (121, 204)

proliferation the necessity, given exclusivity, of creating a new genre to accommodate any work that does not exactly fit any existing genre; a primary problem with essentialist theories of genre. (There are more general meanings.) (51)

prologue (1) an introductory speech or scene; (2) as Prologue, a special rôle, one who speaks a prologue to a play or act, as in Shakespeare's *Henry V*. (61, 158, 215)

promenade a style of acting and/or mode of production in which an audience must move to successive locations during a single performance. (54)

prompt-copy see the Book.

prompt-corner in theatres using a prompter but lacking a prompter's box, a corner of the stage where the prompter sits. (141)

prompter a person whose job is to follow a performance in the book and prompt actors who forget their lines (or dry). (202)

prompter's-box in proscenium-arch (and perhaps later Restoration) theatres, a box built in to the front of the stage for the prompter. (141, 143)

proof-reader in publishing a person (often the author) who checks the proofs, the first set of printed pages, for mistakes, and marks up the proofs for final corrections before the print-run begins. (9)

prop an abbreviation for 'stage-property', any movable object needed on stage by an actor (personal props include walking-sticks, pens, etc., but not costume) or as part of the set (e.g. books, ironing-boards, etc.). (11)

prop-maker a less straightforward job than it sounds: daggers may have to be retractable or sturdy-but-safe, some props are made to be destroyed and others to be indestructible, and theatre has a way of needing unlikely things at short notice. (204)

property-master one responsible for issuing and retrieving props during performance; in larger companies also a property-manager overseeing the general maintenance and hiring-out of props. (205)

proscenium arch in a theatre the proscenium wall divides the stage from the auditorium, and is pierced by the proscenium arch, usually curtained, through which audiences watch framed action. (35, 95)

proscenium door in Restoration theatres, a door on to the forestage. (141)

proscenium wall a wall pierced by the proscenium arch, dividing a theatre into areas restricted to actors/stage-crew and predominantly for audience. (140)

protagonist lit. 'first player'; the first actor/rôle in Greek tragedy upon whom the drama was centred, and hence the leading rôle in any play. (60)

psychological realism the treatment of rôles as real people whose behaviour must be psychologically coherent, plausible, and related to their material circumstances. (98, 183)

psychomachia Greek, traditionally translated as 'The Battle for Mansoul'; a name for a work constructed as a struggle for a human/Christian soul between vices and virtues; also the name of the first such text, by Prudentius (348–405 CE). (73)

pub-theatre a studio-theatre in or above a bar such as the Bush and King's Head in London. (128, 144)

puff an eighteenth-century term for an exaggerated commendation, and as a verb, hyperbolically to commend and promote. (223–4)

Pulcinella a Mask in *Commedia dell'arte*, sometimes one of the *zanni* but also a small trader or shopkeeper, and as such a master rather than a servant. The name lit. means 'little chicken', and he tends to strut and have a big beaky nose, like his main English descendant, Mr Punch. (20, 78–9)

Punch-and-Judy show a traditional English glove-puppet show first recorded in the 1660s; the typical routines featuring nutcracker-faced Mr Punch (hook-nose and hook-chin), his long-suffering and irascible wife Judy, their baby, a policeman, Mr Punch's dog Toby, some sausages and much slapstick had largely been established by the later eighteenth century. Mr Punch is a descendant of Pulcinella in *Commedia dell'arte*. (20, 79, 91)

Q

quarto a book printed on sheets of paper which have been folded twice, giving four pages (eight sides of text) to each sheet. Quartos are usually about the size of modern paperbacks, a suitable format for individual plays.(23, 148–9)

Quem quaeritis (trope) lit. 'Whom do you seek?', words spoken by an angel to the three Marys at the empty tomb of the risen Christ (Matthew 28:1–7, Mark 16:1–7), and used in the Introit to the Easter Mass; subsequently a name for the trope in liturgical drama whereby a Christian seeks Christ. (73)

R

radio-play a play written specifically for radio, i.e. to be heard, not seen.(108–9)

Rake a supposed stock-character in Restoration comedy, a witty libertine, when present often the protagonist. (64, 158)

raked of a stage, angled, so that an actor upstage is physically higher than one downstage; a raked stage helps perspectival illusion. (85, 140, 142)

ratings a system of estimating audience-figures for TV shows. (109)

realist(ic) a complex term used very loosely, and often confused with both **naturalistic** and **Naturalism**, but primarily associated with (post-) fourth-wall theatre and applying to sets and props, such as those for drawing-room drama, which seek to reproduce the real world not by illusion but in fact: thus real furniture, telephones, food and drink, etc. are used, while guns must be able to go 'bang' and swords to be convincingly fenced with. Playwrights assuming a realist *mise-en-scène* will tend to assume naturalistic acting, and the dialogue, costumes, etc. of their plays are by extension sometimes described as realist. (93)

realization of a rôle or play, its physical manifestation on stage or film.(184)

receiving-house a theatre that does not produce shows, but only receives shows produced elsewhere. (204)

reception the critical, public, academic, and commercial response to an edition or a production. (35–6)

reconstruction an attempt to stage a play as it would have been staged originally. (170)

regional new writing organization in the UK, one set up to service the needs of and lobby for new playwrights in the regions, e.g. North West Playwrights (Manchester), Yorkshire Playwrights, and Northern Playwrights (Newcastle). (191)

rehearsal lit. 'repeating aloud'; the process of preparing a performance before opening; a session of preparation. (2, 123–7, 170–1)

rehearsal-period the time allowed for rehearsal before a show opens. (123, 127)

rehearsal-room a room purpose-built for rehearsing, equipped for theatrical convenience and actors' personal safety. (127)

repertoire the performance-stock of a given theatre, culture, or period. (124, 187)

repertory theatre a twentieth-century British form of primarily regional theatre in which permanent companies based in urban theatres maintained a substantial repertoire of classic and new plays, each production typically running for one week. (126)

requiem from Latin *requies*, 'rest', used in the Introit to the Mass for the Dead; a service or art-work commemorating someone or something dead. (69)

resident-dramatist a playwright who 'resides' in a theatre or company and writes specifically for it/them. (158)

Restoration generally, of the time following the Restoration of Charles II in 1660; of drama, the period 1660–1737, including work by Behn, Congreve, Dryden, Etherege, Farquhar, Gay, Otway, Vanbrugh, and Wycherley. (53)

Restoration comedy a period variant characterized by witty dialogue, often set in London. (63–4)

Restoration tragedy a period variant characterized by high stylization of dialogue and heroism, often set abroad. (53)

revenge-tragedy tragedy in which the central action is the taking of revenge, often ending in the death of the revenger; promoted during the Renaissance by the influence of Seneca, major revenge tragedies include Kyd's *Spanish Tragedy* (*c.*1589), *Hamlet* (1600), and Middleton's *Revenger's Tragedy* (*c.*1606). (60)

review a critical account of a new production, usually published in a newspaper or weekly magazine within a few days of the opening. (2, 17)

reviewer one who writes reviews; see **theatre-critic**. (8)

revival any production of a play after the first. (11, 15, 151)

revolve a nineteenth-century development, a part of the stage that can be rotated; technology has now made possible vertical revolves in which a scene or flat can be flipped as well as revolved. (143)

rigger one who rigs lights, sound, etc. (204)

Riverside Shakespeare the market-leader among one-volume editions, both in the 1st (1974) and 2nd (1997) editions; notable for excellent introductions and generous illustration. (4, 234–5)

rôle a part in a play; a sequence of lines and actions that an actor must learn. (10, 13)

Romances a late-nineteenth-century label for Shakespeare's last plays (*Pericles*, *Cymbeline*, *Winter's Tale*, and *Tempest*) which profoundly fuse comedy with tragedy. (63)

Roscius from Quintus Roscius Gallus (*c*.120–62 BCE), a great Roman actor famed for generic versatility; hence a term of praise for a complete actor. (133, 173, 178)

Royal Academy of Dramatic Art (RADA) England's most famous school of acting, founded by Beerbohm Tree in 1904. (182, 185)

Royal Box the best in the house, usually central in the first-circle directly opposite the stage and optimally placed for perspectival illusion; so called from the provision of a box for King Charles II in Restoration theatres. (141)

Royal Court (Theatre) (RCT) built in Sloane Square, London, in 1888; made famous in 1904–7 under the management of J. E. Vedrenne (1867–1930) and Granville Barker; a principal venue for avant-garde playwrights, including Shaw, Ibsen, Robins, Arthur Schnitzler (1862–1931), W. B. Yeats (1865–1939), and Maurice Maeterlinck (1862–1949); its repertoire and ethos provided a model for independent theatre-companies and inspired the repertory-theatre movement. Not in theatrical use 1932–52, but as the home of the English Stage Company under the management from 1956 to 1965 of George Devine, and from 1965 to 1972 of William Gaskill (b.1930), again became the foremost new-writing venue in England, staging work by Osborne, Brecht, Wesker, Ionesco, Arden, David Storey (b.1933), and Bond, and recovering the plays of D. H. Lawrence. Later artistic directors have been Oscar Lewenstein (1972–7), Stuart Burge (1977–9), Max Stafford-Clark (1979–93), Stephen Daldry (1993–9), and Ian Rickson (1999–), and it remains a principal venue for new writers, including Kane, Ravenhill, Crimp, and McDonagh. In the 1990s limited space forced many productions into other theatres, and it reopened in 2000 after major redevelopment with the Jerwood Theatre Downstairs (the main-house) and Jerwood Theatre Upstairs (a smaller space). (97, 208, 237, 248, 250)

Royal National Theatre (RNT) see National Theatre (NT).

Royal Shakespeare Company (RSC) founded in 1960 by Peter Hall with the aim of producing both old (mainly Shakespearean) and modern classics; based in Stratford-on-Avon, where they use the Royal Shakespeare Theatre (RST, known before 1961 as the Shakespeare Memorial Theatre), The Other Place (a small studio-theatre opened in 1974), and The Swan (a thrust-stage theatre opened in 1986), and London, where they have used the Barbican

Centre since 1982; the artistic directors have been Peter Hall (1960–8), Trevor Nunn (1968–86), Terry Hands (1978–90), and Adrian Noble (1990–). In 2001 plans were announced to quit the Barbican and significantly change the structure and operation of the company, but what will actually happen is presently unclear. (12)

royalties an author's percentage of income from performance or print-sales of their work. (159, 164)

rubric (1) the general instructions for an exam, usually printed on the cover, specifying the time allowed, the number of questions to be answered, etc.; (2) the wording of an individual exam-question, including any specific directions. Rubric infringements are usually subject to a formal penalty. (278)

run a sequence of consecutive public performances, the period for which a play is 'on'. In Renaissance practice runs were rarely longer than one night, though a play could remain in the company repertoire for years; but in 1624 Middleton's *A Game at Chess* ran for nine nights, and after the Restoration runs of a week seem to have become more usual. Agatha Christie's *The Mousetrap* has been running in London since 1952. (2)

S

safety-curtain a 'curtain' of fire-resistant material which can be lowered to separate stage from auditorium in proscenium-arch theatres; it may be a legal requirement in larger theatres. (107)

Saints' plays those telling of the lives (and usually martyrdoms) of saints, performed on the proper feast-day. (72)

satire lit. 'art-work in a mixed style'; now usually art that attacks, denounces, mocks, or otherwise urges correction and reform. (52, 58)

satyr-play a classical dramatic genre featuring satyrs, half-bestial servants of Dionysus with permanent erections; always appended to tragic trilogies. (57–8)

Savoy operas light operas by Gilbert and Sullivan staged by D'Oyly Carte at the Savoy Theatre in London in the last quarter of the nineteenth century. (87, 89)

scaena in Roman theatres, the stage itself. (133–4)

scaenae ductiles in Roman theatres, painted canvas panels set into the *frons scaenae* which could be covered by curtains (*siparia*). (134)

scaenae versatiles in Roman theatres, rotatable double- or triple-sided painted canvas panels set into the *frons scaenae*. (134)

Scapino a Mask in *Commedia dell'arte*, one of the *zanni*. *Scappare* means 'to flee, scarper', but though a coward Scapino is also an intriguer and opportunist with an eye for money and love. (79)

Scaramuccia a Mask in *Commedia dell'arte*. The name lit. means 'skirmisher',

and he is a lower-class version of *Il Capitano*, often a servant to an impover-
ished gentleman. (79)

scene (1) the basic units into which plays may be divided. In the 'French' or
'classical' system a new scene begins whenever any main character enters or
exits, or when something important happens; in the 'English' system, always
used for Shakespeare and now much the most common system, a scene ends
only when the stage is clear, and a scene-division often means a change of time
or location. (2) in Restoration play-texts a term used in stage-directions for the
scenic stage, and implicitly for the painted perspectival illusions of buildings
or landscapes created by the flats and shutters of the scenic stage.
(5, 140, 193–4)

scene-division dividing a play into scenes; the break between scenes. In editions of Renaissance plays these are often indicated by editors, but in the English system (see **scene**) there is little doubt about where scene-divisions
fall. (5)

scene-painter one who paints perspectival illusion on flats, a highly skilled
task. See **scene (2)**, **set-painter**. (193–4)

scenic stage (scene) in Restoration theatres the part of the stage behind the
proscenium wall, seen by the audience only through the proscenium arch;
used for perspectival scenery and associated particularly with tragedic performance. In stage-directions 'scene' usually means the (several, collective)
pictorial images on the flats on the scenic stage. (140, 178)

scenography set-decoration, including the provision of perspectival
flats. (131)

screwball comedy a screwball is, in baseball, a pitch thrown with reverse
spin which distorts its natural curve; the term screwball comedy was coined to
describe the 1930s–40s style of film comedy particularly associated with Cary
Grant (Archibald Leach, 1904–86) and Katherine Hepburn (b.1909) in such
films as *Bringing Up Baby* (1938) and *The Philadelphia Story* (1940), and usefully
describes the style of some Restoration comedies. (64)

scribe a professional writer by hand. (28, 147)

script lit. 'something written'; often used as a synonym for 'text', but also
used in opposition to 'text' to distinguish the written from the published, and
the verbal from the performative. (9, 37)

scriptorium a room used by scribes, typically in a monastery. (147)

season an annual period devoted to (new) productions; in Elizabethan and
later English practice usually autumn to early summer (in late summer aristo-
crats returned to their estates and theatre-companies toured). A Christmas
season was associated with the court, and playing was forbidden during Lent
(a rule only intermittently enforced). Modern commercial theatre-practice
may offer several distinct 'seasons', but if unqualified an autumn–to–summer
theatrical 'year' is probably meant. (124)

season-set (also **season-stage**) one used for all plays in a season; an economy, but also a challenge to designers. (200)

second gallery in Jacobethan amphitheatres the middle-gallery. (138)

second tetralogy Shakespeare's *Richard II*, *1* and *2 Henry IV*, and *Henry V*. (40)

seen of passages set in exams for comment (or translation), from previously specified texts which candidates have been able to study. (277)

seen through the press supervised and corrected during printing; editions seen through the press by authors have particular authority. (22)

self-censorship internalized restraint from writing or behaviour that would (or might) be controversial; the expedient lack of curiosity; devotion to not rocking the boat; the aim of much official censorship. (209, 212)

Senecan the adjective from Lucius Annaeus Seneca (*c*.4 BCE–65CE), a great Roman politician, philosopher, and tragic playwright. Senecan tragedy is particularly associated with horrific revenge, and greatly influenced Elizabethan revenge-tragedies including *The Spanish Tragedy* and *Hamlet*. (51)

senex the 'old man', a stock-character in Plautine comedy. See Pantalone. (61)

sensation drama a nineteenth-century genre evolved from early melodrama; extravagant spectacles, often of disasters, were central. (93, 195)

sentence (1) in Jacobethan use sometimes a legal sentence, a judgement, but often 'sententiousness, self-consciously dignified language'. (2) in modern use, the largest unit of syntax, composed of one or more clauses, and normally containing at least one grammatical subject, one transitive or intransitive verb, and if appropriate an object; typographically, sentences begin with a capital letter and end with a full-stop. (29)

sentimental drama prevalent in the eighteenth century, a self-consciously pious drama with an exaggerated insistence on the claims of Christian virtue and socially refined sentiment, especially love. (89–90)

series on TV and radio, a succession of episodes all related to the same unit of meaning, typically a specific (sub)urban location. (110)

set the fixed elements of a design (setting) for a production, including flats, furniture, and impersonal props, etc., but excluding costume and personal props, and distinct from the permanent architecture of the theatre-space. (10)

set-builder a less straightforward job than it sounds: skilled design and carpentry, metalwork, electrical ducting, wallpaper-hanging, and carpet-fitting are often needed, and other skills may be called on. (103)

set-designer one responsible for the overall design of a set for a production or a season. (204)

set-painter a modern term distinguishing set-painting that does not include perspectival illusion; though ephemeral it is more skilled than many think. (204)

set-up the placement of props, etc. before performances. (205)

shadow-theatre different forms exist in Indonesia and China; flat puppets, accompanied by music/words, are moved against a screen, casting shadows. (185)

Shakespeare apocrypha a group of plays at one or another time attributed to Shakespeare but not generally accepted as his nor usually included in *Complete Works* and academic series-editions. (149)

Shakespearean stage the English stage of the period 1576-1642. (77)

sharers in Jacobethan companies, those who (unlike hired actors) owned a 'share' of the company, entitling them to a percentage of the profits; shares could be sold or bequeathed. Shakespeare was a sharer in the Lord Chamberlain's/King's Men. (158)

Sho'ah in Hebrew, 'destruction'; the word normally used by modern Israelis for the events in Germany and elsewhere 1933–45 often called the 'Holocaust'. As 'holocaust' literally means "a sacrifice wholly consumed by fire; a whole burnt offering" (*Sh.OED*) many people prefer the Hebrew word. (65)

shooting-script the script used during the actual shoot, highly technical in nature and including specifics about camera-use, sound, etc. Shooting-scripts are rarely published, but the term is loosely used to describe published scripts of TV-dramas or films given a technical feel by the inclusion of some technical directions. (111)

Short-Title Catalogue (STC) a monumental reference-work listing all books published in the British Isles or in English 1475–1640. (150)

shot in film, one uninterrupted run of the camera, also called a take.

shutters in Restoration theatres paired perspectival flats used on the scenic stage as a back-drop; they could be slid into the wings to reveal a second or third pair showing a different scene. (139, 140, 193)

sight-lines the view of the stage from (any given seat or area of seating in) the auditorium. (131, 135, 144)

siparia in Roman theatres, small curtains covering apertures in the *frons scaenae*, used to cover *scaenae ductiles*. (134)

sitcom situation-comedy, a TV form using a given setting or situation (typically a home or workplace) for multiple episodes (e.g. *MASH, Cheers*). (53)

site-specific of an art-work or performance, articulating itself in relation to the particular site in which it exists and from which it cannot be moved. (272)

skênê in Greek amphitheatres, the rear-wall of the stage, pierced by one door; the equivalent of the *frons scaenae* and tiring-house wall. (130–1, 135)

skênographia the Greek term for scenography. (131)

slapstick originally a wooden clapper used by Arlecchino (in *Commedia dell'arte*) to beat people; subsequently a generic term for comedic violence. (79)

slot the regular placement of a programme in a broadcasting time-table; prime-time slots are heavily contested but on commercial stations the need to protect the value of advertising breaks creates a pressure for uncontroversial prime-time programming. (110)

soap opera a TV or radio series distinguished by long duration (years) involving the same characters and programmed regularly each week.

(111, 113)

soccus a light slipper worn for comedy by Roman actors. (134)

social realism a complex term often used very loosely, and clearly overlapping with realist(ic). Generally, 'social realism' refers to the verisimilar depiction of social conditions in art and literature, but it has strong and persistent associations with Socialist politics. In contemporary British theatre it was popularised by critical responses to plays at the Royal Court in the 1950s–60s, which were understood to follow Osborne's *Look Back in Anger* (1956) in concentrating on current political and social issues. Lacey's *British Realist Theatre* offers a particularly lucid and helpful account. (65, 245, 248–52)

soliloquy lit. 'speaking alone'; a speech, usually of some length, by an actor alone on stage. Brilliantly used by Renaissance dramatists, soliloquies are awkward for naturalistic acting and at odds with Naturalism. It is rare in and after Ibsen; the monologue has since developed in its own right. (143)

sound-box the room, now often high in the auditorium, from where stage- and auditorium-sound is controlled; sound- and lighting-boxes may be adjacent or combined. (144)

sound-technician one responsible for sound during performance. The term could be, but usually is not, applied to the stage-hands and others who must in Renaissance and Restoration performances have been responsible for the thunder-run, etc., and to those who organized sound-effects in sensation drama and still do in radio-drama and soap-opera. (205)

soundtrack of film and TV, the music composed and recorded to accompany the visuals, now often available on CD or tape. (107)

speech-heading an alternative to **speech-prefix**.

speech-prefix the name or other tag indicating the speaker of each line in a printed dramatic text, now usually given in upper-case letters or bold.

(15, 19, 28, 30, 34, 202, 247, 267, 278)

sponsor one who gives money to a theatre or company, or towards a production; rare in purely commercial theatre but critical in subsidized theatre. As in sports, business sponsorship is vitally important but raises ethical issues and tends to inhibit some kinds of experiment/innovation. (204)

spotlight a focusable light, producing a spot to pick out and track an individual actor, or illuminate only a particular area of the stage.

stage-boards the wooden floor of the stage. (30, 134, 137)

stage-business actions worked out in rehearsal, but not usually specified in the text, ranging from individual characteristics (someone who is always fiddling with a particular prop) to the timing and sequencing of comic exchanges or fights. 'Comic business' is sometimes used for sequences of physical, non-verbal action generated by a comic actor. (11, 74–5)

stage-crew those who have to be backstage during performance and have no direct contact with spectators. (10, 205)

stage-design the overall design for a production, usually including set, décor, costume, props, posters, etc.

stage-direction in printed dramatic texts an instruction for action or delivery. *Explicit* stage-directions are distinguished from dialogue by italics and/or brackets; *embedded* stage-directions are implicit in an actor's part, as 'They kneel' is when Volumnia says "Down Ladies: let vs shame him with our knees" (*Coriolanus* 5.3.169).
(13, 16–18, 28, 30–1, 44–5, 71, 99, 124, 159–60, 164, 195–7, 267)

stage-door the rear entrance to a theatre, used by actors and backstage crew but closed to the public. (205)

stage-hand one who assists backstage during performance, particularly with scene-changes; often seen dressed in black moving props and furniture on and off between scenes. See also **super**. (127, 205)

stage-left the left of the stage from the actor's point-of-view; villains often enter from stage-left. (16)

stage-manager one reponsible for the stage and backstage area during performance, in charge of stage-hands, lighting-technicians, etc. (205)

stage-right the right of the stage from the actor's point-of-view; heroes often enter from stage-right. (16)

stage-trap a trap-door set into the stage-boards, which can be used as a part of the set (graves, holes, cellars) or for supernatural dis/appearances of ghosts, demons, etc. (30, 134, 137)

stalls the seating-area on the floor of the auditorium; formerly the pit.
(138, 144)

stand-up a comedian who stands up in front of an audience and performs solo. (211)

start a moment of sudden recognition when an actor/character perceives something provoking horror/surprise, etc.; Garrick was famed for starts. (179)

stereotype in printing, a method (dominant in the nineteenth century) which makes a re-usable plate from the type set by compositors. (151)

stichomythia lit. 'verse-line talk'; a classical form of dialogue, each interlocutor speaking only one line at a time; used and adapted by Renaissance dramatists, it remains in use today, especially in comedy. (68–9)

stoa in Greek amphitheatres, a colonnaded walkway behind the *skênê*, separating the stage-area from the temple behind and perhaps used to store masks, robes, etc.   (127, 131)

stock-character an established rôle in any genre, such as Il Capitano or Pantalone in *Commedia dell'arte*, the lone gunfighter or the bad rancher in Westerns, the teenage child and the mother-in-law in sitcoms, etc.   (61)

stock-companies in the nineteenth and early twentieth centuries, companies of actors who performed the same stock-role in successive formulaic plays.   (92)

straight man an actor who is a foil to another actor, providing the opportunity for laughs rather than generating them him/herself. Comedy pairs often feature a straight man, as Laurel to Hardy.   (251)

strike (a set) to dismantle a set; see also **get out**.   (205)

studio-theatre a versatile modern theatre, without a proscenium wall and with reconfigurable seating.   (144–6, 195)

sub-plot any plot distinct from (even if parallel to) the main plot.   (62)

subtext a Stanislavskian term referring to the reading of a character's motivations deducible from, but not literally stated in, a play; in performance subtext is often to do with an actor's body-language.   (183, 256–8)

supers from 'supernumary (actors)'; stage-hands visible to spectators during (not between) scenes, for example to push a mobile prop about.   (205)

Surreal(ist) of sets, anti-realist, using distortion and inappropriately juxtaposed images and objects to create a dream-like effect. (There are other meanings in criticism and art history.)   (200–1)

suspension-marks three dots (...) indicating omission of some kind, or commonly in drama a voice trailing away (cf. **dash**). Pinter distinguishes three-dot (. . .), four-dot (. . . .), and five-dot (. . . . .) pauses.   (16, 288–9)

Symbolist of sets, anti-realist, abandoning mimesis in favour of indirect suggestion, and symbolizing ideas or states of mind in abstract designs. (There are other meanings in criticism and art history.)   (195–6)

syntactical of punctuation, indicating syntax, not elocutionary.   (149)

the System Stanislavski's name for his approach to direction, rehearsal, and performance; play-texts are broken down into units and objectives, rôles analysed psychologically, and actors required to develop affective memory.
                                                                              (182–3)

T

tableau a group of persons who hold themselves still to create the effect of a picture; the plural is *tableaux*.   (44, 92, 210)

Tartaglia a Mask in *Commedia dell'arte*, a utility figure who is often a minor official such as a policeman, lawyer, or magistrate. *Tartare* means 'to stammer', and the Mask's constant stammering is a source of obscene comedy. Shakespeare adapted the rôle in his malapropizing constables. (78–9)

technical rehearsal one dedicated to setting and checking all light- and sound-cues, etc. (10)

television-drama a general term for television-plays, adaptations, etc. (109)

television-play one written specifically for TV. (109–11)

tetralogy lit. 'four accounts, discourses'; originally the set of four plays (3 tragedies + satyr-play) required from an Athenian tragedian; subsequently any four linked plays, particularly the Shakespearean histories. See **first** and **second tetralogy**. (57)

textual collation in modern editions the block of notes, usually between the play-text and the editor's annotations, which record textual variants, especially of early editions. (31)

text-up of performance, etc., undertaken with text in hand, the lines not yet having been learnt. A normal early stage of rehearsal, text-up performance may also occur if a part has to be recast at very short notice. (241)

Thatcherite concerning the policies and style of Margaret Thatcher (b.1925), Conservative Prime Minister of Great Britain 1979–90, an exceptionally polemical leader whose thinking was characterized by impatience; scorn for socialism, trades union, the welfare state, and the arts; praise for economic efficiency and fiscal prudence; and patriotism amounting to self-righteousness. A three-term winner either loved or loathed, opposition to her funding policies became a major influence in the arts and affects the context of most plays produced in the UK during the 1980s and beyond. (237)

The Theatre the first theatre building specifically designed and built for professional actors and a paying public, erected by James Burbage in Shoreditch in 1576. It stood idle 1597–99, and was then dismantled, moved across the Thames, and reassembled as Globe I. (76)

theatre-clubs in late-nineteenth and twentieth-century London, private theatres open only to members rather than the general public, and as such not requiring a licence; a means of evading censorship. (99, 208)

theatre-complex at its best an architecturally elegant and coherent set of theatre-spaces with associated rehearsal, storage, administrative, and public rooms; at its worst a pseudo-mall somewhere in which is a theatre. Major British examples include the RNT and Barbican in London, the RSC complex in Stratford, Birmingham Rep., and Theatre Clwyd in Mold. (127)

theatre-critic one who writes reviews and articles about theatre; in the UK academic critics often like to distinguish themselves from journalists. (213)

theatre-listings a list of theatres giving details of performances and venue; a quick way to learn what's on where. (223)

Theatre Laboratory (or **Laboratory Theatre**) a company/workshop founded in 1965 by Jerzy Grotowski (1933–99) to explore and teach his ideas about physical theatre; his book *Towards a Poor Theatre* (1968) has been very influential. (185)

theatre-manager one with overall financial responsibility for a theatre building; in producing-houses sometimes the senior staff-producer. (187, 204)

Theatre of the Absurd a term coined by Martin Esslin to describe certain plays by Beckett, Adamov, Ionesco, and Genet; subsequently used to label a style/approach inaugurated in these works. What is absurd is not simply the situation or action, nor the reasonless universe, but the compulsive search for reason when it is known to be fruitless. (245, 252–5)

Theatre of Cruelty a form of theatre confronting spectators with acts of extreme violence, broken taboos, and disturbing images of sexuality; posited but not developed in any detailed theoretical or practical way by Antonin Artaud (1896–1948); a particular influence on Grotowski, Brook, and Kane. (220)

Theatre of Death a set of experiments undertaken in the 1970s by Tadeusz Kantor (1915–90), which explored death, time, and memory. (198)

theatre-space the fixed material environment of performance. (53, 121, 129, 139)

theatrical monopoly the system of 1662–1843 whereby some theatres only were granted patents allowing them to stage performances in London; the basis for the distinction of legitimate and illegitimate drama. (89, 159)

theatrical space the space generated by a performance; the fictional spaces within which the action of a play occurs. (129)

theatrical space-within that part of the theatrical space visible to an audience. (129–30)

theatrical space-without that part of the theatrical space invisible to an audience, whether fictionally adjacent to or distant from the theatrical space within. (129–30)

theatron lit. 'place of viewing'; in Greek amphitheatres the audience-area. (131–2)

Thespian as noun, an actor; as adjective, to do with acting, from the sixth-century BCE Greek Thespis, credited with inventing the solo actor (as distinct from the *coryphaeus*). (59)

third gallery in Jacobethan amphitheatres the uppermost gallery. (138)

three-hander a play for three actors. (268)

thriller a narrative art-work which aims to arouse fear and apprehension in consumers through action, tension, suspense, and surprise. The modern master of thrillers (often turning on primal fears, sexual repressions, and fantasies) was Alfred Hitchcock (1899–1980). (49, 113)

throughline in Stanislavskian and much subsequent acting predicated on one or more of naturalistic style, realism, and psychological realism, the step-by-step, cause-and-effect sequence of feelings, motives, and actions that an actor imagines to make their performance of a rôle 'convincing'.   (48, 180)

Through Line Numbering (TLN) a reference system for F1 established by Charlton Hinman, in which all lines of print, including titles and stage-directions, are sequentially numbered from 1. Thus *Hamlet*, which in act. scene.line referencing is 1.1.1–5.2.403 becomes simply 1–3906.   (4)

thrust-stage a stage partly behind but protruding through a proscenium arch with audience on three sides. The finest recent example is the Swan at Stratford. See **apron-stage**.   (142)

thunder-run in Jacobethan amphitheatres, and Restoration and some proscenium-arch theatres, a metal-lined wooden trough down which cannon-balls could be rolled to simulate thunder; later replaced by large sheets of metal which are struck.   (136)

thymêle in Greek amphitheatres, a small upright stone at the centre or command-point of the *orchêstra*, perhaps used as an altar.   (131)

tiring-house lit. the place where actors attire (costume) themselves; in Jaco-bethan amphitheatres the building of which the front wall forms the rear wall of the stage, the interior the within, and the first floor the above; the tiring-house also provided access to the Heavens and Hell, and storage and adminis-trative space, while accommodating the thunder-run and a platform from which performances could be trumpeted, small cannon fired for battle-scenes, etc.   (127, 135–6)

tiring-house wall in Jacobethan amphitheatres the rear wall of the stage, pierced by two doors and the discovery-space; the equivalent of the Greek *skênê* and Roman *frons scaenae*.   (135)

totalise, totalising referring to all texts or productions of a play, or all audi-ences, etc. as if singular and certain, as opposed to formulations which respect the number/variety of texts, performances, etc.   (278, 284)

traditional essay-question (TEQ) one demanding an answer in continu-ous prose.   (241)

tragedic concerning tragedy as a form and art; a usefully narrower word than 'tragic' (terminal deaths are tragedic but not necessarily tragic).   (56)

tragedy from Greek *tragos*, a billy-goat, + *ode*, a song; one of the two funda-mental Greek genres, the pair of comedy, symbolized by the mask with down-turned mouth. In Aristotelian and other essentialist genre-theory tragedy is supposed to be concerned with the individual rather than society, with high- rather than street-life, and to end in death; in non-essentialist theories it relates to any sad and/or polemic elements of action and dialogue. Shake-spearean tragedy is broadly associated with blank verse rather than prose or song. See also **domestic, Restoration**, and **revenge tragedy**.   (50, 53, 56–66)

tragicomedy when used specifically, a tragedy that averts or transcends its terminal deaths, or a comedy that fails to unite its lovers; more commonly anything that seems to mix the two super-genres in some way.　(63, 80–5)

transition a visible, usually gradual, change of emotion in an actor, considered an important skill from the late eighteenth to mid nineteenth century. Edmund Kean was a notable enactor of sudden transitions.　(179–80)

traverse of a stage, arranged as a strip between two banks of seats, like the choir of a cruciform Christian church.　(69, 145–6)

trust exercise one designed to build absolute trust between members of a company, such as falling backwards from a podium to be caught.　(127)

twist a plot-development that cannot easily be anticipated; a surprise turn-of-events.　(52)

two-hander a play for two actors.　(257)

typecast to be cast for a particular type of rôle, implicitly without regard for range and potential. Actors who have had an outstanding success in one film or in a TV series are vulnerable to typecasting.　(184)

typo from 'typographical error'; a slip of the pen or finger, as distinct from misstatements of fact, spelling-mistakes, grammatical solecisms, etc.　(288)

U

Übermarionette lit. 'super-puppet' (the plural is *Übermarionetten*); a human-size puppet: a term invented by Edward Gordon Craig, who speculated that imperfect actors might be replaced by giant puppets which could be precisely manipulated. The term has been taken too literally and over-analysed: Craig was a polemicist making a deliberatively provocative assault on late-nineteenth-century acting-styles. The film *Being John Malkovich* (dir. Spike Jonze, 1999) powerfully explores Craig's fantasy.　(197)

understudy in theatre, a junior actor who learns a substantial rôle in case the more senior actor playing it is ill or otherwise unable to perform.　(182)

unit from Stanislavski, who argued that play-texts can be scored and broken down into a series of units of action, a mode of analysis that can help actors understand the play and their rôle in more subtle detail.　(183)

unities see Aristotelian (or neo-classical) unities.

unseen of passages set in exams for comment (or translation), from any text, without prior specification or opportunity to study.　(277)

unsolicited (manu)script one sent to a theatre which has not requested it.　(158)

upper-case of type-letters, capitals, LIKE THESE, not lower-case letters. In hand-printing the capitals were in the upper case of type.　(15)

upper-circle in proscenium-arch theatres, a gallery above the circle, usually the highest/cheapest seats in the auditorium; see **gods**. (144)

upper-gallery the upper-circle in Restoration theatre, associated with servants and 'proletarian' audience-members. (142)

upstage on a raked stage, further away from the audience. (142)

utility figure one that serves as needed as a policeman, apothecary, etc. who appears only briefly to advance the plot. (79)

Utopian theatre from *Utopia* ('Nowhere', 1516) by Thomas More (1478–1535), a tale of an impossible paradise; hence theatre which offers a particular ideology, usually socialist, as the cure for all ills. (104)

V

variorum edition from Latin *editio cum notis variorum*, 'an edition with the notes of various people'; a text that presents the annotations of all (major) editors, and usually a full textual collation and bibliography. (233–4)

vaudeville an American form equivalent (but not identical) to **music-hall**. (93)

vela in Roman theatres, a linen awning covering part of the audience in the orchestral area. (133)

Verfremdung, Verfremdungseffekt see alienation.

versurae in Roman theatres a colonnaded gallery encircling the auditorium. (133)

vestibulum in Roman theatres, a small roofed porch distinguishing the middle-door in the *frons scaenae*. (133)

via lit. 'a street'; in Roman theatrical spaces-within the street commonly mapped on to the *platea*, on to which the 'front-doors' piercing the *frons scaenae* opened; hence sometimes an equivalent of *platea*. (133)

Vice an extremely influential stock-rôle originating in Moralities which combined the devils of the Mysteries with aspects of the Fool; the Vice usually dominates when on stage (but may disguise it), addresses the audience directly, and can control (meta)theatrical levels of reality both by providing inset-performances and by encompassing the audience within the play-world. Wisecracking Elizabethan and Jacobean villains are usually descendants of the Vice, as are some clowns, and Shakespeare persistently experimented with the rôle. (73–5, 81)

vocative the use of someone's name or title in a speech addressed to them (Sir, my Lord, churlish Priest, etc.). (29)

voice-coach a specialist in voice-work who helps actors, particularly for rôles that have unusual demands (accent, speech-impediment, etc.) or which will be played in acoustically difficult spaces. (204)

voice-over of film, a spoken narration pronounced 'over' the film images but not audible within those images. (107)

voice-work a general term for everything that an actor must do vocally in rehearsal and performance, including the use of stress, regional or national accents, pitch, projection, and any special effects or particular styles of delivery. (173)

volumes in analysing masks the relative size and distortion or 'normality' of each feature (chin, nose, forehead, cheeks, etc.) are described as volumes. (58)

W

Wakefield Master an unknown playwright-reviser of great skill whose hand has been identified in the Wakefield Cycle; his masterpiece is the *Second Shepherds' Play*. (71)

walk-through a teaching or rehearsal exercise in which actors are assigned parts and walk through a scene or act, physically moving about the stage but not 'acting' as such. A 'text-up' walk-through means texts are carried; 'text-down' walk-throughs abandon print for memorized lines. (10)

wardrobe costumes and personal props for a production or of a theatre/company, collectively. (205)

wardrobe-master one responsible for issuing costumes prior to performance, retrieving them afterwards, and having them repaired or cleaned as necessary; in larger companies also a wardrobe-manager overseeing the general maintenance and hiring-out of costumes. (205)

warm-up exercise an athletic or theatrical exercise preparing actors physically and/or mentally for rehearsal/performance but not relating specifically to the play in hand. (127)

wash the saturation of the stage with light of a particular colour; in stylized productions a murder might be staged in a red wash. On film tinted lenses give the effect of washes. (105–6)

well-made play (pièce bien faite) a term invented by Eugène Scribe (1791–1861) to define a technical structure marked by logical plots delivering neat, causally satisfying resolutions; a major influence on playwrights from the later nineteenth century. (96, 120)

West End the principal theatre district in London, centred on Shaftesbury Avenue, St Martin's Lane, and the Strand; hence a term for all London mainstream theatre. See **Broadway, fringe theatre**. (94)

western a genre, mainly in film and print, featuring the Western American frontier, conflict between pioneers (later cowboys) and Amerindians, etc. (52, 65, 258–9)

white-face any style of performance in which actors wear white facial make-up. Western mime and some comedy (e.g. clowning) still use white-face; some Eastern classical styles also use it. (19)

Whitehall farce lit. those played at the Whitehall Theatre, London, particularly the string of bedroom farces put on from 1950 to 1967 by the actor-manager Brian Rix (b.1924); hence more generally any such bedroom farce. See also **Aldwych farce**. (95)

white hole a simple generally rectangular modern theatre-space, a room draped in white cloth; the Pit in the Barbican in London was redecorated as a white hole for the 2000–1 season. (144)

Windmill Girls Britain's nudest performers 1931–68, but particularly associated with 1939–45; named for the Windmill Theatre, Piccadilly, where they appeared. All but nude, they were not allowed to move when lighted, and presented sequential tableaux separated by blackouts. (210)

Wing a monumental reference-work listing all books published in the British Isles and North America or in English 1640–1700. (150)

wings in Restoration theatres both flats, and the spaces to each side of the scenic stage into which flats could be withdrawn and where actors waited to enter; subsequently and in proscenium-arch theatres restricted to these areas. (139, 141, 142, 193)

within in Jacobethan amphitheatres the unseen space within the tiring-house, from which, e.g., those knocking at doors, or answering from behind a closed door, could call, often as a prelude to entering. (135–6, 141)

workshop in teaching and drama training, a lesson or exercise that involves practical work and activity, not simply sitting and reading, or being told what to think. (162, 241)

writer-in-residence a temporary resident-dramatist; such posts form one part of development schemes and are associated with community projects and outreach theatre. (160)

Z

zanni (1) as Zanni, a Mask in *Commedia dell'arte*, a servant, but more generally (2) as *zanni*, a singular and plural term for the servant Masks, including Arlecchino, Brighella, and Scapino, who also function as messengers who persistently delay or misdeliver their messages. The name is a diminutive of Giovanni (John), and is thought to have entered Venetian *Commedia* with an influx of Bergamese peasants following the conquest of Bergamo in the early fifteenth century. (79)

Select Bibliography and Further Reading

The bibliography is organized in sections corresponding to the text, followed by much fuller sections on play-texts and plays on video. We have tried to include something on every aspect and period of theatre discussed in the text, but not critical or biographical work on individual theatre-makers.

We have not included web-addresses because of their mutability, but students especially are reminded that all major newspapers, most theatre-funding and organizational bodies, most theatres, many companies, some individuals, and a growing number of reference-works maintain web-sites. Reviews, production and biographical data, performing schedules, photographs, and virtual animations are all available: the on-line digital bibliography of Brockett's *History of the Theatre*, is a good starting point; it can presently be found at < http://www.abacon.com/brockett/links.html > .

General/Reference

BANHAM, Martin, ed., *The Cambridge Guide to Theatre* (2nd ed., Cambridge: Cambridge University Press, 1995; ISBN 0–521–43437–8).

BROCKETT, Oscar G., with HILDY, Franklin J., *History of the Theatre* (8th ed., Boston, London, Toronto, Sydney, Tokyo, and Singapore: Allyn and Bacon, 1999; ISBN 0–205–28171–0).

BROWN, John Russell, ed., *The Oxford Illustrated History of Theatre* (Oxford and New York: Oxford University Press, 1995; ISBN 0–19–212997–X).

CUDDON, J. A., ed., *A Dictionary of Literary Terms and Literary Theory* (4th ed., rev. C. E. Preston, Harmondsworth: Penguin, 1999; ISBN 0–14–051363–9).

HALLIDAY, F. E., *A Shakespeare Companion* (rev. ed., Harmondsworth: Penguin, 1969 [Penguin Shakespeare Library]; ISBN 0–14–053011–8).

HARTNOLL, Phyllis, ed., *The Oxford Companion to the Theatre* (1951; 4th ed., with corrections, Oxford, New York, Toronto, and Melbourne: Oxford University Press, 1985; ISBN 0–19–211546–4).

NAGLER, A. M., *A Source Book in Theatrical History: Twenty-five centuries of stage history in more than 300 basic documents and other primary material* (New York: Dover Publications, Inc., 1952; ISBN 0–486–20515–0).

PAVIS, Patrice, *Dictionary of the Theatre: Terms, Concepts, and Analysis* (Toronto and Buffalo: University of Toronto Press, 1998; ISBN 0–8020–8163–0).

PREMINGER, Alex, *et al.*, eds, *The New Princeton Encyclopedia of Poetry and Poetics* (Princeton: Princeton University Press, 1993; ISBN 0–691–02123–6).

WINSLOW, Colin, *The Oberon Glossary of Theatrical Terms: Theatre Jargon Explained* (London: Oberon Books, 1991; ISBN 1–870259–26–2).

Performance, Notation, Text

BRENNER, Alfred, *TV Scriptwriter's Handbook: Dramatic Writing for Television and Film* (Los Angeles: Silman-James Press, 1992; ISBN 1–879505–10–X).

CATRON, Louis E., *The Elements of Playwriting* (Oxford and New York: Macmillan, 1993; ISBN 0–02–522991–5).

DESSEN, Alan C. and THOMSON, Leslie, *A Dictionary of Stage Directions in English Drama, 1580–1642* (Cambridge: Cambridge University Press, 2000; ISBN 0–521–00029–7).

MARCUS, Leah S., *Unediting the Renaissance: Shakespeare, Marlowe, Milton* (London and New York: Routledge, 1996; ISBN 0–415–10053–4).

WELLS, Stanley, *Re-editing Shakespeare for the Modern Reader* (Oxford: Clarendon Press, 1984; ISBN 0–19–812934–3).

WILLIAMS, George Walton, ed., *Shakespeare's Speech-Headings* (Newark: University of Delaware Press/London: Associated University Presses, 1997; ISBN 0–87413–637–7).

Reading Structures

CAUGHIE, John, *Television Drama: Realism, Modernism, and British Culture* (Oxford: Oxford University Press, 2000; ISBN 0–19–874218–5).

CHAMBERS, E. K., *The Mediaeval Stage* (1903; Mineola, NY: Dover Publications, 1996; ISBN 0–486–29229–0).

DUCHARTE, Pierre Louis, *The Italian Comedy* (1929; New York: Dover Publications, Inc., 1966; ISBN 0–486–21679–9).

GOLDHILL, Simon, *Reading Greek Tragedy* (Cambridge: Cambridge University Press, 1986; ISBN 0–521–31579–4).

HAYWARD, Susan, *Cinema Studies: The Key Concepts* (2nd ed., London and New York: Routledge, 2000; ISBN 0–415–22740–2).

HOLLAND, Peter, *The Ornament of Action: Text and performance in restoration comedy* (Cambridge: Cambridge University Press, 1979; ISBN 0–521–22048–3).

LAMB, Andrew, *150 Years of Popular Musical Theater* (New Haven and London: Yale University Press, 2000; ISBN 0–300–07538–3).

MOODY, Jane, *Illegitimate Theatre in London, 1770–1840* (Cambridge: Cambridge University Press, 2000; ISBN 0-521-56376–3).

ORGEL, Stephen, *The Illusion of Power: Political Theater in the English Renaissance* (1975; Berkeley, Los Angeles, and London: University of California Press, 1991; ISBN 0–520–02741–8).

RIGHTER (Barton), Anne, *Shakespeare and the Idea of the Play* (1962; Harmondsworth: Penguin, 1967 [Penguin Shakespeare Library]; no ISBN).

RUDLIN, John, *Commedia dell'Arte: An Actor's Handbook* (London and New York: Routledge, 1994; ISBN 0–415–04770–6).

THOMPSON, Kristin, and BORDWELL, David, *Film History: An Introduction* (New York: McGraw-Hill, 1994; ISBN 0–07–006445–8).

WHITE, Martin, *Renaissance Drama in Action: An introduction to aspects of theatre practice and performance* (London and New York: Routledge, 1998; ISBN 0–415–06739–1).

WILLIAMS, Raymond, *Drama from Ibsen to Brecht* (1952; Harmondsworth: Penguin, 1973 [Pelican]; ISBN 0–14–021492–5).

Defining Architectures

BATE, Jonathan, and JACKSON, Russell, eds, *Shakespeare: An Illustrated Stage History* (Oxford: Oxford University Press, 1996; ISBN 0–19–812372–8).

BEACHAM, Richard C., *The Roman Theatre and its Audience* (London: Routledge, 1995; ISBN 0–415–12163–9).

BROOK, Peter, *The Empty Space* (1968; Harmondsworth: Penguin, 1972 [Pelican]; ISBN 0–14–021415–1)).

EARL, John, and SELL, Michael, *The Theatres Trust Guide to British Theatres 1750–1950: A Gazeteer* (London: A. & C. Black, 2000; ISBN 0–7136–5688–3).

FOAKES, R. A., *Illustrations of the English Stage 1580–1642* (London: Scolar Press, 1985; ISBN 0–85976–684–6)).

GASKELL, Philip, *A New Introduction to Bibliography* (1972; with revisions, Oxford: Clarendon Press, 1985; ISBN 0–19–818150–7)).

GURR, Andrew, *The Shakespearean Stage 1574–1642* (3rd ed., Cambridge: Cambridge University Press, 1992; ISBN 0–521–42240–X).

JOSEPH, Stephen, ed., *Actor and Architect* (Manchester: Manchester University Press, 1964; ISBN 0–7190–0011–4).

KENNEDY, Dennis, *Looking at Shakespeare: A Visual History of Twentieth-Century Performance* (Cambridge: Cambridge University Press, 1993; ISBN 0–521–34655–X).

MULRYNE, J. R., and SHEWRING, Margaret, eds, *Shakespeare's Globe Rebuilt* (Cambridge: Cambridge University Press, 1997; ISBN 0–521–59988–1).

PEACOCK, John, *The Stage Designs of Inigo Jones: The European Context* (Cambridge: Cambridge University Press, 1995; ISBN 0–521–41812–7).

RUTTER, Carol Chillington, ed., *Documents of the Rose Playhouse* (1984; rev. ed., Manchester and New York: Manchester University Press, 1999 [Revels Plays Companion Library]; ISBN 0–7190–5801–5).

SCOLNICOV, Hanna, *Woman's Theatrical Space* (Cambridge: Cambridge University Press, 1994; ISBN 0–521–39467–8).

WILES, David, *Tragedy in Athens: Performance space and theatrical meaning* (Cambridge: Cambridge University Press, 1997; ISBN 0–521–66615–5).

Personnel in Process

ARTAUD, Antonin, *The Theatre and its Double* (trans. Victor Corti, London: Calder & Boyars, 1970; ISBN 0–7145–0703–2).

BARTON, John, *Playing Shakespeare* (London: Methuen, 1984; ISBN 0–413–54790–6).

BENEDETTI, Jean, *Stanislavski & The Actor* (London: Methuen, 1998; ISBN 0–413–71160–9)

BENTLEY, Gerald Eades, *The Profession of Dramatist in Shakespeare's Time 1590–1642* (Princeton: Princeton University Press, 1971; ISBN 0–691–06205–6).

—— *The Profession of Player in Shakespeare's Time* (Princeton: Princeton University Press, 1984; ISBN 0–691–06596–9).

BOAL, Augusto, *Games for Actors and Non-Actors* (trans. Adrian Jackson, London and New York: Routledge, 1992; ISBN 0–415–06155–5).

GOODWIN, John, ed., *British Theatre Design: The Modern Age* (London: Weidenfeld & Nicholson, 1989; ISBN 0–297–83070–8).

GROTOWSKI, Jerzy, *Towards a Poor Theatre* (trans T. K. Wiewiorowski *et al.* London: Methuen, 1969; ISBN 0–413–34910–1).

GURR, Andrew, *Playgoing in Shakespeare's London* (2nd ed., Cambridge: Cambridge University Press, 1996; ISBN 0–521–57449–8).

HARE, David, *Writing Left-Handed* (London and Boston: Faber & Faber, 1991; ISBN 0–571–14334–2).

INVERNE, James, ed., *The Impresarios* (London: Oberon Books, 2000; ISBN 1–84002–135–7).

JOHNSTONE, Keith, *Impro: Improvisation and the Theatre* (1981; London: Methuen, 1989; ISBN 0–413–46430–X).

JONAS, Susan, PROEHL, Geoff, and LUPU, Michael, eds, *The Dramaturgy of the American Theater: A Sourcebook* (Fort Worth: Harcourt Brace, 1997; ISBN 0–15–502586–4).

LECOQ, Jacques, *The Moving Body: Teaching Creative Theatre* (*Le Corps poétique*, 1997; trans. David Bradby, London: Methuen, 2000; ISBN 0–413–75260–7).

MEYER-DINKGRÄFE, Daniel, *Approaches to Acting: Past and Present* (London and New York: Continuum, 2001; ISBN 0–8264–4901–8).

MILLER, Jonathan, *Subsequent Performances* (London and Boston: Faber & Faber, 1986; ISBN 0–571–13928–0).

NELSON, Richard, and JONES, David, *Making Plays: the Writer-Director Relationship in the Theatre Today* (ed. Colin Chambers, London and Boston: Faber & Faber, 1995; ISBN 0–571–16354–8).

PLIMPTON, George, ed., *Playwrights at Work: The Paris Review Interviews* (London: Harvill Press, 2000; ISBN 1–84046–783–0).

RITCHIE, Rob, ed., *The Joint Stock Book* (London: Methuen, 1987; ISBN 0–413–41030–7).

ROACH, Joseph P., *The Player's Passion: Studies in the Science of Acting* (London and Toronto: Associated University Presses, 1985; ISBN 0–87413–265–7).

ROWELL, George, ed., *Victorian Dramatic Criticism* (London: Methuen, 1971; ISBN 0–416–30010–1).

SCHOENBAUM, S., *Shakespeare's Lives* (Oxford and New York: Oxford University Press, 1991; ISBN 0–19–818618–5).

SMALLWOOD, Robert, ed., *Players of Shakespeare 4: Further Essays in Shakespearean Performance by Players with the Royal Shakespeare Company* (Cambridge: Cambridge University Press, 1998; ISBN 0–521–79416–1). [Volumes 1–3 remain available.]

STAFFORD-CLARK, Max, *Letters to George: The Account of a Rehearsal* (1989; London: Nick Hern Books, 1997; ISBN 1–85459–317–X).

STANISLAVSKI, Constantin, *The Actor's Handbook* (London: Methuen, 1990; ISBN 0–413–63080–3). [See also BENEDETTI, Jean.]

TAYLOR, George, *Players and Performances in the Victorian Theatre* (Manchester and New York: Manchester University Press, 1989; ISBN 0–7190–4023–X).

TYNAN, Kenneth, *A View of the English Stage* (St Albans: Paladin, 1976; ISBN 0–586–08234–4).

WARDLE, Irving, *Theatre Criticism* (London: Routledge, 1992; ISBN 0–415–03181–8).

WATSON, Ian, *Conversations with Ayckbourn* (London and Boston: Faber & Faber, 1981; ISBN 0–571–15192–2).

WHITELAW, Billie, . . . *Who He?* (London: Hodder & Stoughton, 1996; ISBN 0–340–61737–3).

WILES, David, *Shakespeare's Clown: Actor and text in the Elizabethan Playhouse* (Cambridge: Cambridge University Press, 1987; ISBN 0–521–32840–3).

WILLIAMS, David, compiler, *Peter Brook: A Theatrical Casebook* (rev. ed., London: Methuen, 1991; ISBN 0–413–66460–0).

WU, Duncan, ed., *Making Plays: Interviews with Contemporary British Dramatists and Directors* (Basingstoke: Macmillan, 2000; ISBN 0–333–91561–5).

Theatre Today

BIGSBY, C. W. E., *Modern American Drama 1945–2000* (Cambridge: Cambridge University Press, 2000; ISBN 0–521–79410–2).

FENNER, Jill, ed., *The Actor's Handbook* (3rd ed., London: Bloomsbury, 1998; ISBN 0–7475–3768–2).

GIANNACHI, Gabriella, and LUCKHURST, Mary, eds, *On Directing: Interviews with Directors* (London: Faber & Faber/New York: St Martin's Griffin, 1999; ISBN 0–571–19149–5 [UK]/0–312–22483–4 [US]).

GOLDBERG, Rose Lee, *Performance Art* (London: Thames and Hudson, 1988; ISBN 0–500–20214–1).

JELLICOE. Ann, *Community Plays: How to Put them on* (London: Methuen, 1987; ISBN 0–413–42150–3).

KAYE, Nick, *Postmodernism and Performance* (London: Macmillan, 1994; ISBN 0–333–51918–3).

—— *site-specific art: performance, place and documentation* (London and New York: Routledge, 2000; ISBN 0–415–18559–9).

LACEY, Stephen, *British Realist Theatre: The New Wave in its Context 1956–1965* (London: Routledge, 1995; ISBN 0–415–12311–9).

LESSER, Wendy, *A Director Calls: Stephen Daldry and the Theatre* (London and Boston: Faber & Faber, 1997; 0–571–19070–7).

LUCKHURST, Mary, and VELTMAN, Chloe, eds, *On Acting: Interviews with Actors* (London & Boston: Faber & Faber, 2001; ISBN 0–571–20656–5).

Play-texts

ANTHOLOGIES

BAINES, Paul, and BURNS, Edward, eds, *Five Romantic Plays* (Oxford and New York: Oxford University Press, 2000 [World's Classics]; ISBN 0–19–283316–2).

BONNEY, Jo, ed., *Extreme Exposure: An Anthology of Solo Performance Texts from the Twentieth Century* (New York: Theatre Communications Group, 2000; ISBN 1–55936–155–7).

BOOTH, Michael R., ed., *The Magistrate and other Nineteenth-Century Plays* (Oxford: Oxford University Press, 1974; ISBN 0–19–881336–8).

—— *The Lights o'London and Other Plays* (Oxford and New York: Oxford University Press, 2000 [World's Classics]; ISBN 0–19–812173–3).

BRADWELL, Mike, ed., *The Bush Theatre Book: 25 Years* (London: Methuen, 1997; ISBN 0–413–71320–2).

CHOTHIA, Jean, ed., *The New Woman and Other Emancipated Woman Plays* (Oxford and New York: Oxford University Press, 1998 [World's Classics]; ISBN 0–19–282427–9).

CORDNER, Mike, and CLAYTON, Ronald, eds, *Four Restoration Marriage Plays* (Oxford and New York: Oxford University Press, 1995 [World's Classics]; ISBN 0–19–282570–4).

DRAKE, Nick, ed., *New Connections: New Plays for Young People* (London and Boston: Faber & Faber, 1997; ISBN 0–571–19148–7).

—— *New Connections 99: New Plays for Young People* (London and Boston: Faber & Faber, 1999; ISBN 0–571–20196–2).

ESSLIN, Martin, ed., *Absurd Drama* (Harmondsworth: Penguin, 1965 [Penguin Twentieth-Century Classics]; ISBN 0–14–018415–5).

FINBERG, Melinda, ed., *Eighteenth-Century Women Dramatists* (Oxford and New York: Oxford University Press, 2000 [World's Classics]; ISBN 0–19–282729–4).

FISCHLIN, Daniel, and FORTIER, Mark, eds, *Adaptations of Shakespeare: A critical anthology of plays from the seventeenth century to the present* (London and New York: Routledge, 2000; ISBN 0–415–19894–1).

HAMPDEN, John, ed., *The Beggar's Opera and other Eighteenth Century Plays* (London: Dent/New York: Dutton, 1974 [Everyman]; ISBN 0–460–01818–3).

HAPPÉ, Peter, ed., *Tudor Interludes* (Harmondsworth: Penguin, 1972 [Penguin English Library]; ISBN 0–14–043062–8).

—— *Four Morality Plays* (Harmondsworth: Penguin, 1979 [Penguin English Library]; ISBN 0–14–043119–5).

KILGORE, Emilie S., ed., *Landmarks of Women's Drama* (London and New York: Methuen, 1992; ISBN 0–413–66220–9).

KINNEY, Arthur F., ed., *Renaissance Drama: An Anthology of Plays and Entertainments* (Oxford: Blackwell, 1999; ISBN 0–631–20803–8).

LAMPORT, F. J., ed., *Five German Tragedies* (Harmondsworth: Penguin, 1969 [Penguin Classics]; ISBN 0–14–044219–7).

LEVY, Deborah, ed., *Walks on Water* (London: Methuen, 1992 [Methuen New Theatrescripts]; ISBN 0–413–67120–8).

LINDLEY, David, ed., *Court Masques: Jacobean and Caroline Entertainments 1605-1640* (Oxford and New York: Oxford University Press, 1995 [World's Classics]; ISBN 0–19–282569–0).

MORGAN, Fidelis, ed., *The Years Between: Plays by Women on the London Stage 1900–50* (London: Virago, 1994; ISBN 1–85381–620–5).

PENMAN, Bruce, ed., *Five Italian Renaissance Comedies* (Harmondsworth: Penguin, 1978; ISBN 0–14–044338–X).

ROWELL, George, ed., *Nineteenth-Century Plays* (2nd ed., Oxford: Oxford University Press, 1972; ISBN 0–19–281104–5).

STIERSTORFER, Klaus, ed., *London Assurance and Other Victorian Comedies* (Oxford and New York: Oxford University Press, 2000 [World's Classics]; ISBN 0–19–283296–4).

TRUSSLER, Simon, ed., *Burlesque Plays of the Eighteenth Century* (1969; Oxford and New York: Oxford University Press, 1995; ISBN 0–19–281055–3).

WALKER, Greg, ed., *Medieval Drama: An Anthology* (Oxford and Malden, MA: Blackwell, 2000; ISBN 0–631–21727–4).

WOMERSLEY, David, ed., *Restoration Drama: An Anthology* (Oxford and Malden, MA: Blackwell, 2000; ISBN 0–631–20903–4).

INDIVIDUAL PLAYWRIGHTS

ADAMOV, Arthur, *Two Plays* (trans. P. Meyer and D. Prouse, London: John Calder, 1962; no ISBN).

AESCHYLUS, *Plays 1* (London: Methuen, 1991; ISBN 0–413–65190–8).

—— *Plays 2* (London: Methuen, 1991; ISBN 0–413–65480–X).

ALBEE, Edward, *Who's Afraid of Virginia Woolf?* (Harmondsworth: Penguin, 1965; ISBN 0–14–048061–7).

—— *The Zoo Story and other plays* (Harmondsworth: Penguin, 1995; ISBN 0–14–025113–8).

ARDEN, John, *Plays 1* (London: Methuen, 1977; ISBN 0–413–68800–3).

—— *Plays 2* (London: Methuen, 1994; ISBN 0–413–68810–0).

ARISTOPHANES, *Birds and Other Plays* (ed. and trans. Stephen Halliwell, Oxford and New York: Oxford University Press, 1998 [World's Classics]; ISBN 0–19–282408–2).

—— and Menander, *New Comedy* (London: Methuen, 1994; ISBN 0–413–67180–1).

ARMIN, Robert, *Collected Works* (2 vols, New York and London: Johnson Reprint Corporation, 1972; no ISBN).

AYCKBOURN, Alan, *Henceforward* (London and Boston: Faber & Faber, 1988; ISBN 0–571–15185–X).

—— *Plays 1* (London and Boston: Faber & Faber, 1995; ISBN 0–571–17680–1).

—— *Plays 2* (London and Boston: Faber & Faber, 1998; ISBN 0–571–19457–5).

BANDELE-THOMAS, 'Biyi, *Resurrections in the Season of the Longest Drought* (Oxford: Amber Lane Press, 1994; ISBN 1–8728–68–4).

BARKER, Howard, *Collected Plays, volume 1* (London: John Calder, 1993; ISBN 0–7145–4161–3).

—— *Collected Plays, volume 2* (London: John Calder, 1993; ISBN 0–7145–4182–6).

BARRIE, J. M., *Peter Pan and Other Plays* (ed. Peter Hollindale, Oxford and New York: Oxford University Press, 1995 [World's Classics]; ISBN 0–19–283919–5).

BARTON, John, *Tantalus: Ten New Plays* (London: Oberon Books, 2000; ISBN 1–84002–160–8).

BECKETT, Samuel, *The Complete Dramatic Works* (1986; London: Faber & Faber, 1990; ISBN 0–571–14486–1).

BEHN, Aphra, *The Rover and Other Plays* (ed. Jane Spencer, Oxford and New York: Oxford University Press, 1995 [World's Classics]; ISBN 0–19–283451–7).

BENNETT, Alan, *Plays 1* (London and Boston: Faber & Faber, 1991; ISBN 0–571–17745–X).

—— *Plays 2* (London and Boston: Faber & Faber, 1998; ISBN 0–571–19442–7).

—— *The Complete Talking Heads* (London: BBC Publications, 1998; ISBN 0–563–38461–1).

BERKOFF, Steven, *Plays 1* (London and Boston: Faber & Faber, 1994; ISBN 0–571–16903–1).

—— *Plays 2* (London and Boston: Faber & Faber, 1994; ISBN 0–571–17102–8).

—— *Plays 3* (London and Boston: Faber & Faber, 2000; ISBN 0–571–20587–9).

BOLT, Robert, *A Man for All Seasons* (London: Methuen, 1995; ISBN 0–413–70380–0).

BOND, Edward, *Plays 1* (London: Methuen, 1977; ISBN 0–413–45410–X).

—— *Plays 2* (London: Methuen, 1978; ISBN 0–413–39270–8).

—— *Plays 3* (London: Methuen, 1987; ISBN 0–413–33890–8).

—— *Plays 4* (London: Methuen, 1992; ISBN 0–413–64830–3).

—— *Plays 5* (London: Methuen, 1994; ISBN 0–413–70390–8).

BOND, Edward, *Plays 6* (London: Methuen, 1996; ISBN 0–413–70400–9).

BOUCICAULT, Dion, *Selected Plays* (Gerrards Cross: Colin Smythe/Washington, D.C.: Catholic University of America Press, 1987 [Irish Drama Selections 4]; ISBN 0–86140–151–4 [UK]/0–8132–0583–2 [US]).

BRECHT, Bertolt, *Plays 1* (London: Methuen, 1994; ISBN 0–413–68570–5).

—— *Plays 2* (London: Methuen, 1994; ISBN 0–413–68560–8).

—— *Plays 3* (London: Methuen, 1997; ISBN 0–413–70460–2).

—— *Plays 4* (London: Methuen, 2001; ISBN 0–413–71520–5).

—— *Plays 5* (London: Methuen, 1995; ISBN 0–413–69970–6).

—— *Plays 6* (London: Methuen, 1994; ISBN 0–413–68580–2).

—— *Plays 7* (London: Methuen, 1994; ISBN 0–413–68590–X).

BRIGHOUSE, Harold, *Hobson's Choice* (London: Heinemann, 1992; ISBN 0–435–23280–0).).

BROME, Richard, *The Antipodes* (1640; ed. Ann Haaker, London: Edward Arnold, 1967 [Regents Renaissance Drama Series]; no ISBN).

BUTTERWORTH, Jez, *Mojo* (London: Nick Hern Books, 1996; ISBN 1–85459–366–8).

CALDERÓN, *Plays 1* (London: Methuen, 1991; ISBN 0–413–63460–4).

CAMERON, Richard, *Plays 1* (London: Methuen, 1998; ISBN 0–413–71660–0). [See also BRADWELL, Mike, ed., *The Bush Theatre Book.*]

ČAPEK, Josef, and ČAPEK, Karol, *R. U. R. & The Insect Play* (Oxford and New York: Oxford University Press, 1961; ISBN 0–19–281010–3).

CARR, Marina, *Plays 1* (London and Boston: Faber & Faber, 1999; ISBN 0–571–20011–7).

—— *On Raftery's Hill* (London and Boston: Faber & Faber, 2000; ISBN 0–571–20549–6).

CARTWRIGHT, Jim, *Plays 1* (London: Methuen, 1996; ISBN 0–413–70230–8).

CHASE, Mary, *Harvey* (London: English Theatre Guild, 1953; no ISBN).

CHEKHOV, Anton, *Five Plays* (ed. and trans. Ronald Hingley, Oxford and New York: Oxford University Press, 1980 [World's Classics]; ISBN 0–19–281548–2).

CHRISTIE, Agatha, *The Mousetrap and Selected Plays*, (London: HarperCollins, 1994; ISBN 0–00–649618–0).

CHURCHILL, Caryl, *Shorts* (London: Nick Hern Books, 1990; ISBN 1–85459–085–5).

—— *Plays 1* (London: Methuen, 1985; ISBN 0–413–86670–6).

—— *Plays 2* (London: Methuen, 1990; ISBN 0–413–62270–3).

—— *Plays 3* (London: Nick Hern Books, 1998; ISBN 1–85459–342–0).

—— *Blue Heart* (London: Nick Hern Books, 1997; ISBN 1–85459–327–7).

CIBBER, Colley, *see* WOMERSLEY, ed., *Restoration Drama*.

CONGREVE, William, *The Comedies* (ed. Eric S. Rump, Harmondsworth: Penguin, 1985 [Penguin Classics]; ISBN 0–14–043231–0).

CORNEILLE, Pierre, *The Cid/Cinna/The Theatrical Illusion* (trans. John Cairncross, Harmondsworth: Penguin, 1975; ISBN 0–14–044312–6).

COWARD, Noel, *Plays 1* (London: Methuen, 1986; ISBN 0–413–46060–6).

—— *Plays 2* (London: Methuen, 1986; ISBN 0–413–46080–0).

—— *Plays 3* (London: Methuen, 1987; ISBN 0–413–46100–9).

—— *Plays 4* (London: Methuen, 1988; ISBN 0–413–46120–3).

—— *Plays 5* (London: Methuen, 1994; ISBN 0–413–51740–3).

—— *Plays 6* (London: Methuen, 1995; ISBN 0–413–73410–2).

—— *Plays 7* (London: Methuen, 1997; ISBN 0–413–73400–5).

—— *Plays 8* (London: Methuen, 1998; ISBN 0–413–75510–X).

CRIMP, Martin, *Plays 1* (London and Boston: Faber & Faber, 2000; ISBN 0–571–20345–0).

—— *Attempts on her Life* (London and Boston: Faber & Faber, 1997; ISBN 0–571–19215–7).

—— *The Country* (London and Boston: Faber & Faber, 2000; ISBN 0–571–20340–X).

DANIELS, Sarah, *Plays 1* (London: Methuen, 1991; ISBN 0–413–64930–X).

de ANGELIS, April, *Plays 1* (London and Boston: Faber & Faber, 1999; ISBN 0–571–19709–4).

—— *A Warwickshire Testimony* (London and Boston: Faber & Faber, 1999; ISBN 0–571–20355–8).

DELANEY, Shelagh, *A Taste of Honey* (London: Methuen, 1982; ISBN 0–413–49250–8 [Methuen Student Editions]).

de MOLINA, Tirso, *The Rape of Tamar* (*La Venganza de Tamar*, trans. and adapted Paul Whitworth, London: Oberon Books, 1999 [Absolute Classics]; ISBN 0–948230–94–0).

de VEGA, Lope, *Three Major Plays* (ed. and trans. Gwynne Edwards, Oxford and New York: Oxford University Press, 1999 [World's Classics]; ISBN 0–19–283337–5).

DEVLIN, Anne, *Ourselves Alone* (London and Boston: Faber & Faber, 1990; ISBN 0–571–14457–8).

—— *After Easter* (London and Boston: Faber & Faber, 1994; ISBN 0–571–17394–2).

DOWIE, Claire, *Why is John Lennon Wearing a Skirt? and other Stand-up Theatre Plays* (London: Methuen, 1996; ISBN 0–413–71090–4).

DRYDEN, John, *All for Love* (ed. N. J. Andrew, London: Ernest Benn/New York: Norton, 1975 [New Mermaids]; ISBN 0–510–33711–2 (UK), 0–393–90006–1 (USA)).

—— *Marriage a la Mode* (ed. Mark S. Auburn, London: Edward Arnold, 1981 [Regents Restoration Drama]; ISBN 0–7131–6356–9).

[*See also* CORDNER, ed., *Four Restoration Marriage Plays*; WOMERSLEY, ed., *Restoration Drama*.]

DURAS, Marguerite, *Four Plays* (trans. Barbara Bray; London: Oberon Books, 1992; ISBN 1–870259–28–9).

EDGAR, David, *Albert Speer* (London: Nick Hern Books, 2000; ISBN 1–85459–485–0).

—— *Plays 1* (London: Methuen, 1987; ISBN 0–413–15220–0).

—— *Plays 2* (London: Methuen, 1990; ISBN 0–413–63050–1).

—— *Plays 3* (London: Methuen, 1991; ISBN 0–413–64850–8).

ELTON, Ben, *Plays 1* (London: Methuen, 1998; ISBN 0–413–73670–9.)

ENSLER, Eve, *The Vagina Monologues* (New York: Villard, 1998; ISBN 0–375–75052–5).

ETHEREGE, George, *The Man of Mode* (ed. W. B. Carnochan, London: Edward Arnold, 1967 [Regents Restoration Drama]; ISBN 0–7131–5247–8).

—— *She Would If She Could* (ed. Charlene M. Taylor, Lincoln, NE, and London: University of Nebraska Press, 1971 [Regents Restoration Drama]; ISBN 0–8032–6700–2).

EURIPIDES, *Bacchae and Other Plays* (ed. and trans. James Morwood, Oxford and New York: Oxford University Press, 2000 [World's Classics]; ISBN 0–19–283875–X).

—— *Orestes and Other Plays* (ed. Edith Hall and James Morwood, trans. Robin Waterfield, Oxford and New York: Oxford University Press, 2000 [World's Classics]; ISBN 0–19–283260–3).

—— *Medea and Other Plays* (ed. and trans. James Morwood, Oxford and New York: Oxford University Press, 2000 [World's Classics]; ISBN 0–19–282442–2).

—— *Trojan Women & Other Plays* (ed. and trans. James Morwood, Oxford and New York: Oxford University Press, 2000 [World's Classics]; ISBN 0–19–283987–X).

FARQUHAR, George, *The Recruiting Officer and Other Plays* (ed. William Myers, Oxford and New York: Oxford University Press, 1995 [World's Classics]; ISBN 0–19–283450–9).

FEYDEAU, Georges, *Four One-act Plays* (trans. Peter Meyer, London: Oberon Books, 1998 [Absolute Classics]; ISBN 1–870529–70–X).

—— *First to Last: Eight One-Act Comedies* (trans. Norman R. Shapiro, Ithaca and London: Cornell University Press, 1982; ISBN 0–8014–1295–1).

FIERSTEIN, Harvey, *Torch Song Trilogy* (London: Methuen, 1984; ISBN 0–413–55580–1).

FO, Dario, *Plays 1* (London: Methuen, 1992; ISBN 0–413–15420–3).

—— *Plays 2* (London: Methuen, 1994; ISBN 0–413–68020–7).

FORD, John, *'Tis Pity She's a Whore and Other Plays* (ed. Marion Lomax, Oxford and New York: Oxford University Press, 1995 [World's Classics]; ISBN 0–19–283449–5).

FRAYN, Michael, *Plays 1* (London: Methuen, 1985; ISBN 0–413–59280–4).

—— *Plays 2* (London: Methuen, 1991; ISBN 0–413–66080–X).

—— *Plays 3* (London: Methuen, 2000; ISBN 0–413–75230–5).

—— *Copenhagen* (London: Methuen, 1998; ISBN 0–413–72490–5).

FRIEL, Brian, *Plays 1* (London: Methuen, 1985; ISBN 0–413–59280–4).

FUGARD, Athol, *The Township Plays* (Oxford and New York: Oxford University Press, 1993; ISBN 0–19–282925–4).

GENET, Jean *The Balcony* (trans. Barbara Wright and Terry Hands, London and Boston: Faber & Faber, 1991; ISBN 0–571–15246–5).

—— *The Maids and Deathwatch* (trans. Bernard Frechtman, London and Boston: Faber & Faber, 1989; ISBN 0–571–14856–5).

GILBERT, William Schwenk, and SULLIVAN, Arthur, *Complete Opera Librettos* (ed. Reginald Allen, London: Chappell & Co., 1958; ISBN 0–903443–10–4).

GODBER, John, *Plays 1* (London: Methuen, 2001; ISBN 0–413–75810–9).

—— *Plays 2* (London: Methuen, 2001; ISBN 0–413–75820–6).

GRANVILLE BARKER, Harley, *Plays 1* (London: Methuen, 1994; ISBN 0–413–67530–0).

—— *Plays 2* (London: Methuen, 1994; ISBN 0–413–67980–2).

GRASS, Günter, *The Plebeians Rehearse the Uprising* (trans. Ralph Manheim; Harmondsworth: Penguin, 1972; no ISBN).

GRAY, Spalding, *Swimming to Cambodia: The Collected Works of Spalding Gray* (London: Picador, 1985; ISBN 0–330–29947–6).

GREIG, David, *Europe & The Architect* (London: Methuen, 1996; ISBN 0–413–70880–2).

GROSSO, Nick, *Real Classy Affair* (London: Faber & Faber, 1998; ISBN 0–571–19592–X).

GUARE, John, *Six Degrees of Separation* (New York: Dramatists Plays Service, Inc., 1992; ISBN 0–8222–1034–7).

HALL, Lee, *Spoonface Steinberg & other plays* (London: BBC Books, 1997; ISBN 0–563–38398–4).

HAMPTON, Christopher, *Plays 1* (London and Boston: Faber & Faber, 1997; ISBN 0–571–17834–0).

HANDKE, Peter, *Plays 1* (London: Methuen, 1997; ISBN 0–413–68090–8).

HARE, David, *The History Plays* (London and Boston: Faber & Faber, 1984; ISBN 0–571–13132–8).

—— *Plays 1* (London and Boston: Faber & Faber, 1996; ISBN 0–571–17741–7).

—— *Plays 2* (London and Boston: Faber & Faber, 1997; ISBN 0–571–17835–9).

—— *Via Dolorosa* (London and Boston: Faber & Faber, 1998; ISBN 0–571–19752–3).

HARRIS, Zinnie, *Further than the Furthest Thing* (London and Boston: Faber & Faber, 2000; ISBN 0–571–20544–5).

HARRISON, Tony, *Theatre Works 1973–1985* (Harmondsworth: Penguin, 1986; ISBN 0–14–058657–1).

—— *The Mysteries* (London and Boston: Faber & Faber, 1985; ISBN 0–571–13790–3).

—— *Plays 3* (London and Boston: Faber & Faber, 1996; ISBN 0–571–17966–5).

HARWOOD, Ronald, *Collected Plays* (London and Boston: Faber & Faber, 1993; ISBN 0–571–17001–3).

—— *Plays 2* (London and Boston: Faber & Faber, 1995; ISBN 0–571–17401–9).

HOCHHUTH, Rolf, *The Representative: A Christian Tragedy* (trans. Robert David MacDonald, London: Oberon Books, 1998; ISBN 1–870259–39–4).

IBSEN, Henrik, *Four Major Plays* (ed. and trans. James McFarlane, trans. Jens Arup, Oxford and New York: Oxford University Press, 1981 [World's Classics]; ISBN 0–19–283387–1).

—— *Brand* (trans. Geoffrey Hill, 1978; 3rd ed., Harmondsworth: Penguin, 1996 [Penguin Classics]; ISBN 0–14–044676–1).

IONESCO, Eugène, *Rhinoceros, The Chairs, The Lesson* (Harmondsworth: Penguin, 1962; ISBN 0–14–118429–9).

JARRY, Alfred, *The Ubu Plays* (trans. Cyril Connolly and Simon Watson Taylor, London: Methuen, 1968; ISBN 0–413–67990–X).

JEFFREYS, Stephen, *The Libertine* (London: Nick Hern Books, 1994; ISBN 1–85459–277–7).

JOHNSON, Terry, *Plays 1* (London: Methuen, 1993; ISBN 0–413–68200–5).

—— *Plays 2* (London: Methuen, 1998; ISBN 0–413–72360–7).

JONES, H. A., *see* BOOTH, Michael, ed.

JONSON, Ben, *The Alchemist and Other Plays* (ed. Gordon Campbell, Oxford and New York: Oxford University Press, 1995 [World's Classics]; ISBN 0–19–283446–0).

—— *The Devil is an Ass and Other Plays* (ed. M. J. Kidnie, Oxford and New York: Oxford University Press, 2000 [World's Classics]; ISBN 0–19–813229–8).

KANE, Sarah, *Complete Plays* (London: Methuen, 2001; ISBN 0–413–74260–1).

KEMPINSKI, Tom, *Duet for One* (London: Samuel French, 1981; ISBN 0–573–11091–3).

KHAN-DIN, Ayub, *East is East* (London: Nick Hern Books, 1996; ISBN 1–85459–313–7).

KOLTÈS, Bernard-Marie, *Plays 1* (trans. David Bradby, Maria M. Delgado, and Martin Crimp, London: Methuen, 1997; ISBN 0–413–70240–5).

KUREISHI, Hanif, *My Beautiful Laundrette and other writings* (London and Boston: Faber & Faber, 1996; ISBN 0–571–17738–7).

—— *Plays 1* (London and Boston: Faber & Faber, 1999; ISBN 0–571–19774–4).

KUSHNER, Tony, *Angels in America, Part One: Millennium Approaches* (London: Nick Hern Books, 1992; ISBN 1–85459–156–8).

—— *Angels in America, Part Two: Perestroika* (London: Nick Hern Books, 1994; ISBN 1–85459–255–6).

LAVERY, Bryony, *Plays 1* (London: Methuen Drama, 1998; ISBN 0–413–72340–2).

LAWRENCE, D. H., *The Widowing of Mrs Holroyd and Other Plays* (ed. Simon Trussler, Oxford and New York: Oxford University Press, 2001 [World's Classics]; ISBN 0–19–283314–6).

LOCHHEAD, Liz, *Mary Queen of Scots got her Head Chopped Off & Dracula* (Harmondsworth: Penguin, 1989; ISBN 0–14–048220–2).

—— *Perfect Days* (London: Nick Hern Books, 1998; ISBN 1–85459–419–2).

—— *Medea* (London: Nick Hern Books, 2000; ISBN 1–85459–602–0).

LORCA, Federico Garcia, *Four Major Plays* (ed. Nicholas Round, trans. John Edmunds, Oxford and New York: Oxford University Press, 1999 [World's Classics]; ISBN 0–19–283938–1).

LOWELL, Robert, *Prometheus Bound* (London and Boston: Faber & Faber, 1971; ISBN 0–571–09274–8).

MacDONALD, Sharman, *Plays 1* (London and Boston: Faber & Faber, 1995; ISBN 0–571–17621–6).

MAMET, David, *Plays 1* (London: Methuen, 1978; ISBN 0–413–39540–5).

—— *Plays 2* (London: Methuen, 1996; ISBN 0–413–67840–6).

—— *Plays 3* (London: Methuen, 1996; ISBN 0–413–68750–3).

—— *Oleanna* (London: Methuen, 1993; ISBN 0–413–62620–2).

MARBER, Patrick, *Closer* (London: Methuen, 1997; ISBN 0–413–70950–7).

MARLOWE, Christopher, *Doctor Faustus and Other Plays* (ed. David Bevington and Eric Rasmussen, Oxford and New York: Oxford University Press, 1995 [World's Classics]; ISBN 0–19–283445–2).

MARSTON, John, *The Malcontent and Other Plays* (ed. Keith Sturgess, Oxford and New York: Oxford University Press, 1997 [World's Classics]; ISBN 0–19–282250–0).

McDONAGH, Martin, *Plays 1* (London: Methuen, 1999; ISBN 0–413–71350–4).

—— *The Cripple of Inishmaan* (London: Methuen, 1997; ISBN 0–413–71590–6).

—— *The Lieutenant of Inishmore* (London: Methuen, 2001; ISBN 0–413–76500–8).

McGUINNESS, Frank, *Plays 1* (London and Boston: Faber & Faber, 1996; ISBN 0–571–17740–9).

McPHERSON, Conor, *The Weir* (London: Nick Hern Books, 1997; ISBN 1–85459–427–3).

MEDOFF, Mark, *Children of a Lesser God* (Ambergate: Amber Lane Press, 1982; ISBN 0–906399–32–7).

MENANDER *see* ARISTOPHANES and MENANDER.

MERCER, David, *Plays 1* (London: Methuen, 1990; ISBN 0–413–63450–7).

—— *Plays 2* (London: Methuen, 1994; ISBN 0–413–65200–9).

MIDDLETON, Thomas, *A Mad World, My Masters and Other Plays* (ed. Michael Taylor, Oxford and New York: Oxford University Press, 1998 [World's Classics]; ISBN 0–19–283455–X).

—— *Women Beware Women and Other Plays* (ed. Richard Dutton, Oxford and New York: Oxford University Press, 1999 [World's Classics]; ISBN 0–19–282614–X).

MILLER, Arthur, *Plays 1* (London: Methuen, 1988; ISBN 0–413–15810–1).

—— *Plays 2* (London: Methuen, 1988; ISBN 0–413–15820–9).

—— *Plays 3* (London: Methuen, 1990; ISBN 0–413–63500–7).

—— *Plays 4* (London: Methuen, 1994; ISBN 0–413–68010–X).

—— *Plays 5* (London: Methuen, 1995; ISBN 0–413–69830–0).

MINGHELLA, Anthony *Plays 1* (London: Methuen, 1992; ISBN 0–413–66580–1).

—— *Plays 2* (London: Methuen, 1997; ISBN 0–413–71520–5).

MOLIÈRE, *Don Juan and Other Plays* (ed. and trans. Ian Maclean, trans. George Gravely, Oxford and New York: Oxford University Press, 1999 [World's Classics]; ISBN 0–19–283551–3).

—— *The Misanthrope, Tartuffe, and Other Plays* (ed. and trans. Maya Slater, Oxford and New York: Oxford University Press, 2000 [World's Classics]; ISBN 0–19–283341–3).

MÜLLER, Heiner, *Theatremachine* (ed. and trans. Marc von Henning, London: Faber & Faber, 1995; ISBN 0–571–17528–7).

MUNRO, Rona, *Bold Girls* (London, New York, Toronto, and Hollywood: Samuel French Ltd, 1991; ISBN 0–573–13006–X).

—— *Your Turn to clean the Stair & Fugue* (London: Nick Hern Books, 1995; ISBN 1–85459–248–3).

—— *The Maiden Stone* (London: Nick Hern Books, 1995; ISBN 1–85459–243–2).

NEILSON, Anthony, *Plays 1* (London: Methuen, 1998; ISBN 0–413–72460–3).

NICHOLS, Peter, *Plays 1* (London: Methuen, 1987; ISBN 0–413–64870–2).

—— *Plays 2* (London: Methuen, 1991; ISBN 0–413–65070–7).

NORTON-TAYLOR, Richard, ed., *The Colour of Justice: Based on the transcripts of the Stephen Lawrence Inquiry* (London: Oberon Books, 1999; ISBN 1–84002–107–1).

Oh What a Lovely War see THEATRE WORKSHOP.

O'NEILL, Eugene, *Complete Plays* (ed. Travis Bogard, New York: Literary Classics of the United States, 1988; ISBN 0–940–45062–3).

O'ROWE, Mark, *Made in China* (London: Nick Hern Books, 2001; ISBN 1–85459–627–6).

ORTON, Joe, *The Complete Plays* (London: Methuen, 1976; ISBN 0–413–34610–2).

OSBORNE, John, *Plays 1* (London and Boston: Faber & Faber, 1993; ISBN 0–571–17766–2).

—— *Plays 2* (London and Boston: Faber & Faber, 1998; ISBN 0–571–17846–4).

OTWAY, Thomas, *The Orphan* (1680; ed. Aline Mackenzie Taylor, London: Edward Arnold, 1977 [Regents Renaissance Drama Series]; ISBN 0–7131–5948–0).

—— *Venice Preserved* (1682; ed. Malcolm Kensall, London: Edward Arnold, 1969 [Regents Renaissance Drama Series]; ISBN 0–7131–5471–3).

[*See also* CORDNER, ed., *Four Restoration Marriage Plays*.]

PASCAL, Julia, *The Holocaust Trilogy* (London: Oberon Books, 2000; ISBN 1–8400–2094–6).

PENHALL, Joe, *Blue/Orange* (London: Methuen, 2000; ISBN 0–413–75270–4).

PINERO, Arthur Wing, *Trelawny of the 'Wells' and Other Plays* (ed. Jacky Bratton, Oxford and New York: Oxford University Press, 1995 [World's Classics]; ISBN 0–19–282568–2).

PINNOCK, Winsome, *Mules* (London: Faber & Faber, 1996; ISBN 0–571–19022–7).

PINTER, Harold, *Plays 1* (London and Boston: Faber & Faber, 1991; ISBN 0–571–17844–8).

—— *Plays 2* (London and Boston: Faber & Faber, 1991; ISBN 0–571–17744–1).

—— *Plays 3* (London and Boston: Faber & Faber, 1991; ISBN 0–571–19383–8).

—— *Plays 4* (London and Boston: Faber & Faber, 1993; ISBN 0–571–19384–6).

—— *Remembrance of Things Past by Marcel Proust adapted by Harold Pinter and Di Trevis* (London and Boston: Faber & Faber, 2000; ISBN 0–571–20760–X).

PIRANDELLO, Luigi, *Three Plays* (London: Methuen, 1985; ISBN 0–413–57560–8).

PLAUTUS, *Four Comedies* (ed. and trans. Erich Segal, Oxford and New York: Oxford University Press, 1996 [World's Classics]; ISBN 0–19–283896–2).

POTTER, Dennis, *Waiting for the Boat: On Television* (London and Boston: Faber & Faber, 1984; ISBN 0–571–13081–X).

—— *The Singing Detective* (London and Boston: Faber & Faber, 1986; ISBN 0–571–14590–6).

PRICHARD, Rebecca, *Yard Gal* (London: Faber & Faber, 1998; ISBN 0–571–19591–1).

PRIESTLEY, J. B., *An Inspector Calls* (Harmondsworth: Penguin, 1995; ISBN 0–14–118535–X).

RACINE, Jean, *Andromache and Other Plays* (trans. John Cairncross, Harmondsworth: Penguin, 1967 [Penguin Classics]; ISBN 0–14–044195–6).

RATTIGAN, Terence, *Plays 1* (London: Methuen, 1981; ISBN 0–413–49070–X).

—— *Plays 2* (London: Methuen, 1985; ISBN 0–413–54670–9).

RAVENHILL, Mark, *Plays 1* (London: Methuen, 2001; ISBN 0–413–76060–X).

RIDLEY, Philip, *Plays 1* (London: Methuen, 1997; ISBN 0–413–71100–5).

ROSE, Reginald, *Twelve Angry Men* (1955; London: Methuen, 1996; ISBN 0–413–70610–9).

ROWE, Nicholas, *The Tragedy of Jane Shore* (1714; ed. H. W. Pedicord, London: Edward Arnold, 1975 [Regents Renaissance Drama Series]; ISBN 0–7131–5784–4).

RUSSELL, Willy, *Educating Rita and Others* (London: Methuen, 1986; ISBN 0–413–41110–9).

SANDFORD, Jeremy, *Cathy Come Home* (London: Marion Boyars, 1976; ISBN 0–7145–2515–4).

—— *Smiling David: The Story of David Oluwale* (London: Calder & Boyars, 1974; ISBN 0–7145–1049–1).

SARTRE, Jean-Paul, *Three Plays* (trans. Kitty Black, Sylvia and George Leeson, Ronald Duncan, Harmondsworth: Penguin, 1969; ISBN 0–14–048083–8).

SENECA, *Four Tragedies and Octavia* (trans. E. F. Watling, Harmondsworth: Penguin, 1966 [Penguin Classics]; no ISBN).

—— *Thyestes* (trans. Jasper Heywood, 1560; ed. Joost Daalder, London: Ernest Benn/New York: W. W. Norton, 1982 [New Mermaids]; ISBN 0–510–39010–2 (UK)/0–393–95237–1 (USA)).

SHAFFER, Peter, *Three Plays* (Harmondsworth: Penguin, 1976; ISBN 0–14–048128–1).

—— *Amadeus* (Harmondsworth: Penguin, 1981; ISBN 0–14–048160–5).

—— *The Royal Hunt of the Sun* (London: Penguin, 1981; ISBN 0–14–048163–X).

SHAKESPEARE, William, *Mr. William Shakespeares Comedies, Histories, & Tragedies. Published according to the True Originall Copies* (London: Isaac Jaggard & Ed. Blount, 1623).

—— *The Applause Facsimile. The First Folio of Shakespeare.* 1623 (Prepared and Introduced by Doug Moston, New York and London: Applause, 1995; ISBN 1–66783–184–X).

—— *The Riverside Shakespeare* (1974; 2nd ed., ed. G. B. Evans *et al.*, Boston and New York: Houghton Mifflin, 1997; ISBN 0–395–75490–9).

SHANGE, Ntozake, *Plays 1* (London: Methuen, 1992; ISBN 0–413–67370–7).

SHAW, George Bernard, *Plays Pleasant* (Harmondsworth: Penguin, 1946; ISBN 0–14–045020–3).

—— *Plays Unpleasant* (Harmondsworth: Penguin, 1946; ISBN 0–14–045021–1).

—— *Pygmalion* (Harmondsworth: Penguin, 1941; ISBN 0–14–045022–X).

—— *Three Plays for Puritans* (Harmondsworth: Penguin, 1946; ISBN 0–14–048002–1).

SHEPARD, Sam, *Plays 1* (London: Methuen, 1996; ISBN 0–413–70830–6).

—— *Plays 2* (London and Boston: Faber & Faber, 1997; ISBN 0–571–19074–X).

—— *Plays 3* (London: Methuen, 1996; ISBN 0–413–70840–3).

SHERIDAN, Richard Brinsley, *The School for Scandal and Other Plays* (ed. Michael Cordner, Oxford and New York: Oxford University Press, 1998 [World's Classics]; ISBN 0–19–282567–4).

SIMPSON, N. F., *One Way Pendulum* (London: Samuel French, n.d.; ISBN 0–573–01321–7).

—— *Resounding Tinkle* (London: Samuel French, n.d.; ISBN 0–573–02229–1).

SOPHOCLES, *Antigone; Oedipus the King; Electra* (ed. Edith Hall, trans. H. D. F. Kitto, Oxford and New York: Oxford University Press, 1998 [World's Classics]; ISBN 0–19–283588–2).

SOYINKA, Wole, *Collected Plays 1* (Oxford and New York: Oxford University Press, 1973; ISBN 0–19–281136–3).

—— *Collected Plays 2* (Oxford and New York: Oxford University Press, 1974; ISBN 0–19–281164–9).

STEIN, Gertrude, *Last Operas and Plays* (ed. Carl Van Vechten, Baltimore and London: Johns Hopkins University Press, 1995; ISBN 0–8018–4985–3).

STEPHENSON, Shelagh, *An Experiment with an Air Pump* (London: Methuen, 1998; ISBN 0–413–73310–6).

STOPPARD, Tom, *The Plays for Radio 1964-1991* (London and Boston: Faber & Faber, 1994; ISBN 0–571–17209–1).

—— *Plays 1* (London and Boston: Faber & Faber, 1996; ISBN 0–571–17765–4).

STOPPARD, Tom, *Plays 2* (London and Boston: Faber & Faber, 1996; ISBN 0–571–19008–1).

—— *Plays 3* (London and Boston: Faber & Faber, 1999; ISBN 0–571–19428–1).

—— *Plays 4* (London and Boston: Faber & Faber, 1999; ISBN 0–571–19750–7).

—— *Plays 5* (London and Boston: Faber & Faber, 1999; ISBN 0–571–19751–5).

STOREY, David, *Plays 1* (London: Methuen, 1992; ISBN 0–413–67350–2).

—— *Plays 2* (London: Methuen, 1994; ISBN 0–413–68610–8).

STRINDBERG, August, *Miss Julie and Other Plays* (ed. and trans. Michael Robinson, Oxford and New York: Oxford University Press, 1998 [World's Classics]; ISBN 0–19–283317–0).

SYNGE, J. M., *The Playboy of the Western World and Other Plays* (ed. Ann Saddlemyer, Oxford and New York: Oxford University Press, 1995 [World's Classics]; ISBN 0–19–282611–5).

TAYLOR, C. P., *Good* & *A Nightingale Sang* (London: Methuen, 1984; ISBN 0–413–63910–X).

TERENCE, *The Comedies* (trans. Betty Radice, Harmondsworth: Penguin, 1976 [Penguin Classics]; ISBN 0–14–044324–X).

THEATRE DE COMPLICITE, *The Street of Crocodiles* (based on stories by Bruno Schulz, adapted by Simon McBurney and Mark Wheatley; London: Methuen, 1999; ISBN 0–413–73870–1).

—— *Light* (based on the book by Torgny Lindgren, adapted by Simon McBurney and Matthew Broughton, devised by the Company; London: Oberon Books, 2000; ISBN 1–84002–203–5).

THEATRE WORKSHOP, *Oh What a Lovely War* (ed. Joan Littlewood, London: Methuen, 2000; ISBN 0–413–30210–5).

THOMAS, Brandon, *Charlie's Aunt* (London: Heinemann, 1969; ISBN 0–435–22115–9).

THOMAS, Dylan, *Under Milk Wood* (London: Dent, 1977 [Everyman]; ISBN 0–460–87765–8).

TRAVERS, Ben, *Five Plays* (Harmondsworth: Penguin, 1979; ISBN 0–14–048146–X).

UPTON, Judy, *Bruises* & *The Shorewatcher's House* (London: Methuen, 1996; ISBN 0–413–70430–0).

—— *Confidence* (London: Methuen, 1998; ISBN 0–413–77290–X).

VANBRUGH, John, *Four Comedies* (ed. Michael Cordner, Harmondsworth: Penguin, 1988; ISBN 0–14–043276–0).

WALCOTT, Derek, *Dream on Monkey Mountain and other plays* (New York: Farrar, Straus and Giroux, 1970 [Noonday Press]; ISBN 0–374–50860–7).

—— *Remembrance* & *Pantomime* (New York: Farrar, Straus and Giroux, 1980; ISBN 0–374–24912–1).

—— *The Joker of Seville & O Babylon!* (London: Jonathan Cape, 1979; ISBN 0–224–01669–5).

—— *Three Plays* (New York: Farrar, Straus and Giroux, 1986; ISBN 0–374–51883–1).

WALSH, Enda, *Disco Pigs & Sucking Dublin* (London: Nick Hern Books, 1997; ISBN 1–85459–398–6).

WEBSTER, John, *The Duchess of Malfi and Other Plays* (ed. René Weis, Oxford and New York: Oxford University Press, 1996 [World's Classics]; ISBN 0–19–283453–3).

WEDEKIND, Frank, *Plays 1* (trans. Edward Bond and Elisabeth Bond-Pablé, London: Methuen, 1993; ISBN 0–413–67540–8).

WERTENBAKER, Timberlake, *Our Country's Good* (1988; London: Methuen, 1995 [Methuen Student Editions]; ISBN 0–413–69230–2).

—— *Plays 1* (London and Boston: Faber & Faber, 1996; ISBN 0–571–17743–3).

—— *The Break of Day* (London and Boston: Faber & Faber, 1995; ISBN 0–571–17679–8).

—— *After Darwin* (London and Boston: Faber & Faber, 1998; ISBN 0–571–19584–9).

WEISS, Peter, *The Persecution and Assassination of Marat as Performed by the Inmates of the Asylum of Charenton under the Direction of the Marquis de Sade* (1964, as *Der Verfolgung und Ermordung Jean Paul Marats Dargestellt durch die Schauspielgruppe des Hospizes zu Charenton unter Anleitung des Herrn de Sade*; trans. Geoffrey Skelton and Adrian Mitchell, London and New York: Marion Boyars, 1965; ISBN 0–7145–0361–4).

—— *The Investigation* (1965, as *Die Ermittlung*, trans. Jon Swan and Ulu Grosbard, New York: Atheneum, 1973; ISBN 0–689–10287–9).

WESKER, Arnold, *Plays 1* (London: Methuen, 1964; ISBN 0–413–75830–3).

—— *Plays 2* (London: Methuen, 1976; ISBN 0–413–75840–0).

WILDE, Oscar, *The Importance of Being Earnest and Other Plays* (ed. Peter Raby, Oxford and New York: Oxford University Press, 1995 [World's Classics]; ISBN 0–19–283444–4).

WILLIAMS, Tennessee, *Sweet Bird of Youth, A Streetcar Named Desire, The Glass Menagerie* (Harmondsworth: Penguin, 1959; ISBN 0–14–048015–3).

WILSON, August, *Fences & Ma Rainey's Black Bottom* (Harmondsworth: Penguin, 1988; ISBN 0–14–048217–0).

WILSON, Snoo, *Plays 1* (London: Methuen, 1999; ISBN 0–413–74180–X).

WOOD, Charles, *Plays 1* (London: Oberon Books, 1997 [Modern Playwrights]; ISBN 1–870259–83–1).

—— *Plays 2* (London: Oberon Books, 1999 [Modern Playwrights]; ISBN 1–870259–84–X).

—— *Tumbledown* (Harmondsworth: Penguin, 1987; ISBN 0–14–048215–6).

WRIGHT, Nicholas, *Cressida* (London: Nick Hern Books, 2000; ISBN 1–85459–454–0).

WYCHERLEY, William, *The Country Wife and Other Plays* (ed. Peter Dixon, Oxford and New York: Oxford University Press, 1996 [World's Classics]; ISBN 0–19–283454–1).

Videos

Videos come and go at high speed and catalogue numbers are constantly changing. We have given the most recent information we could find but some films may have been reissued in other packaging or deleted. For video it is important to check both US and UK availability; most new video-recorders will play both VHS and NTSC formats. The format of all videos listed is VHS unless otherwise stated; DVDs are also indicated. Both Amazon.com and blackstar.co.uk maintain detailed searchable on-line catalogues.

SHAKESPEARE

Names in parenthesis are those of principal actors. The associated films to which cross-references are provided appear after the list of plays. The BBC Shakespeare films of all 37 non-collaborative plays are unavailable to buy, and therefore excluded; some remain available in libraries and to rent. A full Shakespeare cineography appears in Kenneth S. Rothwell, *A History of Shakespeare on Screen: a century of film and television* (Cambridge: Cambridge University Press, 1999; ISBN 0–521–00028–9).

Anthony and Cleopatra

dir. Lawrence Carra, 1999 (Dalton, Redgrave, Carradine), Quantum Leap QL0167, 2001.

As You Like It

dir. Paul Czinner, 1936 (Olivier, Bergner); Video Yesteryear 447, 1980 (NTSC).

dir. Christine Edzard, 1992 (Fox, Croft, Rhys Jones, Margolyes), Buena Vista Home Video D515672, n.d.

Hamlet

dir. Laurence Olivier, 1949 (Olivier, Holloway), Rank Home Video 0002, n.d.

dir. John Gielgud, 1964 (Burton, Drake, Cronyn), 2 vols, BMG Entertainment International BMG 74321-403603, 1996.

dir. Grigori Kozintsev, 1964 (Smoktoenovski, Vertinskaya), Moskwood Video 2644, n.d.

dir. Franco Zeffirelli, 1990 (Gibson, Close, Bates, Bonham Carter), Columbia Tristar Home Video CVR22762, 1992.

dir. Kenneth Branagh, 1996 (Branagh, Christie, Jacobi, Winslet), Columbia Tristar Home Video CVR86033, 1997.

dir. Michael Almereyda, 2000 (Hawke, McClachlan, Shepard, Murray), FilmFour/Video Collection International VC3871, 2001.

See also *Hamlet Goes Business, In the Bleak Midwinter.*

Henry V

dir. Laurence Olivier, 1944 (Olivier, Asherson, Robey, Aylmer), Carlton 0010, 2001.

dir. Kenneth Branagh, 1989 (Branagh, Jacobi, Scofield, Thompson), Columbia Tristar Home Video CVR22761, 1991.

Julius Caesar

dir. Joseph L. Manckiewicz, 1953 (Gielgud, Mason, Brando), Warner Home Video S050274, 2001.

dir. Stuart Burge, 1970 (Heston, Robards, Gielgud, Rigg), 4-Front Video 045-516-3, 1997.

King John

dir. W.-K. L. Dickson, 1899 (Beerbohm Tree, Senior): see *Silent Shakespeare.*

King Lear

dir. G. Lo Savio, 1910 (Novelli): see *Silent Shakespeare.*

dir. Peter Brook, 1970 (Scofield, Worth), Columbia Tristar Home Video CC7623, 1998.

dir. Grigori Kozintsev, 1970 (Yarvet, Dal, Volchek), Tartan Video PAL TVT 1262, 1997.

dir. Michael Elliot, 1983 (Olivier, Rigg, McKern), Granada Media GV0201, 2000.

dir. Richard Eyre, 1998 (Holm, Flynn, Redman, Lyon), 2 vols, WGBH Boston Video/BBC SV10632.

See also *Ran, A Thousand Acres.*

Love's Labour's Lost

dir. Kenneth Branagh, 1999 (Branagh, Lester, Silverstone), Pathé P8987S, 2001.

Macbeth

dir. Orson Welles, 1947 (Welles, Nolan), Second Sight 2nd1011, 1996.

dir. Roman Polanski, 1971 (Finch, Annis, Shaw), Columbia Tristar Home Video CVR20668, 1991.

dir. Trevor Nunn, 1978 (McKellen, Dench), Thames Television International/Video Collection International TV8124, 1991.

See also *Throne of Blood.*

The Merchant of Venice

dir. G. Lo Savio, 1910 (Novelli): see *Silent Shakespeare*.

dir. Jonathan Miller, 1974 (Olivier, Plowright), Polygram Filmed Entertainment 29279, 1998.

A Midsummer Night's Dream

dir. J. S. Blackton/C. Kent, 1909 (Ranous, Costello): see *Silent Shakespeare*.

dir. Max Reinhardt/William Dieterle, 1935 (Cagney, de Havilland, Rooney), Warner Home Video 65114, 2000 (NTSC).

dir. Adrian Noble, 1996 (Jennings, Duncan, Barrit, Lynch), FilmFour CC8151, 2000.

dir. Michael Hoffman, 1998 (Kline, Pfeiffer, Everett), Twentieth Century Fox Home Entertainment 14252S, 2000.

dir. Christine Edzand, 2001 (all-child cast), Sands Films Nut Ltd, no catalogue no., 2001.

Much Ado About Nothing

dir. Kenneth Branagh, 1993 (Branagh, Washington, Thompson), Entertainment in Video EVS1134, 1994.

Othello

dir. Orson Welles, 1952 (Welles, MacLiammoir), Castle Hill Productions BRP6018, 1992.

dir. Sergei Yutkevich, 1955 (Bondarchuk, Popov), Moskwood Video HEN2210, n.d.

dir. John Dexter/Stuart Burge, 1964 (Olivier, Finlay, Smith), British Home Entertainment, no catalogue no., n.d.

dir. Trevor Nunn, 1990 (White, McKellen, Stubbs), Pickwick Video RPT2030, n.d.

dir. Oliver Parker, 1995 (Fishburne, Branagh), Columbia Tristar Home Video CVR34497, 1997.

Richard III

dir. F. R. Benson, 1911 (Benson, Brydone): see *Silent Shakespeare*.

dir. Laurence Olivier, 1955 (Olivier, Gielgud, Richardson), Video Collection International CC1146, 1994.

dir. Richard Loncraine, 1996 (McKellen, Hawthorne, Bening), Guild Pathé Cinema G8873S, 1997.

See also *Looking for Richard*.

Romeo and Juliet

dir. Baz Luhrmann, 1997 (Di Caprio, Danes, Postlethwaite), Twentieth Century Fox Home Entertainment 4143S, 1998.

dir. William Woodman, 1999 (Hyde-White, Baker, Rolle, Hamilton), Revelation Films PAR50068, 1999.

See also *West Side Story, Shakespeare in Love*.

The Taming of the Shrew

dir. Franco Zeffirelli, 1967 (Burton, Taylor, Hordern), Columbia Tristar Home Video CC7453, 1997.

See also *Kiss Me Kate, McLintock, Ten Things I Hate about You.*

The Tempest

dir. Percy Stow, 1908: see *Silent Shakespeare.*

dir. Derek Jarman, 1979 (Williams, Wilcox, Birkett), Art House Productions AHP5029, 1995.

See also *Forbidden Planet, Prospero's Books.*

Titus Andronicus

dir. Julie Taymor, 1999 (Hopkins, Lange), Hollywood Pictures Home Video D611331, 2001.

Twelfth Night

dir. Charles Kent, 1910 (Turner, Kent): see *Silent Shakespeare.*

dir. John Sichel, 1981 (Guinness, Richardson, Plowright, Steele), Polygram Video 29289, 1998.

dir. Kenneth Branagh, 1988 (Briers, Langrishe), Thames Television International/Video Collection International TV8123, 1991.

dir. Trevor Nunn, 1996 (Hawthorne, Bonham Carter, Grant, Stubbs), Entertainment in Video EVS 1227, 1997.

Associated Films

Forbidden Planet, dir. Fred M. Wilcox, 1956 (Pidgeon, Nielsen, Francis), Warner Home Video S052321, 1995.

Hamlet Goes Business, dir. Aki Kaurismaki, 1987 (Petelius, Salminen, Outinen), Electric Pictures 0579603, 1998.

In the Bleak Midwinter, dir. Kenneth Branagh, 1995 (Briers, Farrell, Maloney, Sawalha), Columbia Tristar Home Video CVT24496, 1996.

Kiss Me Kate, dir. George Sidney, 1953 (Grayson, Miller, Fosse), Warner Home Video S052325, 2001.

Looking for Richard, dir. Al Pacino, 1996 (Pacino, Rider, Spacey), Twentieth Century Fox Home Entertainment 4142W, 1998.

McLintock, dir. Andrew McLaglen, 1963 (Wayne, O'Hara, Powers), IMC Vision IMC314, 2001.

Prospero's Books, dir. Peter Greenaway, 1991 (Gielgud, Clark, Bell, Blanc), Polygram Filmed Entertainment 6357583, 1996.

Ran, dir. Akiro Kurasawa, 1985 (Nakadai, Terao, Nezu, Ryu), Warner Home Video S038403, 2000.

Shakespeare in Love, dir. John Madden, 1998 (Fiennes, Paltrow), Universal 0610443, 1999.

Silent Shakespeare, British Film Institute BFIV046, 1999.

Ten Things I Hate about You, dir. Gil Junger, 1999 (Stiles, Ledger, Gordon-Levitt), Touchstone Home Video D610611, 2001.

A Thousand Acres, dir. Jocelyn Moorhouse, 1997 (Pfeiffer, Lange, Robards), 4-Front Video 0551303, 2001.

Throne of Blood, dir. Akiro Kurasawa, 1957 (Mifune, Yamada), Conoisseur Video CR043, 1998. (The Japanese title, *Kumonosu-Jo*, lit. = 'Cobweb Castle'.)

West Side Story, dir. Robert Wise and Jerome Robbins, 1961 (Wood, Beymer, Tamblyn), MGM Home Entertainment 15930S, 2001.

OTHER PLAYS ON VIDEO

ALBEE, Edward, *Who's Afraid of Virginia Woolf?* (dir. Mike Nichols, 1966); Warner Home Video S001056, 1998.

BARNES, Peter, *The Ruling Class* (dir. Peter Medak, 1971); Momentum Pictures Home Entertainment MP055D, 2000 (DVD).

BENNETT, Alan, *The Madness of King George* (dir. Nicholas Hytner, 1994); Columbia Tristar Home Video CC7822, 1999.

—— *Talking Heads*, British Broadcasting Corporation BBCV6309, 1997.

—— *Talking Heads 2*, British Broadcasting Corporation BBCV6718, 1998.

BOLT, Robert, *A Man for All Seasons* (dir. Fred Zinneman, 1966); Video Collection International CVR30013, 1991.

BOUBLIL, Alain, and SCHÖNBERG, Claude-Michel, *Les Misérables* (dir. Trevor Nunn and John Caird, 1985); Video Collection International VC6528, 1995.

BRECHT, Bertolt, and WEILL, Kurt, *The Threepenny Opera* (dir. G. W. Pabst, 1931); Janus Films/Public Media Home Vision THR110, 1981.

BRIGHOUSE, Harold, *Hobson's Choice* (dir. David Lean, 1953); Warner Home Video S038164, 2000.

CARTWRIGHT, Jim, *Little Voice* (dir. Mark Herman, 1998); Miramax Home Entertainment D610890–1, 1999.

CHASE, Mary, *Harvey* (dir. Henry Koster, 1950); Universal 902–2563, 2000.

CHEKHOV, Anton, *The Three Sisters* (dir. Laurence Olivier, 1970); Warner Home Video S038253, 1993.

—— *Uncle Vanya* (dir. Laurence Olivier and Stuart Burge, 1962); British Home Entertainment, no catalogue no., n.d.

COWARD, Noël, *Blithe Spirit* (dir. David Lean, 1945); Video Collection International CC7069, 1993.

DELANEY, Shelagh, *A Taste of Honey* (dir. Tony Richardson, 1961); Samuel Goldwyn Home Entertainment VHS CAS9084, 1990.

Elizabeth R (1971); 3 vols, BBC Video BBCV 5585/5641/5642, 1995.

EURIPIDES, *Medea* (dir. Pier Paolo Pasolini, 1970); Connoisseur CR005, n.d.

FIERSTEIN, Harvey, *Torch Song Trilogy* (dir. Paul Bogart, 1988); New Line Home Video N4110V, 1995.

FORD, John, *'Tis Pity She's a Whore* (dir. Giuseppe Patroni Griffi, 1973); Redemption RED003, n.d.

FRIEL, Brian, *Dancing at Lughnasa* (dir. Pat O'Connor, 1998); FilmFour FDV065, 1999.

GAY, John, *The Beggar's Opera* (dir. Peter Brook, 1953); Warner Home Video S039021, 1999.

GILBERT, W. S., and SULLIVAN, Arthur, *The Gondoliers* (Executive Producer George Walker, 1982); Polygram 6325183, 1994.

—— *HMS Pinafore* (Executive Producer George Walker, 1982); Polygram 6325143, 1994.

—— *Iolanthe* (Executive Producer George Walker, 1982); Polygram 6325103, 1994.

—— *The Mikado* (Executive Producer George Walker, 1982); Polygram 6325243, 1994.

—— *The Pirates of Penzance* (Executive Producer George Walker, 1982); Polygram 6325283, 1994.

—— *Princess Ida* (Executive Producer George Walker, 1982); Polygram 6325123, 1994.

—— *Ruddigore* (Executive Producer George Walker, 1982); Polygram 6325303, 1994.

GUARE, John, *Six Degrees of Separation* (dir. Fred Schepisi, 1993); MGM Home Entertainment 159085, 2000.

HARWOOD, Ronald, *The Dresser* (dir. Peter Yates, 1983); Video Collection International CC7084, 1993.

JOHNSON, Terry, *Insignificance* (dir. Nicolas Roeg, 1985); no name, PVC2085, n.d.

KESSELRING, Joseph, *Arsenic and Old Lace* (dir. Frank Capra, 1944); Warner Home Video S099316, 2000.

KHAN-DIN, Ayub, *East is East* (dir. Damien O'Donnell, 1999); FilmFour VC3775, 2000.

LLOYD-WEBBER, Andrew, *Cats* (dir. David Mallet, 1981); Polygram 0587963, 1998.

MACDONALD, Sharman, *The Winter Guest* (dir. Alan Rickman, 1997); FilmFour CC8399, 2001.

The Mahabharata (dir. Peter Brook, 1989); 3 vols, British Film Institute/Argos Films CR180, n.d.

MAMET, David, *American Buffalo* (dir. Michael Corrente, 1996); FilmFour CC8102, 2000.

—— *Glengarry Glen Ross* (dir. James Foley, 1992); Video Collection International CCD8240, 2000 (DVD).

MARCUS, Frank, *The Killing of Sister George* (dir. Robert Aldrich, 1966); The Film Collection PTVID1321, 2001.

MARLOWE, Christopher, *Doctor Faustus* (dir. Richard Burton and Nevill Coghill, 1967); Columbia Tristar Home Video 60824, 1995.

—— *Edward II* (dir. Derek Jarman, 1992); New Line Home Video N4085, 1992.

MEDOFF, Mark, *Children of a Lesser God* (dir. Randa Haines, 1986); Paramount BRP4347, n.d.

MILLER, Arthur, *The Crucible* (dir. Nicholas Hytner, 1996); Twentieth Century Fox Home Entertainment 4144BD, 2000.

—— *Death of a Salesman* (dir. Volker Schlödorff, 1985); Warner Home Video PEV35017, n.d.

Oh, What a Lovely War! (dir. Richard Attenborough, 1969); Paramount VHN2121, n.d.

MINGHELLA, Anthony, *Truly, Madly, Deeply* (dir. Anthony Minghella, 1991); MGM Home Entertainment 159225, 2000.

O'NEILL, Eugene, *Long Day's Journey into Night* (dir. Sidney Lumet, 1962); 4 Front Video 0451223, 1997.

ORTON, Joe, *Entertaining Mr Sloane* (dir. Douglas Hickox, 1969); Warner Home Video S038090, 1994.

—— *Loot* (dir. Silvio Narizzano, 1970); Warner Home Video S038122, 2002.

OSBORNE, John, *The Entertainer* (dir. Tony Richardson, 1960); W. H. Smith 0858663, n.d..

—— *Look Back in Anger* (dir. Tony Richardson, 1959); W. H. Smith 0858703, n.d.

PINTER, Harold, *Betrayal* (dir. David Jones, 1982); 4 Front Video 0580543, 1998.

—— *The Birthday Party* (dir. William Friedkin, 1968); PT Video PTVID 1367, n.d.

—— *The Dumb Waiter* (dir. Robert Altman, n.d.); no name IVA 004, n.d.

POTTER, Dennis, *The Singing Detective* (1986), 2 vols, 1994, BBC Video BBCV 5445, 5446.

RATTIGAN, Terence, *The Browning Version* (dir. Anthony Asquith, 1951); Universal Pictures Video CFV06412, n.d.

—— dir. Mike Figgis, 1994; Paramount Home Entertainment BRP0122, 2001.

—— *The Winslow Boy* (dir. Anthony Asquith, 1948); DD Video, DD3390, 2000.

—— dir. David Mamet, 1998; Columbia Tristar Home Video CC8482, 2001.

ROSE, Reginald, *Twelve Angry Men* (dir. Sidney Lumet, 1957); MGM Home Entertainment 16232S, 2001.

RUSSELL, Willy, *Educating Rita* (dir. Lewis Gilbert, 1983); Carlton Home Entertainment RCC3062, 1998.

Seven Brides for Seven Brothers (dir. Stanley Donen, 1954); Warner Home Video S050091, 2000.

SHAFFER, Anthony, *Sleuth* (dir. Joseph L. Manckiewicz, 1972); Video Collection International CC7568, 1998.

SHAFFER, Peter, *Amadeus* (dir. Milos Forman, 1984); Warner Home Video S036218, 2000.

—— *Equus* (dir. Sidney Lumet, 1977); MGM Home Entertainment 15804S, 2000.

SHAW, George Bernard, *My Fair Lady* (dir. George Cukor, 1964); Twentieth Century Fox Home Entertainment 8166C, 2000.

SHEPARD, Sam, *Fool for Love* (dir. Robert Altman, 1975); no name, 0243, n.d.

STOPPARD, Tom, *Rosencrantz and Guildenstern are Dead* (dir. Tom Stoppard, 1990); Second Sight 2nd1071, n.d.

WILDE, Oscar, *An Ideal Husband* (dir. Oliver Parker, 1998); Pathé P8966S, 2000.

—— *The Importance of being Earnest* (dir. Anthony Asquith, 1952); Rank Video RCC3070, 1998.

WILLIAMS, Tennessee, *Cat on a Hot Tin Roof* (dir. Richard Brooks, 1958); Warner Home Video S050060, 2000.

—— dir. Jack Hofsiss, 1984; First Independent Video VA14213, n.d.

—— *A Streetcar Named Desire* (dir. Elia Kazan, 1951); Warner Home Video S035442, 2000.

—— *Suddenly Last Summer* (dir. Joseph L. Manckiewicz, 1959); Video Collection International CC7612, 1998.

—— *Sweet Bird of Youth* (dir. Richard Brooks, 1961); Warner Home Video S050793, 2000.

Index of Persons

Index of Plays

Films, adaptations, etc. are included, but prose-fiction, poetry, and criticism are not. Initial articles are omitted in all languages. Shakespearean titles appear in modern form.